Outside, Looking In: Critiques of American Policies and Institutions, Left and Right

Outside, Looking In: Critiques of American Policies and Institutions, Left and Right

DOROTHY BUCKTON JAMES
Herbert H. Lehman College of
The City University of New York

Harper & Row, Publishers
New York, Evanston, San Francisco, London

To Douglas and Anne, Corland and Ella Judith
(reading from left to right).

**Outside, Looking In: Critiques of American
Policies and Institutions, Left and Right**
Copyright © 1972 by Dorothy Buckton James

Standard Book Number: 06-043265-9
Library of Congress Catalog Card
Number: 75-188201

Contents

Preface

This volume developed out of the need of my students of American political thought and interested laymen for an accessible, interesting, and informative work in which the basic contemporary controversies and problems of the American system could be understood. There are some books of readings on radical criticism and some on conservative criticism, but not one that pulls the two together within the type of intellectual framework presented here. Furthermore, most books of readings suffer from a disjointed coverage because the articles were originally intended for another purpose and setting. A major asset of this anthology is that it is primarily composed of original pieces written especially for the work. The few reprinted articles have been revised by their authors and the editor for this volume. Therefore, it presents the problems of the 1970s from divergent viewpoints that stimulate the reader's independent thought. For this, the editor is most grateful to each of her contributors, whose thoughtful articles made editing this volume intellectually stimulating and whose gracious cooperation made it personally rewarding as well.

The editor is deeply indebted to Walter Lippincott, Editor-in-Chief of the College Division of Harper & Row for his encouragement and assistance, and to Mrs. Ida Fialkin and her able assistants Elizabeth Figueroa and Laura Goldenberg for valiant typing efforts. It is impossible to express her deep, continuing appreciation to Judson Lehman James, husband, teacher, and friend.

D. B. J.

Part I

American Values

Introduction: The American Right and Left, "Old" and "New"

Most analysts agree that throughout its history the United States has been dominated by a single ideology, that of liberalism. This has been a source of bitter frustration to those who have held the minority views that have always existed outside that mainstream, because it has severely restricted the range of alternatives on which public policy has been based. To its critics on the left it has appeared immorally restrictive of the degree to which government would act to meet their demands for substantive change toward an egalitarian society. To critics on the right it has

1

appeared immorally active in expanding government power over individual life, liberty, and property. To understand the nature of this conflict, it is useful briefly to consider the nature of the liberal, conservative, and socialist traditions as they have developed in English thought (because England was the primary influence on American thought), the dominance of liberalism in American thought, and the nature of contemporary criticism of this ideology.

Three English Traditions

In England the three major traditions of political thought since the eighteenth century have been liberalism, conservatism, and socialism. At the risk of oversimplification, their basic differences may be seen in Table I.

Of particular importance to American thought was the fact that in England liberalism developed through three stages. Throughout this development it aimed at "liberating," or freeing, the individual from restraints on his personal development, but liberals differed in their conception of the source of individual oppression and the functions legitimate to government.

In 1690, when John Locke wrote *The Social Contract,* the most obvious source of individual oppression was the traditional, hierarchical authority of the State. Consequently, he held that the State had to be deprived of its power to coerce individuals; this was to be done by severely restricting the functions that it might legitimately perform. Thus, in Locke's thought government's *sole* purpose was to protect individuals in their inalienable rights to life, liberty, and estate. Essentially, this entailed little more than maintaining adequate defenses against foreign aggression, a legal-judicial system to defend individuals against the occasional aggression of their neighbors, and an administrative apparatus sufficient to provide those types of services necessary for protection of life, liberty, and estate that individuals could not themselves provide (such as lighthouses or post roads).

As English liberalism developed through the eighteenth century, it shifted from supporting individual equality on the ground used by Locke (that it was part of a Natural Law that governed the universe) to supporting it on utilitarian grounds (that men are equal in their capacity to experience pleasure and that the equal pleasures of any two or more men are equally good). Thus, early liberals justified human freedom on the ground of human equality as a universal natural principle, whereas later liberals justified freedom on the ground that it was useful ("utilitarian") in maximizing pleasure. For utilitarians the sole legitimate function of government was the maximization of pleasure and minimization of pain for the greatest possible number of people. In practice, utilitarians gave government the same restricted responsibilities as had earlier liberals, because they believed that the way to provide the greatest happiness for the greatest number was for government solely to protect individual life, liberty, and property.

Among those utilitarians particularly anxious to prevent government interference in economic matters was Adam Smith, author of *The Wealth of Nations* (1776). He maintained that there was a natural harmony in the economic order expressed by the image of an "invisible hand." If left unrestrained that natural harmony would work for the greatest good of the greatest number. Consequently, government should not interfere in the economy, because any such interference would destroy the balance maintained by the "invisible hand." The government should leave people free to do for themselves (laissez-faire).

Although laissez-faire economics had thus been intended as a means to advance the greatest good of the greatest number, during the nineteenth century many liberals came to view it as a bulwark of reaction and privilege. They attributed this discrepancy between theory and practice to the erroneous assumption that a free enterprise system *could* exist. To have a truly free enterprise system individuals must be able to bargain freely, and critics claimed that in reality such a great discrepancy existed in bargaining power between major industrialists and the unorganized individuals working for them that most men could enjoy neither individual freedom nor equality.

T. H. Green was well within the liberal tradition in *Principles of Political Obligation* (1882), where he stressed individual freedom and equality, but in his conception of the source of oppression and the legitimate functions of government, he departed significantly from

Table 1: *Comparison Among English Traditions of Political Thought*

	Liberalism	*Conservatism*	*Socialism*
1. Concept of the nature of man	Inherent equality.	Inherent inequality as a result of the natural division of labor and unequal distribution of mental and physical attributes.	Inherent equality has been obscured by exploitative economic organization.
	Inherent right to seek private ends.	Individuals are created *by* their society as part of an organic whole; therefore, the social order is superior to privately determined individual rights.	The general well-being is more important than individual goals.
	Men are capable of rational choice; men share similar values and goals that can be the basis of public policy.	Most men are selfish and short sighted.	Men are created by their societies.
2. Concept of property	Because man may seek private ends, he must enjoy full freedom to have and use private property. (Initially, liberal thought emphasized unrestricted use of private property; later it restricted usage that interfered with others' ability to develop morally.)	The inherent inequality of human nature justifies economic inequality.	The general well-being is incompatible with any social order based on a competitive struggle for the means of living.
	Capitalism is the appropriate economic system. (Later liberals preferred to soften its harsh edges with welfare capitalism.)	The economic system of a society is part of its organic development; consequently, varied forms are acceptable, including capitalism.	Each person should contribute as much as he can to the general good and should receive whatever he needs from the general store.

3. Concept of the legitimate function of government	Initially favored government solely to protect individuals in the full enjoyment of their life, liberty, and property and perhaps to provide those types of services necessary for their protection that they could not themselves provide. Later added idea that government should actively seek to create social conditions that make individual moral development possible.	The constitution of a society cannot be "made"; it is the product of the slow, invisible working of history. Thus, the tradition of a society's constitution should be held in religious awe, because it forms part of a collective intelligence and civilization that forms an organic whole requiring the devotion and sacrifice of individuals. Government should conserve this heritage and transmit it to succeeding generations.	Once the socialist State is achieved, government needs to engage in comprehensive planning of public policy for the general good. But eventually the state will wither away, because under socialism, all will work without any necessity of coercion.
4. Concept of social change	Social change *could* result from individual deliberation and choice.	Social change is an evolutionary, not a deliberative process; consequently, whatever is the *existing* constitution is the true constitution.	Social change depends on economic development; as the means of production change, the new group that controls them must become self-conscious and wrest political power from its previous wielders.
5. Concept of the appropriate organization of the State	Only democracy is acceptable if men are inherently equal and free.	The natural aristocracy of men of ability, birth, and wealth should rule.	At any given era the political system will merely reflect a nation's economic development. Whoever controls the means of production controls the political system. Thus, a government of the few is appropriate in an agricultural society; bourgeois democracy is appropriate during the early stages of industrialism; and socialism is appropriate to advanced industrial societies.

earlier liberal thought. Green maintained that earlier liberals had focused solely on "negative" freedom, that is, freedom *from* governmental restraint. Yet when a man is freed from governmental restraint, he still may not be able to develop his moral and intellectual potential, because social or economic factors may restrain him. Therefore, Green believed that freedom should not be merely negative; to be truly free an individual must also have "positive" freedom, that is, freedom *for* development. Although he conceded that moral and intellectual development could never be accomplished through government legislation because it is the act or character of a free agent, Green maintained that it *is* possible for a government to *create conditions* under which it can occur. Thus, he held that although government cannot *make* people moral, it can *remove obstacles* to their moral development.

Unlike earlier liberals who had focused solely on individuals, Green conceived of society as an organic whole in which all the parts interact. This philosophy has been labeled "organic liberalism" in distinction to liberalism based on natural rights or utilitarianism. Organic liberals held that for moral development men require at least subsistence and protection from economic exploitation such as factory safety laws, wage and hour protections, regulations concerning child and woman labor, pure food and drug laws, public health service, sanitation, and education, and that it was *government's legitimate responsibility* to provide them. However, the State could not regulate individuals beyond the necessities for individual growth and development. Thus, private ownership of the means of production was compatible with organic liberalism, as were large differences in the distribution of individual wealth. These developments in English liberal thought were very influential for Americans.

One Dominant American Tradition

When we say that America has been dominated by a single ideology—liberalism—we should add that American liberals have followed the path of development taken by English liberal thought but added some distinctive elements as well.

During the eighteenth century American thought was dominated by the natural-law liberalism of John Locke, which was the basis for the Declaration of Independence. Though the Constitution permitted greater governmental regulation than had the Articles of Confederation, it was still based on the premises of individual freedom, equality, the right of men to create and alter (preferably through prescribed means) their social contract, the right of individuals to pursue private ends (which entailed the right to possess and enjoy private property), and limited government power (checked by internal balances as well as by popular will). However, in practice Federalists added two functions for government that were not compatible with restricting its scope to the narrowest possible range. They added active government encouragement of "infant" industries and various subsidies to commerce, and they enabled government to legislate on questions of personal conduct and morals (e.g., statutes relating to sex, marriage, alcoholic consumption, public education, and the Alien and Sedition Acts). Their successors, the Jeffersonians, were closer to laissez-faire principles in their attempt to dismantle subsidies and laws relating to morals, but there were many slips between Jeffersonian principles of limited government and actual practice (e.g., the Louisiana Purchase, embargoes). The Jacksonians unabashedly took the path that succeeding administrations followed until the 1930s of preaching the illegitimacy of government regulation of business and industry while actively assisting and encouraging both. Various forms of limitation of personal conduct and morals were also sanctioned. Thus, as Murray Rothbard's article indicates, complete free enterprise capitalism has never been tried in America.

Laissez-faire theory remained dominant until the turn of the century, when the Progressive movement began to champion some of the principles of organic liberalism, but progressives were essentially ambivalent, combining a laissez-faire attack on trusts, monopolies, and party bosses with some welfare reforms to ease urban blight and poverty. For an extensive analysis of their ideology see the article by Susan and Norman Fainstein.

The struggle to combine the two philosophies lasted for several decades during which the primary emphasis was placed on laissez-faire. Finally, the New Deal era marked the successful emergence of organic liberalism as a major American ideology. Nevertheless, the struggle to combine laissez-faire and organic liberalism persisted well into F.D.R.'s second term, and his actions were more a matter of expedient response to crisis than the reflection of an organic liberal ideology.

Since the mid-1930s America has increasingly moved toward welfare capitalism, which entails the coupling of private ownership of the means of production with government regulation attempting to create the conditions within which individual development might be possible. Thus, the operating tenets of those who have formulated much American public policy through the last three decades have increasingly moved toward the tenets of organic liberalism. The Kennedy and Johnson Administrations came closer to these tenets than had earlier ones, but the Nixon Administration generally has withdrawn. Nevertheless, as the Fainsteins have noted, American reform movements of the twentieth century, including the Kennedy and Johnson eras, have been heavily influenced by Progressive thought, with its attendant ambivalent combination of laissez-faire and organic liberalism. Thus, while we have progressed toward welfare capitalism, each step has been grudging and frequently so ambivalent that it has created a burden for the already disadvantaged— for example, welfare.

Since liberalism has been the dominant ideology throughout American history, a much narrower spectrum of public policy alternatives has been advanced in America than in other western nations. While there have been a few individuals who have been philosophic conservatives in the English tradition, there has been no significant conservative movement in those terms. What is labeled "conservatism" in America has little relation to philosophic conservatism. Rather, it is eighteenth- and nineteenth-century liberal thought continuing to do battle with organic liberalism. This can be seen in the contrast between the articles by Peter Viereck and M. Stanton Evans.

Peter Viereck presents a Burkean argument emphasizing inherent human inequality; the essential function of tradition and structure in holding together that fragile organism, a society; and the consequent need to support those who fill a conservatizing function (such as trade unions, the New Deal, Eugene McCarthy for the young) With Burke, he believes that the existing Constitution is the true

Constitution and that the alternative to evolutionary social change is chaos. (Robert Booth Fowler's article makes a similarly conservative argument about evolutionary social change when he considers the American future.)

In contrast, M. Stanton Evans emphasizes the rights of individuals as opposed to any organic conception of man and society. One could hardly fault him with a Burkean reverence "akin to religious awe" when he views the present society. Rather, his article is a challenging cry for a repeal of most of the philosophic developments and governmental regulations of the twentieth century. Thus, as a spokesman for the American right, Evans stands for a position with regard to government economic regulation that allies him with English laissez-faire liberalism.

However, it should be noted that the basic political thought of the traditional American right (the "old" right) is not fully consistent with laissez-faire principles. Although it stands for limited government in terms of regulation of business and industry, it has always encouraged active government programs on their behalf. Furthermore, it has never supported laissez-faire principles with regard to public morals. In that sense the Old Right has been closer to Burke and conservative thought, as they have supported a vast array of government restrictions of individual practices with regard to such matters as sex, marriage, drug use, alcoholic consumption, praying in schools, sabbath closing of businesses, pledging allegiance to the flag, and obscenity. As a result of their commitment to capitalism and Christianity, the old right has always been actively anti-Communist, and has therefore supported an aggressive (therefore, expensive) military stance toward Communist nations. It is these four factors (limited government economic regulation, active government economic encouragement for business and industry, active government protection of public morals, and militant anti-communism) that unite the disparate elements of the old right, such as William Buckley, the Daughters of the American Revolution, Ronald Reagan, Barry Goldwater, Young Americans for Freedom, the John Birch Society and the *Chicago Tribune*.

Because of the emergence of organic liberalism since the 1930s, the old right has felt that it was ignored and an "outsider" looking in on much of the decision making that has occurred on public policy in America. Its adherents feel particularly threatened by and antagonistic to welfare reforms, the government's increasing tolerance of moral diversity (especially recent rulings of the United States Supreme Court on school prayer and obscenity), and what Anthony Bouscaren's article describes as an increasingly weak posture toward communism.

The "New" Right

On the right a relatively new group of critics has emerged, critical of both the old left and old right. The "new" right presents a proposal for radical change: institute a truly laissez-faire system. That would require the end of all government assistance to business and industry and the end of all legislation regulating individual morals. Furthermore, the new right rejects the militant anti-communism of the old right on two grounds. First, that it leads to a massive governmental war machine that restricts personal freedom (taxes and the draft) and engages in futile and immoral use of power (the Vietnamese War). Second, that it is blind to the realities of the Communist world, which they perceive to be splintering and changing in the direction of "creeping capitalism." Fundamentally, they argue, the way to conquer communism is to provide subject peoples with the example of true individual freedom and they will choose it.

During the late 1960s and early 1970s this New Right developed what is called the "libertarian" movement aimed at freeing individuals from all manner of governmental restraint—that is, absolute laissez-faire liberalism. Libertarians tended to attract a diverse following of people from the right (those suspicious of the degree of state control inherent in old right philosophy) and from the left (those who were concerned about contemporary policies and institutions and who conceived of human freedom in terms of very limited governmental power). It is this union to which Rod Manis refers in his article, "Beyond Left and Right." Libertarian analysis in this volume also includes the articles by Murray Rothbard, Tibor Machan, and Robert Poole.

The "New" Left

Three different lines of thought comprise the new left: organic liberalism, anarchism, and socialism. Just as radicals of the right claim that laissez-faire liberalism has never been tried in America, many people on the left claim, in effect, that organic liberalism has never been tried. (Though this point is generally implicit in their work, not consciously stated.) Spokesmen for true organic liberalism generally consider themselves to be radicals, although this is disputed by anarchists and socialists who claim that nothing from the liberal tradition demands sufficiently sweeping change to be considered radical. However, in the sense of Webster's *Third New International Dictionary* definition of a radical as one who advocates a decided change from existing views and methods, those who advocate true organic liberalism offer a radical alternative, though one that is less sweeping than the alternatives proposed by libertarians, anarchists, or socialists.

The basic philosophy of these radicals is outlined in Charles Frankel's article. Essentially, it revolves around what Frankel labels a distinctive *weltanschauung*: a sense of the complexity of human existence plus a recognition that every social system weighs more heavily on some people than on others, and that public policy should work to correct such inequities. In their sense of human diversity and complexity they share an organic view of society with conservatives like Burke and Viereck, but they differ from conservatives in believing that man is capable of constructing and implementing programs for substantial social change, and they aim at a more truly egalitarian society. For them the old and new right are hopelessly naive about the possibilities of a free enterprise system actually existing, and immorally callous in not recognizing its implications for a differential impact on individuals. They find anarchists irrelevantly nostalgic about an unstructured universe that never has or could exist, and view socialists as wholly doctrinaire in ascribing all human relations to economic factors. Furthermore, organic liberals are suspicious of the capacity of any group of men to have sufficient wisdom for the type of comprehensive social planning necessary to most socialist thought.

Organic liberals are critical of the old left on the ground that despite its rhetorical concern for human freedom its ambivalence with regard to laissez-faire and organic liberalism led it to construct government policies and expand government power in a manner that actually limited human capacity for moral and intellectual development. Moreover, they agree with the new right, anarchists, and socialists that since the 1940s the old left has been involved in a cold war policy of containment of communism that has led to a huge military-industrial machine that coerces individuals (through taxes and the draft) to engage in immoral acts (e.g., the Vietnamese War). All four of these groups of radicals perceive the Communist world to be fragmenting and moving toward greater freedom. Therefore, they call for an end to militarism abroad. Organic liberals also call for the decentralization of government power at home so that the people who are affected by government policies can have a voice in formulating them. They believe that only through this strategy can America develop a truely egalitarian society based on individual freedom that would allow for moral and intellectual development.

Because organic liberals attempt to construct social programs that can both move the country toward a more truly egalitarian society and win sufficient assent to be enacted and administered in America, they emphasize tolerance, negotiation, and compromise. This makes their position wholly unacceptable to the rest of the new left, who view it as "selling out." However, organic liberals maintain that they are forced to work through imperfect existing institutions because they doubt that there is any realistic possibility of overthrowing these institutions in the politically significant future. For example, the article by Philip Brenner advocates making fundamental changes in the school system and then using it as a lever to effect broader social change. Other articles expressing this viewpoint include those by Ira Katznelson, Paul Piccard, and Henry Kariel.

Perhaps nothing better proves the point that America has been dominated by liberalism than the fact that there are so few conservatives, and that the old and new right, old left and part of the new left are within the liberal tradition. Only two groups on the left are outside this spectrum, and their numbers are quite limited.

The smallest of all groups (though certainly highly vocal) are the anarchists who find any form of regulation whatsoever to be antithetical to human freedom. Theirs is a total denial of the legitimacy of any form of structure and framework, and a faith that in the absence of such structures people would relate to each other freely and lovingly. Thus, freedom and love are the only essentials for the "Yippies."

Socialists are the final group of outsiders critical of American policy and institutions. They view capitalism as economically outmoded and morally evil because it depends on competition for profit which inevitably leads to exploitation of all workers (particularly racial minorities and women), imperialism, and war. They maintain that conservatives, the old and new right and organic liberals are merely apologists for middle class interests and that anarchists are foolish, irrelevant romantics. For socialists, the only means to end human exploitation is for the exploited to become conscious of their class interests and act to end their oppression by establishing a true socialist state based on the principle of each person making the contribution of which he is capable and receiving only those goods that he needs from the common store. Socialists envision the possibility of a truly egalitarian society in which modern technology liberates mankind from labor, thereby permitting the fullest possible development of human potential. Such a goal is similar to that of organic liberals, but socialists maintain that it requires a total restructuring of all America's institutions (economic, social, and political) and of human consciousness itself. Thus, the piecemeal approach of organic liberals appears to be a disguised perpetuation of the existing order.

Among articles presenting this position there are differences in the degree of centralized planning and institutional structure that is acceptable. For example, Hyman Lumer would seem to require a well coordinated planning structure, whereas Andrew McLaughlin and Susan and Norman Fainstein would seem to prefer a more decentralized decision-making process. However, because none of these articles addressed themselves directly to this point only tentative distinctions should be made here.

Part I begins with articles by M. Stanton Evans, Charles Frankel and Peter Viereck that set forth the basic critiques of American policies and institutions made respectively by the old right, new left organic liberals, and conservatives. This is followed by four articles on the nature and implications of capitalism. The first two articles analyze it in economic terms, with Murray Rothbard taking a libertarian position and Hyman Lumer a socialist one. The last two articles analyze capitalism in philosophic terms, with the libertarian position taken by Tibor Machan and the socialist one by Andrew McLaughlin.

These are by no means the only discussions of capitalism in this volume. Its benefits and defects are raised by several other authors. (For example, Robert Poole's solution to the environmental crisis is a return to a true laissez-faire system, whereas Clifford Humphrey blames the environmental crisis on the naïveté of laissez-faire economics.) What these four articles provide is a basic outline of the debate whose ramifications may be seen in many areas of American policy and institutions, as the articles in Parts II and III indicate.

Conservatism versus Liberalism

The Death
of Liberalism

M. STANTON EVANS

Affirmative discourse on the subject of freedom must begin from a profoundly negative observation—that we are living in the most despotic century in the history of the world. No discussion about the prospects for liberty can be taken seriously if it does not come to grips with this unhappy fact of record, account for it in some fashion, and attempt to devise a remedy.

M. Stanton Evans is the editor of the *Indianapolis News,* was formerly assistant editor of *The Freeman,* and managing editor of *Human Events Newsletter.* He is currently an associate editor and regular columnist for the *National Review.* He has co-authored two books and authored several, including *The Liberal Establishment, Revolt on the Campus, The Politics of Surrender, The Lawbreakers,* and *The Future of Conservatism.* He is chairman of the American Conservative Union and a commentator on CBS News "Spectrum."

One wonders what the eighteenth-century philosophers of progress would have thought about our era—or whether their modern descendants think very much at all. Far from experiencing an ever-rising level of liberty and enlightenment, we have witnessed the collapse of society into brutality and barbarism. More people have been killed in wars, murdered by secret police, liquidated by state-induced starvation, locked up in dungeons, and herded into labor camps in the twentieth century than in any other epoch known to man. It is not improbable that something like 100 million human beings have been exterminated by one or another of these methods since the advent of the 1900s.

The proximate source of all this misery is of course well known—the fact that ours has been the century of totalitarianism, of movements that claim an absolute lien on the energies and affections of man, that in pursuit of this claim have wrought the characteristic horrors of the age. But totalitarianism itself is not a final cause, an unmoved mover without further source or origin. Its repeated appearance on the stage of modern history suggests, on the contrary, that it is the result of certain fundamental tendencies of our time and place—tendencies that are by their nature hostile to freedom. If we would preserve the liberties we have and entertain the hope of enlarging them, we must set about to understand these forces and repel them.

We are accustomed in America to think of totalitarianism as an alien thing, appropriate to Europe or Asia but inapplicable to the United States. And because American conditions are in many ways distinctive, this characterization is to a degree correct. In the most important sense, however, it is obviously false. We are part of Western society, and, as Hannah Arendt observes, the totalitarian movements have arisen *within* the society. They have not been imposed by any outside agent. The totalitarian phenomenon is part of a general movement of thought and practice that has encompassed all of Western culture, ourselves included.

The Development of Totalitarianism

With all their many differences, the totalitarian movements have certain major features in common. The most crucial of these is that, in the realm of value metaphysics, each is essentially relativist and nihilist, rejecting all standards of right and norms of conduct external to the will of the totalitarian rule. The form in which this nihilism is propounded varies from case to case. With communism, it takes the shape of a full-blooded materialism, the argument that right and wrong are functions of the material flux of things, without ontic status. With nazism, it was a haphazard approximation of the Nietzschean superman and his indomitable will to power. With the Fascists, a slightly milder version of the latter. In all three instances, however, the result is the same.

A striking statement from Mussolini suggests the indebtedness of fascism to the relativist and nihilist drift of twentieth-century thought. "If relativism signifies contempt for fixed categories and men who claim to be the bearers of an external objective truth," he asserted:

> then there is nothing more relativistic than Fascist attitudes and activity . . . We fascists have always expressed our complete indifference toward all theories . . . From the fact that all ideologies are of equal value, that all ideologies are mere fictions, the modern relativist deduces that everybody is free to create for himself his own ideology and to attempt to carry it out with all possible energy.

It will be observed that this is a very modern statement indeed, and one that, taken literally, extinguishes the hope of freedom. By destroying norms of behavior it removes all limits on the power of the State and the actions of the ruler. If there is no higher measure of right, who is to say a Hitler or a Stalin is wrong? If there are no fixed standards of conduct, who may criticize a Dachau or Vorkuta? Nihilism releases appetite and impulse, making the greatest enormities allowable: "When nothing is true, everything is permitted." The monstrous crimes routinely practiced by the totalitarian movements are more than sufficient proof of Nietzsche's statement.

As nihilism unleashes the power of the State, so does it desanctify the life of the citizen. The Judaeo-Christian conception of the individual as a creature of God, possessed of a distinctive soul and personality, is lost. He can be and increasingly is conceived of as a thing or animal, a product of the natural energy flow and therefore a proper object of manipulation. When the religious grounds of personality are abandoned, the stable Western view of man, fixed between certain upper and nether limits, is abandoned as well. The totalitarian despot rises up to become a kind of god, the ordinary citizen descends to the status of thing.

If nihilism *permits* the rise of totalitarian rule, it may also be said to *demand* it. Men cannot live without criteria of decision. Considered in terms of intellectual choice or psychological need, our race requires a sense of ultimate certitude. This yearning for standard feeds both sides of the totalitarian phenomenon—the boundless fantasies of rulers who imagine themselves as godlets, and the readiness of the normless masses to accept such rulers as the arbiters of social right. The rule of force cuts through the Gordian knot of nihilist confusion, supplying "existentially" the necessary grounds of choice. A messianic tyranny provides the assurance that has been removed from the realm of metaphysics.

To these tendencies the totalitarian movements have joined a characteristic type of social organization. They have consistently sought to develop mechanisms that would allow the ruler or ruling cadre to indulge the yearning for god-like power to the fullest, and to exercise the greatest possible control over the life of the citizen. As Franz Neumann demonstrated, the key to totalitarian practice has been to eliminate as systematically as possible all competitive sources of social decision. To spread the power of the ruler or ruling class pervasively, it is necessary to close off all practical alternatives. Thus the striking affinity of all the totalitarians for highly centralized controls of economic life. Just as each is relativist and nihilist in ethical theory, so each is collectivist in matters of politics and economics.

That communism is a species of collectivism is self-evident, but the fact that nazism and fascism were also collectivist in their fashion seems not to be generally understood. The rhetoric of the Marxists has created the impression that the Nazis and Fascists were somehow "capitalistic" in inspiration, which is emphatically not the case. If one examines the early platforms of these two parties, he will find both replete with social-welfare ideology, proposals for extensive government regulation in the interests of leveling, and demands for collectivist controls on the economic life of the individual. Both were predicated on the idea of a tightly controlled economy in which business was made to conform to rules laid down from above by political planners. As Peter Drucker observed:

> It is not true that "big business" promoted fascism. On the contrary, both in Italy and Germany the proportion of fascist sympathizers was smallest in the industrial and banking classes. It is equally untrue that "big business" profits from fascism; of all the classes it probably suffers most from totalitarian economics and *Wehrwirtschaft* . . . The businessman is as unfree as his workers. He can neither hire nor fire without a government permit. He must not try to entice an employee away from a competitor. He is told what wages to pay. The price at which he sells his products is arbitrarily fixed . . . In the case of government orders the industrialist is simply commandeered and told what to produce and at what price. Incidently, up to 80 per cent of all orders are government orders . . . In a closed economy like the fascist state, which forbids capital exports and enforces compulsory investment, profits are reduced to the status of a bookkeeping entry.

Without pretending that we have exhausted the list of contributing factors in the development of totalitarianism, we may thus observe that the phenomenon is invariably marked by nihilism in the realm of value, and collectivism in the sphere of political organization. The first supplies the will to power, the second the means by which that will attains its goal. It is precisely because these have been the leading tendencies of modern philosophy and politics that our century has been such a continuing horror. And it is precisely because these identical tendencies are at work in our own society that liberty is increasingly threatened in America. At our own pace and in terms of our own institutions, we have been travelling the totalitarian road.

The Implications of Relativism

There can be no discussion of political subjects at large without recognizing the general tendencies of Western thought, and there can be no discussion of political events in the United States without first considering the dominant trend of thought in America. This is the point of view loosely described as "liberalism," which has held almost exclusive dominion in the academic spheres and wielded extensive influence in the councils of government for the past four decades.

Liberalism is the movement in American society and Western Europe that parallels, in philosophical origin and ultimate effect, the totalitarian phenomenon. This is not to say that Western liberals either want or recognize in their own performance the likelihood or even the possibility of a totalitarian outcome. The Western liberal hates and fears totalitarianism and holds a sentimental attachment to the ideal of freedom, although the ideal as we shall note has become increasingly attenuated. The difficulty is that liberalism is a product of the same general movement of modern thought discussed in the preceding passages. Indeed liberalism might best be described as an attempt to hang suspended between the "old" values of the West and the "new" conceptions of the nihilist-collectivist movements, to adopt the premises of the totalitarians but to avoid the totalitarian result. The illusion that such a feat is possible has been encouraged by the fact of cultural momentum—the fact that habits of mind and notions of right implanted by two millennia of Judaeo-Christian thought and several centuries of libertarian practice do not vanish overnight, even when the metaphysical roots are severed. Liberalism has subsisted over the span of several generations on the inherited moral capital of the West—as Renan put it, on "the perfume of any empty vase."

From the eighteenth century forward, the particular content of liberal error has varied a great deal, but the general formula has not. The liberal mistake is always the same—the assumption that specific ideas about human nature and conduct derived from the religious tradition of the West can be set up on their own account and made self-validating. Such ideas as the dignity of man, the liberty of the person, limited government, progress over linear time—these and other distinctively Judaeo-Christian conceptions are assumed to be scientific or logical propositions that can be made secure on purely rational premises, detached from the faith that gave them birth.

The clearest statement of this view is given us by John Stuart Mill, who asserts that the supernatural assumptions of Christianity are no longer tenable, and that rejection of those assumptions would in no sense jeopardize our hopes for humane and principled politics. The ethical benefit of Christianity, he asserted, had entered into the "permanent possession" of mankind, and was in no danger of being lost. We could do far better with liberalism's favorite secular substitute—a fabricated "religion of humanity."

Had he lived into the twentieth century with its daily slaughters and pervasive slaveries, Mill would have found his complacent assurance completely shattered. His belief that people would go on acting charitably toward each other, that ethical considerations would inform the councils of government, that liberty could be sustained on the grounds of utilitarian calculation—all this has crumbled in the inferno of modernity. The totalitarian rampage shows us the destruction of value on these assumptions, compressed into a relatively brief interval. The history of liberalism itself shows us the same procedure drawn out by institutional and other resistance over a longer span of time, but the same procedure nonetheless.

It would be tiresome to document at length the degree to which Western liberalism has embraced the premises of modern relativism. Anyone who has had a college course in sociology or anthropology is acquainted with the doctrine of "cultural relativism"—the notion that since things are viewed in different ways in different societies, it is impossible to render universal judgments. The most famous statement of this conception is that provided by Ruth Benedict, who says that the various cultures of the world have "coexisting and equally valid" approaches to the business of living. Another anthropologist spells it out in more detail, asserting that "with the possible exception of technological aspects of life, the proposition that one way of thought or action is better than another is exceedingly difficult to establish on the grounds of any universally acceptable criteria."

Perhaps the most common species of relativism is the historical variety—the doctrine that what was true a hundred years ago, last year, or yesterday is no longer true today, simply by virtue of the passage of time. This attitude is promoted in countless ways. In the argument that a Constitution drafted in 1787 is obsolescent in the twentieth century; that values deemed appropriate for an agricultural society are inappropriate for an industrial one; that "conditions" dictate abandonment of certain ethical absolutes; that norms of conduct preferred by an older generation are no longer "relevant" for the young. This is the meat and drink of numberless professors, pop culture analysts, and leading writers for the mass magazines.

The ultimate relativism is the "value free" or "scientific" approach of the behaviorists, culminating in the doctrines of "logical positivism"—the view that no statement can be considered "true" unless it is empirically verifiable. Thus Professor A. J. Ayer asserts that "if I generalize and say 'stealing is wrong,' I produce a statement which has no factual meaning—that is, expresses no proposition that can be either true or false." The meaning of this value-free approach for all ethical judgments whatsoever is apparent. The logical positivist can tell you how many liters of gas it takes to kill 6 million Jews, but he cannot tell you whether it is wrong to kill them.

Any one species of such relativist thought, propounded steadily enough, would go far to destroy our conceptions of personal liberty. When we consider that all of them have been preached incessantly over a period of decades, the erosion of freedom in our society should hardly be astonishing. For our libertarian notions are distinctive to Christian culture, the Christian value system, and the Christian epoch in history. Any doctrine that teaches us that there are no grounds for preferring a particular culture, value system, or historical epoch in effect tells us, among other things, that there are no grounds for preferring freedom.

The Totalitarian Trend of American Liberalism

Once such premises are adopted slippage from the corpus of Western social value sets in almost immediately. For the past century and more, liberalism has been steadily surrendering the ideas it inherited from Western faith, as its "scientific" quest for the proper social objectives has wound its way into the void. First to go were the classical liberal notions of economic liberty, appreciation of the volitional order of the market, and the conception of the strictly limited state. All of these things were perfectly logical and self-evident to Bentham and the early John Stuart Mill; they were less so to Mill later; they are now completely anathema to Bentham's and Mill's descendants.

Having abandoned the classical liberal view of personal liberty and limited government in matters pertaining to economics, our modern liberals have attempted to cling to certain other remnants of

Western belief—vestiges of libertarian political thought, a species of egalitarianism, the goal of economic progress. But in latter years we have seen that even these commitments, confused as they are, have been abandoned as well. The effect is to bring us out exactly where the totalitarian movements have found themselves—adrift in metaphysical emptiness, without criteria of choice, and with ever-increasing amounts of power piled up in the hands of an unlimited state.

The nature of this slippage is suggested by the career and opinions of Oliver Wendell Holmes, the prototype of the modern liberal mentality. Holmes was, of course, a thoroughgoing relativist, author of what is perhaps the most famous off-hand statement of liberal relativism on record. As he wrote to William James, "I can't help preferring champagne to ditch water—I doubt if the universe does." He went on to assert that "in fact there are as many truths as there are men," that our personal conceptions of truth were merely expressions of our limitations, and that "the attempt to make these limitations compulsory on anything outside our dream—to demand significance, etc., of *the* universe [is] absurd."

This is often depicted as a wonderful starting-point for a libertarian approach to government, on the grounds that one so modest and humble as to foreswear acquaintance with truth is not likely to impose his opinions on others. Holmes himself in the course of his judicial labors made it plain, however, that the consequences of such a view are anything but libertarian, for the logical deduction from the Holmesian premises is that one has no certain reason for objecting to anything, and therefore must drift in whatever direction superior power may take him. Consider, for example, the following 1873 statement by Holmes, subsequently reaffirmed in his later writings:

> It has always seemed to us a singular anomaly that believers in the theory of evolution and in the natural development of institutions by successive adaptations to the environment should be found laying down a theory of government intended to establish its limits once for all by logical deduction from axioms. . . .
> All that can be expected from modern improvements is that legislation should easily and quickly, yet not too quickly, modify itself in accordance with the will of the *de facto* supreme power in the community, and that the spread of an educated sympathy should reduce the sacri-

fice of minorities to a minimum. . . . The more powerful interests must be more or less reflected in legislation . . . It is necessarily made a means by which a body, having the power, put burdens which are disagreeable to them on the shoulders of somebody else.

There is no substantial difference between this view and the reign of the Nietzschean superman except the intercession of Holmes' "educated sympathy." This is an almost perfect epitome of the liberal enterprise over the course of modern history—to embrace the totalitarian premises, but to attempt to forestall the totalitarian result by an exercise in manners. Beneath the veneer of Beacon Street propriety, the effect is apparent. Such formulations abolish the notion of restraint upon the use of power through divine or natural law or the guidelines of a limited constitutional order. Since the epoch of the New Deal, at least, government in our society has come increasingly to rest on precisely these grounds.[1]

Liberal relativism has also degraded, as it must, the value of the individual. Given the emphasis liberal rhetoric has placed on the dignity of man, this may seem paradoxical, but it is rather a simple matter of cause and effect. Having abandoned the premises of Western religion, liberalism has, like its totalitarian precursors, abandoned as well the distinctively Western idea of personality. Man in the modern conspectus is not a creature of God, bearing the image of his Maker and endowed with a soul and therefore with an imperishable value. He is an intelligent animal, the result of purely natural and evolutionary forces whose development is a product of chance and whose future may be determined by applying to him the devices of science. Few themes are stressed more insistently in modern social theory or contemporary proposals for action by government. For example, anthropologist Alfred Kroeber, opines that:

Man, to every anthropologist, is an animal in the given world of nature; that and nothing more—not an animal with a soul or destiny or anything else attached to him beforehand, but an animal to be compared, as to structure and as to function, with other animals; and with the unshakeable conviction that any special traits and qualities which may be ultimately assigned to him are to eventuate from inquiry instead of being supposed.

In some further modulations man is assimilated not merely into animal nature but into the elemental order of physical forces. Carl Becker asserted that the conclusions of modern science lead us to believe that man is "little more than a chance deposit on the surface of the world, thrown up by the same forces that rust iron and ripen corn."

Placed on a level with natural phenomena, objects and animals, man is no longer considered "free" and freedom in fact is viewed as an illusion. Man is determined by the play of natural forces. Psychologist B. F. Skinner puts it that "the hypothesis that man is not free is essential to the application of scientific method of human behavior." He concludes that: "All the causes of human behavior lie outside the individual." Dr. Robert Knight asserts: "Whatever human actions or decisions seem to indicate the operation of a free will, or a freedom of choice, can be shown, on closer inspection and examination and analysis, to be based on unconscious determinism."

From this belief it is only a step to the conclusion that man is like other natural phenomena a suitable object for manipulation and experiment, and modern liberal thought has not been hesitant to take that final step. Social science theory and a good deal of political literature as well has been rife with suggestions that human behavior should be subject to scientific planning and made amenable to prediction and control—that man's essential nature can be changed by the assorted wonders of "science."

The notion of reshaping humanity by tinkering with external material factors has long been characteristic of the liberal program in general. In almost every field liberal policies have incorporated the idea that by making some change in the environment we can bring about a corresponding change in human nature and conduct. This rather vague and diluted environmentalism, however, has of late been getting itself converted into an actual hard-line determinism that may be discerned in every department of political controversy.

For years social theoreticians have expressed the desirability of scientific manipulation of human behavior. Hadley Cantril, for one, suggests that "the only way to bring about the kind of human nature we want is to plan scientifically the kind of social and economic environment offering the best conditions for the development of human nature in the direction we would specify . . ." Harold Lasswell, for another, tells us that "among the tasks of political science is to describe situations which recur with sufficient frequency to make prediction useful as a preliminary to control." Yet another liberal writer asserts that one must ask of abstractions in the field of economics, "is the abstraction a useful one—does it, that is to say, yield the increased power to predict and control which is the aim of all science"?

While the ordinary man is thus reduced to the level of a scientific datum it will be observed that *some* men are implicitly exempted from the general devaluation. These are, of course, the planners and "scientists" themselves. They are the elite who understand the intricate nature of the planning process, of the physical and psychological forces that determine everything. As masters of these forces, they are also the masters of other men. They are entitled by their superior knowledge to direct the lives of everyone else, and in many cases are not bashful about laying claim to such prerogatives. They are, in the Saint-Simonian description of one scientific publicist, "the new priesthood." In some statements, they appear in fact as surrogates of God himself, the nearest approach in an apostate world to a form of divinity.

The last several years have seen a burst of commentary on precisely this theme. Through genetic science, it is now considered possible not merely to alter the direction of human development, but to create new forms of life. "When that time comes," says one commentator, "man's powers will be truly godlike. He may bring into being creatures never before seen or imagined in the universe. He may even choose to create new forms of humanity—beings that might be better adapted to survive on the surface of Jupiter, or on the bottom of the Atlantic Ocean." Another commentator, the late Leroy Augenstein, stated the matter even more explicitly. His 1969 book on this topic was entitled, *Come, Let Us Play God*. Another writer puts it that "at this point, man will be remolding his own being. Theologians will protest but it is certainty itself that man will play God." Reading over enough such statements, one becomes aware that the use of the word "man" is a euphemism; it is the planners and scientists who are supposed to play God. The rest of us will play clay.

Simultaneously with all this, we have been building up the concentration of political and economic power through a collectivist social organization that permits pervasive control of human life. We need not at this point consider whether the power government exerts in this respect is of itself right or wrong. We need simply observe that it is enormous. In matters of personal income, housing, schooling, wages, health care, retirement plans, welfare, consumer protection, food and drugs, advertising, pollution control, job training, and an infinite variety of industrial regulations, government today has a point of entry into virtually every phase of national life. Through the machinery of taxation and subsidies, plus the rules and guidelines that accompany the latter, it has immense potential leverage over all of us. The question of immediate urgency is whether it is seeking to use that leverage, and if so for what purpose.

Three issues of contemporary political debate suggest an answer. These are the issues of sex education in the schools, "busing" for purposes of racial balance, and population control. Ordinarily these are debated as totally separate matters with public attention focused on such questions as whether children are being exposed to pornographic material, whether "racial balance" is a desirable objective, whether there are too many people in our society, and so on. These are, needless to remark, all important issues. But I would contend that they are not the *central* issues in any of these controversies.

The central issue in each case is the same: the idea that the state has a paramount interest over the life of the individual—an interest that entitles it to supersede the authority of the family and wield the major shaping influence in the life of the child. This is most obvious, perhaps, in the case of the "sex education" dispute, in which it is routinely contended that experts in the school must perform this task because the parents are not properly trained and are incompetent to instruct their children. In some cases this view is carried to the point where the experts in the schools actively prevent parents from finding out what their children are being taught. And, as we shall note, the "sex education" dispute has other implications that carry this conception of state control even further into the realm of explicit "social engineering."

The motivation is less apparent in the case of "busing," but it is there nonetheless. Controversy about racial percentages, the neighborhood school, and the like, while perfectly justified, has distracted attention from the underlying purpose and rationale of the whole "busing" enterprise, which embraces a number of other issues as well. This is spelled out at some length by authorities like Professor James Coleman, author of the famous *Coleman Report* which is the constitutive document of the "busing" movement In essence, the point is to get the Negro child out from under the influence of his home, his parents, and his neighborhood, and placed as fully as possibly under the control of the government. Only thus, it is assumed, can he achieve assimilation into the larger society.

Coleman's thesis is that the Negro child loses the good effects of his expert schooling when he returns to his family environment. Thus, "a more intense reconstruction of the child's social environment than that provided by school integration is necessary to remove the handicap of a poor family background. It is such reconstruction that is important—whether it be provided through other children, through tutorial programs, through artificial environments created by computer consoles." And again: "For those children whose family and neighborhood are educationally disadvantaged, it is important to replace this family environment as much as possible by an educational environment—by starting school at an early age, and by having a school that begins very early in the day and ends very late." Hence, Operation Headstart, day care centers, and busing—any device that gets the child away from his parents and under the influence of the official experts.

The same motivation, even more intense, runs through the controversy over population control. Again the surface discussion, although clearly connected to the fundamental issue, has a way of obscuring it. That issue is whether the experts having intruded themselves into the most intimate questions of family life and having asserted the right to remove the child from the suasion of his parents, may now claim the most terrible power of them all—the power to decide who shall live and who shall not, who shall be allowed to have children and who shall be prevented. It is in the dispute over population control that we may discern most clearly the totalitarian advance.

For the would-be shapers of a new humanity, population control is the essential issue. If we are to be bred into a race of super-beings, someone will have to make the essential decisions—weeding out the unfit, mating the fit, conducting experiments with the human material to get the proper mixture of characteristics. Increasingly one finds populationists talking not merely of numbers, but of eliminating "unwanted" or "unfit" children from the ranks of humanity—in which pursuit abortion and sterilization are viewed as essential tools. Consider, in this connection, a recent article in *Time* that tells us:

> Other problems are still in the far future, but how the dilemmas of population control are handled will set important patterns for later issues. Population pressures increase the likelihood of widespread government drives, or even coercion, to limit births. Couples who are warned by genetic counseling that they risk producing deformed offspring would face far greater pressure than they do now to avoid having children; those with defective genes could become, in effect, second-class citizens, a caste of genetic lepers.
>
> One current example illustrates the problem. Amnicentesis can now quite accurately predict whether a fetus is mongoloid; women carrying such abnormal fetuses are now encouraged, where it is legal, to have abortions. Already a number of medical planners are pointing up the cost-effectiveness of abortion in those cases. Unless the birth rate of mongoloid children is reduced, their care by 1975 may well cost some $1.75 billion annually.

These and other such data suggest that the effort to weed out the "unfit" and to limit human reproduction by abortion and sterilization is already upon us. The "sex education" drive, in addition to its assumption that experts rather than parents must be placed in charge of developing the child, is an essential component of this campaign. As one spokesman for these programs has phrased the matter, such classes help the student to relate his "role as a producer of children to the larger social role of human control of population size." Another states that the program "is an essential aspect of what might be termed total contraception," and adds that "this is a new aspect in human engineering."

Agitation on the population question has produced suggestions for coercion of almost every type. Scientist dreams of human engineering, breeding people on eugenic principles, and "expert" abridgement of fundamental freedoms are finding their way increasingly into popular political discourse. Consider, for example, the statement of liberal publicist Gore Vidal on the related questions of government power and population control. "I would like to replace our present system with an Authority—with a capital A—that would have total control over environment," Vidal says. "And environment means not only air, earth, and water but the distribution of services and products, and the limitation of births." This authority would be compatible with personal freedom, Vidal suggests, because "the thing should be run like a Swiss hotel, with anonymous specialists going about their business under constant review by a council of scientists, poets, butchers, politicians, teachers—the best group one could assemble." (Saint-Simon again.) Under this system:

> only certain people would be allowed to have children. Nor is this the hardship that it might at first appear. Most people have no talent for bringing up children and they usually admit it—once the damage is done . . . The right to unlimited breeding is not a constitutional guarantee. If education and propaganda failed, those who violated the birth control restrictions would have to pay for their act as for any other criminal offense. I suspect that, eventually, the whole idea of parenthood will vanish, when children are made impersonally by the laboratory insemination of ova . . . I would favor an intelligent program of eugenics that would decide which genetic types would be continued and which allowed to die off. It's within the range of our science to create, very simply, new people physically healthier and intellectually more competent than ourselves. After all, we do it regularly in agriculture and in the breeding of livestock, so why not with the human race?

If this all sounds vaguely familiar, it should. Compare Vidal's remarks with the following:

> The state has to make the child the most precious possession of the people. It has to take care that only the healthy beget children; that there is only one disgrace; to be sick and to bring children into the world despite one's own deficiencies; but one highest honor: To renounce this . . . It has to put the most modern medical means at the service of this knowledge. It has to declare unfit for propagation everybody who is visibly ill and has inherited a disease and it has to carry this out in practice . . . By education it has to teach the individual that it is not a disgrace but only a regrettable misfortune to be sick and weakly, but that it is a crime and therefore at the same time a disgrace to dishonor this misfortune by one's egoism by burdening it again upon an innocent being . . . The state has finally to succeed

in bringing about that nobler era when men see their care no longer in the better breeding of dogs, horses, and cats, but rather in the uplifting of mankind itself . . .

Those are, of course, the words of Adolf Hitler.

Conclusion

Vidal's conclusion, so similar to Hitler's, is fully congruent with the beginning liberal assumption about the nature of man. If, in fact, humanity is simply a "chance deposit" cast up on the shore of earth by "the same forces that rust iron and ripen corn," if man is that and nothing more, then the broad road down to eugenic breeding and human reengineering and all the rest of it, is open before us. We do it with agriculture and livestock, why not with human beings? Why not indeed? The monstrous conclusion is implicit in the original premise. With these delusions of god-like power, the remolding of humanity, and Authorities with a capital A, the liberal effort to construct a libertarian order on totalitarian premises has obviously collapsed, and liberalism itself therefore expires.

Note

1. That we have entered a period in which the predominant power alone determines the reach of government authority has long been contended, of course, by critics of New Deal and other liberal programs. We now have, however, the testimony of a principal New Deal architect that in the hey-day of liberalism the restraints of the written Constitution were effectively overthrown, leaving us with a central power operated on the general principles enunciated by Holmes. According to Rexford Guy Tugwell, the Constitution "was a negative document meant mostly to protect citizens from their government, not to define its duties to them or theirs to it." In the New Deal, all this was changed so that we moved "from competition to mutuality," to "stability and discipline." Such things, Tugwell says, "were tortured interpretations of a document intended to prevent them." Even by those who favored the alteration, "it really had to be admitted that it was done irregularly and according to doctrines the framers would have rejected."

The Continuing Claims of Liberalism

CHARLES FRANKEL

My first reaction to the question, "After liberalism, what?" is to wonder what radicals and conservatives will do with themselves if liberalism goes. They will be wandering around without a purpose in life.

The first thing, I suppose, in discussing liberalism and its assumed or desired demise is to try to be a bit clear about what "liberalism" means. And to do this, it is necessary to make a distinction between what I would call "critical liberalism" and "pop liberalism."

Almost all important social outlooks tend in the course of time to develop on two levels. At one level, there is a solid core of ideas resting on a tradition of sophisticated discourse and argument; if the outlook has been more than the creed of an insulated sect, these ideas also carry the imprint of practical experience, of the decisions that governments, courts or significant political movements have had to make when they were seeking to attain or use power and were not merely engaged in symbolic or play-acting gestures. However, a social outlook, as it moves out into the political arena and cultural marketplace, inevitably picks up a large number of adherents whose

Reprinted by permission of the *National Review*, 150 East 35th Street, New York City. Charles Frankel (Ph.D., Columbia University) is Professor of Philosophy at Columbia University and was Assistant Secretary of State for Educational and Cultural Affairs (1965–1967). He is an editor-at-large of the *Saturday Review* and author of numerous articles and books including *High on Foggy Bottom*, *The Case for Modern Man*, *The Democratic Prospect*, *The Love of Anxiety*, and *Education and the Baricades*.

relation to it is like Pavlov's dogs to their bell. They simply salivate when they hear the right sounds. Accordingly, there arises at a second level, a cheapened version of the original outlook, louder but flabbier. If a core outlook expresses skepticism about human wisdom or goodness, its debased version will be cynical; if it is marked by compassion for suffering, its shrill partner will turn this into a belief in the superior virtue of those who suffer.

Liberalism operates on these two levels. Critical liberalism has tried to look at social issues as *problems,* to be approached without fixed preconceptions or empty arguments over political labels like "Left" and "Right," but rather with a view to determining the facts and finding a fair and workable solution. Pop liberalism turns this into the astonishing notion that a cure lies ready at hand for any problem that exists, and that the mere presence of the problem is a sign of the wickedness or benightedness of the powers that be. Critical liberalism makes the elementary point that the reform of institutions is necessary to their health. The pop liberal turns this into a feeling of shame in the presence of anyone who seems to want change more than he, and constantly worries about being outflanked on the Left. This process of removing all modulation, complexity and sense of fact from a body of ideas is called, I believe, "telling it like it is."

But liberalism is anything but unique in this respect. It is not foolproof, but neither is any other point of view. Accordingly, when we compare the merits and demerits of liberalism to other outlooks, we ought to be sure which version of it we have in mind. I would not confuse Edmund Burke with a leader of the John Birch Society, and I would not try to refute Karl Marx or Professor Genovese by discussing the views of Jerry Rubin or analyzing the thought-processes of those who, to strike a blow for liberty, throw bombs at libraries. Similarly, it is a far cry from the ideas of John Stuart Mill, John Dewey or Louis Brandeis to the views of pop liberals.

To be sure, a social outlook has to be judged, if we are measuring its actual historical and political significance, not only in terms of its core of developed ideas, but in terms of the distinctive kind of deformation to which it is prone. Pop liberalism has to be assessed as part of the total phenomenon known as "liberalism." But if we do so, the alternatives against which it must be weighed, at least within the framework of the present discussion, are pop conservatism and pop radicalism. And I would ask the reader to consider, as the first step in our discussion, whether these poisons, all in all, are not perhaps even worse than the poison of pop liberalism.

List a few of the traits of radicalism in its critical version: a politically oriented critique of science, art and culture; an analysis of social issues in terms of class conflict; an emphasis on the importance of achieving its goals combined with suspicion of the restrictions that liberals place on the means that should be used; a deliberate vagueness about the actual character of these goals; and an optimism that endemic problems of modern society, such as bureaucracy and the management of the economy can be solved or by-passed if only people have the right ideological stance and have been made over as new men with a new ethic. Give the top radical a crack at these notions, and he turns them, as we know, into philistinism, a Manichean view of society, a mindless retreat to theatrical actions for their own sake, and a view of government and politics in which hypostasized abstractions play the parts of real people. I am not impressed.

Nor does pop conservatism do better. The critical conservative stresses the importance of continuity with the past, of fixed principles, of loyalty; the pop conservative greets dissent with indignation, and sees conspiracy as the great cause of social disturbances. The critical conservative, in the last half century, has argued that the free market is the most rational means for allocating social resources and determining social utilities; the pop conservative falls into platitudes whose effect is to defend privilege, the manipulation of the consumer, and the arrangements that permit industry to pass off to the rest of us its costs in pollution, ugliness and inconvenience. And he seems incapable of even formulating the question whether there are social and cultural values with respect to which the marketplace is an inadequate judge.

When we turn to the issue of violence, domestic and international pop radicalism and conservatism look, if possible, even worse. Pop radicalism sleepwalks in a dream of revolution that is at once unrealistic and internally incoherent. The revolution won't happen, and if it did happen the industrial machine wouldn't produce the goods required to achieve peace and plenty because the people who know enough or care enough to run the machine will have been alienated or exterminated. In an advanced society, a "revolution" is just what the word implies: one full turn around, accompanied by dizziness and nausea.

As for pop conservatism, its indignation at protest at home merely hardens the protest and makes it worse. And its preoccupation abroad with ideological confrontations and military measures freezes the international scene in a state of hopelessness and terror which imposes intolerable strains on human beings. It is unreasonable to think that this condition can indefinitely endure without exploding into violence or collapsing into nihilism. The process has already started. Unless we are really prepared to talk about hydrogen bombs as though they were large bows and arrows, there is therefore something to be said for the desire, even of jejune liberals, to stand in between the warring fanaticisms and exercise a moderating influence.

But let us turn to more promising subjects. The current scene is dominated by the kinds of superstition I have been describing. The problem is to see whether we can reconstruct critical social philosophies—radical, conservative, liberal or unlabeled—that might remove some of the contamination from the intellectual air. Does a critical liberalism have anything to contribute to this task? I am inclined to think that even conservatives and radicals, if they are critical-minded and if they are prepared to look into their own minds candidly, will agree that they want and need this kind of liberalism.

Obviously, no brief account of what I have called "critical liberalism" can be more than a sketch. But I would suggest that it is a composite of three things: a general attitude toward life or *Weltanschauung*; a belief in certain political practices and moral norms; and a set of particular social programs, which change as conditions alter and new knowledge emerges. Let us speak about the *Weltanschauung* first. It has two strands—a sense of the many-sidedness of the human scene, and a sense that every social system weighs more heavily on some people than on others and that this should be corrected to the extent that it is possible.

The first strand in the liberal attitude is suggested by the meaning we attach to the word "liberal" when we speak of a liberal education or of a man of liberal intelligence or disposition. What the word "liberal" designates, I take it, when it is used in this way is a certain breadth of interests and sympathies, a recognition of diversity and variety, a sense of the inevitable limitations of any man's situation or perspective. Conservatives and radicals, of course, can be liberal in this sense, and political liberalism cannot be credited with having invented this attitude. However, it is the political outlook that has attached the greatest social value to it, and that has tried most deliberately to develop the political forms and strategies calculated to support and spread it.

The second strand in the liberal *Weltanschauung* comes from its historical role as the outlook of groups struggling to break through an inherited system of power and privilege. In the course of its history, accordingly, liberalism has split in half. A liberal philosophy developed which spoke for the interests of groups and classes that had managed to arrive, and which interpreted the broad liberal ideals of liberty and equality in such a way as to restrict their practical application to the protection of the liberties and powers possessed by these groups and classes. However, there also remained another branch of liberalism which retained the tradition of speaking for those shut out from the protection and opportunities offered by the existing social order. This variety of liberalism interpreted the general ideals of liberty and equality as imposing a continual requirement for social reform in the interests of those who bear an undue proportion of a society's burdens. This is the source of the egalitarian strand in the liberal *Weltanschauung*.

Accordingly, although the specific social programs favored by critical liberals change from one period to another, there tends to be continuity in their views about the political forms and moral norms within which such programs should be realized. Translated into political and moral terms, the liberal *Weltanschauung* calls for making tolerance the keystone on which social cooperation depends. In education and government, in the relations between classes, in styles of culture, it favors choices that are likely to promote rational communication and criticism, a fluid social structure and a dispersion of power sufficient to give the curious and the restless room to turn around. And because liberalism's outlook is dominated by a sense of the many-sidedness of the individual and of any sophisticated society, it stresses the virtues of negotiation and compromise, within a framework of civil liberty about which there can be no compromise. It does so not simply because negotiation and compromise are "realistic," but because they reflect the moral respect that should be shown to people whose interests and views are different from one's own.

The two strands in the liberal *Weltanschauung* also explain some of the problems that have characterized the internal history of liberalism. In moments of crisis, liberals have often split between those for whom liberty and tolerance are crucial and those for whom the cause of the weak is more important. Moreover, in its concern to speak to and for the people who are shut out, liberalism has collected allies whose roots go back to traditions of evangelical social reform or to Calvinistic or Prophetic struggles against flesh and the devil. Thus, the distinctive tradition of political liberalism, with its anti-Utopian bias and its distaste for absolutisms that divide people into the camps of the saved and the damned, has lived in the recurrent danger of being submerged in the heat of the battle.

There are two morals which are often drawn from this story by conservatives and radicals. One is that liberalism had better decide whether it cares more for liberty or for equality, for negotiation or for justice. But the choice cannot be made. Liberty and tolerance are not likely to survive in crowded modern societies unless there is a serious effort to remove major reasons for social discontent. Conversely, equality without liberty or individual or cultural variety is a stifling prospect, and not a very good bet even for achieving equality. The libertarian and egalitarian strands in liberalism produce an inner tension, but without that tension each would be incomplete.

The second false moral is that liberalism should stay out of coalitions because it loses its purity in them. However, the practical success of liberalism has derived mainly from its power to work in coalitions with people not all of whom are liberals pure and simple. While there are dangers in this, and liberalism has sometimes succumbed to the dangers, the alternative is for liberals to emulate ideological conservatives and radicals and remain pure and simple. Surely a political philosophy has another purpose besides giving its adherents a sense of their superiority to the rest of the world.

Accordingly, I would ask a question of thoughtful conservatives and radicals: When they advocate the death of liberalism, are they also advocating the death of the liberal attitudes and political-moral beliefs that I have described? Do they want no liberty and tolerance and no institutions to protect them, or no concern for a widening equality and for public goods on which everyone's individual welfare depends? These are straight questions, and they should not hedge like the proverbial liberals they describe. If, as I suspect, the answer of many of them would be that, of course, they wish these attitudes and concerns kept alive, they should then ask themselves what they are willing to pay to do so. The price, I believe, is the substantial modification, in tone and substance, of their positions.

For myself, I do not see how toleration or compassion can be kept alive, except perhaps in a few monastic retreats, if we accept the radicals' belief that conflict between different classes or ideologies are irreconcilable and can be settled only by total victory for one side. Nor do I see how they can be kept alive in the world as it is if we adopt the conservative view that the free market, if only we leave it alone, is capable of providing us with livable cities, a decent countryside, an enforceable system of law and order, or an economy that does not leave millions as public charges. In the abstract, there is perhaps the dim possibility that the conservative theory of the free market can be defended. But it is not politically viable, and it could be put into practice only at the expense of draconic forms of social control.

The problem, indeed, for conservatives and radicals, as for liberals, at any rate if all are interested in maintaining a liberal civilization, is not to engage in abstract polemics but to construct social programs capable of winning assent and of dealing with the quite unprecedented problems we face. In this regard, both conservatism and radicalism, it seems to me, are unequivocally nostalgic. They breathe the preconceptions of a world that no longer exists, if ever it did. But I confess that liberalism, in its concrete social programs, is only a little less fixed on the past. It is still living fairly largely on the inherited capital of the Thirties.

This momentum from the past is not sufficient to keep it going; and neither are arguments, no matter how successful, which show that its basic attitudes and principles are sound. What will count for the future of liberalism is the attractiveness and strength of character of its leadership, and the appeal and effectiveness of its practical programs. A major task of renovation lies ahead of liberalism. Its problem thirty years ago was to increase the productivity of the economy.

Its problem now—everybody's problem—is to create ways to bring the economy under the control of a humane system of social cost-accounting that will be sensitive to the costs, in anxiety, disorder and inanity, of the idolatry of GNP. Liberalism's problem three decades ago was to get people back to work. Its problem now is to reorganize work so that more of those who engage in it will enjoy it and believe that its purpose is useful, and fewer will be apathetic or hostile. And in every other field—the cities, education, race relations, welfare policy, foreign affairs—liberalism's situation is similar: The old assumptions no longer hold, and what is needed is the capacity to think through to new ones.

Indeed, liberalism, if it wishes to survive, is under a special obligation to develop workable programs. In this sense it is weaker than either radicalism or conservatism. Radicalism has a way of surviving irrelevance and failure, for what it offers is escape to another world. And conservatism is not likely to notice that it is anachronistic. For when the solutions it offers are no longer workable, it condemns the world and not itself.

It may be, as the radicals say, that liberalism is too patient and polite to do what needs to be done to relieve human misery. But radicals are the last ones who should talk, in the United States, of getting things done and getting them done fast. Liberalism's past record of effectiveness and speed in lessening human misery is better than radicalism's. And it may be, as the conservatives say, that liberalism listens too much and bends too easily. But rigid structures break more easily than flexible ones, and unless conservatives are prepared to stand fast, and to pay the price in force and intimidation that this will probably cost, they will need liberals to nudge them a bit. If liberalism goes, what follows? What follows, I think, is a radicalism turned wholly doctrinaire, a conservatism turned irretrievably callous, and an illiberal society.

Conservatism

PETER VIERECK

Once upon a time a student at the British Museum said to the librarian, "Fetch me a copy of the French Constitution." She primly replied, "Sorry, Sir, but we don't stock periodicals."

That seemingly simple sentence is the best summary of organic Burkean conservatism versus mechanical liberal enlightenment. On the one hand, there is a freedom deeply rooted in an unwritten British constitution, embodying centuries of historical experience. On the other hand, a freedom having such shallow roots as the grand abstract slogans of written French rationalism, requiring every few years an ever newer constitution, listing ever grander Rights of Man, only to be repeatedly superseded because these are top-of-the-brain abstractions without roots in human nature or historical experience.

We can embody freedom but cannot engineer it. We can live it but cannot write it down. Every attempt to blueprint it, whether in 1789 or 1917, has resulted in a bed-of-Procrustes, a bloodbath, and a new form of police state.

Let us try to make a basic distinction between two viewpoints, a distinction not narrowly political but based on a philosophy of human nature. Conservatism (like the British Constitution) is the organic relationship of concrete to concrete, evolved like living trees from deeply-experienced historical roots. Rationalist liberalism (like the many French constitutions) is the mechanical piling-up of abstrac-

Peter Viereck (Ph.D., Harvard University) holds the Alumnae Chair in Modern History at Mount Holyoke College. He is a Pulitzer Prize winning poet as well as the author of numerous articles and books in history and political theory. His more recent prose books include *Conservatism, Shame and Glory of the Intellectuals,* and *Conservatism Revisited.* His most recent book of poetry is *New and Selected Poems.* He was twice the recipient of a Guggenheim Fellowship to write poetry and has been a guest lecturer at many European and American universities.

tion on abstraction, moving its institutions around like separate pieces of furniture, contrived from top-of-the-brain blueprints.

Conservatism serves "growingness" and moves inarticulately and ritualistically, like the recurrent four seasons. Liberalism serves "progress" and moves more consciously and more systematically, like geometry or a logical syllogism. Conservatism sees history as a spiraling circle, a cycle; liberalism sees it as an ever-advancing straight line. Both are needed insights, equally inherent in the human condition, liberalism on a more rational level, conservatism on a perhaps somewhat deeper level, more intuitive and human and less mechanical.

The word "conservative," and the concept of the "American conservative," can have so many different meanings, both good and bad, that the first question on reading this article ought to be: "What does this author stand for specifically, who are his philosophical teachers and political heroes, through whom we can more specifically classify him?" As a Burkean conservative, the thinkers whom I admire are the Englishmen Winston Churchill, Samuel Coleridge, Benjamin Disraeli, and Edmund Burke, the Frenchman Alexis de Toqueville, the Swiss Jakob Burckhardt, the Norwegian Lars Roar Langslet, and the American John Adams, plus the authors of *The Federalist Papers* of 1787. I emphatically do not admire right-wing radicals like Barry Goldwater and Ronald Reagan. The psychological key to these reactionaries from Arizona and California is perhaps that they are not only right of center but west of center.

In American journalistic usage today, the word "conservative" is often used for such reactionaries rather than for genuine Burkean conservatives. This is because of the notorious Goldwater campaign of 1964, which took over the word "conservative" in order to make the unrespectable seem respectable. Thereby a good word became temporarily lost in the labyrinth of journalistic politics. But in the field of serious political philosophy, conservatism can still be used in its correct Burkean meaning; that is how I shall try to use it here.

I belong to no political party, conservative or otherwise, and have felt no enthusiasm for any American politician since the late Adlai Stevenson. In contrast with the unethical present politics of escalation in Vietnam, Stevenson combined the best of liberalism with the best of conservatism, a blending of Thomas Jefferson with Edmund Burke.

Those few books of mine that have reached a fairly large student audience via paperback, such as *The Unadjusted Man* and *Conservatism Revisited*, do not propagandize for conservatism as a systematized political credo—unlike Marxism there is no such animal—but rather for certain conservative insights into history and human nature. These insights aim to change not your political party but your way of thinking. They aim to challenge whatever is your particular form of conformity, especially that fashionable and stylized conformity that calls itself radical nonconformity.

Back in 1937 or 1938 during my student days at Oxford, I heard a socialist speaker, G. H. D. Cole, praise what he called "the inevitability of gradualness." At that moment I realized that Burkean conservative principles are most useful not via the triumph of any self-styled conservative party, but via an equal nonpartisan diffusion through all parties. Beside the phrase "the inevitability of gradualness," that I first learned from the socialist Cole, I should like to place these two sentences learned from Edmund Burke:

> Men are qualified for civil liberties in exact proportion to their disposition to put moral chains on their own appetites. Society cannot exist unless a controlling power upon will and appetite be placed somewhere, and the less of it there is within, the more there must be without.

It may be generalized that the conservative mind does not like to generalize. Conservative theory is antitheoretical. The liberal and rationalist mind consciously *verbalizes* abstract blueprints, but the conservative mind semi-consciously *embodies* concrete traditions. Liberal formulas very brilliantly *define* freedom, with irrefutable open-minded logic. Conservative traditions unbrilliantly *live* freedom, with unbeatable bigoted stubborness. Here the contrast is between Churchill's England and the fall of France during the Nazi onslaught of 1940.

Why did Churchill not yield? Because he was rooted in an old tradition going back to his ancestor, the Duke of Marlborough, who had similarly stood stubbornly against the earlier tyrant of Europe, Louis XIV. The British people as a whole were similarly rooted not in French Rights of Man or slogans of "liberty, equality, fraternity," but in centuries of a shared past, shared provinces and tombstones and landmarks. During the French Revolution, France had eroded its shared past by the brilliant logic of its metric systems that replaced traditional stupid measurements, and by its logically shaped *départments,* that replaced the old awkward historical provinces. Thus England threw back the Nazis, as a deeply-rooted tree throws back a storm, whereas France went down because its roots were no deeper than the thin topsoil of the eighteenth century. Who the devil wants to die fighting for some artificial, geometric-shaped province?

Similarly, the late Senator Joseph McCarthy was not defeated by the clever arguments of our liberals, who were right about his lies but were ineffective against him. He was defeated by the Senate conservatives, like Watkins, Ervin, and Flanders, who effectively "censured" and destroyed him because they were rooted in that traditional American Constitution including its Fifth Amendment which McCarthy had violated but which liberals had long mocked as outdated.

Similarly, in his 1968 campaign for the Presidency, America's leading anti-Negro racist and economic Populist radical, Governor George Wallace of Alabama, made a special point of denouncing the Supreme Court as a small, meddling aristocracy. He demanded that its laws on Negro rights be replaced by popular plebiscites and what he called "democratic majority rule," meaning rule by white lynch law. Here is a 1971 sample of Wallace populism:

> I would ask the Supreme Court: if you're so interested in busing, why don't you bus some of this money of the ultra-rich into the Treasury instead of little children. . . . That banking crowd in Wall Street and the foundations are more dangerous to the United States than any militant group I ever heard of.

Similarly, in the France of 1899 the innocent Captain Dreyfus was saved by an unpopular, unelected group of judges from the majoritarian antisemitic mob, who at first supported the militarists who had framed him. If the Dreyfus case had been decided by a vote, in "fair and free elections," instead of by anti-majoritarian aristocracy of dedicated jurists, an innocent man would have rotted on Devil's Island.

When threatened by rightist thought-controllers today, American liberals rightly cling to the Supreme Court and Constitution, both of which can legally overrule a majority vote of Congress or of the people. Yet in the 1930s liberals discredited the Supreme Court—this was the part of Roosevelt's New Deal that I oppose on conservative grounds—by calling them "the nine old men" and demanding elective or democratically responsive judges instead. Thank God that the American Supreme Court is aristocratic and not democratic, that it is not elected nor subject to a majority vote. Suppose that 90 percent of America, in a fair and free election, voted to lynch all members of one minority, be it Negroes or Catholics or Jews, be it millionaires or be it socialists. The unelected Supreme Court of nine aristocrats, true to the *noblesse oblige* of administering civil liberties and the equal rights guaranteed by our Constitution, would have the legal right to stop the lynching—and in actual practice has often exercised that right, notably on behalf of Negroes and minorities.

Better the nine black robes of a traditional aristocracy of judges, conserving the Constitution against McCarthyite tyrants of right or left, than the white robes of that very democratic alternative—the Ku Klux Klan. What defeated Joseph McCarthy as well as the racist persecutors of Dreyfus, was not democracy but aristocracy, not modern rationalist enlightenment but ancientness of framework.

Even a seemingly useless or parasitic framework, such as aristocracy and monarchy, may serve freedom by the sheer conservative magic of possessing roots. For example, why has no one ever pointed out the following facts? In World War II the three chief enemies of liberty were the plebeians Hitler, Mussolini, and Stalin. The three chief defenders of liberty, not merely for themselves but for all victims of Hitler, were the aristocrats Churchill, Roosevelt, and De Gaulle. The only major attempt against Hitler inside Germany came not from the masses, who worshipped him, but from aristocrats like von Stauffenberg and von Moltke.

Except for Italy, where the monarchy eventually dismissed Mussolini, the two worst despotisms in history were republics based on mass plebiscites: namely Nazi Germany and Stalinist Russia. In World War II the overwhelming majority of governments fighting against Hitler and for parliamentary liberty and racial tolerance were not republics but monarchies. The monarchies of Norway, Denmark, Holland, Greece, Rumania, Yugoslavia, and Great Britain all resisted the Nazi mass armies. Not one of these kings or queens collaborated with Hitler, but the masses—an overwhelming majority of the German masses—did collaborate with Hitler.

In short, the voice of the people can be the voice of Satan, not of God. The future of freedom may depend on whether this generation realizes that freedom and mass welfare are threatened by majority dictatorship as much as by aristocratic minorities. Jakob Burckhardt, de Tocqueville, Nietzsche, Bertrand de Jouvenel, John Adams, Alexander Hamilton, and the magnificent tenth *Federalist Paper* have all warned against majority dictatorship. Here is a typical passage from America's ablest founding father, President John Adams: "Depotism, or unlimited sovereignty, or absolute power is the same in a majority or a popular assembly . . . and a single emperor. Equally arbitrary, cruel, and bloody, and in every sense diabolical. . . . The multitude therefore, as well as the noble must have a check."

To offer such a check on majorities as well as minorities is the purpose of that very conservative institution, the American Constitution and its Supreme Court. Supporting Burke and attacking that liberal demigod Rousseau, Adams wrote in 1814 to the liberal Jefferson, "I never could understand the doctrine of the perfectability of the human mind . . . I am not of Rousseau's opinion."

Even though in the reverse direction of counter-revolution, the radical right is as violent as any "red." In contrast, the Burke-Adams core-conservative favors steady, gradual, *un*revolutionary change. So, of course does the moderate liberal. But the conservative does so without the liberal's optimism, his faith in progress and abstract formulas and in the reasonableness of man and mass. Whether with religious literalness or as a metaphor for the Freudian id, conservatives apply to man and mass the assumption of the great Christian pessimists (from Augustine on) about man's inherent moral weakness. Herein lies the profoundest philosophical distinction of all between the otherwise often similar central position of moderate liberals and moderate conservatives. Call conservative politics a religious axiom made secular (original sin); call liberal politics a secular axiom made into a religion (natural goodness of man).

According to conservatives, men are not born naturally free or good, but naturally prone to evil, folly, anarchy, pride, and mutual destruction. Rousseau's *Social Contract* of 1762, the bible of the

Jacobian dictator Robespierre and other secular saints of leftist ideology, denounces as chains the traditional restrictions of society on the ego of man and mass. These chains hinder man's natural goodness according to liberals. Oh, no, these same chains (so reply conservatives) are in reality the framework enabling man to be at least partly good and free, despite his fallible nature. Without such a stable, durable framework, ethical behavior and responsible use of liberty are impossible. "Man is born free yet everywhere in chains," laments Rousseau in his famous opening sentence. "Thank God for the chains," interrupts the conservative, perhaps adding Goethe's comments that all increases in liberty lead to self-destruction unless accompanied by an equal increase in self-restraint.

Depending on the country or the time, this necessary framework may be monarchy, aristocracy, established church, property, constitution, or supreme court. We must peacefully alter that antiquated framework in accordance with more ideal blueprints, say moderate liberals like Jefferson and John Stuart Mill. We must throw that wicked framework overboard, say radicals like Tom Paine or the new left. No, we must canalize change within that framework, say conservatives, lest change without traffic lights end up in left or right concentration camps.

Radicals of left or right want to uproot the framework—those so-called "chains"—for the sake of some Rousseauistic "noble savage." The noble savage of right or left is supposedly free of original sin and hence should follow his so-called "healthy instincts" rather than the wisdom of the past. This noble savage may be the right-wing redneck of George Wallace, or the somewhat imaginary left wing proletarian of Karl Marx. Both are equally examples of what Ortega y Gasset called "the revolt of the masses." Bloodiest of all were the "healthy instincts" of that noble savage known as the German *Volk*.

Radicalism often means a violent physical uprooting, via the leftist barricades or the rightist counter-revolution. Liberalism sometimes means a chic intellectual uprooting, via what was once called the salon. A viable new conservatism must build on a living traditionalism, true to the real and not dead or imaginary roots of America and the west.

The right wing of both Republicans and Democrats are trying to invent a past that really never existed in America, an imaginary tradition of heartless laissez-faire in economics, ignoring those humane religious principles of compassion that are indeed deep-rooted. Economic materialism is equally uprooting whether called capitalist or socialist.

One kind of liberalism was so eager to prove all values "relative" that it undermined the ethical heritage and Judaeo-Christian restraints of the West, as well as the organic traditional institutions that served as a unifying social cement. Thereby liberalism unintentionally paved the way for Hitlerism and Stalinism. Liberalism always begins attractively by liberating men from absurd old prejudices and aristocratic excesses. It ends tragically by putting all men in the position of those few illuminati who, when initiated into the seventh circle of Syria's medieval Order of Assassins, were told the Order's secret of secrets: *"There is no truth; everything is permitted."* Or, to cite an unconscious Broadway jazz echo of the Assassins: "Anything goes." No wonder that Fascist and Communist mass-murder, based on the assumption that every means is permitted to achieve one's ends, followed a century of relativist liberalism and of the most modern "scientific" enlightenment.

Gertrude Himmelfarb, a refreshingly undoctrinaire liberal, writes: "The defense of liberalism has unfortunately been left to philosophers too busy demonstrating the *relativity* of values to establish the *fact* of values." That's just the point, isn't it? The philosophical new conservatism may in part be defined as the rediscovery of values. Values not just for one class or party, but shared by society as a whole, shared voluntarily without rigid ideology or coercion.

Six aspects of our shared roots seem (among many others) of particular interest to Americans of the second half of the twentieth centry. On them depend the prospects of a new conservatism. (Space limits decree that their treatment here can only be cursory and superficial, justified only if it stimulates further and deeper independent thought, if only to disagree, by the reader.)

Aspect   I: Framework
Aspect II: Western heritage
Aspect III: Relative versus absolute
Aspect IV: Property
Aspect V: Conservatizing function of nonconservatives

Aspect VI: The fight against robotization, in the context of the worldwide secession of youth

(In the days of Burke, Maistre, and John Adams, Aspect VI did not yet exist, and today most conservatives continue to act as if it did not exist. Being the problem least discussed in conservative thought and the hardest for either revolutionaries or conservers to solve, let it here be the last and longest.)

In politics moderate conservatives and moderate liberals, even when they disagree, share a common parliamentary framework, so do social democrats, but not communists or fascists; far right and far left are outside the framework. It therefore becomes a measure of the health of our society if both liberals and conservatives gravitate toward the center in a crisis. Conversely it becomes a symptom of fatal illness in any democratic society if, in crisis, the center parties becomes polarized, moving away from the center to the outside left if they are liberals or social democrats, and moving away from the center to the outside right if they are conservatives. The two extremes cause each other, feed on each other; the more communists you have outside the framework on the left, the more you will have fascists outside the framework of decency on the right, which in turn will drive more liberals to the far left, in an unending circle. Therefore, the center parties of the framework, whether liberal, conservative, or social democrat, must stick together against the two mirror-image extremes.

The Concept of Western Man

More important, less narrow than politics is the concept of Western man; his are the values the conservative tries to conserve. Western civilization is an amalgam of four different strands, often mutually in conflict yet all equally needed; their conflict helps give Western man his *élan vitale*. The four strands are the stern moral awareness of Judaism, the universalism and transcendent spirituality of Christianity, the sense of free play of intellect and imagination that Athens promoted, and the respect for law and equality before the law that Rome developed. The conservative will not violate the law even for noble purposes because bad means corrupt good ends, as we learned when Lenin's noble purposes became corrupted, via his lawless violence, into ignoble Stalinism.

Concrete examples are needed to avoid generalities. A concrete example of what Western civilization means was provided by the dying words of Thomas More when executed by the King of England: "I die the King's good servant, but God's first." There speaks Western man. The adolescent type of rebel, who refuses to be the king's servant in anything at all, would say: "I die the king's bad servant; I refuse to render unto Caesar even those things that are Caesar's." And for "king" substitute today whatever is the established framework in society. Thomas More was a relatively conservative type of rebel because he did loyally serve the king (the establishment) up to a point. In other words, Western man is not otherworldly but attached (up to a point) to the earthly realities around him.

Relative Versus Absolute

The reversal of these two categories by Marxists and other economic determinists has been one of the most successful and least-noticed intellectual revolutions. What deserves a book must be hinted at in a paragraph, as the base of the conservative ethical case against these revolutionists. Marxism treats as absolute what is relative (namely the question of what degree you have of capitalism or socialism) and treats as relative what is absolute (namely the means used toward whatever may be your ideological ends). Grandiose or utopian ends—anything beyond concrete piecemeal reforms—will probably never be attained anyhow. So in practice what matters are the means used *en route*; these indeed are attained, indeed only too much so. And the means used to bring a new movement to power are usually the base used to maintain it in power (ponder the road from Lenin to Stalin) regardless of lip-service to this or that end. In effect, the means *are* the movement. Conclusion: don't listen to the words, the programs, the theories of society's magicians; watch what they have up their sleeves, watch what their fingers are doing in your pockets—in short, watch means, not ends.

Property

Anti-conservative crusades often attack it. The French socialist Proudhon defined it as theft. Marx defined it as the weapon of some exploiting class ("expropriate the expropriators" makes fine rhetoric). Even many liberals enjoy wallowing in feelings of delicious ghastly guilt about it. Conservatives take pride in it. They argue that private property shields not merely one class but all citizens from chaos.

Admittedly, any unfair profiteer may, when indicted ethically involve property arguments as a facade. Here lies the source of the bad name deservedly given to the meaner, narrower kinds of conservatism. Far from being a shield against revolution, a conservatism of the pocketbook, having nothing but its selfserving materialism to conserve, becomes a provoker of revolution, a justification for radicalism. More responsible conservatives, as in the pro-labor legislation of Shaftesbury and Disraeli, give property a moral base, a *noblesse oblige* of community service.

Still, this is an area where conservative practice would succumb to ever greater hypocrisy, were it not for the indispensable gadfly-function of continuous radical and socialist criticism. Conservatives will not last long unless they learn to see criticism not as a threat but as a fruitful dialogue that may save them from themselves.

The Conservatizing Function

Just as property cannot be justified without community service, including responsibility to consumers, so society as a whole cannot be justified in theory or soundly based in practice unless the ever-increasing class of industrial workers are given a stake in the *status quo*, a sense of community within the inherited framework. "Workers of the world unite, you have nothing to lose but your chains"—this slogan of the *Communist Manifesto* fails if workers *do* have something to lose: material property plus moral or psychological community-links. Let us define the conservatizing function as the diffusion of both material and moral property among an ever broader base.

Ironically this function is often most effectively performed by

anti-conservatives who, by increasing the stake of the masses, con-
servatize them quite unintentionally, thereby eventually losing their
vote.

Roosevelt's support of trade unionism and social reform made the
American workers immune to Marxist propaganda and re-rooted them
in our traditional constitutional framework. Had our American
President in 1933 been Herbert Hoover, not Roosevelt, the American
worker would today be a radical, and we would have a large American Communist party, like that of France. Instead, America has no
working-man support for communism, only support from café intellectuals. When the Soviet dictator Khrushchev visited America, he
admitted that his toughest opposition came not from businessmen
but from trade union leaders, who demanded to know why the Soviet
worker was so poor, so oppressed, and without the right to strike.
Therefore, philosophical conservatives ignore party labels in politics
and support the conservatizing function rather than necessarily any
self-styled "conservative" party.

Though our free trade unions may hate and misunderstand the
word "conservatism," they unconsciously represent it in a still deeper
sense than giving physical property to the masses. I refer to the
moral property known as organic unity, the old medieval voluntary
organic unity, grown historically and not imposed by force (as in
fascism) or by mechanical abstract unhistorical blueprints (as in
democratic socialism). This unity, whose absence leads to alienation
and demoralization, was often sacrificed by the excessive individualism of liberalism and by the laissez-faire economics of capitalism
before the New Deal reforms made capitalism humane and open to
all. Yet unlike the free trade unions, who are independent of the
State, socialism overcomes the alienation of capitalism by state action.
Who today has not somewhere seen in person the terrible mischief
done when the State is too powerful? Even the Soviets, who like the
Nazis used to ignore this mischief, are now trying (no matter how
reluctantly) to decentralize state power by the Liberman Plan; this
fact is a tremendous admission of the bankruptcy of statism, a tremendous renewal of conservative prospects for the future. Even our
Communist enemies have had tacitly to admit—by their part-way
de-Stalinizing and by their Liberman Plans—that we conservatives
were right about the inherent evil of excessive state power.

Not that the valid alternative to coercive statism is the atomized society of laissez-faire and Manchester liberalism. The valid alternative is a voluntary non-coercive organic unity, found in America not only in trade unions but also among countless other kinds of unifying yet nonstatist activities of the community, even in such matters as artistic and cultural festivities, charitable organizations, parent-teacher associations, public libraries, consumer cooperatives, all kinds of nonpolitical social institutions, and among young people the volunteer committees of the civil rights and anti-war movements at home, and the Peace Corps abroad. Here are three more examples among the many:

1. Neighborhood task forces: volunteers to prevent poverty riots and racial riots and to rebuild the slums by non-government community effort (their superiority to heavy-handed inflexible government-action was proved in New York City by preventing a new Watts in the racial crisis of April, 1968.)

2. The Black Power movement: not in its destructive hate-mongering negative aspect but in the positive aspect of black communities running their own affairs, socially, economically, and humanely, without either the repression or the condescending and humiliating paternalism of a far-off central white government. Such local, intimate groupings of achievement are not only of economic but psychological gain; they give that self-respect that is won by self-reliance.

3. Our churches: fulfilling individual spiritual needs. These needs might be manipulated by official state or party propaganda (as in tsarist Caesaro-papism and its heir: the "statizing" and centralizing of ideology and philosophy by the Communists), were it not for the American principles of separation of church and state and of voluntary pluralism, allowing free choice among religions.

Of all the various voluntary associations (equally outside the coercive unity of socialist statism and the anomie of atomistic deracinating capitalism) the trade unions clearly have the most political weight. But the trade unions serve this purpose best when partly decentralized and locally controlled rather than when they are a mirror-image of overcentralized big business—and when they give not only the necessary cold cash of high wages but a sense of non-economic belongingness also, via warm relations in all kinds of cooperative associations, celebrations, and cerebrations between fellow craftsmen. Parallel associations can be encouraged in depersonalized big business, on a more human and less philistine level than that which sometimes caricatures the Sinclair Lewis world of Rotary Clubs. Whether labor, business, or consumer, such associations of mutual friendship and respect, being nonstatist, achieve the same rerooting effect of which nationalism boasts—and without these three negative by-products of nationalism: intolerance, chauvinism, militarism.

The urging of decentralization on big trade unions is often construed by them as a capitalist gain, and *vice-versa* in the case of decentralization of big business. It need not be so. Rather, we thereby put the small, the local, and the human above the vast, the abstract, and the socialist-bureaucratic. As Burke said, loyalty and roots begin (though they do not end) with one's own small platoon.

In conclusion and in the context of the worldwide uprooting of youth, consider Aspect VI: the fight against robotization. This in turn requires us to search for a nonpolitical cultural continuity that can help conserve what politics can no longer maintain, namely, the individual human spark in a mechanized ant-hive. First, let us take an example from the classical past of conservative roots in their simplest physical sense. Then let us see what happens when, in the rootless mechanized present, we replace that physical loss by a moral or psychological equivalent.

Conserving the Human Element in a Machine Age

The nonpolitical core of the conservative philosophy is man's need for growing roots in a particular concrete place and time. That this need was once fulfillable we learn by reading the following passage by the Greek scholar, Sir Alfred Zimmern; he is evoking the feeling of an ancient Athenian or any community of organic growingness. Zimmern writes:

> He loved every rock and spring in the folds of her mountains, every shrine and haunt within the circuit of her walls. He had watched every day from his childhood the shadow creeping slowly across the marketplace and the old men shifting their seats when the sun grew

too hot. He could tell the voice of the town-crier from the other end of the city. . . . He never forgot the festival of a god or a hero. . . . And when his city brought forth not merely fighters and bards, but architects and sculptors, and all the resources of art reinforced the influence of early association and natural beauty, small wonder that the Greek citizen, as Pericles said, needed but to look at his city to fall in love with her . . .

To maintain this kind of rooted organic society has become almost impossible for modern industrial man. Partly, it is because of the uprooting effect of liberal relativism. Even more it is because of that alienation via technology that the future conservative Disraeli and the socialist Marx both predicted during the 1840s. In contrast with the above passage on Athens, think only of Los Angeles—need more be said?

We cannot undo industrialism, and we cannot afford to be machine-smashers or suicidal Luddites. So it may be argued quite effectively that our increasing industrial centers, unlike our smaller communities, cannot conserve the physical continuity that Zimmern described. In that case the hope (for without continuity men are cavemen again) is to substitute a psychological continuity (moral, religious, or cultural) for the lost physical continuity. Through the new educational possibilities of the same technology that uproots us, perhaps we can preserve cultural rootedness for a wider audience than ever before in history.

Technology has repeatedly misused culture. Today let culture deliberately misuse technology for nontechnical ends: to rescue psychologically the roots we lose physically to the mobility and urbanization of that same technology. The Nazi bully, Goering, was said to boast: "When I hear the word 'culture,' I reach for my pistol." The modern scholar, artist, and humanist can reply: "When I hear the word 'pistol' I reach for my 'culture.' "

The great liberal-materialist dream of the nineteenth-century progressives was that a creative flowering would automatically follow, if only living standards were raised and the masses given the needed leisure. For this, technology had to triumph. But with its higher living standards, its triumph has not brought any higher level of creativity. The masses—and I mean rich as well as poor masses, I don't use the term snobbishly—the masses use their leisure to listen to television, hardly to compose Beethoven sonatas. Cultural *consumption* has increased; this is another matter and involves the status given to culture in an affluent society. But regardless of cultural consumption and its mass paperback sales in America, Europe, and Russia, cultural creativity has not proportionately increased.

Let us apply a crude test as follows: a mere 100,000 Athenians with low living standards and no bath tubs or plumbing or danger of overweight from overeating, achieved more cultural creativity—think of Aeschylus, Socrates, Phidias, I do not need to complete the list—than did 200 million Americans plus 220 million Russians put together. Similarly 100,000 Florentines achieved more cultural creativity—think of Leonardo, Michelangelo, Cellini, again I do not need to complete the list—than did some 500 million Americans and Russian masses with their fatter bellies and more leisure and more literacy and greater technology. If we divide 500 million by 100,000 to attain the proportionate difference in population, we should not have just one Faulkner or Dostoyevsky but 500,000 such equivalents of Aeschylus or Leonardo.

What went wrong with this liberal-materialist dream? The answer lies in the fact that industrial society goes through not one but two stages of technological development. In stage one, man is freed *by* technology. In stage two, he must fight to be freed *from* technology.

In stage one, the stage at which Africa and Asia and some of our own American slums find themselves, technology is a force for good; it builds roads, drains swamps, clears slums, abolishes disease and hunger. No decent person will oppose stage one for the so-called third world. Most of the world right now is clamoring to enter this stage, whether on a socialist or capitalist model, as shown by the behavior of African and Asian nations today, by Russia in 1917, and by America in the 1800s.

But in stage two, the stage reached by the larger part of America and Russia and much of Europe, the admitted material benefits of technology are now outweighed by the spiraling harm. The harm consists of turning individuals into organization men and subjecting us all to faceless bureaucracy. The robotization is not accidental but inherent in stage two, as proved by the fact that it cuts across ideological and economic and political lines and takes place equally in capitalist and socialist countries. Both countries, in consequence, are facing the secession of youth. Not all youth, not those eternal squares who are always with us, but the most gifted and sensitive youth of east and west are—to use the tiresome but useful cliché—alienated. As students in universities or as workers in factories, they feel that they are being treated as cogs in a machine, as objects on a conveyor belt rather than as subjects possessing the proper dignity of man. Today a humanistic nonpolitical conservatism can serve all parties equally as an arithmetic of the soul. It calculates the cultural and spiritual price paid for material progress. Quality pays for quantity.

My thesis is that stage two explains the reason why 500 million robotized American and Russian masses today, with leisure and plumbing, are less creative than our 100,000 pre-industrial Athenians, or Florentines, or for that matter Elizabethans. Stage two explains why the current unrest of youth all over the world is not a product of some temporary condition like Vietnam or the race problem but is inherent in a conveyor-belt bureaucracy that destroys the spontaneity needed to be creative.

In stage one such remarks can be callous reactionary nonsense. The starving man of stage one rightly has other worries than these and will put up with conformity and loss of creativity in order to get food. In stage one a rise of living standards is legitimate, being based on real physical needs. To oppose this rise in the undeveloped countries, or in our slums, would be wickedly inhumane. However, in stage two a rise in living standards (and both the capitalist and socialist worlds are competing for such a rise), means a rise in imaginary needs, induced by Madison Avenue or the snob status of keeping up with the Joneses. Like the monster that grows two heads when you cut off one, such needs (unlike real ones) keep multiplying twice as fast as they are satisfied, as proved by the billions of dollars spent on advertising slogans to make the public ever more discontented. So in stage two it is discontent, not just real need, that multiplies; note the increased rate of insanity, suicide, and alienation among the rich industrial nations.

Therefore, when the materialist tells you "Never mind the loss of creativity and individualism so long as my living standards rise," when he tells you gleefully "I cried all the way to the bank," it is really his miserable suicidal discontent and his ever doubling insatiable artificial needs that are rising in that bank. If you have a fraction—say, one-half—and you double both sides of it, getting two-fourths or four-eighths, are you really getting more than you had before? Double the new satisfactions in an advertising age, and you merely double the new needs by which they are divided. And the great advertising dream of the future is to use subliminal advertising on TV that invents needs and perhaps even opinions, politics, and morals, via concealed radiations from the TV screen, radiations you are not even aware of, while seemingly hearing something else. The time to take a stand against invasions of your soul is now, today.

In every age there is one kind of fight that is the key fight for its generation. Other fights are also important and not to be neglected but they are not the key fights. Today the key fight is for the private life, the fight to remain human, to remain individual in a machine age. In politics the abstract public ideologies on both sides have become as dry as the Sahara; the "isms" have become "wasms." During stage one and early stage two of technology, the fight for political ideology still counted. The last time it was the key fight of the age, was the fight of freedom against the totalitarianism of Hitler and Stalin, a true battle of right against wrong. But now the industrial worlds of communism and capitalism are converging in a common nonpolitical or postpolitical world of rule by faceless technocrats; these are no longer evil like Hitler and Stalin, nor decent like the resistance heroes of World War II, whose fight was still the key fight. As we enter this late stage two, the key fight is no longer political nor economic nor ideological (though many important non-key fights are political and economic). In late stage two, the political and economic leaders become more alike on all sides. They become mere expert technicians of the McNamara and Kosygin type, whose ideological differences were camouflage for an unofficial dictatorship by technocrats. A boss of General Motors and a Socialist commissar are equally technocrats and resemble each other more than they do the alienated unbureaucratic individualists whose key fight for the private life is crushed in either society.

Thus, the true world-wide battleline is drawn: between rootless robots and the conservers of the human spark; between those who have machine oil in their veins and those who still have blood; between the mechanical and the spontaneous. And remember that poetry, music, and the arts are the one remaining area that conserves spontaneity in a machine age. This is why young people today no longer ridicule the arts as "sissy" or useless or antisocial. Instead, in both America and Russia, students flock by the thousands, as never before, to the nonpolitical public poetry readings. They sense, by unconscious wisdom, that only thus can they conserve man's oldest tradition, that spontaneity that distinguishes man from the ant-hive, or bee-hive, with its stress on raising production quotas. Beauty, creativity, inwardness, the private life, these have replaced the Molotov cocktail as the new international guerilla warfare against both communist and capitalist organization men of late stage two. If this is a revolution it is a conservative one, a post-political and post-ideological conservatism with its roots in all that is oldest and best in unrobotized man.

In an age of quantitative production quotas, the qualitative, creative act of spontaneity is the ultimate sin, the only obscenity that still shocks. It is, therefore, the only act that today must be sublimated and kept unconscious as sex once used to be in the nineteenth-century Victorian world that Freud reflected. The nineteenth century also used to conceal and sublimate not only sexual motives but economic motives, as in the motto: "They say God and they mean Cotton." Today these two dirty secrets of the nineteenth century, sex and economics, have become open and overt. Instead, the individual human impulse is today the forbidden dirty secret that must be kept unconscious or sublimated by American or Soviet organization men.

Therefore, when students in Berkeley thought that they had revolted against capitalism—and in Moscow and Prague against communism—both were using outdated political slogans to sublimate unconsciously their real nonpolitical grievances. Their real grievance was that they were being treated not as humans but as IBM cards by the multi-versity that had replaced the free university, and by the faceless technocracy that had replaced human individuals.

Usually there is a time lag of a generation between the new motive and its conscious stale old slogan. In this case the new motive is from the 1970s, the slogan from the stale ideological 1930s. According to my own interpretation of the worldwide secession of youth, its conscious political slogan of revolution (anti-capitalist in the West, anti-Communist in the East), is an unconscious sublimation of a nonpolitical new conservatism—a conservative revolt of man against robots.

There is no solution in being a Luddite, a machine smasher. You cannot solve the problems of stage two by going back to stage zero, to a machineless middle ages, but only by going into and through stage two, and coming out on the other side, fighting every inch of the way (even if against odds), for a possible stage three, a stage when at last machines will serve man instead of the other way around; when atomic energy is there not to destroy us but to express the creative flowering of the human spirit. The odds are against our reaching stage three. (I am pessimistic about human nature.) Yet our duty is to fight anyhow, even if we go down fighting, to remain men and not robots.

We must fight for confused goals and on inadequate hunches. Our light is admittedly a fallible and flickering one, the Judaeo-Christian heritage in religion and our great literary and philosophic classics of Western civilization. It is an inadequate, superstitious, fitful light but the only one we have and less dark, less deadly than the materialist superstitions of shallow progress and its gadgets.

Deprived of the seeming clarity of eighteenth-century rationalism or nineteenth-century materialism, we orphans of the twentieth century must admit that we fight on Matthew Arnold's darkling plain, "where ignorant armies clash by night." Acting under flickering torches, knowing that surprise is the rule and that there are no predictable blueprints for progress and no sure allies, we must, nevertheless, make our fallible yet morally necessary choices.

And when we have made enough mistakes and when revolt and counter-revolt and counter-conservatism are all behind us and turn out to be but different mirrors that distort always the same homesick, urban, twentieth-century face, then at last we may learn the honorable humility of these words by a man half medieval-conservative and half modern-socialist, the poet-philosopher William Morris: "Men fight and lose the battle, and the thing they fought for comes about in spite of their defeat; and when it comes, turns out to be not what they meant; and other men have to fight for what they meant under another name."

Capitalism

Capitalism Versus Statism

MURRAY N. ROTHBARD

From the very first we run into grave problems with the term "capitalism." When we realize that the word was coined by capitalism's most famous enemy, Karl Marx, it is not surprising that a neutral or a pro-"capitalist" analyst might find the term lacking in precision. For capitalism tends to be a catchall, a portmanteau concept that Marxists apply to virtually every society on the face of the globe, with the exception of a few possible "feudal-

Murray N. Rothbard (Ph.D., Columbia University) is Professor of Economics at the Polytechnic Institute of Brooklyn and the editor of *Libertarian Forum*. He is the author of numerous articles and several books including *Men, Economy and State*, *America's Great Depression*, *The Panic of 1819*, and *Power and Market*.

ist" countries and of the Communist nations (although, of course, the Chinese consider Yugoslavia and Russia "capitalist," while many Trotskyites would include China as well). Marxists, for example, consider India as a "capitalist" country, but India, hagridden by a vast and monstrous network of restrictions, castes, state regulations, and monopoly privileges is about as far from free-market capitalism as can be imagined.[1]

If we are to keep the term "capitalism" at all, then, we must distinguish between "free-market capitalism" on the one hand, and "state capitalism" on the other. The two are as different as day and night in their nature and consequences. Free-market capitalism is a network of free and voluntary exchanges in which producers work, produce, and exchange their products for the products of others through prices voluntarily arrived at. State capitalism consists of one or more groups making use of the coercive apparatus of the government—the State—to accumulate capital for themselves by expropriating the production of others by force and violence.

Throughout history, states have existed as instruments for organized predation and exploitation. It doesn't much matter *which* group of people happen to gain control of the State at any given time, whether it be oriental despots, kings, landlords, privileged merchants, army officers, or Communist parties. The result is everywhere and always the coercive mulcting of the mass of the producers—in most centuries, of course, largely the peasantry—by a ruling class of dominant rulers and their hired professional bureaucracy. Generally, the State has its inception in naked banditry and conquest, after which the conquerors settle down among the subject population to exact permanent and continuing tribute in the form of "taxation" and to parcel out the land of the peasants in huge tracts to the conquering warlords, who then proceed to extract "rent." A modern paradigm is the Spanish conquest of Latin America, when the military conquest of the native Indian peasantry led to the parcelling out of Indian lands to the Spanish families, and the settling down of the Spaniards as a permanent ruling class over the native peasantry.

To make their rule permanent, the State rulers need to induce their subject masses to acquiesce in at least the legitimacy of their rule. For this purpose the State has always taken a corps of intellectuals to spin apologia for the wisdom and the necessity of the existing system. The apologia differ over the centuries; sometimes it is the priest-craft using mystery and ritual to tell the subjects that the king is divine and must be obeyed; sometimes it is Keynesian liberals using their own form of mystery to tell the public that government spending, however seemingly unproductive, helps everyone by raising the GNP and energizing the Keynesian "multiplier." But everywhere the purpose is the same—to justify the existing system of rule and exploitation to the subject population; and everywhere the means are the same—the State rulers sharing their rule and a portion of their booty with their intellectuals. In the nineteenth century the intellectuals, the "monarchical socialists" of the University of Berlin, proudly declared that their chief task was to serve as "the intellectual bodyguard of the House of Hohenzollern." This has always been the function of the court intellectuals, past and present—to serve as the intellectual bodyguard of their particular ruling class.

In a profound sense, the free market is the method and society "natural" to man; it can and does therefore arise "naturally" without an elaborate intellectual system to explain and defend it. The unlettered peasant *knows* in his heart the difference between hard work and production on the one hand, and predation and expropriation on the other. Unmolested then, there tends to grow up a society of agriculture and commerce where each man works at the task at which he is best suited in the conditions of the time, and then trades his product for the products of others. The peasant grows wheat and exchanges it for the salt of other producers or for the shoes of the local craftsman. If disputes arise over property or over contracts, the peasants and villagers take their problem to the wise men of the area, sometimes the elders of the tribe, to arbitrate their dispute.

There are numerous historical examples of the growth and development of such a purely free-market society. Two may be mentioned here. One is the fair at Champagne, that for hundreds of years in the Middle Ages was the major center of international trade in Europe. Seeing the importance of the fairs, the kings and barons left them unmolested, untaxed, and unregulated, and any disputes that arose at the fairs were settled in one of many competing, voluntary courts, maintained by church, nobles, and the merchants themselves. A more sweeping and lesser known example is Celtic Ireland, which for a thousand years maintained a flourishing free-market society without a State. Ireland was finally conquered by the English State in the seventeenth century, but the statelessness of Ireland, the lack of a governmental channel to transmit and enforce the orders and dictates of the conquerors, delayed the conquest for centuries.[2]

The American colonies were blessed with a strain of individualist libertarian thought that managed to supersede Calvinist authoritarianism, a stream of thought inherited from the libertarian and antistatist radicals of the English revolution of the seventeenth century. These libertarian ideas were able to take firmer hold in the United States than in the mother country owing to the fact that the American colonies were largely free from the feudal land monopoly that ruled Britain.[3] But in addition to this ideology, the absence of effective central government in many of the colonies allowed the springing up of a "natural" and unselfconscious free-market society, devoid of any political government whatever. This was particularly true of three colonies. One was Albemarle, in what later became northeastern North Carolina, where no government existed for decades until the English Crown bestowed the mammoth Carolina land grant in 1663. Another, and more prominent example was Rhode Island, originally a series of anarchistic settlements founded by groups of refugees from the autocracy of Massachusetts Bay. Finally, a peculiar set of circumstances brought effective individualistic anarchism to Pennsylvania for about a decade in the 1680s and 1690s.[4]

While the purely free and laissez-faire society arises unselfconsciously where people are given free rein to exert their creative energies, statism has been the dominant principle throughout history. Where State despotism already exists, then liberty can only arise from a self-conscious ideological movement that wages a protracted struggle against statism, and reveals to the mass of the public the grave flaw in its acceptance of the propaganda of the ruling classes. The role of this "revolutionary" movement is to mobilize the various ranks of the oppressed masses, and to desanctify and delegitimize the rule of the State in their eyes.

It is the glory of Western civilization that it was in Western Europe, in the seventeenth and eighteenth centuries, where, for the first time in history, a large-scale, determined, and at least partially successful self-conscious movement arose to liberate men from the restrictive shackles of statism. As Western Europe became progressively enmeshed in a coercive web of feudal and guild restrictions, and of state monopolies and privileges with the king functioning as the feudal overlord, the liberating movement arose with the conscious aim of freeing the creative energies of the individual, of enabling a society of free men to replace the frozen repression of the old order. The Levellers and the Commonwealthmen and John Locke in England, the *philosophes* and the Physiocrats in France, inaugurated the Modern Revolution in thought and action that finally culminated in the American and the French Revolutions of the late eighteenth century.

This Revolution was a movement on behalf of individual liberty, and all of its facets were essentially derivations from this fundamental axiom. In religion, the movement stressed separation of Church and State, in other words the end of theocratic tyranny and the advent of religious liberty. In foreign affairs, this was a revolution on behalf of international peace and the end to ceaseless wars on behalf of State conquest and glory to the ruling elite. Politically, it was a movement to divest the ruling class of its absolute power, to reduce the scope of government altogether and to put whatever government remained under the checks of democratic choice and frequent elections. Economically, the movement stressed the freeing of man's productive energies from governmental shackles, so that men could be allowed to work, invest, produce, and exchange where they wished. The famous cry to power was "laissez-faire": let us be, let us work, produce, trade, move from one jurisdiction or country to another. Let us live and work and produce unhampered by taxes, control, regulations, or monopoly privileges. Adam Smith and the classical economists were only the most economically specialized group of this broad liberating movement.

It was the partial success of this movement that freed the market economy and thereby gave rise to the Industrial Revolution, probably the most decisive and most liberating event of modern times. It was no accident that the Industrial Revolution in England emerged, not in guild-ridden and State-controlled London, but in the new industrial towns and areas that arose in the previously rural and therefore unregulated north of England. The Industrial Revolution could not come to France until the French Revolution freed the economy from the fetters of feudal landlordism and innumerable local restrictions on trade and production. The Industrial Revolution freed the masses of men from their abject poverty and hopelessness—a poverty aggravated by a growing population that could find no employment in the frozen economy of pre-industrial Europe. The Industrial Revolution, the achievement of free-market capitalism, meant a steady and rapid improvement in the living conditions and the quality of life for the broad masses of people, for workers and consumers alike, wherever the impact of the market was felt.

An undeveloped and sparsely populated area originally, America did not begin as the leading capitalist country. But after a century of independence it achieved this eminence, and why? *Not*, as the common myth has it, because of superior natural resources. The resources of Brazil, of Africa, of Asia, are at least as great. The difference came because of the relative freedom in the United States, because it was here that the free-market economy more than in any other country was allowed its head. We began free of feudal or monopolizing landlord class, and we began with a strongly individualist ideology that permeated much of the population. Obviously, the market in the United States was never completely free or unhampered; but its relatively greater freedom (relative to other countries or centuries) resulted in the enormous release of productive energies, the massive capital equipment, and the unprecedentedly high standard of living that the mass of Americans not only enjoy but take blithely for granted. Living in the lap of a luxury that could not have been dreamed of by the wealthiest emperor of the past, we are all increasingly acting like the man who murdered the goose that laid the golden egg.

And so we have a mass of intellectuals who habitually sneer at "materialism" and "material values," who proclaim absurdly that we are living in a "post-scarcity age" that permits an unlimited cornucopei of production without requiring anyone to work or produce, who attack our undue affluence as somehow sinful in a perverse recreation of a new form of Puritanism. The idea that our capital machine is automatic and self-prepetuating, that whatever is done to it or not done for it does not matter because it will go on perpetually—this is the farmer blindly destroying the golden goose. Already we are beginning to suffer from the decay of capital equipment, from the restrictions and taxes and special privileges that have increasingly been imposed on the industrial machine in recent decades.

We are unfortunately making ever more relevant the dire warnings of the Spanish philosopher Ortega y Gasset, who analyzed modern man as:

> finding himself in a world so excellent, technically and socially, [he] believes that it has been produced by nature, and never thinks of the personal efforts of highly-endowed individuals which the creation of this new world presupposed. Still less will he admit the notion that all these facilities still require the support of certain difficult human virtues, the least failure of which would cause the rapid disappearance of the whole magnificent edifice.

Ortega held the "mass-man" to have one fundamental trait: "his radical ingratitude towards all that has made possible the ease of his existence." This ingratitude is the basic ingredient in the "psychology of the spoiled child." As Ortega declares:

> Heir to an ample and generous past . . . the new commonalty has been spoiled by the world around it . . . the new masses find themselves in the presence of a prospect full of possibilities, and furthermore, quite secure, with everything ready to their hands, independent of any previous efforts on their part, just as we find the sun in the heavens. . . . And these spoiled masses are unintelligent enough to believe that the material and social organization, placed at their disposition like the air, is of the same origin, since apparently it never fails them, and is almost as perfect as the natural scheme of things . . .
>
> As they do not see, behind the benefits of civilization, marvels of invention and construction that can only be maintained by great effort and foresight, they imagine that their role is limited to demanding these benefits peremptorily, as if they were natural rights. In the disturbances caused by scarcity of food, the mob goes in search of bread, and the means it employs is generally to wreck the bakeries. This may serve as a symbol of the attitude adopted, on a greater and more complicated scale, by the masses of today towards the civilization by which they are supported.[5]

In an era when countless numbers of irresponsible intellectuals call for the destruction of technology and the return to a primitive "nature" that could only result in the death by starvation of the

overwhelmingly greatest part of the world's population, it is instructive to recall Ortega's conclusion:

> Civilization is not "just there," it is not self-supporting. It is artificial
> and requires the artist or the artisan. If you want to make use of the
> advantages of civilization, but are not prepared to concern yourself
> with the upholding of civilization—you are done. In a trice you find
> yourself left without civilization. . . . The primitive forest appears in
> its native state, just as if curtains covering pure Nature had been
> drawn back.[6]

The steady decline in the underpinnings of our civilization began
in the late nineteenth century, and accelerated during the World
Wars I and II and the 1930s. The decline consisted of an accelerating
retreat back from the Revolution, and of a shift back to the old order
of mercantilism, statism, and international war. In England, the
laissez-faire capitalism of Price and Priestly, of the Radicals and of
Cobden and Bright and the Manchester School, was replaced by a
Tory statism driving toward aggressive Empire and war against
other imperial powers. In the United States the story was the same,
as businessmen increasingly turned to the government to impose
cartels, monopolies, subsidies, and special privileges. Here as in
Western Europe, the advent of World War I was the great turning
point—in aggravating the imposition of militarism and government-
business economic planning at home, and imperial expansion and
intervention overseas. The medieval guilds have been re-established
in a new form—that of labor unions with their network of restrictions
and their role as junior partners of government and industry in the
new mercantilism. All the despotic trappings of the old order have
returned in a new form. Instead of the absolute monarch, we have
the President of the United States, wielding far more power than any
monarch of the past. Instead of a constituted nobility, we have an
Establishment of wealth and power that continues to rule us regardless of which political party is technically in power. The growth of a
"bipartisan" civil service, of a bipartisan domestic and foreign policy,
the advent of cool technicians of power who seem to sit in positions
of command regardless of how we vote (the Achesons, the Bundys,
the Baruchs, the McCloys, the J. Edgar Hoovers), all underscore our
increasing domination by an elite that grows ever fatter and more

privileged on the taxes that they are able to extract from the public hide.

The result of the aggravated network of mercantilist burdens and restrictions has been to place our economy under greater and greater strain. High taxes burden us all, and the military-industrial complex means an enormous diversion of resources, of capital, technology, and of scientists and engineers, from productive uses to the overkill waste of the military machine. Industry after industry has been regulated and cartellized into decline: the railroads, electric power, natural gas, and telephone industries being the most obvious examples. Housing and construction have been saddled with the blight of high property taxes, zoning restrictions, building codes, rent controls, and union featherbedding. As free-market capitalism has been replaced by state capitalism, more and more of our economy has begun to decay and our liberties to erode.

In fact, it is instructive to make a list of the universally acknowledged problem areas of our economy and our society, and we will find running through that list a common glaring leitmotif: government. In all the high problem areas, government operation or control has been especially conspicuous.

Let us consider:

Foreign policy and war: Exclusively governmental.

Conscription: Exclusively governmental.

Crime in the streets: The police and the judges are a monopoly of government, and so are the streets.

Welfare system: The problem is in government welfare; there is no special problem in the private welfare agencies.

Water pollution: Municipally owned garbage is dumped in government owned rivers and oceans.

Postal service: The failings are in the government owned Post Office, not, for example, among such highly successful private competitors as bus delivered packages and the Independent Postal System of America, for third-class mail.

The military-industrial complex: Rests entirely on government contracts.

Railroads: Subsidized and regulated heavily by government for a century.

Telephone: A government-privileged monopoly.

Gas and electric: A government-privileged monopoly.

Housing: Bedeviled by rent controls, property taxes, zoning laws, and urban renewal programs (all government).

Excess highways: All built and owned by government.

Union restrictions and strikes: The result of government privilege, notably in the Wagner Act of 1935.

High taxation: Exclusively governmental.

The schools: Almost all governmental, or if not directly so, heavily government subsidized and regulated.

Wiretapping and invasion of civil liberties: Almost all done by government.

Money and inflation: The money and banking system is totally under the control and manipulation of government.

Examine the problem areas, and everywhere, like a red thread, there lies the overweening stain of government. In contrast, consider the frisbee industry. Frisbees are produced, sold, and purchased without headaches, without upheavals, without mass breakdowns or protests. As a relatively free industry, the peaceful and productive frisbee business is a model of what the American economy once was and can be again—if it is freed of the repressive shackles of big government.

In *The Affluent Society*, written in the late 1950s, John Kenneth Galbraith pinpointed the fact that the governmental areas are our problem areas. But his explanation was that we have "starved" the public sector and that therefore we should be taxed more heavily in order to enlarge the public sector still further at the expense of the private. But Galbraith overlooked the glaring fact that the proportion of national income and resources devoted to government has been expanding enormously since the turn of the century. If the problems did not appear before, and have appeared increasingly in precisely the expanded governmental sector, the judicious might well conclude that perhaps the problem lies in the public sector itself. And that is precisely the contention of the free-market liberterian. Problems and breakdowns are inherent in the operations of the public sector and of government generally. Deprived of a profit-and-loss test to gauge productivity and efficiency, the sphere of government shifts decision-making power from the hands of every individual and cooperating group, and places that power in the hands of an overall governmental

machine. Not only is that machine coercive and inefficient; it is necessarily dictatorial because whichever decision it may make, there are
always minorities or majorities whose desires and choices have been
overridden. A public school must make *one* decision in each area: it
must decide whether to be disciplined or progressive or some blend
of the two; whether to be pro-capitalist or pro-socialist or neutral;
whether to be integrated or segregated, elitist or egalitarian, etc.
Whatever it decides, there are citizens who are permanently deprived.
But in the free market, parents are free to patronize whatever private
or voluntary schools they wish, and different groups of parents will
then be able to exercise their choices unhampered. The free market
enables every individual and group to maximize its range of choice,
to make its own decisions and choices and to put them into effect.

It is ironic that Professor Galbraith does not seem to be very happy
about the public sector as it has lately been manifesting itself: in the
military-industrial complex, in the war in Vietnam, in what Galbraith
has himself properly derided as President Nixon's "Big Business
Socialism." But if the glorious public sector, if expanded government,
has brought us to this pretty pass, perhaps the answer is to roll
government back, to return to the truly revolutionary path of dis-
mantling the Big State.

Indeed, American liberals—who for decades have been the main
heralds and apologists for big government and the welfare state—
have increasingly become unhappy at the results of their own efforts.
For just as in the days of oriental despotism, state rule cannot endure
for long without a corps of intellectuals to spin the arguments and
the rationale to gain the support and the sense of legitimacy among
the public, and the liberals (the overwhelming majority of American
intellectuals) have served since the New Deal as the celebrants of big
government and the welfare state. But many liberals are coming to
realize that they have been in power, have fashioned American society, for four decades now, and it is clear to them that something
has gone radically wrong. After four decades of the welfare state at
home and "collective security" abroad, the consequences of New Deal
liberalism have clearly been aggravated breakdowns and conflicts at
home and perpetual war and intervention abroad. Lyndon Johnson,
with whom liberals became extremely unhappy, correctly referred to
Franklin Roosevelt as his "Big Daddy"—and the parentage on all

foreign and domestic fronts was quite clear. Richard Nixon is scarcely distinguishable from his predecessor. If many liberals have become strangers and afraid in a world *they* have made, then perhaps the fault lies precisely in liberalism itself.

If, then, there is to be a rollback of statism, there will have to be another ideological revolution to match the rise of the classical radicals of the seventeenth and eighteenth centuries. Intellectuals will have to shift, in large part, back from their role as apologists for the State to resume their function as upholders of the standards of truth and reason as against the *status quo*. In the last several years, there have been signs of disenchantment by the intellectuals, but the shift has been largely a wrongheaded one. As a result, in the current split between liberals and radicals among the *intelligentsia, neither* side provides us with the requisites of civilization, with the requisites for maintaining a prosperous and free industrial order. The liberals have offered us the spurious rationality of technocratic service to the Leviathan State, of fitting in as manipulated cogs in the bureaucratic government-industrial machinery. Liberalism's solution to every domestic problem is to tax and inflate more and to allocate more federal funds; its solution for foreign crises is to "send the Marines" (accompanied, of course, by politico-economic planners to alleviate the destruction that the Marines cause). Surely we cannot continue to accept the proferred solutions of a liberalism that has manifestly failed. But the tragedy is that the radicals have taken the liberals at their face value: identifying reason, technology, and industry with the current liberal-mercantilist order, the radicals, in order to reject the current system, have turned their backs on the former necessary virtues as well.

In short, the radicals, feeling themselves forced into a visceral rejection of the world of liberalism, of Vietnam and the public school system, have adopted the liberals' own identification of their own system with reason, industry, and technology. Hence the radicals raise the cry for the rejection of reason on behalf of emotions and vague mysticism, of rationality for inchoate and capricious spontaneity, of work and foresight for hedonism and dropping out, of technology and industry for the return to "nature" and the primitive tribe. In doing so, in adopting this pervasive nihilism, the radicals are offering us even less of a viable solution than their liberal enemies. For the murder of millions in Vietnam they would, in effect, substitute the death by starvation of the vast bulk of the world's population. The radicals' vision cannot be accepted by sane people, and the bulk of Americans, their ignorance or errors otherwise, are astute enough to recognize this fact and to make loud, clear, and sometimes brutal their rejection of the radicals and their alternative ethic, society, and life-style.

The point of this essay is that the public need not be forced to choose between the alternative of repressive and stifling welfare-war-fare state monopoly liberalism on the one hand, or the irrational and nihilistic return to tribal primitivism on the other. The radical alternative is evidently not compatible with a prosperous life and indus-trial civilization; this much is crystal clear. But less clear is the fact that corporate state liberalism is in the long run also not compatible with an industrial civilization. The one route offers our society a quick suicide; the other a slow and lingering murder.

There is, then, a third alternative—one that has still gone un-heeded amid the great debate between liberals and radicals. That alternative is to return to the ideals and to the structure that gen-erated our industrial order and that is needed for that order's long-run survival—to return to the system that will bring us industry, technology, and rapidly advancing prosperity *without* war, milita-rism, or stifling governmental bureaucracy. That system is laissez-faire capitalism, what Adam Smith called "the natural system of liberty," a system that rests on an ethic that encourages individual reason, purpose, and achievement. The nineteenth century libertarian theorists—men like the Frenchmen of the Restoration era, Charles Comte and Charles Dunoyer, and the Englishman Herbert Spencer— saw clearly that militarism and statism are relics and throwbacks of the past, that they are incompatible with the functioning of an in-dustrial civilization. That is why Spencer and the others contrasted the "military" with the "industrial" principle, and judged that one or the other would have to prevail.

What I am suggesting, in short, in the oversimplified categories made popular by Charles Reich, is a return to "Consciousness I"—a Consciousness that is brusquely dismissed by Reich and his readers as they proceed to take sides in the great debate between Conscious-nesses II and III. To Reich, Consciousness I was made obsolete by the growth of modern technology and mass production, which made the turn to the corporate state inevitable. But here Reich is not being radical *enough*; he is simply adopting the conventional liberal historiography that big government was made necessary by the growth of large-scale industry. If he were familiar with economics, Reich would realize that it is precisely advanced industrial economies that require a free market to survive and flourish; on the contrary, an agricultural society can plod along indefinitely under despotism provided that the peasants are left enough of their produce to survive. The Communist countries of Eastern Europe have discovered this fact in recent years; hence, the more they industrialize the greater and more inexorable their movement away from socialism and central planning and toward a free market economy. The rapid shift of the East European countries toward the free market is one of the most heartening and dramatic developments in the last two decades; yet the trend has gone almost unnoticed, for the left finds the shift away from statism and egalitarianism in Yugoslavia and the other East European countries extremely embarrassing, while the conservatives are reluctant to concede that there may be *anything* hopeful about the Communist nations.

Furthermore, Reich is clearly unaware of the findings of Gabriel Kolko and other recent historians that completely revise our picture of the origins of the current welfare-warfare state. Far from large-scale industry forcing the knowledge that regulation and big government were inevitable, it was precisely the *effectiveness* of free-market competition that led big businessmen seeking monopoly to turn to the government to provide such privileges. There was nothing in the economy that objectively required a shift from Consciousness I to Consciousness II: only the age-old desire of men for subsidy and special privilege created the "counter-revolution" of statism. In fact, as we have seen, this development only cripples and hampers the workings of modern industry; objective reality would require a return to Consciousness I. In this world of remarkably swift changes in values and ideologies, such a change in consciousness cannot be ruled out as impossible; far stranger things have been happening.

In one sense, the adoption of libertarian values and institutions would be a return; in another, it would be a profound and radical advance. For while the older libertarians were essentially revolutionary, they allowed partial successes to turn themselves strategically and tactically into seeming defenders of the *status quo*, mere resisters of change. In taking this stance, the earlier libertarians lost their radical perspective; for libertarianism has never come fully into being. What they must do is to become "radicals" once again, as Jefferson and Price and Cobden and Thoreau were before them. To do this they must hold aloft the banner of their ultimate goal, the ultimate triumph of the age-old logic of the concepts of free market, liberty, and private property rights. That ultimate goal is the dissolution of the State into the social organism, the privatizing of the public sector. In contrast to the dysfunctional vision of the New Left, this is a goal wholly compatible with the functioning of an industrial society—and with peace and freedom as well. All too many of the older libertarians lacked the intellectual courage to press on—to call for total victory rather than settle for partial triumph—to apply their principles to the fields of money, police, the courts, the State itself. They failed to heed the injunction of William Lloyd Garrison that "gradualism in theory is perpetuity in practice." For if the pure theory is never held aloft, how can it ever be achieved?

References

1. For a view of India by free-market economists, see P. T. Bauer, *United States Aid and Indian Economic Development* (Washington, D.C.: American Enterprise Association, 1959) and B.R. Shenoy, *Indian Planning and Economic Development* (Bombay and New York: Asia Publishing House, 1963).
2. In a similar way, the British in the late nineteenth century had a great deal of difficulty in establishing their rule over the stateless, free-market tribe of the Ibos of West Africa. On Ireland, see Joseph R. Peden, "Stateless Societies: Ancient Ireland," *The Libertarian Forum* (April 1971) and the references therein.
3. On the ideological inheritance from Britain, see Bernard Bailyn, *The Ideological Origins of the American Revolution* (Cambridge, Mass.: Harvard University Press, 1967).
4. See Murray N. Rothbard, "Individualist Anarchism in the United States: the Origins," *Libertarian Analysis* (Winter 1970), pp. 14–28.

5. José Ortega y Gasset, *The Revolt of the Masses* (New York: Norton, 1932), pp. 63–65.
6. *Ibid.*, p. 97.

Capitalism Outmoded

HYMAN LUMER

In contrast to its predecessors, capitalism appeared on the historical scene as a highly dynamic socio-economic system, one whose watchword was ceaseless innovation and change. In 1848 Karl Marx and Frederick Engels expressed it in the *Communist Manifesto* in these words:

> The bourgeoisie cannot exist without constantly revolutionizing the instruments of production, and with them the whole relations of society. Conservation of the old modes of production in unaltered form was, on the contrary, the first condition of existence for all earlier industrial classes. Constant revolutionizing of production, uninterrupted disturbance of all social conditions, everlasting uncertainty and agitation distinguish the bourgeois epoch from all previous ones.[1]

The foundation of capitalism is production for the market, and with this goes competition for the market and the endless striving of every entrepreneur after new, more efficient productive techniques with which to outstrip his rivals. Thus, modern science had its birth with capitalism, and that within its few centuries of existence capitalism gave rise to an Industrial Revolution and to a flowering of sci-

Hyman Lumer (Ph. D., Western Reserve University) was formerly the National Educational Director of the Communist party in America, and is presently editor of its journal, *Political Affairs.* He has taught biology at Western Reserve University and was Educational Director of the Ohio-Kentucky district of the United Electrical, Radio, and Machine Workers Union. He is author of numerous pamphlets, articles, and books, of which the more recent are *Is Full Employment Possible?* and *Poverty: Its Roots and Its Future.*

ence and technology that has changed the face of the earth vastly more than in all the millennia of human existence preceding it.

Nowhere has this dynamic quality manifested itself more than in the United States. Here, we find the most modern forms of production and acknowledged world leadership in technology and productive efficiency. And here, too, we find the social, political and ideological aspects of capitalist development in their fullest expression.

Contradictions of Modern American Capitalism

Today a new scientific and technological revolution is under way. It is as yet only in its infancy, but the rise of automation and cybernation, of computerized production, already holds forth the possibility of producing an abundance of material goods hitherto undreamed of. Indeed, the day is not far off when it will be possible to supply every individual with everything he or she needs, and this with an ever diminishing amount of human labor.

Yet these very achievements bring with them a growing multiplicity of paradoxes and contradictions. Thus, it has already become commonplace to speak of the "paradox of plenty." A recent government study is characteristically entitled *Poverty Amid Plenty: The American Paradox*. It states that:

> At the end of 1968 there were 25 million poor Americans as measured by the Federal Government's poverty index. This index allows a non-farm family of four $3,553 per year, or $2.43 per person per day, to meet all living expenses. In contrast to the poverty index, a recent Department of Labor study found that an urban family of four needed at least $4.05 per person per day to meet its needs.[2]

In short, a considerable proportion of our population lives below the level of economic adequacy—and this by conservative standards. Moreover, of those classified as poor, from one-third to one-half suffer increasing malnutrition and hunger, in not a few cases extending to literal starvation.[3] And this in a country where the production of agricultural surpluses is habitual, and where well-to-do farm operators are paid considerable sums for restricting their plantings.

It will be objected by some that the incidence of poverty has been steadily declining and that poverty is actually on its way out, though its departure can be greatly hastened by suitable anti-poverty measures. Government estimates, it is true, show a considerable drop— from 32 percent in 1950 to 13 percent in 1968. But these figures are greatly misleading. They are based on the use of a fixed standard of measure, corrected only for price changes (and even that inadequately). This is at best a highly dubious procedure, since living standards and assessments of needs change with time. If income status is measured against a variable yardstick that takes these changes into account in addition to price changes—for example, the Bureau of Labor Statistics estimate of the annual income required by an urban family of four for minimum adequacy—it is found that the percentage of the population living below adequacy has remained almost unchanged over the past two decades. The most striking feature of poverty in the United States is not its decline but its persistence.[4] The paradox is not newly discovered; its existence has been recognized for quite some time. And it has expressed itself in a variety of forms.

That technological advance in our capitalist economy brings with it an ever-growing problem of displacement of workers and joblessness is an old story. The term "technological unemployment" dates back to the 1920s. And during the depression years of the 1930s there were numerous advocates of a moratorium on scientific and technological research. The new upsurge in science and technology has only rendered the problem more acute. Since World War I actual full employment has not existed except in periods of all-out war, and since World War II, despite the absence of major depressions, the rate of unemployment as officially estimated has never fallen significantly below 4 percent except during the wars in Korea and Vietnam. The problem of unemployment, once periodic, is now chronic.

These and other contradictory features of modern capitalism, that emerge in increasingly sharp relief as technology advances, suffice to show that the phenomenal rise in our ability to produce abundance for all leads instead to persistent poverty and hunger and to growing insecurity for many millions of Americans. We shall deal with these contradictions more fully later.

Growing Socialization of Production versus
Private Appropriation of the Product

The immediate question is: why these paradoxes, these contradictions? Marxist theory holds that they are not mere temporary blemishes on our society but inevitable consequences of the fundamental contradiction that lies at the heart of capitalism, that in fact defined it as a mode of production. That is the contradiction between the socialized character of the process of production and the private appropriation of the product.

Industrial capitalism grew out of the individual handicraft production of feudal times. The individual producer, having provided the raw materials, the tools and the labor, was clearly the owner of the product. This earlier form of ownership was carried over into capitalist production although the labor was performed not by the capitalist, who owned the tools and raw materials, but by others employed by him as wage workers. The history of capitalism, with its ceaseless revolutionizing of the instruments of production, has correspondingly been one of growing socialization of production. The constantly rising complexity of machinery has led to growing division of labor, increasing size of enterprises and involvement of greater and greater numbers of workers in turning out even the simplest of products. And with this the history of capitalism has been one of mounting incompatibility of this ever more socialized production with its integument of private ownership.

The social character of the means of production increasingly demands social ownership. Within the framework of capitalism this pressure has given rise to a process of socialization of *capitalist* ownership. As the scale of the necessary capital investment has grown, larger numbers of small capitalists have been progressively replaced by smaller numbers of big capitalists. And with their further growth, means of pooling capitals were sought, giving birth to the modern corporation. One of the most striking features of U.S. capitalist development during the past century has been the rise of corporate giants far outstripping in size their counterparts in other capitalist countries.

American Telephone and Telegraph, the largest corporation in the world, reported assets of nearly $44 billion in 1969, up from $28 billion in 1964. This mammoth enterprise has well over 700,000 employees, equal to the population of a good-sized city, and a gross annual income that exceeds the combined revenues of the five richest states—California, New York, Pennsylvania, Texas and Michigan. It operates 85 percent of all telephones in the United States, as well as extensive telegraph and other communications services, and its subsidiary, Western Electric, manufactures all the equipment involved.[5]

General Motors, largest of the industrial giants, recorded sales of $24 billion and assets of nearly $15 billion in 1969. These assets had grown from $4.4 billion in 1950 and $10 billion in 1962. Similarly, the assets of Standard Oil of New Jersey, next-largest in terms of sales, grew from $4.2 billion in 1950 to $11.5 billion in 1962 and $17.5 billion in 1969.[6]

These and other giant corporations account for a huge and growing share of assets, sales and profits. In 1948 the 200 biggest manufacturing corporations owned 48 percent of all manufacturing assets. By 1969 this had risen to nearly 59 percent, and it is anticipated that by 1975 it will reach 75 percent. The seventy-eight industrial giants with assets of $1 billion or more alone accounted for 43 percent of all assets and 49 percent of all profits in 1968.[7] This represents a concentration of capital without equal, and its pace has been accelerating, thanks to the progress of the scientific-technological revolution.

With the rise of the giant corporation, competitive capitalism gives way to monopoly capitalism. In industry after industry a few top corporations come to dominate production and the market. In the automobile industry, for example, four firms account for the total domestic production of automobiles. General Motors alone accounts for more than half. In the electrical industry General Electric and Westinghouse dominate the field, in the aluminum industry Aluminum Corporation of America and a few other enterprises, and so on. Under these circumstances it becomes possible to fix prices at levels above those that would prevail if competition existed, and so to raise profit levels above the average.

The question rises: who owns all of this immense corporate wealth? In business circles it has become fashionable to refer to present-day capitalism as "democratic capitalism" or "people's capitalism," on grounds of the wide diffusion of stock ownership (recent

estimates place the total number of stockholders in the neighborhood
of 20 million). But this is a myth, designed to conceal the real distribution of ownership. Various studies indicate that less than 1 percent of all families own as much as 80 percent of all publicly owned
stocks.[8]

To be sure, with the ownership of the shares in a corporate enterprise spread over a large number of stockholders, we can no longer
speak of its outright ownership by a particular individual or group.
But we *can* speak of its *control* by such an individual or group, and
because of the very diffusion of stock ownership such control can
frequently be exercised through the possession of a relatively small
percentage of the outstanding stock. Thus, General Motors is controlled by the du Pont family, which owns approximately 20 percent
of its stock.

The Du Pont interests do not end with General Motors, however.
They include controlling interests in E. I. du Pont de Nemours and
Company, the largest American chemical firm, United States Rubber
Company, and North American Aviation, as well as in a number of
banks, insurance companies and other financial and industrial enterprises. The du Pont clan thus constitutes a financial grouping controlling a corporate empire of substantial proportions.

But the du Ponts are not the only such group, and are far from
being the largest. Top position is contested for by the Morgan and
Rockefeller groups. The Morgan Empire includes such corporate
giants as Guarantee Trust Company, Prudential Insurance Company,
American Telephone and Telegraph, United States Steel Corporation,
General Electric, International Business Machines and many others.
The Rockefeller sphere of influence embraces the Chase Manhattan
Bank, Metropolitan Life Insurance Company, American Telephone
and Telegraph (shared with the Morgan interests), Westinghouse
Electric and, of course, the immense complex of Standard Oil com-
panies.

Other leading interest groups include the Mellon group, the First
National City Bank group, the Cleveland group, the Chicago group
and the California group. These and one or two other leading financial interest groups control virtually all of the top industrial and
financial corporations in the United States. Some few thousand members of corporate boards of directors, representing these groups, are

today the country's economic rulers. It is they who dispose of the huge accumulations of capital provided by the multitude of investors in corporate stocks and bonds.[9]

As the socialization of production proceeds further, the required scale of investment comes to exceed even these vast aggregates of private capital. Now the economic resources of the government are invoked. "Partnerships" of the giant monopolies and the state emerge in which the latter provides the research, the patents and the plant and equipment, which are turned over to the former to operate at lucrative fees. Such, for example, is the arrangement between the government and General Electric, Union Carbide and Carbon, Westinghouse and other corporations in the field of atomic energy. And such is the arrangement between the government and American Telephone and Telegraph and others in the space communications field.

There takes place a union of monopoly capital and the state, with the latter acting to bolster the profits and power of the former through subsidies, government orders, tax concessions and a host of other devices. To insure this largesse, growing numbers of representatives of finance capital enter the executive departments of the federal government at various levels up to the Cabinet itself. This process found its most blatant expression in the "Cadillac Cabinet" of President Eisenhower, which was described as consisting of "fourteen millionaires and a plumber." John Foster Dulles, secretary of state, was chairman of the board of the Rockefeller Foundation and member of a law firm that represented the Rockefeller interests among others. C. E. Wilson, secretary of defense, was president of General Motors. George M. Humphrey, secretary of the treasury, was president of the M. A. Hanna Company and a kingpin in the Cleveland Finance capital group—and so on. President Kennedy replaced Dulles with Dean Rusk, another head of the Rockefeller Foundation; Wilson with Robert MacNamara, president of the Ford Motor Company, and Humphrey with Douglas Dillon, head of Dillon, Read and Company, one of the top Wall Street investment houses. Today representation at the Cabinet level is less direct, but the lower ranks of these departments continue to be honeycombed with representatives of big business.

By far the greatest outpouring of government funds into the coffers of big business is the $40 billion a year handed out in contracts for military goods (of which we shall have more to say below) whose unholy offspring is the highly publicized industrial-military complex. Here the tie between business and the state apparatus is reflected in the extensive influx of retired military brass into top executive positions in leading corporations. Senator William Proxmire states:

> At present, more than 2,100 retired officers of the rank of colonel or higher are holding jobs with firms doing defense work. The ten companies employing the largest number of them had 1,065 on their payrolls, an average of 106, three times the average number employed in 1959.[10]

Thus monopoly capitalism develops into state monopoly capitalism. The growing socialization of production results in the bringing together of ever more enormous quantities of capital, obtained from a growing number of private sources and now increasingly from the federal treasury. But the disposal of these huge masses of capital remains in the hands of a small number of individuals. Ownership is no less private than before and the antagonism between private ownership and socialized production is not a whit diminished; on the contrary, it is increased.

Accelerated Concentration

Is this process of concentration coming to an end? Not at all; it is, in fact, accelerating. The biggest corporations continue to grow bigger, as the figures presented above show. But the most striking manifestation of the accelerated pace of concentration today is the colossal flood of corporate mergers and takeovers that has developed in recent years. According to the Federal Trade Commission, the number of mergers rose from 219 in 1950 to 955 in 1966 and 2,655 in 1968. This is the biggest merger boom in U.S. history, and it is marked especially by the rise in mergers of larger corporations.

Most significant is the spectacular rise in conglomerate mergers, mergers of firms producing totally unrelated products. From less than 40 percent of the total in 1948–1951, these jumped to 90 percent in 1968. To some extent the rise is due to an increase in such mergers effected by older corporations. A number of these, such as General

Electric and Union Carbide and Carbon, have through such mergers evolved into conglomerate corporations. But in recent years they have involved mainly a mushrooming group of new conglomerate corporations, typified by Ling-Temco-Vought and Litton Industries, consisting mainly or entirely of collections of enterprises in quite unrelated fields and constantly striving to expand by swallowing up additional enterprises.

Conglomerate mergers do not contribute to increased efficiency of production. Why, then, have they become so widespread? Initially, they were motivated primarily by a desire to provide, through diversified operations, greater financial stability in the face of economic fluctuations. Subsequently they became a device for effecting tax savings by acquiring firms that had sustained losses and writing these off against the profits of the rest of the corporation. More recently they have been motivated principally by the quick profits to be obtained through the stock manipulations and tax concessions that such mergers make possible.[11]

With the birth of the joint stock company there comes into being the institution known as the stock market and of speculation in stocks as the road to wealth. With the growing role of the banks as concentration of capital proceeds, and the emergence of finance capital, the quest for financial control of corporations as a source of profits becomes a predominant form of capitalist operation. To these forms of economic parasitism the rise of conglomerate corporations adds a new dimension. To a growing degree, profits are sought through financial manipulations rather than through the production of goods or services. Increasingly the nation's productive resources and the workers employed in them become a means for clever operators to make a fast buck. The mushrooming of conglomerates is therefore only a crowning demonstration of the growing parasitism and decay of capitalism in the face of the mounting socialization of production.

Inevitable Class Struggle

The antagonism between socialized production and capitalist ownership expresses itself also in the antagonism between the two social classes involved in the productive process: capitalists and wage workers. Like its more immediate predecessors, capitalism is an exploitative system. In ancient slave society the slaveowner lived on the labor of the slave and himself did no work. In feudal society the noble lived in indolence on the labor of the serf. In capitalist society, similarly, the capitalist lives on the fruits of wage labor.

Profit is not payment to the capitalist for his own labor. He receives it by virtue of his ownership of the means of production even if he chooses to live in complete idleness. If he does participate actively in the management of the enterprise he is paid for doing so in addition—and generally very handsomely.

What, then, is the source of capitalist profit? Marxism holds that the sole source of the exchange value of commodities is human labor, that the new value created in the process of production is due entirely to the labor expended by the wage worker. But he must share that value with the capitalist, and therein lies the exploitative nature of capitalism. Because the worker owns no means of production and can live only by selling his labor power to the capitalist, the latter can compel him to work enough hours to turn out a surplus beyond his own means of subsistence as embodied in his wages. That surplus, the capitalist pockets. The source of his profit, therefore, is unpaid labor by the wage worker.

That profit is the motive force of capitalist production, the sole reason for the capitalists's existence. And to safeguard that existence he is driven to extract the largest possible profit from his operations —to keep both the number of workers he employs and the wages he pays them at a minimum. The workers, on the other hand, are compelled to strive ceaselessly to maintain or increase the share of the product that they receive. Hence the existence of the class struggle as a built-in feature of capitalism.

The bulk of the profits extracted become, in turn, fresh capital to be invested to produce yet more profits, and so on. The aim of capitalist production, in short, is the unending accumulation of capital. Out of this, interlinked with continual technological innovation, grows the process of concentration of production and ownership that we have already noted.

As this proceeds there takes place a growing polarization of society into a handful of big capitalists at one end and a growing mass of wage and salaried workers on the other. Today the latter comprise more than 82 percent of the gainfully employed population as against 64 percent in 1900 and 72 percent in 1940.

With the rise of monopoly capital, and especially with its development into state monopoly capital, the profits secured by the big monopoly corporations through the direct exploitation of wage labor are augmented through other channels. They are added to by "administered" prices, by subjecting farmers to the price scissors (compelling them to pay high monopoly prices for their needs while paying them low prices for their product), by making inroads on the profits of the smaller capitalists and of small business generally, and by subjecting sections of the working class to super-exploitation.

Especially notorious is the super-exploitation of black workers, who are habitually confined to the most menial, dirtiest, most dangerous and poorest paying jobs, who are widely paid less than white workers for the same work, who are last hired and first fired, and who are present in grossly disproportionate numbers among the poor, the hungry and the unemployed. This economic discrimination is part of the whole Jim Crow pattern of discrimination and segregation to which black Americans are subjected in every aspect of life, and which in turn rests on the ideological foundation of an all-pervading racism, worse here than in any other country except possibly South Africa.

The source and the prime beneficiary of the oppression of black people is monopoly capital. Indeed, it was with the penetration of the South by the newly rising trusts in the 1890s that the present Jim Crow pattern had its beginning. Concerning this, W. E. B. DuBois states:

> The power of private corporate wealth in the United States has throttled democracy and this was made possible by the color caste which followed Reconstruction after the Civil War. When the Negro was disfranchised in the South, the white South was and is owned increasingly by the industrial North. Thus, caste which deprived the mass of Negros of political and civil rights and compelled them to accept the lowest wage, lay underneath the vast industrial profit of the years 1890 to 1900 when the greatest combinations of industrial capital took place.[12]

If we were to add together the total differential in pay received by black and white workers, the amount by which the existence of a mass of low-paid black labor drags down the wages of white workers generally, and the added North-South wage differential, the resulting sum, running into many billions of dollars, would approximate the added profits obtained by big business through job discrimination against black workers. To this should be added the differences arising from the extortionate rents and prices paid by black ghetto residents.

This discrimination could be ended almost overnight if the big corporations practicing it chose to do so. As Gabriel Kolko correctly notes: "The low economic status of the Negroes could be radically changed in short order if the 2,000 or so men who control the major American corporations really desired such changes."[13] But clearly they do not desire them, for this would mean the loss of considerable sums in extra profits.

The racist practices that so disgrace our country in relation to black Americans extend also to other groups, notably the Chicanos (Mexican-Americans), the Puerto Ricans and the Indian population. The oppression of these peoples is a further source of extra profits.

To this racial and national oppression must be added the flagrant discrimination against women workers, who comprise nearly 40 percent of the labor force. It is well known that women are largely or completely excluded from many fields of work and that they are generally paid less than men on identical jobs. Here, too, is a considerable source of extra profits. In a word, modern capitalism not only directly exploits wage labor but in one way or another enlarges its profits at the expense of every other section of the population.

Imperialism and War

The drive for profits does not end at the water's edge; on the contrary, it extends over the whole face of the earth. The growth of monopoly capital and the exceptionally high profits of the monopolies led to an accumulation of surplus capital that could not be profitably invested at home but sought investment abroad. The aim of these foreign investments was to gain control of sources from the exploitation of extremely low-paid wage labor.

This led to the rise of modern imperialism and in the case of a number of capitalist countries, most notably Britain and France, to the acquisition of extensive colonial empires. The United States acquired few colonies but nevertheless built its own empire, chiefly in the rest of the Western Hemisphere. Though the Latin American countries are nominally independent, their economic resources are mainly in the hands of U.S. corporations and their governments are dominated by that of the United States. In Canada, a highly industrialized country, the key industries are controlled or owned outright by U.S. monopolies. Together with a handful of top Canadian capitalists, linked with them as junior partners, they control the whole of Canada's economic life. Thus, despite its lack of outright colonies, some time ago the United States became a leading imperialist power.

Here we encounter a further expression of the antagonism between private appropriation and socialized production. The growing division of labor and socialization of production is not confined within the boundaries of individual countries. Early in the history of capitalism there were already the beginnings of a world economy with growing inter-dependence between nations. Of this, V. I. Lenin wrote:

> Developing capitalism knows two historical tendencies in the national question. The first is the awakening of national life and national movements, the struggle against all national oppression, and the creation of national states. The second is the development and growing frequency of international intercourse in every form, the break-down of national barriers, the creation of the international unity of capital, of economic life in general, of politics, science, etc.[14]

For capitalism these two tendencies pose an irreconcilable contradiction, since the only economic relations capitalism knows are those of exploitation and national oppression. Its motivation is profits from foreign trade and foreign investment, higher than those to be made at home. Hence it is that with the growing tendency toward world intercourse came the rise of imperialism and, by 1900, the division of the world into a handful of imperialist powers and a worldwide mass of oppressed colonial and semi-colonial countries, containing the bulk of the world's population. And hence it is that there arose, side by side with the class struggle, movements of national liberation throughout the world.

Following World War II, taking advantage of its improved position, United States imperialism set out to extend its empire and to establish its domination on a world scale. This was to be accomplished in the name of anti-communism, of saving the world from an alleged menace of "Soviet aggression." Under these banners the cold war was launched.

The effort was not without a degree of success. United States foreign investments have vastly increased. Private United States assets abroad have risen from $12 billion in 1940 to $100 billion in 1968. They have grown not only in underdeveloped regions but in advanced industrial areas such as Western Europe. The United States has indeed become by far the most powerful of the imperialist states.

But the effort has also converted the United States into the most highly militarized of the major countries of the world. Richard J. Barnett writes:

> Since 1946 the taxpayers have been asked to contribute more than one trillion dollars for national security. Each year the federal government spends more than 70 cents of every budget dollar on past, present and future wars. The American people are devoting more resources to the war machine than is spent by all federal, state and local governments on health and hospitals, education, old-age and retirement benefits, public assistance and relief, unemployment and social security, housing and community development, and the support of agriculture. Out of every tax dollar there is about 11 cents left to build American society.[15]

United States troops and military installations are spread around the world. According to General David M. Shoup, retired in 1963 as a member of the Joint Chiefs of Staff: "We maintain more than 1,517,000 Americans in uniform overseas in 119 countries. We have 8 treaties to defend 48 nations if they ask us to—or if we chose to intervene in their affairs."[16] Aside from Vietnam the troops stationed abroad are located in 3,401 military installations girdling the globe.

Cold war has turned into hot war, first in Korea, now in Indochina. Allegedly these wars have been waged to protect the peoples of Southeast Asia from a Communist takeover. But in reality United States ruling circles had their eyes on this part of the world for other reasons. A report in *The New York Times* of February 12, 1950 noted that: "Indochina is a prize worth a large gamble. In the North are exportable tin, tungsten, zinc, manganese, coal, lumber, and rice, and in the South are rice, rubber, tea, pepper, cattle and hides." A few years later President Eisenhower, speaking to the Conference of State Governors in Seattle, declared that:

> When the U.S. votes $400,000,000 to help that war [the French war in Indochina] we are not voting a giveaway program. We are voting for the cheapest way we can to prevent the occurrence of something that would be of a most terrible significance to the U.S.A., our security, our power and ability to get certain things we need from the riches of the Indonesia territory and from Southeast Asia.[17]

In 1965 the same idea was expressed by Secretary of State Dean Rusk, who said:

> With its archipelagos, Southeast Asia contains rich natural resources and some 200 million people. . . . more is at stake than preserving the independence of the peoples of Southeast Asia and preventing the vast resources there from being swallowed by those hostile to freedom.[18]

Southeast Asia is already a major area for United States corporate investment. Frm $309 million in 1950, direct private investments have grown to nearly $3 billion in 1968. They have grown most rapidly in Taiwan, South Korea and Thailand, countries ruled by United States—imposed puppets, in which extremely cheap labor provides a source of lavish profits.

It is the drive to expand United States corporate control of the rich sources of raw materials in the area and to swell the profits to be made by exploiting its inhabitants that had led to the full-scale United States invasion of South Vietnam, the bombing of North Vietnam, and now the spread of the war to the rest of Indochina. Standard Oil, the Chase Manhattan Bank and other top corporations have some time ago moved into South Vietnam behind the troops, and despite the uncertain situation, the influx has grown. The war, therefore, is not a fight in defense of the liberty of the Vietnamese people (it is well known that the corrupt puppet regime in Saigon could not last a week without U.S. military support); on the contrary, it is an act of imperialist aggression in the interests of U.S. monopoly capital.

A significant feature of the post-World War II period, and especially of the past decade, is the rise of international (or multinational) industrial corporations. This is an outcome of the enormous rise in direct foreign investment, which increased 5½ times between 1950 and 1968. Especially striking is the rise in investments in Western Europe; since 1950 these have increased tenfold.[19] And here they have gone chiefly into the most technologically sophisticated fields of manufacture, such as automobiles and computers. Today a considerable part of the Western European output in these fields comes from American-owned or American-controlled firms.

What is involved in the internationalization of *production*? Instead of producing goods in the United States and supplying foreign markets by exporting them, the international corporation produces the goods wherever the conditions and costs of production are most favorable and exports them from there—to the United States as well as to other countries. A report by Sidney E. Rolph notes that in 1968 the estimated value of the output of these foreign holdings of U.S. corporations was about $120 billion. This is more than three times the value of U.S. exports. Moreover, it exceeds the gross national product of any other capitalist nation.[20]

The extent to which major U.S. corporations have become internationalized is indicated by the following figures: Standard Oil Company of New Jersey has facilities in 45 foreign countries, amounting to 56 percent of its total assets. Some 68 percent of its sales and 52 percent of its net income come from abroad. International Business Machines has assets in fourteen foreign countries, amounting to 34 percent of its total assets, and obtains 30 percent of its sales and 32 percent of its net income abroad.[21] With this growing export of capital goes the export of jobs and the growing insecurity of American workers. This only serves to aggravate the problems created by the displacement of workers from their jobs as a result of automation.

To be sure, other capitalist countries also have considerable foreign investments, a substantial part of them in the United States. But the total of all these countries combined is much less than the volume of U.S. investments. In 1966, according to an OECD estimate, their combined direct foreign investments came to less than 64 percent of the U.S. total. Thus, it is American monopoly capital that predominates, that increasingly makes inroads into the economies of other countries and exploits wage labor on a world scale.

But this meets with mounting resistance and leads to a sharpening conflict between the United States and other imperialist powers. And it is sharpened all the more by the fact that the position of the United States in the capitalist world economy, in terms of rate of economic growth, share of world trade and other features, has for a number of years been declining, a decline that the American monopolists seek to offset through stepping up foreign investments.

As the basic contradiction inherent in capitalism has deepened, we have endeavored to show that the various derivative contradictions and antagonisms have become more and more acute. Today they have reached a critical stage.

The advance of technology, now more rapid than ever, has made available a growing wealth of material goods. And it is true that in the years since World War II a substantial section of the working class has succeeded in measurably improving its lot and achieving an increasing possession of such goods. Ownership of homes, cars, television sets, refrigerators and many other means of material comfort has indeed become widespread.

But this has been accompanied by a mounting degree of economic insecurity and a spreading fear that these possessions may all too easily be lost. Thus, one's job may be wiped out by the introduction of automation, by the closing down of a plant, by recession, and one may be left stranded, especially in late middle age, with little hope of again finding comparable employment. The reality of such a danger is sharply demonstrated by the recent wave of layoffs of skilled, technical, professional and managerial personnel, with many of those laid off being compelled eventually to abandon their fields and seek much lower-paying jobs.

Moreover, the earnings of the average worker are not sufficient to provide him and his family with what is regarded as an adequate American living standard. According to the Bureau of Labor Statistics a "modest" standard of living for an urban family of four requires an annual income of roughly $11,000 a year. But in 1970 the yearly earnings of workers in manufacturing averaged less than $7,000. Hence to achieve the BLS standard requires a second job or a second breadwinner in the family. Or it requires the mortgaging of future income by buying on credit.

Indeed, the "affluence" of the postwar years has been maintained largely by a rapidly expanding volume of credit buying. The volume of consumer credit outstanding rose from $8.4 billion at the end of 1946 to $122.2 billion at the end of 1969. In 1947 consumers used 6 percent of their after-tax income to repay installment debt; in 1969 they used 15 percent.[22] With this the precariousness of ownership and the danger of loss through repossession has steadily grown.

This insecurity is the consequence not of technological advance itself but of the ownership of today's colossal forces of production by a handful of financiers for whom they represent not a means of making life better for everyone but only a source of profit and aggrandizement for themselves. The drive· for profits compels every capitalist, in his competition with others, to strive to expand his production and his share of the market to the maximum as the condition of his survival. But the very same drive compels him, in the name of holding his production costs down, to keep wages at a minimum and to utilize every advance in technology to get rid of as many "superfluous" workers as possible, and thus to restrict the ultimate market for all the goods being poured on the market.

Capitalism thus gives rise to the phenomenon of overproduction expressing itself in periodic crises in which production falls off and unemployment shoots up because "too much" has been produced. For some time now American capitalism has been able to cope with the mounting surplus only through various forms of wasteful consumption, of which the principal form is military spending. Since World War II, as we have already noted, the militarization of our economy has proceeded apace, with well over half the federal budget and roughly 10 percent of the national product going down the drain each year. And because of the sums consumed in this sheer waste, we are told, money is not available for social needs. Moreover, today not even this huge waste suffices and we witness the unprecedented phenomenon of a recession during a period of large-scale warfare.

Capitalism, Marxism contends, is long outmoded as a social system. Far from being the dynamic force of its youth, it becomes increasingly an obstacle to progress. Above all, it cannot encompass the production of abundance that today's scientific-technological revolution promises. For abundance means the cheapening of commodities as the labor time required for their production decreases. And ultimately, as technological development continues, as the labor time consumed per unit of production becomes infinitesimal, the prices of commodities must tend toward zero. That is, an end is put to their existence as commodities, and with this an end is put to the basis for existence of an economic system founded on the buying and selling of commodities. In particular, the basis for extracting profits from the unpaid labor of others vanishes.

But to capitalists the very idea of falling prices for their products is anathema. On the contrary, they strive always to get the highest possible price; for them the most desirable state of affairs is one of constantly rising prices. Hence we encounter the paradox of inflation coupled with the ability of the monopoly corporations to "administer" prices.

Since World War II the consumer price index has fallen only twice, in 1949 and 1955, and in both cases only slightly. Today (early 1971) American workers are confronted with both rising unemployment and rising prices, and with falling real wages.

These are some of the main contradictions inherent in capitalist production as they manifest themselves in the present stage of capitalism in the United States. They are expressions of the growing incompatibility of the capitalist mode of production with the present-day level of the forces of production. They indicate that capitalism, having played the historic role of bringing these gigantic productive forces into being, now comes increasingly into conflict with them and must sooner or later give way to a new socio-economic system that is in harmony with these productive forces and serves their further development. That new system is socialism.

Socialism

Our society is today in a state of pervsasive crisis. There is a crisis of foreign policy, stemming from the fact that despite the slaughter and maiming of untold numbers of Vietnamese, despite the destruction of much of their country, despite the invasion of Cambodia and Laos, no U.S. military victory in Indochina is possible. The crisis finds expression in the rise of a mass popular opposition to this aggressive war that is unmatched in U.S. history.

There is a crisis of the ghettos, marked by the outbreaks of ghetto rebellions, the rise of black militance and other expressions of the unshakeable determination of black Americans to put an end to the inhuman, degrading racial oppression imposed on them. There is a crisis arising from the social and economic impact of the scientific-technological revolution, to which we have already referred. Coupled with this are the effects of the growing burden of paying for armaments and war which is being placed on the American working people. This has led to rising demands for higher wages and to a spreading rank-and-file revolt against the extreme conservatism of the top trade union leadership.

There is a crisis of education, of decaying school systems and backward institutions of higher learning, giving birth among other things to the student revolts of recent years. There is a crisis of the cities, rotting at their cores. There is a crisis of environmental pollution. There is a crisis of morality, marked by growing resort to violence and repression, extending even to assassination, by the alarming rise in crime, in drug use, in pornography, and by the tendency of growing numbers of young people to "drop out."

This multi-faceted crisis evidences the sickness of a society in decay. It represents an advanced stage of a chronic general crisis that has afflicted all of the capitalist world since the days of World War I. At that time the October Revolution of 1917 in Russia established the world's first socialist state and precipitated the world-wide conflict between socialism and capitalism—a conflict that takes place on the economic, political and ideological planes.

The ideology of capitalism is an ideology based on the private ownership of the means of producing wealth. It places the acquisition of personal wealth as a prime objective in life, as the measure of success. It is an ideology of individualism, that sees relations between people as relations of competition, and success in life as something to be sought on an individual basis, in competition with and at the expense of others. It is an ideology of division among men, of national chauvinism and racism, of justification of the oppression of other peoples on the grounds of their alleged inferiority.

Capitalist ideology views capitalism not as a stage in the evolution of human society but as eternal and as the best of all possible socio-economic systems. It looks on any serious departure from capitalism as a dangerous aberration to be condemned and dealt with harshly.

But this is the ideology of an outmoded system, in which individual ownership of the means of production and appropriation of the product clashes ever more sharply with the socialized, cooperative character of the productive process itself and the increasing degree of economic interdependence among people, nationally and internationally. This character of the productive process calls for a society based on social relationships of cooperation, not competition, and it gives rise to an ideology based on that concept. And such an ideology develops of necessity among the workers in the gigantic enterprises that capitalism has brought into being.

These workers soon come to see that they cannot effectively defend their interests against the employers by acting as individuals, that they must confront the employers as an organized body—as a trade union. In the course of these battles they are increasingly brought to recognize that they can advance their individual interests only to the extent that the working class as a whole advances, and to understand that it can do so only through struggle against the capitalist class as a whole—against the class of its exploiters. Finally, a growing section of the working class is led to see that this exploitation lies not in the extraction of "unfair" profits but in the very *existence* of the profit system, and that it can be ended only by the workers themselves becoming the owners of the means of production and using them to produce for their own use, not for someone else's profit. But because the means of production are operated collectively, not individually, it follows that ownership by the workers means collective ownership.

In opposition to capitalist ideology, therefore, there arises a working-class ideology—an ideology of socialism. Only through the establishment of socialism—of socialized ownership—can the antagonism between private appropriation and socialized production be abolished, and with it all of its harmful consequences. Only socialism can end the exploitation of man by man and do away with the accumulation of fabulous wealth at one pole and mass poverty at the other. Only socialism can abolish the anarchistic character of production that exists under capitalism and make possible rational planning for the benefit of the people as a whole. And only socialism can remove the roots of racial oppression and of war.

Not surprisingly, therefore, the movement for socialism has grown vastly throughout the world since 1917. A number of countries, embracing one-third of the world's population, have already taken the socialist path. In addition, many former colonial countries have won their political independence and a number of these have embarked on a path leading toward socialism. The ideological conflict between the capitalist class and the working class has acquired a new dimension; today it exists on a world scale in the context of the competition between the two systems. In this competition, adherents of Marxism-Leninism maintain that it is socialism that represents the future and will be victorious throughout the world.

References

1. Karl Marx and Frederick Engels, *Manifesto of the Communist Party* (New York: International Publishers, 1948), p. 12.
2. *Report of the President's Commission on Income Maintenance Programs* (Washington, D.C.: U.S. Government Printing Office, 1969).
3. *Hunger, U.S.A.*, A Report by the Citizens' Board of Inquiry into Hunger and Malnutrition in the United States (Boston: Beacon Press, 1968), p. 34.
4. For a further elaboration of this point see: Hyman Lumer, *Poverty: Its Roots and Its Future* (New York: International Publishers, 1966), pp. 25–28.
5. *Fortune* (May 1970).
6. *Ibid.*
7. *Fortune* (May 15, 1969).
8. G. William Domhoff, *Who Rules America?* (Englewood Cliffs, N.J.: Prentice-Hall, 1967), pp. 44–46.
9. For a detailed account of these financial interest groups and their holdings, see Victor Perlo, *The Empire of High Finance* (New York: International Publishers, 1957). See also Domhoff, *op. cit.*, and Ferdinand Lundberg, *The Rich and the Super-Rich: A Study in the Power of Money Today* (New York: Lyle Stuart, 1967).
10. "The Pentagon vs. Free Enterprise," *Saturday Review* (January 31, 1970).
11. For a detailed account of the devices employed, see *Economic Report on Corporate Mergers* (Washington, D.C.: U.S. Government Printing Office, 1969).
12. W. E. B. DuBois, *The Battle for Peace: The Story of My 83rd*

Birthday (New York: Masses & Mainstream Publishers, 1952), pp. 184–185.

13. Gabriel Kolko, *Wealth and Power in America*, (London: Thomas & Hudson, 1962), p. 109.

14. V. I. Lenin, "Critical Remarks on the National Question," *Collected Works* (Moscow: Progress Publishers, 1964), Vol. 20, p. 27.

15. Richard J. Barnett, *The Economy of Death* (New York: Atheneum, 1969), p. 5.

16. David M. Shoup, "The New Militarism," *The Atlantic* (April 1969).

17. *The New York Times* (August 3, 1953).

18. U.S. Department of State, *Why Vietnam* (Washington, D.C.: U.S. Government Printing Office, 1965).

19. U.S. Bureau of the Census, *Statistical Abstract of the United States: 1970* (Washington, D.C.: U.S. Government Printing Office, 1970), p. 766.

20. Sidney E. Rolph, *The International Corporation* (International Chamber of Commerce, 1969).

21. *Fortune* (September 15, 1968).

22. *Statistical Abstract of the United States: 1970*, p. 541.

Freedom Through Capitalism

TIBOR R. MACHAN

Though this essay is directed to political science students and the layman, the specifically *philosophical* defense of the position that I am taking must at least be outlined. I am not an economist and am not well equipped to deal with capitalism as a

Tibor R. Machan (Ph.D., University of California at Santa Barbara) is Assistant Professor of Philosophy at California State College at Bakersfield, the author of numerous articles, a columnist for the *Santa Ana Register*, and associate editor of *Reason*. He was co-director of the First and Second Annual Conference on Political Philosophy. He came to the United States from Hungary.

purely economic concept or system. I disagree, in the main, with those who want to analyze capitalism outside of the context of a political-legal system. (Both economists and political scientists have become methodological positivists in the last fifty years, boasting of being *"wertfrei"* or value-free. Such a methodology is, in the final analysis, however, indefensible in connection with fields of study that deal with specifically human institutions.)

My essay focuses on the ideological groundwork for capitalism as a socio-economic-legal system, especially the ethical groundwork. Capitalism is widely viewed as a social order and not merely as an economic theory. Yet in virtue of its etymological roots[1] and the primarily economic scrutiny that the system has received, the examination of capitalism must begin with an emphasis on its relationship to man's economic life.

Economists define capitalism as the economic system based on the free exchange of goods and services among individuals and groups within a given society. The crucial feature of capitalism is free trade.[2] The freedom referred to in this context means freedom from coercive action by individuals and groups, including (and especially) governments. The phrase that calls to mind the kind of relationship enjoyed between those acting in the market place of goods and services and the governments that administer the laws of society is "laissez-faire" (the expression is French and means literally "let act"). In the context of economic activity, the phrase serves as a demand or command put to governments to abstain from interfering with the uncoerced interactions between individuals and groups in their trading and other business undertakings.[3]

To think of capitalism in economic terms is not, however, entirely accurate unless the concept of "economics" is broadened to include reference to all of man's interactions.[4] It is more useful to retain the traditional economic reference of the concept of "capitalism" and point out that, in order to make possible capitalism (as a condition of free trade), certain other elements of a social system would have to be secured. The political system in the context of which capitalism can obtain is called, loosely, the free society. The crucial legal features of such a society would have to be certain fundamental constitutional provisions that make it illegal to practice coercion either by individuals and groups, or by governments. The concept of "coercion" in this context refers to acts of force *initiated* by the actor. In order that such coercion could be legally identified, the constitutional foundations of a legal system would have to spell out certain rights that all individuals of the society possess. These rights would serve as the legal guides to the definition and identification of crimes either by individuals and groups or by governments. The government of a free society is, in terms of the political philosophy underlying the present approach to law, the *agent* of citizens in their efforts to secure justice, namely the correct identification of culprits in coercive action, which is to say actions that constitute a violation of the rights of individuals.[5]

Historically the philosopher John Locke came closest to identifying those basic features of a legal system that spell out the rights all men (*served* by the law) possess.[6] Locke's natural rights (and law) doctrine is recognized as the most influential intellectual impetus underlying the American system of government.[7] American society, in turn, is the closest approximation, to date, of the societal system of a free society, and it is in the context of this social-legal system that capitalism has come closest to operating as an economic system—that is, to the conditions of acting within the market place of goods and services where trading occurs.

Underpinnings

In this essay I will not discuss how closely American society and the American economic life has approximated laissez-faire capitalism and its legal framework, the fully free society. Though it is widely believed that American capitalism has been responsible for evils that in its absence could have been avoided, the *merits* of (the approximation of) laissez-faire capitalism and the system of law required for a free society have not received the recognition that they deserve.[8] Fortunately, recent revisionist economic historians have shown this to the satisfaction of any reasonable investigator.[9] The task of my essay will be to discuss the philosophical basis for the political system of the free society, first, and to show its viability as a social system for human beings.

The ethical principles that properly underlie a free society and

from which its political principles derive are based on certain statements about human beings that identify human nature. Human
nature is in part properly and truly characterized by two mutually
entailed crucial features of man: his capacity for rational, conceptual
thought and awareness, and his freedom to be or not to be aware.
Man's "volitional consciousness"[10] is the basis for the ethical principles that are right for him. Because man is distinctive in that he
can think and know by thinking—by using his mind—and because
he is ultimately free to exercise a choice between being or not being
fully aware, fully conscious, it is here that his moral nature must be
uncovered, because morality logically depends on human freedom.
Because man is free, ultimately, only in his capacity to choose to
think or not to think, it is whether or not he chooses to think that
must determine whether or not he is doing the right thing, the
morally right thing, that is.[11]

Ethics is the science that discovers the principles that should
govern human action; and man's freedom (i.e., his nature as a free
agent of his actions) makes it possible for him to discover what
these principles are. Is a man morally blameworthy if he fails to
make the effort to discover the ethical principles that must guide
human action? We have already pointed out that human life requires thinking and knowledge; so the use of his mind is the primary
responsibility of every man, one that he needs in order to live even
at a minimum level of humanity. And because a sound code of ethics
contains the most basic principles of human actions, the discovery
of these is every man's prime responsibility. On the whole this is
well acknowledged in our daily lives. To be ignorant of moral principles is far more blameworthy an act for everyone, even those who
are experts in some special and otherwise important field of human
knowledge, than to be ignorant in any other realm of life.

The right of every man to be free from coercion by others and
groups of others, including governments, is based on the fact that
it is *wrong* to incapacitate a person in his ability to exercise choice
and to aspire, possibly, to moral goodness. This is a *human* right
that everyone possesses by virtue of his being human and thus having
the capacity for choice and the capacity for making himself a *good*
man. It makes sense to assert this right only to other people—thus

only in society—because only other people have the freedom to abstain from interfering with one's freedom.

The political philosophy that underlies the theory of a free society is based on the (fundamental) human right to be free from coercion. The laws of such a society must be based on the statement of what condition is right for every man *in society*, namely to be free. This freedom is not the basic moral value of a man's life, of course, but it is the basic *political* value of every man's life. Political freedom would be of no value unless each man's life were of value. Because it is only in freedom that one can make of his life a good (or bad) life, a society that recognizes man's moral nature, his capacity for goodness or evil, must be based on the principle that each man's freedom is inviolate. In other words, there cannot be any *legal* and moral sanction to the coercion of men by men. No matter how important some may feel that it would be to violate this principle, the laws of a free society must stand firmly against the impulse to sanction such violation. In terms of what we know of human beings, this is the most reasonable conclusion we can establish.

Capitalism in Practice

I do not believe that there has been a laissez-faire capitalist society in existence in the world known to us. I do believe, however, that American society has come closest to instantiating such a state of affairs, at least for a considerable period of time in its history. The contradictions that plagued our system were very severe, however. As an example, the legal tolerance of slavery, that explicitly contributed to the violation of the human rights of millions of people, can only be considered as a very severe and tragic contradiction to the theoretical provisions of a free society. Though there will be many who will maintain that slavery was not only consistent but an inherent part of laissez-faire capitalism[12] the fact is that such contentions could only be made by those who have no understanding of the nature of a free-market economy and the legal framework that is necessary for its maintenance.[13]

Aside from slavery, there were many other inconsistencies about

American society and law that prevented the existence of the free society that was sketched earlier. These and other inadequacies of our political system, including ones that developed later in domestic and foreign policies through the various governmental actions of the executive, legislative, and judicial branches of our government, have contributed much to the nature of the problems we now face. For instance, the existence of slavery is clearly responsible in great measure for the "racial" problems that exist today. The immense responsibilities that the various governments have assumed contribute directly to the equally immense powers that reside in governmental bodies. The military draft, which is also in direct contradiction not only to the tenets of the system that I presented but to the system that has been the nominal foundation of law in the United States, accounts for some of the most pressing difficulties that we face throughout our culture. And while the present economic situation is widely considered to be a direct outgrowth of capitalism,[14] there is overwhelming evidence to bear out the judgment that the prevailing economic ills, from widespread poverty to the existence of monopolistic and oligopolistic economic practices and institutions of businesses, stem not from what is central to laissez-faire capitalism but what has been the *statism* (governmental intervention) tolerated and introduced in the last 150 years of America's economic history.[15] The special favors that legislators were permitted to carry out for enterprises that were said to serve the "public interest," the fusion of business with politics both in law and, as a result of this, outside the law (e.g., the actions of politicians on behalf of business that could only be performed because their power to interfere with the market was legally politically secured),[16] and outright nationalization of such purely economic practices as the printing of money, banking, building of highways, securing public parks, forests, beaches, and educational facilities—all these have contributed drastically to the problems that we now face.

In a free society man's problems would have to be solved *without* recourse to unprovoked coercion (initiated force) and *with* every other avenue that could possibly be utilized. How, for example, would air pollution be treated in a free society?[17] Because violations of the rights of citizens would include the violation of their property rights, the pollution of an individual's or firm's property whether home, backyard, ocean or lake front real estate, water supply, park, road, or airspace), would be a criminal act. The various categories of criminality—malice aforethought, negligence, violation of contract, fraud, theft, etc.—would all be available to prosecute law breakers and the courts would authorize the legally justifiable protection necessary to prevent such violations from occurring. As to how manufacturers of cars and other polluting machinery would have to cope with the legal prohibition against violating somene's rights pertaining to acts of pollution, *this* would be a technological problem totally unrelated to law and the operations of governments. Just as now, when in order to travel from my home to a friend's party I am not legally entitled to cross over my next door neighbor's backyard without his permission and must, therefore, *solve my problem* without violating his property rights, so, with a more elaborate understanding and definition of human rights, the solution of problems would take on the appropriate characteristics. Undoubtedly, difficulties yet unheard of would arise. But once we know what human rights people possess, it would be *unjust* and illegal to tolerate their evasion and invasion in favor of some person's or group's special aim that could perhaps be carried out more "efficiently" without the "obstacle" of refraining from violating a man's human rights.

As a list of examples of what would be absent from the present legal system, were it consistent with the theoretical foundations of a society based on man's rights, the following should suffice: All laws pertaining to gambling; the practice of religious rituals that do not involve harming others; drug usage; the reading and selling of pornography; the acquisition of wealth; the development of large firms or corporations; foreign trade; the granting of special financial privileges to businesses or individuals (via subsidies, welfare, depletion allowance, governmental insurance, governmental contracts); prices of goods; wages of people; the practice of medicine, barbering, dentistry, etc.; service in the military; VISTA or the Peace Corps; broadcasting; the arts; education; and so forth would be barred in a free society. In all cases laws pertaining to such matters would be disallowed by the consistent application of the underlying legal principles of the system, namely the list of human rights that the government (i.e., law interpreter and implementor) and the people would be required to observe. This is not so much a prediction as a description of how such a system would have to operate. It would, of course, also contain many of the legal features of our present system, including the bulk of its criminal code pertaining to *crimes with victims*. But these features of the system would be improved and highly efficient since *only* these would be attended to by legal theorists, jurists, and the courts themselves. The administration of such just laws of the society would be the sole concern of the legal apparatus, granting, of course, that mistakes could and would at times occur. Of course, a commitment to the basic features of the system would generate much impetus toward the correction of mistakes in line with these features, namely man's rights.

The entire legal structure cannot be discussed here, of course. As the system develops from what it is toward what it should be, in line with the present discussion, the mechanism for handling situations in terms cf the principles advanced herein would also have to be developed. There is ample evidence that human beings versed in the problems of the law stand ready to provide the necessary talent and know-how to aid in this development. There is a massive library of theoretical material waiting on bookshelves, and there are men's minds to be used for such a purpose.[18]

Needless to say, the development of such a society requires that sufficient individuals today begin to gain an understanding of its merits and begin to work toward their realization. There are some signs that movement in this direction is regaining its momentum, i.e., that which has been lost since the beginning of the undermining of the basic principles of the American political system. Not all people need to agree to the full viability or even desirability of such a system, but at least a politically and intellectually active minority is necessary. There are, of course, no *guarantees* about the eventuality of such matters in the light of the existence of human freedom. Unlike Marxists, libertarians (i.e., those advocating these ideas) do not claim that some mysterious "history" is on their side. They are counting on themselves and other people, only.

At this point a couple of contemporary issues will be considered from within the frame of reference of the present point of view: the actions of the Federal Communications Commission and state teaching of sex. The treatments should be considered a case of libertarian analysis of present social-political problems.

Present Problems

The defenders and proponents of the welfare state—and its logical extension, socialism—argue that capitalism, the uncontrolled market-economy, cannot take care of some important needs of the public, therefore government must step in to accomplish that end. An example of how the public interest is to be upheld is provided by the actions of the Federal Communications Commission, the guardian of the electromagnetic spectrum—the TV and radio broadcast airwaves.

The FCC was set up because in 1927 Congress *declared* that the airwaves belonged to the public. At that time called the Federal Radio Commission, the agency was promoted mainly on the grounds that the allocation of frequencies had to be supervised by some expert judicial body—though even then some had in mind the *advancement* of various public goods through the governmental control of broadcasting. (There was, incidentally, no legal ground on which to base the declaration of the airwaves as public property since "the Ether," then thought to comprise such property, has been shown not to exist by the Michelson-Morley experiments.) The work invested by inventors and their sponsors in broadcasting was ignored while the general public (which had nothing at all to contribute to the broadcasting technology), was designated the owner and controller of broadcasting. Broadcasters were relegated to the status of tenants. (This is why the First Amendment cannot have real bearing on broadcasting: broadcasters are not dealing in private publication and expression of ideas but are said to be using a "publicly owned" medium to get rich at the public's expense.)

The example of advancing the public good that I would like to present is the infamous "Fairness Doctrine" of the FCC. According to this rule, broadcasters cannot present "controversial issues of public concern" on the air without freely providing airtime to those who are ruled by the FCC to be "responsible representatives of opposing points of view."

When the "Doctrine" was first advanced and approved, an atheist attempted to get on the air in opposition to some theistic sermon on the grounds that fairness dictated an airing of his side, also. His appeal was rejected. Clearly, it would have been consistent with the intent of the "Doctrine" to force the broadcasters to give the atheist air time. But as governments are wont to do, justice must bow to popularity or advantage, or whatever else is politically relevant, and atheists could not get, at that time, fairness under the "Fairness Doctrine."

Some years ago a New York lawyer filed a complaint against WCBS, N.Y., claiming that cigarette advertisements constituted a "controversial issue of public concern." The FCC agreed with the complaint and ruled that broadcasters must give free time to the American Cancer Society's "public service" announcements. At this time the FCC is going even further and is proposing to ban all cigarette ads from the air—that is, to use its regulatory powers to censor the content of broadcasting in behalf of its conception of the "public good." (Interestingly enough, the anti-smoking ads are not in danger of being barred.)

It is clear that there are thousands of controversial issues on the air each day, including newscaster's biased reports, beer ads (which some religious groups would oppose), movies (the themes of which make one's blood boil), comedy shows (the materials of which are very offensive to some), and commentaries submerged in so-called documentary programs (which to some people's minds advance highly spurious notions of how to deal with social, economic, political, diplomatic and other ills). It is obvious that consistent with the "Fairness Doctrine" the FCC must require the presentation of opposing views in each of these cases—yet it cannot do so and will not do so for various reasons. To pick just one of the many issues on which to take a stand on behalf of one or the other side is, accordingly, blatantly unjust—it constitutes the *inequal* application of the law to the citizenry!

But this is what happens when the welfare of the people is dictated to them not through their own best judgments and voluntary associations, but through the rules and regulations of political, social, and moral reformers in Washington and in other political territories. A similar problem is posed by state teaching of sex. There has been much fervor recently about sex education in our public schools. When "right-wingers" object to sex-education they are easily dismissed as being paranoid and unnecessarily puritanical—surely, it is claimed, there is nothing really wrong about teaching sexology to young people; in fact, there is everything right with it.

The problem about sex education stems, however, from something that is far deeper than puritanical ethics. The problem stems from a basic belief on the part of Americans that all education dealing with ethics and morality should be kept out of the State's reach. Because the State is supposed to be neutral about the morality of private behavior, the inference is properly drawn that State-run educational institutions should avoid treating such a morally pregnant subject as sex in the curriculum. Just as we would not want the State to teach the "proper" religion or philosophy, so we are rightly concerned about the teaching of "proper" sex on the part of state-run educational institutions.

The fact is, however, that virtually no subject-matter can be taught value-free. History, biology, government, and even mathematics are open to the insertion of controversies or value-judgments when taught to children. It is hardly possible, therefore, to begin to draw the line with sex-education when, in fact, the line should have been drawn at education in general. In other words, the State should not be involved in education at all; whenever the job of bringing knowledge to the young is put into the hands of politicians who are subject to all the pitfalls of seeking power (wanting to please instead of wanting to tell the truth as best known) the political authority cannot be kept far from the vehicle of teaching. (Teaching is itself a morally loaded activity; it *cannot* be neutral.)

Though it may not always be taken advantage of, the opportunity to make use of the classroom as a political, moral, or religious podium always exists. It is no accident that both the right and the left wing is anxious to make use of the schools on behalf of their own philosophies. The John Birch Society wants to use schools to teach its conception of Americanism; leftists, on the other hand, see the classroom as their vehicle to make people aware of the "evils of the American system of government"—the SDS included the infiltration of high schools and universities as a major goal in its attempt to implement its vaguely-held political philosophy.

While we may quite legitimately say that being educated about sex is a good thing, we must say, prior to this, that being free to teach one's children the truth, as best known by the parents *or their chosen* educators, is even more important for the maintenance of a free society. In other words, even when the State would indeed tell the truth about sex through public schools, the State should not be allowed to do this for it can, thereby, tell falsehoods as well. And because education is compulsory up to a certain age, the State (the politically active majority) has special access to the young, whether the parents or children like it or not.

The practical implications of an approach to political realities from within the libertarian (capitalist) framework have been indicated by the above examples. The case of the FCC should point up at least some of the reasons why federal intervention into the activities of so called crucial industries cannot achieve the goal of securing virtue and wisdom on the part of such industries. Quite the contrary usually happens, as evidenced by the current crises in broadcasting. That education is in dismal shape is not perceived by libertarians alone, but the political approach to education is nowhere more radical than within libertarian circles. Here the total separation of state and education is acknowledged to be the only truly viable solution to those problems of education that are politically related. (Others, like Ivan Illich and Paul Goodman, have also suggested this. In official circles, however, the suggestion is completely ignored.)

In essentials the question about the practical implications of the libertarian viewpoint has been answered. The only additional matter that could arise in this connection is whether under the conditions of political freedom people *would* or *would not* solve the problems they face. In terms of the present view there cannot, of course, be a guarantee that people who are free will do the things that are necessary for their proper survival. Let's ask the question clearly: "Will free people do the right things?" No one knows this, although there is ample evidence to *suggest* that they will do more things right than will people who are not free. Constraints upon the actions of people who are innocent of violating others' rights have not produced much progress in the improvement of the human condition. Even though the American system is far from having adhered to the principles of a free society, to the extent that it has come the closest of any known culture to approximating the legal system that, based on

Locke's theory of natural human rights, protected the rights of individuals against violations by individuals or groups or governments, its record is not something that we can divorce from its form of government. And the record of the United States, in making possible the fulfillment of the aspirations of its citizens on a relatively equal basis (though it *could have been* better), is commendable when *comparatively* assessed. It is unwise to rely on what could be construed as primarily emotional appeals, but one cannot in justice evade the fact that American culture is held in high esteem *especially* by the most unfortunate peoples throughout the world. And while European sophisticates may castigate the American way of life for a variety of its alleged cultural and intellectual failings, as far as providing a setting in which individuals of innumerable variety of backgrounds can aspire to and often reach a form of life that at least they judge desirable, there is really no country that can compare with it. At least not if we examine American history in its full context and make our comparisons in terms of the relative success of various forms of political systems to make possible the development of the lives of its citizens individually and collectively.

The broad generalizations above can be shown to be just that, but they do succeed in identifying what they are meant to identify, namely *general* truths. With the evidence in stock, as it surely is by any standard of judgment that considers the lives of *individuals* of prime value, the relative practicability of the American system is certainly borne out. This is to say, within the framework of a semi-free system of government, people have, on the whole, succeeded in the achievement of their own goals on a wider scale—in greater number and at less expense to others—than elsewhere.

Capitalism and the Critics

A very persistent belief, held by Ralph Nader, for instance, that people entertain about the free market is that unrestrained by governmental controls, producers of goods and services will manage to sell what people either do not desire or desire in entirely different forms. Today this belief manifests itself in the numerous attempts by politicians to regulate the packaging of merchandise and the prices of goods and services in different locations. Why, they say, should company X sell its breakfast food in a big, fancy box, while company Y sells it in a small and plain one? Why should gasoline cost 38 cents in service station A, when it costs only 31 cents in station B? There have also been attempts to impose controls on grocery store operators and owners in order to equalize prices between various regions of a community. In general, there is a stigma attached to the free market because of the alleged injustice that its existence perpetuates.

It cannot be denied that in a free, uncontrolled economy producers would be free to *ask* anything for their products, while buyers could offer anything for what they wanted to purchase and, as a result, the differences within the market would be many, both in regard to the price for which a certain good would sell and the price that different people would pay for it. But further thought on the matter will make it clear that no massive injustice occurs within a free market—none, that is, that could be eliminated by centralized political control. Furthermore, if anything, the free market is far more just in precisely these regards than any other economic arrangement could be.

One of the basic ideas that underpin the political system of a free society is that men have but a few universal qualities that they share among each other, and that they have even fewer features or characteristics in which they enjoy quantitative equality. Thus, in most healthy people we will find the capacity to reason, so we can assert with certainty, that all men, excepting only borderline cases, share in this characteristic, namely rational thought. Yet, even in something as central to being a human being as this, men do vary considerably in their capacity for exercising rational thought. Men are significantly different in their mental, intellectual capacities.

In other matters the situation is even more revealing. Some men are good athletes, others poor; some are tone deaf, others sing beautifully; in talents, traits, potentialities, etc., men vary drastically. Yet, the idea that they are *all equal* in an important respect is of course a true one. Each man is equal as a being of moral worth, as an end in himself not to be used for the purposes of others. It is possible for men to bring upon themselves just punishment, when they commit a violation of others' rights, for instance; but unless proved otherwise, all men are equal in deserving the respect of their human rights. But this very specific sort of equality is not to be confused with the far broader notion of equality implied in the objections against the free market. There is no justice in anything but that sort of standardization which arises out of voluntary consent and exchange.

Then there are those critics who account for America's success in terms of such "accidents" as its natural resources—minerals, land, wilderness, oceans, varieties of terrain, etc. Others claim that American society flourished indeed "at the expense of others," namely non-Americans whose wealth has been exploited by the enterprising Yankees.

There are many reliable, scholarly sources that invalidate these charges and that can be investigated by those who are honestly interested in finding out the answers and solutions to problems.[19] With the first charge, however, there is the logical/verbal problem that those who attribute America's well being to "natural" resources are simply unable to account for the failure of other nations to make use of resources that exist within *their* geographical areas. In fact, those making this charge are generally the ones who accuse the American semicapitalistic system of imperialism, meaning that U.S. business took advantage of the relative underdevelopment of, for instance, Latin American and Middle Eastern countries (in industrial technology), and "exploited" these foreign lands by virtue of its technological superiority and money. This accusation, though presented in a very biased manner (is it *really* exploitation to import (often by invitation) business into a country with a state of permanent economic depression and to utilize the untapped resources?), admits that just having natural (potential) resources does little good. Human ingenuity is required to make these resources *for* something, namely human use, which is precisely the point of the libertarian contention; in a political-legal system based more than less on individual liberty, the goals of people can more successfully be accomplished than elsewhere. Just imagine what a completely free society could do for its individual members by securing for them the one truly public good, namely human liberty! But, still, one cannot offer guarantees. To be free to succeed is to be free to fail.

Skepticism in a Free Society

When giving answers to those who inquire about the free society, individuals who hold freedom in high esteem can find themselves in many difficulties. It is, after all, not easy to predict how *free* men would cope with the problems that *they* might encounter. Few people realize how much distortion exists in society as a result of the multitude of intrusions upon the lives of individuals from government. Who can tell what *might have happened* if people had been allowed to pursue their own aims with the income they earned instead of having to finance undertakings designated by the politicians in Washington?

Because we never had the opportunity to find out what free men do in the face of the problems of contemporary society, the confidence that they could handle these problems without having others doing it for them does not exist in our culture today. People not familiar with the philosophy of freedom simply look around, find that numerous feats have been started and carried out hand in hand with various governments, and conclude that these feats could be accomplished *only through* governments. It rarely occurs to them that not only might the same feats have been attained by free men as well or better than by governments, but that even if the achievements we do witness today—such as space flights to the moon—had not been chosen by free men, other, equally great, and most likely more meaningful and relevant achievements would have taken their place.

To argue the foregoing point to interested people is a difficult task. Today's rather pessimistic view of human nature often contributes to the dogmatic skepticism one finds among those who most often reject the viability of a free society. In such instances one must choose whether it is worth pressing on with the educational endeavor or whether it might be more valuable to seek out other tasks through which the prospects of freedom (or other values) could be enhanced.

There is, however, one common "objection" to the viability of a free society that should not be left unanswered. This is not really an objection at all but rather a skepticism based on bad reasoning. It occurs most often when one explains why freedom would flourish without all the governmental intervention in the economic life of the society. The skeptic often counters this explanation not with any evidence to the contrary—from history—but with the remark: "This is all well and good, but it is still *possible* that in a free society certain businesses would act in such a way as to bring about the kind of oppression you all fear from government today." When one presses the person to offer grounds upon which he bases this possibility, he merely reasserts his claim that it *might*, after all, turn out that way, whatever the evidence does or does not show.

But certainly one need not be dissuaded by such an "argument." Simply because we cannot on the spot prove that something—in this case coercive monopolies in a free society—is impossible, we need not believe that it is likely or even possible. The burden of proof is on he who contends that freedom breeds coercion—he is the one who is putting forward the strange theory, after all. It is an absurd request to have to disprove something for which no evidence and proof has been offered. It is like asking one to disprove that there *might* be quacking ducks on Venus; it is he who contends that there *are* or could be such a phenomenon who is responsible for proof.

At this point I want briefly to touch upon the possible challenge that the system for which I have argued is utopian and fails like all utopian systems. Namely, a utopia assumes that there can be a final, unchanging, timeless conception of society that yields the solution to all of man's problems and guarantees human happiness. In its essentials the Marxian conception of the communist society is, accordingly, utopian, for example. To begin with, the system discussed above guarantees nothing for people individually except a continual effort to secure their freedom to do as they judge best with what is theirs, including their lives, property, and talents.[20] Just in this respect alone the system does not meet the standards of ordinary utopias.

More importantly, however, in terms of the political tenets discussed in this essay, there is no evidence of utopian thinking. No claim was made to the effect that the free society *will forever* be the best political arrangement to serve the lives of individual men in their associations. It is simply the best that can be *reasonably* conceived. That perhaps in some future time a different system would be an improvement on the presently conceived one cannot be ruled out, even though to the best of our ability we cannot reasonably conceive of such a system *now*. But, of course, all of human knowledge is in evolution, including the knowledge concerning what is politically right for man. Furthermore, we cannot say now that the nature of man (in terms of which what is right for him politically or otherwise must be conceived and ascertained), will remain forever in time what it is now. Though we have no grounds now for believing that it will change, and cannot say anything informative about whether it could or would or will change, we must allow that human nature need not always remain what it presently is. But only when we have evidence to suggest its change will we be responsible to consider what is best for man in terms of his *new* nature. Accordingly, the present discussion cannot reasonably be regarded as utopian venturesomeness.

Capitalism and the Future

Finally, I must discuss briefly a most important question, namely how would it be possible to progress(!) toward the state of affairs judged above to be right for man, namely toward a fully free society based on individual human rights?[21] The question, like many of those treated earlier, cannot be answered simply. First of all, "how would it be possible to progress" *for whom*? Which is to say, there is no *one* answer to the question if what is required is that one outline certain policies or programs. As mundane as it may seem, each man, once he has considered and agreed to the above analysis, must appraise his own situation and make the appropriate moves within his own life to further the goals at issue. Once a person agrees with the above analysis one thing *must be* clear for him: at no point must he resort to coercion or aggression in his attempt to achieve any of his aims, whether they be the satisfaction of some short term goal or the achievement of the transformation of the society. Thus, violent revolution (which is not a wide-scale protective measure against tyrant(s) but a move to wrest political power from some and bestow it on others), is *not* a step toward the attainment of the ends of a libertarian. (Revolution can be justifiable, of course, but only when it consists of retaliatory action against a state!)

Perhaps the best slogan characterizing the proper approach to building a libertarian political system is "First, liberate yourself!"

In more specific terms, a libertarian owes it to himself to abstain from all actions and associations that contribute to the maintenance of institutions that violate human rights. This, at least, is the first principle that must guide such a person in his *social* and *political* relations. And this is the only area where one can justly give general advice in this matter. For in all other matters individuals are just that, individuals who have their own specialties by which to contribute to their own liberation and to the improvement of their lives within present day society. Libertarianism most emphatically does not call for martyrdom! It is, after all, the value of human life that gives the libertarian political philosophy its ethical foundation. Because, at least now, the likelihood of actually attaining the desired political end of instituting a free society based on individual human rights is very remote (though opinion is divided among libertarians on this matter), the life of a libertarian is very often extremely complex, especially as regards the advancement of his ideas. He is, very often, an educator.[22] He is also involved in the building of avenues of solving problems outside the framework of the State.[23] Frequently libertarians who engage in profitable businesses contribute heavily to the scholarship of young libertarian educators.[24] On the whole, libertarians attempt to work for the realization of their ideas in both personal and political context through intellectual and entrepreneurial efforts, including education, scholarship, art. (The novels of Ayn Rand, the scholarship of Ludwig von Mises, the teaching of Milton Friedman, and similar examples testify to this.)

Through these methods, and through occasional efforts to resist the State overtly (tax strikes, the challenge of draft laws, the support of more rather than less libertarian political candidates) libertarians believe that their goals *can* be achieved. Naturally, each new day suggestions come to the fore as to additional methods. Only one approach is unacceptable—coercing or deceiving others into accepting the libertarian position.

Underlying this approach to social change is the libertarian's basic view of human nature. He views man as fundamentally free and capable of rational thought, something that he is not only responsible to exert but requires for his proper existence. The libertarian does not regard men out of context of the present world and does not deny the immense complexity of the world. On the contrary, it is *because* of his recognition of complexity and difficulty that he urges rational thought for everyone. He may give advice and recommendations but only with reasonable comprehension of someone's special situation, individual context. Since, however, he is not interested in running peoples' lives, he is satisfied with as much.

Finally, because he rests his case on reason, the libertarian also holds that, if he cannot achieve his ends through reason, it is unfortunate. And when he is wrong in wanting to achieve certain ends, he will fail to achieve them and that is exactly the *just* development of events. As a libertarian, one does not believe in entertaining unreasonable doubts. Which is what it would take, at this point, for one to fail to acknowledge the correctness of the position for which I have argued in this essay.

References

1. The term gained popularity in the nineteenth century. The Oxford English Dictionary lists W. M. Thackeray as having used it in *Newcomes II* (75) ; "The sense of capitalism sobered and dignified Paul de Florac." (1854) Pall Mall G. II (Sept. 6/1.1877) mentioned capitalism as moving in on Christian communism. The term "capitalist" is recorded to have been used even earlier. A. Young called "moneyed men . . . (who) escape all taxation" by the term in 1792. In both instances the sense of the term is not strange to us.
2. Adam Smith, the father of modern economics, for example, did not advance a completely free economic system but he did propose what came closest to it to date. Smith's task, however, was to a large extent critical; it is English mercantilism that provoked his opposition to government management of business activity.
3. The concept "laissez-faire" comes to us from French political history. Legendre, who when asked by Colbert to say what the state might do to help business responded with *"laissez-nous faire,"* is supposed to have originated the phrase. Frederic Bastiat was the most ardent exponent of *laissez-faire* economics in France. All through the few years of his adult life from 1840 to 1850 he did the most to present a lucid exposition of the political economy of a free society. Bastiat's *Selected Essays on Political Economy, Economic Harmonies,* and *Economic Sophisms* have recently been

published by D. Van Nostrand Company. His work, *The Law*, published as a pamphlet in the year in which he died (1850) has been studied by libertarians throughout this country for many years (published by Foundation for Economic Education, Irvington-on-Hudson, New York, 10533).

4. Cf., Ludwig von Mises, *Human Action: A Treatise on Economics* (Chicago: Henry Regnery Co., 1966). Von Mises' works comprise an eloquent library of scholarly defense of free market economics from the famous Austrian School of economic thought's point of view. Miss Bettina Bien of the Foundation for Economic Education, Inc., Irvington-on-Hudson, New York, has compiled a small volume, *The Works of Ludwig Von Mises*. Any serious defender or opponent of free market economics should have some familiarity with von Mises' works.

5. Within the circles of those who advocate a society based on individual rights (to life, liberty and property) there is debate, of course, as to the precise form such a society might take. Most important of the differences that separate libertarians is the one between anarcho-capitalists or individualist anarchists and limited or consensual governmentalists. Murray N. Rothbard, *Man, Economy, and State* (Van Nostrand), and *Power and Market* (Institute for Humane Studies), James J. Martin, *Men Against the State* (Ralph Myles Publisher), and their students defend the anti-governmentalist conception of society, while Ayn Rand, *Capitalism: The Unknown Ideal* (New American Library), *The Virtue of Selfishness* (New American Library), and in lectures and articles; Nathanial Branden in recorded lectures; John O. Nelson, *The Personalist* (forthcoming); Ludwig von Mises; F. A. Hayek, L. Peikoff, and others, including the present writer, argue that it is possible to conceive of government as a purely defensive and retaliatory social agency, operating entirely through the consent of the governed. The proceedings of the First Annual Conference on Political Philosophy, held at the University of Southern California in September 1970, to be published in *The Personalist*, includes an informative symposium concerning the differences between the anarcho-capitalists and voluntary anarchists.

6. In addition, cf., Ezra Heywood, William B. Greene, J. K. Ingals, Lysander Spooner, Benjamin R. Tucker, Josiah Warren, *et al.* These and other contributors to early American anti-statist thought are discussed by James J. Martin in *Men Against the State* (Colorado Springs: Ralph Hyles Publisher, Inc., 1970). The ideal of

absolute freedom from state coercion has found supporters from many different sources, including such major figures of Western philosophy as Spinoza, John Locke, Immanuel Kant, and Herbert Spencer.

7. Some claim that the Founding Fathers had only "selfish" economic interests in mind when they forged the legal system of this country. Cf., Charles A. Beard, *An Economic Interpretation Of The Constitution Of The United States* (New York: Macmillan, 1941). No doubt, those who opt for a free legal system must also be thinking of what is good for them. What is wrong with that kind of "selfishness" anyway?

8. Exceptions are the many semi-nationalist tracts emanating from "America First" circles in behalf of "free enterprise." Today such material is put out by so-called conservative groups and the John Birch Society. While some of this material is sound within the realms of economics (as far as it goes), libertarians part company with it concerning such important matters as civil liberties, foreign policy, protectionism, *etc.* More useful are such works as John Chamberlain's *The Enterprising Americans* (New York: Harper & Row, 1961) and *The Roots of Capitalism* (Princeton, N.J.: Van Nostrand, 1962), and F. A. Hayek's *Capitalism And The Historians* (Chicago: University of Chicago Press, 1954). Ludwig von Mises' small volume, *The Anti-Capitalist Mentality* (Princeton, N.J.: Van Nostrand, 1956), offers an interesting analysis of widespread hostility toward capitalism by academicians and intellectuals.

9. Murray N. Rothbard, *America's Great Depression* (Van Nostrand), *Power and Market* (Institute for Humane Studies); Milton Friedman, *Capitalism And Freedom* (Chicago: University of Chicago Press); F. A. Hayek, *Capitalism And The Historians* (University of Chicago Press); also, *The New Individualist Review* (1961–1968), *The Journal Of Law And Economics, The Intercollegiate Review, Left And Right,* and *Reason Magazine.*

10. Ayn Rand, "The Objectivist Ethics," in *The Virtue Of Selfishness* (New York: New American Library, 1964).

11. Ayn Rand, *Atlas Shrugged* (New York: Random House, 1957); Nathaniel Branden, *The Psychology of Self-Esteem* (Los Angeles: Nash Publishing Company, 1969).

12. Eugene D. Genovese, *The Political Economy of Slavery* (New York: Pantheon Books, 1965).

13. Gordon Tullock, "The Economics of Slavery," *Left and Right*, vol. iii, no. 2, pp. 5–16.
14. Cf., Galbraith, Samuelson, Keynes, and hundreds of others.
15. *Op. cit.*, Rothbard, Friedman, Hayek, *et al.*
16. Cf., Oscar Lewis, *The Big Four;* David Marshall, *Grand Central;* Yale Brozen, "Is Government the Source of Monopoly?", *The Intercollegiate Review*, vol. 5, no. 2. pp. 67–78.
17. Robert Poole, "Infinite Sink No More," *Reason*, Vol. 2, No. 7/8; Steve Goldstein (ed.), *Cleaning House Inside The Ecology Revolution* (Los Angeles: Aware Publications, 1970).
18. *The Journal Of Law And Economics*, Gabriel Kolko's Works, Historical Investigations by F. A. Hayek, *et al.*
19. *Ibid.*
20. Even here no perfect administration is guaranteed or predicted—though, unlike in statist systems, the model of perfection would not be impossible to satisfy in principle.
21. Tibor R. Machan, "A Rationale for Human Rights," *The Personalist* (Spring 1971).
22. University of Chicago, Department of Economics, Graduate School of Business; University of California as Los Angeles, Department of Economics; University of Virginia, Department of Economics; etc.
23. For example, out of court arbitration agencies (The American Arbitration Association), protection agencies (guards, security forces, insured protection devices, etc.), private mails (used where the United States Post Office not only cannot break even but simply cannot deliver; yet these private groups bring in profits), private schools, charities, better business bureaus, private fire departments (in Scottsdale, Arizona), etc.
24. The Foundation for Economic Education has embarked on what it calls a mission of "conservation"; it is investing in the reprinting of liberterian literature such as the works of Bastiat, von Mises, Henry Hazlitt, Rothbard, *et al.*

Freedom Versus Capitalism

ANDREW McLAUGHLIN

It has been suggested by capitalism's proponents that capitalism is itself an element of human freedom. What I want to argue is that capitalism and human freedom are in fact, antithetical. Because I take human freedom to be a moral good, this amounts to a moral argument against capitalism. While capitalism does provide the illusion of a certain sort of freedom, in a more fundamental sense it is a system built upon manipulation and coercion.

Two different types of arguments can be offered about the proper economic organization of society. One can try to argue only in economic terms, suppressing moral considerations as much as possible. (However, no purely "economic" argument on this issue can wholly avoid some value commitments.) Alternatively, one can focus upon moral issues, discussing economic issues briefly and only in passing. Ideally, both the moral and the economic aspects need to be considered, but this would necessitate a very lengthy discussion. The reason why *both* the moral and the economic dimensions of economic organization need to be considered is that while it would be foolish to try to adopt the morally best economic system if it were economically impossible, it would be impossible to justify adopting an economic organization that, though feasible, was morally worse than other available alternatives. Fortunately, it is possible to short-circuit some of the difficult questions of economics by noting the fact of abundance in contemporary post-industrial societies. I want to

Andrew McLaughlin (Ph.D., State University of New York at Buffalo) is Assistant Professor of Philosophy at Herbert H. Lehman College of the City University of New York, and at the C.U.N.Y. Graduate Center. His writings have focused on reason and scientific inquiry, and he is currently working on the idea of social rationality.

briefly show why I think that this fact allows one to sidestep the economic questions involved in assessing capitalism.

The economic case for capitalism might be made along the following lines. It has been claimed by some that capitalism is the most efficient mode of economic organization—meaning roughly that the capitalist mode of organization is the one that produces the most economic goods. Now such an argument contains a hidden moral premise concerning the unlimited desirability of economic goods so that it is not "purely" an economic argument. To do justice to this and other economic arguments for and against capitalism raises some difficult questions. To mention only one, what precisely is capitalism? Some theorists equate "true" capitalism with an economic system that has large numbers of relatively small independent producers and consumers and a relatively weak government that does not significantly interfere in the economy. Such a system was reasonably descriptive of some economies in the nineteenth century. However, modern capitalist systems bear little resemblance to that image, because they are typically composed of large producers who can significantly control market conditions. Moreover, governments often attempt to manipulate the economy. Some theorists see this system as capitalism. Which of these two quite different economic systems is to be called capitalism is not an easy question. What does seem clear is that modern technology is conducive to the development of relatively large productive organizations.[1] Whether technology *requires* economic organizations with gigantic corporations is a subject involving difficult questions concerning the nature of technology.[2] Hence, it is unclear whether it is possible to return to nineteenth century capitalism, even if that were desirable. This is but one of the issues that would have to be faced if a wholesale appraisal of the economic arguments concerning capitalism were to be undertaken.

However, as suggested above, the difficult economic arguments can be sidestepped if the fact of economic abundance is granted. It seems clear to me that whatever may be the pressing problems of today, they do not include the problem of economic efficiency. By this I mean that it is no longer necessary to worry about producing the *maximum* or anything near the maximum amount of material goods. Man's productive capacity has developed to the point that it simply is not plausible to claim that morally objectionable social systems must be supported in order for man to produce the material goods necessary for survival—or even the "good life," unless "goodness" is equated with the maximum of material goods. This does not mean that capitalism is not justified. Rather it only shifts the question from one of economics to one of morality. The growth of man's productive capacity widens his options as to economic organization so that what once may have been necessary now becomes a matter for human decision. If capitalism is morally acceptable, then its alleged economic efficiency is fine, but if capitalism is morally objectionable, then given the abundance of material goods, the economic argument becomes irrelevant.

The claim that economic abundance is a fact might be contested. One could point to poverty, both within the United States and worldwide, as evidence that scarcity is still a profound problem. Without pursuing this issue fully, two questions need to be raised about poverty. First, it is obvious that one way poverty could be greatly reduced, if not eliminated, would simply be to redistribute wealth from the rich to the poor. Of course, radical social change and the redistribution of political power are necessary steps toward achieving such a redistribution in the United States. Secondly, what constitutes "poverty" is very much dependent upon the way society is organized and it may be that poverty can be eliminated by simply reorganizing society. An example might make this point clearer. Generally, in the United States a family that could not afford a car would be considered poor. Given the prevailing structure of society, a car is often desirable or necessary because mass transit is inadequate. However, if mass transportation were adequate, then much of the necessity for a car would disappear. Nevertheless, there would still be times when one wanted to go someplace that was not served by mass transit. It is possible to imagine a society that simply provided public cars (built to last, not to become obsolete) located near population centers that were available for use by anyone who needed them. It is true that such a plan would be contrary to the interests of automobile manufacturers, but the benefits for others would be enormous. Life in cities would be greatly enhanced. People would not have to spend so much time working to pay off their cars, nor would they have to spend as much time on an assembly line making the cars. Yet people would still be able to travel when they wanted to. Of course it is obvious that such a transit system would require a radical social change away from capitalism, but notice that such a change would result in the elimination of poverty (at least as far as cars go) while requiring *less* human labor. The general point I am making is that poverty and its causes can be seen as resting within a social context. The amount of material production that is required within capitalism to eliminate poverty is far greater than that required to eliminate poverty within a more humanely organized economic system. This indicates that we may well be in a time of economic abundance right now, and that radical social change rather than increased material production is the solution for poverty. Considerations such as these indicate that economic abundance is a fact—and that fact frees us to appraise economic systems in terms of their moral worth, rather than in terms of alleged "economic necessity."

The Capitalist Idea of Freedom

Rather than attempt to canvas all the possible moral arguments concerning capitalism, it may be more interesting to look simply at the argument that relates capitalism to human freedom. The basic moral argument put forward for capitalism is that capitalism is itself an essential element of human freedom and, moreover, that such an economic system preserves other dimensions of freedom. Now because I take freedom to be a fundamental human value, if capitalism were an integral aspect of freedom, I would be at least somewhat persuaded that capitalism was a justifiable economic arrangement—but, in fact, I think that capitalism is far from being an element of freedom, and is directly opposed to it. It seems to me that one has to choose between capitalism and freedom since they are mutually exclusive. Showing that this is so will involve first a look at the idea of freedom embodied in the capitalist credo, and then a look beyond this toward a more adequate notion of human freedom.

The most obvious sense in which capitalism might be said to be essential to human freedom, involves the notion of economic freedom. Such a freedom might be defined as the right to use one's resources as one pleases or that one can make economic choices without being coerced in any particular situation. That is, a person can consume what he has, or save, or invest. Of course, this requires some modification since not *every* use of resources will be permitted by the capitalist. For example, capitalist theorists do not grant such rights as the right to form monopolies, or break valid contracts. Milton Friedman and others argue that it is the mechanism of the market-place in capitalism that translates this freedom into effective social coordination.[3] The freedom involved here is simply the freedom to decline to enter into any particular transaction. The preservation of this freedom is claimed to insure the absence of coercion:

> The consumer is protected from coercion by the seller because of the presence of other sellers with whom he can deal. The seller is protected from coercion by the consumer because of other consumers to whom he can sell. The employee is protected from coercion by the employer because of other employers for whom he can work, and so on.[4]

Whether these conditions are significantly present in contemporary capitalism is questionable in the extreme.[5] But present or not, there is a conception of freedom implicit within capitalist ideology that calls for examination. The essential notion of freedom seems to be that a person is free if he is not coerced. This notion of freedom can be applied in all realms, not just the economic. Thus, political freedom, too, can be defined as the absence of coercion in the political realm.

It is important to distinguish this conception of freedom (which is not unique to Friedman) from some of his other views. He thinks that the justifiable role of government is quite narrow, ruling out tariffs, rent controls, minimum wage laws, compulsory old-age insurance, licensing of professions, conscription, national parks or publicly owned toll roads from the realm of legitimate governmental activity. Not all who espouse the fundamental idea of freedom as simply the absence of coercion take such a narrow view of the role of the government. Thus many capitalist theorists think that the government has a responsibility to manipulate the economy to achieve the possibly incompatible goals of the reduction of inflation, full employment and economic growth. But what unites these "left-wing" capitalists and "right-wing" capitalists such as Friedman is the belief that the notion of human freedom can be adequately developed by reference to the absence of overt coercion. This general definition of freedom has been called "negative freedom" which means that a person is free if he is not coerced and "coercion implies the deliberate interference of other human beings within the area in which I could act."[6]

Essentially, then, the ideal of freedom as envisioned by capitalism is one in which a person can do as he pleases without interference by other people. But, of course, all such theorists recognize that *some* constraints must be imposed upon individuals. The traditional suggestion is that a person's actions must be limited to the extent that he cannot take away from other people's freedom to act. Exactly where such a line is to be found is a sticky problem, but one upon which we need not dwell here. The general idea is that one may have to surrender some freedom to act in order to have a viable society. How much freedom and what sorts of actions must be curtailed depend upon empirical questions as to the probable consequences of allowing various sorts of actions to be permitted within society. Berlin states the position of proponents of this sort of freedom well:

> Most modern liberals, at their most consistent, want a situation in which as many individuals as possible can realize as many of their ends as possible, without assessment of the values of these ends as such, save in so far as they may frustrate the purposes of others. They wish the frontiers between individuals or groups of men to be drawn solely with a view to preventing collisions between human purposes, all of which must be considered to be equally ultimate, uncriticizable ends in themselves.[7]

This position coincides nicely with Friedman's claim that a free competitive capitalist economy achieves well the goal of giving "people what they want instead of what a particular group thinks they ought to want."[8] This is both the major moral argument for capitalism and a sketch of the ideal of freedom embodied in such an argument, but that ideal needs serious examination. To do this it is first necessary to digress a bit and examine the idea of human choice.

The Dimensions of Human Choice

One fruitful way of looking at human choice is to separate the choice situation into an objective aspect and a subjective aspect. By the objective aspect, I am referring to the range of alternatives that an agent finds available to him. By the subjective aspect, I am referring to the agent himself, his desires, wants, values, etc. Now a choice can be seen as the result of the interaction between the objective and subjective aspects of the choice situation. What the capitalist idea of human freedom claims is that a person's choice is free (or not coerced) if there is no compulsion by some other person to choose one particular alternative. This view of human freedom is seriously inadequate and overlooks essential elements that must be present in a choice situation before it can really be called free.

In a choice situation a person surveys the alternatives open to him and elects that alternative which best (or adequately) suits him. Which alternative suits him depends importantly upon the subjective element such as his goals, desires, and values. Obviously, it also depends importantly upon what alternatives are available to him. Now one way of coercing someone is to simply structure the situation so that he has only one alternative. One could do this by threatening him with disastrous results (punishment) if he fails to elect the option desired by the coercer. To restrict a person's range of alternatives down to only one option constitutes the extreme case of coercion and coercion can be covertly accomplished by systematically structuring alternatives.

It is possible to deny that even in the most extreme of cases, such as the presence of the threat of death, that a person is not "free." For even the threat of death does not eliminate alternatives—but only substitutes the alternative of death for all but the oppressor's desired alternative. If merely the presence of options implies that the agent is free, then the political prisoner (given the option of death or confession) is still "free." Such a notion of freedom, while of interest to existentialists in analysing the nature of the human situation, has little relevance to the question of economic or political freedom, because we surely want to have a notion of freedom where sometimes people are free and sometimes they are not. But if freedom is taken to be merely the presence of options, then we are always free. Even where there are no "objective" options—such as the prisoner's situation when he is about to be executed—people still have the "option" of the mental attitude they decide to take toward their situation. Such attitudes themselves can become objects of choice—and this means that if freedom is simply the presence of options, everyone is always free, and always will be, at least until there are attitude-determining chemicals that can coerce the mind as effectively as bullets can coerce the body. The upshot is that the mere presence of alternatives is not sufficient to indicate that a person is free.

In the schema of choice that I have adopted here, the capitalist's notion of freedom is that if the range of alternatives is not restricted by other agents, then a person is free. Of course, there is a recognition that there are degrees of freedom and that the necessities of the social system may require that some alternatives be foreclosed, e.g., by attaching punishments to certain types of actions. But it remains true that the essence of the capitalist ideal of freedom is simply that whatever alternatives exist, the degree to which people are free is solely a function of whether other humans prevent an agent from pursuing the alternative of his choice.

What is totally missing in this analysis of freedom is a critical analysis of the types of alternatives open to the agent. This aspect of choice is simply taken for granted by the capitalist and he does not hold up for criticism the ranges of actions open to each individual— yet such a consideration of the types of alternatives is essential in any adequate idea of human freedom. Perhaps this point can be made clearer by looking at one type of coercion that is wholly overlooked by the capitalist idea of freedom.

Systematic Coercion

Overt coercion seems fairly unproblematic to define. Someone is coerced when he is threatened with injury unless he acts in some particular way, or refrains from some particular action. But there is another type of coercion that is probably much more important in understanding the degree of freedom within a society. It is extremely difficult to run a society simply on the basis of overt coercion. To do so would require a policeman at every corner and if a society really required that many policemen, it is likely that it would be upon the verge of dissolution. Most forms of social control are much less obvious. Thus, the forces of social pressure, in a small face-to-face community can function much more effectively than can overt coercion, except in extreme cases. Now one important type of coercion involves *the systematic structuring of alternatives that the individual faces in a choice situation.* It is the nature of the alternatives available that is neglected by the capitalist ideal of freedom, yet this is an exceedingly important aspect of coercion. An example may make the nature of this form of coercion clearer.

The following passages are quoted from an *official* Selective Service document entitled "Channeling":

> While the best known purpose of Selective Service is to procure manpower for the armed forces, a variety of related processes take place outside of delivery of manpower to the active armed forces. Many of these may be put under the heading of "channeling manpower." Many young men would not have pursued a higher education if there had not been a program of student deferment. Many young scientists, engineers, tool and die makers, and other possessors of scarce skills would not remain in their jobs in the defense effort if it were not for a program of occupational deferments. . . .
>
> The club of induction has been used to drive out of areas considered to be less important to the areas of greater importance in which deferments were given, the individuals who did not or could not participate in activities which were considered essential to the defense of the nation. . . .
>
> Since occupational deferments are granted for no more than one year at a time, a process of periodically receiving current information and repeated review assures that every deferred registrant continues to contribute to the overall national good. This reminds him of the basis for his deferment. . . .
>
> The psychology of granting wide choice under pressure to take action is the American or indirect way of achieving what is done by direction in foreign countries where choice is not permitted. Here, choice is limited but not denied, and it is fundamental that an individual generally applies himself better to something he has decided to do rather than something he has been told to do. . . .
>
> Delivery of manpower for induction, the process of providing a few thousand men with transportation to a reception center, is not much of an administrative or financial challenge. It is in dealing with the other millions of registrants that the system is heavily occupied, developing more effective human beings in the national interest.[9]

A lot of interesting points are made in this document, such as the idea of indirect pressure being more effective as a means of social control than direct pressure. But the essential point to note is that "channeling" is simply a way of coercing people into various activities by structuring the nature of the alternatives available to them. Such coercion, while not overt and readily visible, *is* coercion—systematic coercion. Now I do not mean to suggest that such systematic coercion is wholly avoidable—social control is, at least until we develop a wholly voluntary community, simply necessary. What I want to emphasize very strongly is that any analysis of human freedom must recognize that systematic coercion is just as real a form of coercion as a club. But if this is so, this means that an adequate appraisal of how free a person is must involve looking critically at the range of alternatives that he faces. It is in refusing to face up to this question that the capitalist idea of freedom shows its inadequacy. And, moreover, it is apparent why the capitalist does not focus upon this dimension of freedom. If he were to look at this dimension, it would become apparent that different social classes have, in fact, widely divergent ranges of alternatives in their choice situations. The alternatives available to the worker and those open to the owner are widely divergent. Yet the capitalist idea of freedom would lead one to believe that the worker and the capitalist are equally free, because they both can make their choices without overt coercion. But to call them equally free is to take an important ideal—human freedom—and twist it into a tacit defense of capitalism.

Marx remarks in the first volume of *Das Capital* that the capitalist needs "free laborers,"—that is, those who are free in a double sense. First they are free from the constraints of feudalism with the traditional obligations that prohibit the worker from changing employers. That is, the system of capitalism requries that workers can go from one employer to another. *This* is the only sort of freedom envisioned by Friedman when he touts the freedom of competitive capitalism as embodied in the worker's freedom from coercion by employers because he can change jobs (see the quotation from Friedman above). But Marx presses on to note with irony that the worker in capitalism has also another "freedom." "Free workers" are also free in the sense that they are "free from, unencumbered by, any means of production of their own." The point he is making is simply that workers under capitalism find themselves with options as to whom to work for, but they *are* forced to work. They *must* hire themselves out to those who own the means of production. Their range of alternatives simply is narrowed by the social structure within which they live. And this must be seen as an important dimension of unfreedom under capitalism. Moreover, as I will suggest below, to eliminate this form of "unfreedom" in capitalism would require its abolition.

The essential point that is worth emphasis is that it is not enough to look at a choice and to decide that it is free if it is not a result of overt coercion. One must also call into question the nature of the alternatives that are present within a choice situation. And to talk of meaningful freedom for a person requires that the range of alternatives he can select must be judged adequate. Human freedom involves much more than simply the absence of overt coercion. While this is one element of freedom, another is the absence of what I have called systematic coercion. Whether this form of coercion can be wholly eliminated is a question that requires constructing alternative forms of society and seeing whether they are possible. Rather than trying to do justice to such a vast subject here, let me briefly indicate the direction in which any social system must move if it seriously wants to enhance the realm of freedom through the reduction of systematic coercion.

Any choice that involves ceasing to survive as one of its real alternatives cannot be a free choice, because the choice between labor and starvation is not a free choice. It is not a free choice because the presence of one alternative—death—is such as to *require* the agent to elect one of the other alternatives, and this requirement introduces the objectionable element of coercion. Thus, it would seem that to provide really free choices between alternatives, one must insure that the agent is not only free to elect one of the proffered options, *but is also free to walk away from the deal altogether*. This means that free choices cannot obtain where the question of survival is involved. Consequently, the range of human freedom can be greatly extended by insuring that all have the means for survival. This means that providing the means for the satisfaction of all survival needs is a prerequisite for providing the genuine possibility for human freedom, in the sense under discussion. To a large extent, providing for survival needs eliminates the element of systematic coercion from a social system. The line between survival needs and what might be called psychic needs is not sharply defined. However, the absence of sharp boundaries does not mean that there are no boundaries, and what counts as an item necessary for survival in any given society can be decided with some precision.

The question now arises whether it is feasible under capitalism to provide a reasonable life for every human being, whether or not he has functioned effectively within the economic system. The range of alternatives offered under capitalism for those who do not choose one of the socially defined "productive" alternatives is quite small. Unemployment insurance is only a temporary means of support when a worker has been fired and can find no other suitable job. Hence, this is not really a viable alternative. The various welfare programs do not even come close to providing what amounts to an adequate living. Hence, they are not viable choices, although they are an alternative into which many find themselves forced. The only ones who do voluntarily choose welfare as a means of life are those who have resigned themselves to voluntary poverty and find a suitable life-style. These people have created a viable option out of welfare by changing their own aspirations and values (the subjective dimension of choice) sufficiently to survive on welfare allotments. Indeed, these people— the voluntary dropouts—constitute a significant threat to the capitalist system, in pointing out an alternative life-style. But I want to defer discussion of the subjective aspect of the choice situation for the moment. In essence, the basic coercion on which the capitalist system operates is the necessity to enter into the economy in some way. There are, of course, other coercions (exemplified by channeling) but the basic one is to enter in some way into the market system and earn a living—or else live a life of poverty.

This point might be brushed aside on the ground that the necessity for human labor is a characteristic of the human situation and does not really constitute a basis for objecting to capitalism. The mere fact that to live one must survive, and survival requires labor, is the element of coercion and this is common to all economic systems. There is some force to this objection because it is true that labor is necessary for survival. Nevertheless, it is first important to recognize that this *is* a constraint upon the range of alternatives available to man. Recognition of this fact leads to the idea that freedom really requires the abolition of labor. Consequently, to move toward reducing required labor is to move toward freedom. Absolute freedom *might* not be possible, but the direction toward increasing freedom is clear. Yet capitalism and its image of freedom entirely obscures this.

A second and more important reply that lessens the force of the objection is that capitalism does nothing to diminish this element of systematic coercion and, in fact, thrives upon it. Notice that the fact of abundance makes the *possibility* of the reduction of socially required labor a real one. Yet there is little indication that post-industrial society is moving in a direction that uses the possibility of abundance in a way to enhance human freedom. Capitalism's great contribution, as Marx pointed out many times, was that it made the possibility of abundance real through its immense increase in man's productive ability. The simple reason why capitalism cannot utilize the possibility of abundance to increase freedom is that capitalism is based upon production for profit. Profit is made when goods are sold, hence it is essential for capitalism to have an ever increasing demand for goods. This can be met in several ways—by building cars that rapidly deteriorate, by going to the moon, by fighting wars, building missiles, creating demand for "new and improved" products, and so on. But these methods of creating demand do little, if anything, for increasing human freedom. Indeed, when it is seen that capitalism depends upon ever increasing the demand for goods (hence, the possibility of profit), the American definition of the "good life" as one of never-ending consumption (and thus of never-ending labor) comes to look like a definition of happiness that is highly functional for capitalism. Notice that an alternative principle of production—namely, production for needs—would lead to the gradual reduction in the need for labor as needs were met. Thus, under that principle, the idea of an automobile that lasted for twenty years would be a liberating idea, whereas under capitalism it spells joblessness and hard times. The production for need would lead to an increase in the realm of human freedom, as it would raise the alternative for people that they could choose to work less and pursue other activities. The need for systematic coercion would decline and the realm of freedom would increase.

Yet, even if a policy were immediately instituted whereby every person were entitled to a reasonable life (say a guaranteed income of $7,000 per year) without having to work, its effect upon capitalism is not obvious. It might be that there would be a massive walkout from such institutions as factories or schools, but that might not happen. This latter possibility leads us to the second dimension of any free choice—the subjective dimension. The subjective dimension of choice entails such factors as aspirations, goals, values and desires that lead a person to select one of the alternatives with which he is presented in a choice situation. Thus, in the most trivial of cases, a person is presented with the option of an apple or a pear and he selects one or the other on the basis of his own preferences. Another person, given the same option, might choose otherwise and the different choices would be the result of different subjective preferences.

Manipulation

It is when we consider the subjective dimension of human choices that the most profound weakness of the capitalist idea of freedom becomes apparent. As previously quoted, Isaiah Berlin considered negative freedom to involve granting that the ends of people (what I am calling the subjective dimension) are "uncriticizable" in themselves. Now this seems fine and is pleasantly permissive, yet an important issue must be raised. What happens to the idea of accepting people's aspirations uncritically when we raise the question "why do people come to have the desires that they do?" This question becomes rather more pressing when we realize that a complex industrial society with a large number of people depends for its very continuance on the intermeshing of large numbers of individual choices. Now the capitalist argument is that it achieves such coordination without coercion. We have already discussed the element of systematic coercion involved in a society, but I want now to direct attention to an even more profound aspect of social control that goes beyond simply the structuring of alternatives. The socialization process is a process that implants socially necessary values, goals, or aspirations within individuals. By insuring that people come to desire what society wants them to desire, their "free" choices can be influenced. It is this socialization of the subjective dimension of human choice that I call manipulation. Knowing what we do know about the ways society

implants values within members of that society, it becomes less reasonable to accept uncritically the particular expressions of preference
as necessarily showing what people "really" want. Rather, preferences and values must be subjected to critical scrutiny. Man is molded
by his society through many modes of socialization, such as the
family, schools, television, religion, films, peer groups, and so on.
And lo and behold, at the end of this process he comes out a good
citizen, active consumer, and having the aspirations needed by the
society. Recognizing these facts requires us, I think, to look rather
more critically at the ends people have and not to accept them as
"uncriticizable."

The general point about socialization can be made simply by
noting how society brings "physiological autonomy" under cultural
control.[10] The young infant's physiological autonomy is culturally
channeled in at least the following ways: he learns to transform the
reduction of blood-sugar levels (hunger) into appetite, which is
partially dependent upon external stimuli, and the hunger is directed
towards culturally approved foods; he learns to regulate urine and
feces evacuation in accordance with culturally acceptable behavior;
his emotional reactions are channeled to accord with culturally approved modes of expression. These are but a few of the profound
modifications we all learn in going from child to adult. From this
perspective, when we ask how it comes to pass that a relatively predictable number of people will desire a new Ford automobile in a
particular year, we realize that consumer behavior in the market
place is highly conditioned. This does not mean that people are
coerced into making the purchases they actually do make, but it does
raise the question of why people come to want the things they do
want. The manipulation of subjective desires is not coercion, but is
rather a much more subtle form of social control.

We should look, then, with a critical eye to the values adults in
any particular society have. By looking at those values, we can see
that they are a product of the socialization process of a society and,
if those values are judged inadequate, then this constitutes a condemnation of the society that produces them. In other words, the
question is shifted from the individual to the social level. We look
at the sort of person that various societies "grow" and judge societies
upon the worth of the types of people they create. The notion of the

sort of people societies grow and, in particular, the type of person grown by capitalism is discussed at some length by Erich Fromm. He uses the term "social character" to describe the way in which societies:

> shape the energies of the members of society in such a way that their behavior is not a matter of conscious decision as to whether or not to follow the social pattern, but one of *wanting to act as they have to act* and at the same time finding gratification in acting according to the requirements of the culture.[11]

The basic point is that societies *do* in fact socialize their members in ways that cause those people to want what society needs them to want. And this means that we cannot uncritically accept the particular values and desires that people happen to have. If those values are not such as to withstand critical examination, we can decide to restructure society to make other sorts of people. In refusing to raise this question, the weakness of the concept of negative freedom becomes apparent. In fact, if we take freedom to be highly valuable, then we can try to socialize people so that they can be autonomous. This is why I would suggest that, in the name of human freedom, we must subject the society's socialization process to critical scrutiny.

The realm of manipulation becomes most important when a society moves to a stage of relative abundance. When choices are made that relate to physical survival, the needs of each person are fairly clear and not subject to much manipulation—when you are hungry, you need food and it is hard to be convinced to spend money instead upon luxuries.[12] But once choices are to be made that do not have any close relation to survival needs, certain types of social characters are vulnerable to extensive manipulation. For example, the insecure person who derives his self-esteem from his relative status in his neighborhood can easily be convinced that it is important to be "the first on his block to have . . . ." (fill in whatever you want). There is a great deal that could be said about the process of manipulation involved in capitalism. Markets *must* be found for the increasingly numerous goods that are produced—"must" because otherwise there are no profits. This means that abundance is a problem, and people must be forever convinced that there is something more that they "need," something that they are willing to sacrifice some of their money to get. New markets are forever needed. They can be gotten in foreign lands (along with raw materials) or they can be created. The American "fear" of body odor helps to sell deodorant, yet it remains conceivable that we could have a very happy world without such a "fear." But, of course, it is quite understandable how, under capitalism, creating a fear of body odor simply creates a whole range of new products. Rather than dwell at length on this point, I shall simply quote from a quite successful advertising executive who is surprising in his candor:

> Feminine hygiene is going to be a big business for agencies. Our stuff, Feminique, is selling well. FDS is doing well. Johnson & Johnson came out with Vespré and it's doing well. The American businessman has discovered the vagina and like it's the next thing going. What happened is that the businessman ran out of parts of the body. We had headaches for a while but we took care of them. The armpit had its moment of glory, and the toes, with their athlete's foot, they had the spotlight, too. We went through wrinkles, we went through diets. Taking skin off, putting skin on. We went through the stomach with acid indigestion and we conquered hemorrhoids. So the businessman sat back and said "what's left?" And some smart guy said, "The vagina." We've zeroed in on it. And this is just the beginning. Today the vagina, tomorrow the world. I mean, there are going to be all sorts of things for the vagina: vitamins, pep pills, flavored douches like Cupid's Quiver (raspberry, orange, jasmine, and champagne). If we can get by with a spray, we can sell anything new. And the spray is selling.[13]

Capitalism and Its "Values"

Rather than trying to canvass all the values that capitalism requires for its existence, I shall only briefly look at two of them. First, capitalism requires a competitive individual, one who gets his satisfaction from outdoing others. Capitalism does not run on love and cooperation. The second value required by capitalism is materialism, or the idea that one becomes happy by possessing more and more material things. Both of these values make a person who is willing to sacrifice most of his waking time to either working to earn money to buy things or using the things he buys.

The training of the individual for competitive behavior starts quite young. The typical elementary schoolroom experience is one of competition. The teacher asks a question and the children put up their hands. The children are excited by the prospect of being called upon and showing that they know the answer, but they are even more delighted by the prospect of being able to correct another child who has given the wrong answer. Slowly, the children learn that their happiness depends upon the other's failure. Thus, they learn to feel bad when another does well. This is simply the sort of training that *must* be carried out if you wish to maintain a stratified society with a pyramid shape. The lovely thing about a pyramid is that it is narrow at the top so there is not much room there. Therefore, "success" is something that can only be had by a few. Hence, it becomes necessary to train people to accept that fact. The way to do that is to train them to be competitive.[14]

The other value that supports the hierarchical structure essential to capitalism is materialism. To train people to judge their self-esteem by reference to the size of the pile of things they accumulate fits in very nicely with capitalism's requirement of ever increasing consumption. Materialism as a definition of the good life also fits in well with the need for some means of differential reward necessary for a pyramidal social structure because material goods can always be divided into larger and smaller piles, thereby making it possible to dole out different amounts to different people. To see this point clearly, just imagine what would happen to society if we insisted that every person was of equal worth and that the good life consisted in warm interpersonal relations, after the basic physical needs were met.

It is hard to convince someone who is committed to the values of competition and materialism to see the emptiness of the life to which such values leads. It is always hard, in the realm of values, to make progress toward agreement when there is fundamental disagreement. Those who have grown up in America have the whole culture on their side when they respond with disguised hate, when they look at a new car with the throb of desire, when they respond to a friendly gesture with nastiness, and so on. Yet progress can be made. This society and capitalism become a little hard to defend when you strip away the platitudes about "individual achievement" and see how that achievement is rarely an achievement of some personally decided upon goal, but is rather defined in terms of social needs. When a person really becomes conscious of the fact that many of the things that he "wants" are the result of social manipulation, those things lose a little of their charm. Hence, it is important to become conscious of being manipulated. This process of becoming conscious of the shallowness and, finally, loneliness of the competitive and materialistic life can lead to new experiences—of the values of cooperative action and mutual affection. And those experiences lead to further ones. What is required is a new learning process involving the emotions as well as the mind—but once that new learning begins, the values necessary for capitalism no longer have much appeal. Once this process of freeing one's self from the values required by capitalism is begun, one can start to see the terrible poverty involved in the life that capitalism has to offer, not only for the poor and the hungry, but also for the rich and "successful." R. H. Tawney's "tadpole philosophy" provides an alternative perspective from which to view capitalism:

> It is possible that intelligent tadpoles reconcile themselves to the inconveniences of their position, by reflecting that, though most of them will live and die as tadpoles and nothing more, the more fortunate of the species will one day shed their tails, distend their mouths and stomachs, hop nimbly on to dry land, and croak addresses to their former friends on the virtues by means of which tadpoles of character and capacity can rise to be frogs.[15]

To work through the manipulation of capitalism leads to the insight that one might decide to be neither a tadpole nor a frog. That's a step towards a new world.

In the end, then, the choice is between capitalism and freedom. Only if the idea of human freedom is made into a trivial concept can capitalism be thought of as a system of freedom. It must necessarily rely upon systematic coercion because it must prohibit the provision of a decent life for all, and to provide such a life would eventually deprive the capitalist of his workers. But even more profoundly antithetical to human freedom is capitalism's need to breed a type of person chained to material goods as tokens of his self-esteem and a person locked into competitive relations with others. It is only in shedding those values that mankind can begin to see a whole

of confidence in its institutions and policies that
bly to tear the fabric of American life asunder. It
ial change was accelerating, particularly among
but the direction of that change remained unclear.
and conservatives fought to hold the pieces to-
they could buy enough time for the whirlwind to
ll persuasions were contesting for control of the
rocess. They tended to be similar in demanding
of political power to the community level. Thus,
ke in terms of ending "Big Government," while
nic liberals, and socialists spoke of the need of
o the people. While this was considered a moral
was also expedient. As an "outsider" each group
ower to exert a steady influence upon the national
he high motivation and organization of its followers
n a smaller sphere. Furthermore, radical groups
raphically concentrated so that although they might
verage on the national scene they could often hope
ve role at the community level. This concern for
and community control is expressed in most of the
olume.

ders" raised the key question: What *is* government?
riters appearing in this volume have used a narrow
eby government is equated with formal institutional
cutive, legislative, judiciary, and bureaucracy.) Be-
nition of government is so narrow, these writers gen-
advocate ending the problems that governments pose
erts in an area formulate policies, or having "the
Such a narrow definition of government often tends
fact that *whoever* sets goals, determines public policy
esources is exercising power—is governing. That is why
s been an *inescapable* fact of human existence ever
as given a companion. Even in the animal world there
n of values and enforcement of group norms (e.g., a
r") as recent studies by Konrad Lorenz have shown.
to have or not have government is an irrelevant ques-
questions are:

new realm of human freedom begin to open up. It is hard to prove,
but if we structured a society wherein people were not manipulated,
but rather were allowed to grow as they pleased, capitalism would
crumble. People, allowed to develop freely, would not have the
desires and goals necessary for capitalism. The experience of A. S.
Neill at Summerhill school shows this. When students are allowed
to learn *what they want when they want to,* they grow up to be
happy, yet they are not usually the sort of people that capitalism
needs. If this is true, then it brings to light the most fundamental
way in which capitalism and freedom are opposed—for capitalism
must manipulate people into being what the profit system needs,
rather than letting them be.

Unfortunately, the problems of human liberation are more complicated than simply eliminating capitalism. I have tried to argue
here that capitalism and freedom, far from going together, are antithetical. But simply to eliminate capitalism would not thereby make
people free. There are after all, other forms of society that strive to
enslave people to the needs of the social system. When we begin to
think seriously about how to arrange ourselves so that we can all be
free to be ourselves, we find that we really do not know much. For
example, to eliminate capitalism and yet leave untouched sexual
liberation for men and women would be to stop short of freedom.
But, as we know so clearly now, the difficulties of sexual liberation
are profound. It is just too optimistic to think that if we only tran-
scended capitalism toward a more humane economic system, that the
problems of human freedom would then be solved. What I can only
hope to have shown here is that capitalism *does* stand in the way of
human freedom; I can't claim to have discovered all of what stands
in the way of humanity becoming fully human.

References

1. See John Kenneth Galbraith, *The New Industrial State* (Boston:
   Houghton Mifflin, 1967).
2. For a summary of much of this problem see V. C. Ferkis, *Technological Man* (New York: Braziller, 1969).
3. Perhaps the most accessible statement of this position can be

found in Milton Friedman, *Capitalism and Freedom* (Chicago: University of Chicago Press, 1962).

4. *Ibid.*, pp. 14–15.
5. See Galbraith, *op. cit.*
6. "Two Concepts of Liberty," Isaiah Berlin, *Four Essays on Liberty* (New York: Oxford University Press, 1969), p. 122.
7. *Ibid.*, p. 153.
8. Friedman, *op. cit.*, p. 15.
9. Quoted from Mitchell Goodman, *The Movement Toward a New America* (New York: Knopf, 1970), pp. 444–445.
10. The term and this dimension of manipulation are drawn from Lawrence K. Frank, "Cultural Control and Physiological Control," in C. Kluckhohn and H. Murray, *Personality in Nature, Society and Culture* (New York: Knopf, 1954).
11. Erich Fromm, *The Sane Society* (Greenwich, Conn.: Fawcett Publications, 1965), p. 77.
12. See Galbraith, *op. cit.*, chapter 18.
13. Jerry Della Femina, *From Those Wonderful Folks Who Gave You Pearl Harbor* (New York: Pocket Books, 1971), pp. 37–38.
14. Jules Henry has some poignant descriptions of schoolroom behavior in *Culture Against Man* (New York: Knopf, 1963).
15. R. H. Tawney, *Equality* (New York: Barnes & Noble, 1964), Ch. 3.

Part

tion faced a crisis
threatened irrevoca
was clear that so
those under thirty,
While the old left
gether, hoping tha
pass, radicals of
decision-making
a decentralization
the old right sp
libertarians, org
bringing power
good by many, i
lacked sufficient
government, but
could assist it
tended to be geo
lack sufficient le
to play a decis
decentralization
articles in this v
These "outsi
Many of the w
definition wher
structures (exe
cause their defi
erally tend to
by having exp
people" do it.
to overlook the
and allocates r
government h
since Adam w
is an allocatio
"pecking orde
Thus whether
tion. The rea

Int
Am
and

Less th
academ
as a "m
consensu
cally de
in a cult
leaders
demonstr
forced to
Much of
in the tu
1970s mo

Who should govern?

Why should that person or group exercise power over others— should power be based on expertise, heredity, talent, or selection by one's peers?

To whom should the governors be *responsible*—to other experts, all those affected by their decisions, only those who selected them or solely those with the economic means for influence?

What *degree of institutional structure* will be necessary to accomplish this?

Whether implicitly or explicitly, all of the contributors to this volume raise these questions.

Part II has been divided into five policy sections: racism, urban policy, poverty, environment and foreign and military policy. These issues are raised in other articles throughout the volume, but here they are the central focus. In each section a spokesman for the right and left presents his or her position. The following introduction does not discuss individual articles at length because their authors have effectively communicated their positions. Therefore, summarizing them would be both redundant and liable to oversimplification. It has, however, seemed useful to indicate their position within the basic framework of American political thought that has been indicated in the introduction to Part I. The terms conservative, old and new right, old and new left, organic liberal, and socialist are being used in the sense in which they were defined in that introduction.

In considering racism Ernest Van den Haag demonstrates conservative skepticism about the liberal assumption of the equality of all men in all ways. He presents this in the context of genetic and psychological studies of racial differences in native intelligence. From a position in the new left Ira Katznelson assumes inherent human equality. Both are critical of American racial policies: Ernest Van den Haag criticizes what he considers to be an overemphasis on policies of school integration, and Ira Katznelson criticizes the values and institutions that he considers to have structured racial inequality in the north. In this section there is no intention of ascribing racism to one or the other side of the ideological spectrum. The left has generally ascribed it to the American right, but the vast array of research during the last decade by psychologists, sociologists, political scientists and various government commissions and agencies has clearly documented the fact that racism is too widespread a phenomenon in America to be the monopoly of any one political persuasion (though it may be expressed more openly by some than others). Furthermore, both the old right and old left are implicated in developing the policies and institutions that this research finds to have structured American racism. This is a point on which all of the new radicals agree—libertarians, organic liberals, anarchists, and socialists are explicitly antagonistic to any form of discrimination based on race, ethnicity, or gender. Often these radicals also fight discrimination against those who engage in what society has traditionally considered to be deviant sexual or drug practices. Thus all these groups support the end of imperialism abroad and support domestic movements of "black power," "brown power" (Mexican-Americans and Puerto Ricans), "red power" (American Indians), "gold power" (orientals), and woman's liberation. Libertarians, anarchists, and some members of the other two new left groups also champion "gay liberation" (homosexuals and lesbians) and users of all forms of drugs.

In the section on urban policy Edward Banfield writes of the inherent inferiority of the "lower class" as the major urban problem, while Paul Piccard raises the organic liberal argument that our urban policy has a differential impact on people and should be reformed in the direction of greater equality. Because he maintains that the problems are inherent in the people, Banfield is critical of any governmental policies that have been tried. Rather, he maintains that the only effective solution to urban problems is to prevent children from being raised in a "lower class" culture by encouraging their parents to give or sell them to parents outside that culture or by having the state place them in orphanages. Needless to say, Piccard's solutions differ markedly.

Under the topic of poverty Rose Friedman presents an argument that is very popular with the old right: the question of poverty in America is relative, and so no one starves in America. In contrast, Susan and Norman Fainstein present a socialist analysis of the situation of the poor. (See the discussion of their article in the introduction to Part I.)

In their analysis of the environmental crisis Robert Poole, Jr., and Clifford Humphrey differ markedly on a number of points, particularly the function of government with regard to environment. Poole presents a libertarian argument that ascribes the problem to governmental acts and omissions, while Humphrey argues from the new left that the fault lies in a naïve economic system in which traditional market economics have forced and led Americans into a situation that rewards them for jeopardizing their future. Thus, while Poole advocates the development of a "full-liability society" in which "rational technologists" decide on what constitutes an environmental hazard, Humphrey contends that the level of education, planning and coordination necessary to meet the environmental crisis can only be provided through the assistance of national and local governments.

The final policy section in Part II considers the problems of American foreign and military policy. Anthony Bouscaren's history of the last quarter century presents the old right argument that our policy should be an aggressive, "forward" one with regard to Communist power rather than the weak containment policy of the old left. For him communism is monolithic. Hans Morgenthau views the same period of history as a disaster because it went too far. He makes the new left argument that the government has gained far too much power and that public policy is now formulated by the technological elites rather than popular will. He argues that this has led to policies that are counter to the national ethos, and that have had a disruptive and disintegrative impact upon the society. Richard Barnet makes a similar argument, analyzing the background of the men who actually design American foreign policy to suggest the shared, unchallenged (and, he maintains, dangerous) assumptions on which it has been based.

Racism

Intelligence or Prejudice?

ERNEST VAN DEN HAAG

Q. Melvin Tumin, a Princeton sociologist, has interviewed experts on Testing, Psychology, Sociology, and Anthropology, about Negro intelligence. His questions, the answers and his introduction have been published (by the Anti-Defamation League) under the title "Race and Intelligence: A Scientific Evaluation." What do you think of it?

A. Well, Mel Tumin is a good man; at least his heart is in the

Ernest Van den Haag (Ph.D., New York University) is Adjunct Professor of Social Philosophy at New York University, Lecturer in Sociology and Psychology at the New School, and a practicing psychoanalyst. He received a Guggenheim Fellowship, and is the author of an extensive number of articles and numerous books, of which the most recent is *The Jewish Mystique*.

right place—left of center. According to science, that's where the heart ought to be.

Q. What about his mind?

A. It's where his heart is.

Q. Do you mean he's prejudiced?

A. On the contrary. He's against all prejudices he doesn't share. (So am I, and most social scientists. But we don't share the same prejudices.) If "prejudiced" means nasty or deliberately dishonest, I think he is neither.

Q. Would he go wherever science leads?

A. On racial matters he'd always be able to convince himself that science leads him where he wants to go.

Q. Suppose the experts he questioned had answered: "science proves that Negroes are innately inferior." Would he have published this result, would most scientists today?

A. An interesting question. Ask one that I can answer with facts rather than hopes and wishes. But the Jensen case—of which more later—suggests that many psychologists today are capable of stridently and unfairly attacking scholars who publish data suggesting that there are genetic differences of intelligence among groups.

Testing Native Intelligence

Q. O.K. let me ask you first about a statement that startled me. Dr. Henry C. Dyer, a big shot in "educational testing," says that: "There are no tests of native intelligence. In fact the concept of native intelligence is essentially meaningless. Every response to the stimulus material in intelligence tests is of necessity a *learned* response." Elsewhere he adds: "You cannot make inferences about something that is meaningless." Because in his view the concept of innate intelligence is meaningless, he insists that test results cannot (not *do not*, but *cannot*) measure it. What about that?

A. Perhaps Dr. Dyer speaks *pro domo sua* when he denies native intelligence. I do not see why a learned response could not be used to test native intelligence, i.e., innate ability to learn. If we can standardize the learning opportunities (and motivation) we test native intelligence, without isolating it, by testing the learned responses. (Conversely, if we can standardize genetic inheritance, we can test the influence of learning.) I certainly agree that it is very difficult to standardize learning opportunities. I do not think it is impossible though. Moreover, difficulties in testing something do not make whatever is hard to test "meaningless"—they just make it hard to test. If we had no way of testing the temperature of the moon, it would not follow that the concept of lunar temperature would be "meaningless." Any person endowed with native intelligence could figure that out—even if he were not an astronaut.

Dyer's assertion also is—and quite clearly—contrary to fact. H. G. Eysenck (Professor of Psychology at the University of London, and a well known expert on testing) concludes that:

> Do tests of mental ability in fact tap innate factors? The evidence is by now quite conclusive that they are surprisingly successful in doing so. Consider a recent study by James Shields, in which he administered two intelligence tests to groups of fraternal twins brought up together, and to identical twins some of whom had been brought up separately. Identical twins share completely a common heredity, while fraternal twins are only 50 percent alike with respect to heredity; on the tests the identical twins were found to be more than twice as similar to each other, *whether brought up together* or *separate*, than were the fraternal twins.[1]

Research on identical (monozygotic) twins—that is, persons known to share exactly the same genetic inheritance—permits us to separate the effect of environment (learning) and of inheritance on the intelligence of the subjects. The results yielded by this research indicate that "[the intelligence test results of] the average pair of identical twins reared together [are] almost as similar as are the two scores of a single person tested twice [i.e., differences do not exceed what may be attributed to testing errors, usually accounting for about five points] and *that those reared apart show a difference not very much greater.*"[2]

Thus, whereas the IQ of the population varies from about 50 to 80, the variation in IQ among identical twins reared separately does not exceed a few points, even when the difference in environmental advantages is known to be marked.

Q. What do you conclude?

A. The evidence so far yielded by twin studies indicates:

1. Intelligence (even if we define it simply as that which is measured by IQ tests) is very largely genetically inherited.

2. Even when environments differ very markedly (e.g., when one identical twin is highly educated and the other is hardly educated at all), the difference in test results among individuals known to have the same genetic endowment remains very small.

3. It follows that differences in environment account only for a very small part of the observed differences in test results among individuals who do not have the same genetic endowment.

4. It seems unlikely also that environmental differences can account for all the observed differences of test results among groups, including ethnic ones.

Q. Does that settle the question?

A. No, I don't think so. There are many unanswered questions on the relation of IQ tests to intelligence, and the legitimacy of the concept of general intelligence. Further, there are many questions on the relationship between performance in actuality and test performance, etc.

Q. Then Dr. Dyer and the many psychologists who discount genetic endowment as far as intelligence is concerned may be right after all?

A. They are clearly and overwhelmingly wrong. We know enough to be certain of the correct answer, in quantitative terms, to the question they are known to answer wrongly.

Odd Silence

Q. Why didn't Dr. Dyer tell about the observations on monozygotic twins—or was he ignorant of them?

A. I find his silence on this odd myself.

Q. Odd?

A. I can say no more. After all, perhaps he was in ignorance and thus innocent (if we discount culpable neglect). Or, perhaps he interprets the observations on twins so that they are not inconsistent with his ideas—though I wish he had told us how he does it.

Q. Let me return from facts to logic. If Dr. Dyer were right, that "there are no tests of native intelligence," would it follow that the difference in test results among ethnic groups (on the average) is due to environmental differences, and that native intelligence is equal (as well as meaningless)?

A. The Tumin panel seems to assume that if one cannot show (or has not shown) by tests that there are innate differences in intelligence among ethnic groups, it follows that there are no such differences. At least that seems to be the clear implication. But it does not follow—it only follows that we cannot show, etc. Our inability to prove native inferiority or superiority is, of course, no proof of native equality.

If we did not, or could not test the temperature of the moon, it would not follow that it must be the same as that of earth. If native intelligence of ethnic groups has not been tested, or is untestable, it would not follow that it does not exist, is meaningless, or that it is the same in all ethnic groups. (Actually the temperature of the moon can be tested; so can native intelligence.)

Cultural Differences

Q. You seem to assert, then, that native intelligence exists, that it is measurable, and that if it weren't, it wouldn't follow that it is equal among groups or individuals. That leaves little of the Dyer argument, does it?

A. Nothing. Dr. Dyer first confuses demonstrability with existence (or meaningfulness). Then he asserts, contrary to the evidence, the nondemonstrability of native intelligence because of our alleged inability to measure it, ignoring the fact that we have been "surprisingly successful" in measuring it. But let me add an important point here. Certainly, measurement is desirable and we should work toward quantitative specification where possible and significant. Yet love, honor, and happiness—most of the important things in life—cannot be measured. It does not follow that they are meaningless concepts, or that they do not exist; at least not to me.

Q. I understand. Now, forgive me for laboring this point once more—I want to get it quite clear: if innate intelligence—except for identical twins—is so hard to isolate and measure, shouldn't we attribute differences in test results among ethnic groups to environmental factors, at least as a practical matter?

A. This is an illicit inference. From the fact that intelligence—the innate ability to learn—is hard to test because it is hard to isolate without contamination by unstandardized amounts of learning and by variable motivation, we cannot infer that differences in test results *must* be attributed to differential cultural opportunities or other uncontrolled factors. Only that they can be. We do not know whether the differences that tests find occur because of differences in cultural opportunities or because of differences in native intelligence.

The existence of differences in cultural opportunities does not preclude the existence of differences in native intelligence as well. Suppose we take a number of people to a dark room and ask them to distinguish colors. They cannot. Are we to infer that the darkness prevented them? Possibly. But it is also possible that they are color blind. We can draw conclusions only after we have tested them in a lighted room. Similarly, the native intelligence of groups that experience uncontrolled amounts and kinds of learning opportunities or desirabilities, is not determined by, or identical with, these opportunities (or meaningless, or nonexistent) however hard it may be to test it separately.

Environment

Q. But what about a practical guess? I don't doubt your logic. Yet people might feel that common sense tells them what science cannot demonstrate (even though some rash scientists think it can).

A. A practical guess would permit us to attribute as much of the difference in the test performance of ethnic groups to environmental differences as can be shown to have been produced by environmental differences in the test performance of identical twins reared apart. If the differences in the environments of the twins are reasonably parallel to the two ethnic groups, we might make not a conclusive, but a tentative estimate of how much of the difference in the average test performance of the ethnic groups can be imputed to the enviroment.

Q. Well, can you?

A. I'm reluctant. There are very few studies of monozygotic twins reared apart that show much of a difference in test results—even with radically different environments. When the environmental difference appears to be about what it is between white and Negro children on the average, the difference in the test results of the twins remains insignificant. Yet there are too few studies, and too many unanswered questions: I feel uneasy about guessing.

Q. Nonetheless you conclude that (1) all or (2) most or (3) much of the average difference in test results between white and Negro children indicates innate differences?

A. This is very possible but not certain. I should be inclined to believe that (3) is true. Eighty percent of tested intelligence differences among individuals seem genetic. This, and other factors, suggest that many group differences may be similarly accounted for. But there are too few twin studies as yet; and the differences between the environments of twins reared apart, and of Negroes and whites, are hard to compare. Finally there are intangible differences. The Negro-white environmental difference simply does not parallel the environmental difference experienced by twins reared apart.

Q. What then is your conclusion?

A. I hate to strain your patience, but I must stick to science: I cannot at present reach conclusions that go beyond the common-sense guess already offered.

Q. I think you have satisfied me on the *possibility* of differences in innate intelligence among ethnic groups—despite the Tumin claims to the contrary. But I want to know more about the actuality. For instance, I know some very intelligent Negroes.

A. So do I. We may say correctly:

1. There are some very intelligent Negroes. (This is probably true for any randomly selected large human group of any color.)

2. The performance of some Negroes equals or exceeds that of some whites. (This would be true in comparing any two large enough randomly selected groups of whatever color.)

3. Whatever the intelligence of groups of Negroes, their performance improves when their opportunities do—when they move from a less to a more propitious environment. (This would be equally true for any group, including retarded children.)

These propositions though often confused with it are obviously irrelevant to the issue: do Negroes as a group have, on the average, a lower native intelligence, at least in certain respects, than whites? If, and only if, the total Negro test performance equaled that of whites *ceteris paribus*, genetic differences could be excluded by comparison of test performances.

I do not think that in this matter we have conclusive evidence one way or the other, though the indications are that the two groups have different aptitudes (or a different distribution of aptitudes). Please note that I am not saying that I have proved genetic inferiority of Negroes. I am asserting that Tumin's respondents have not disproved the claim of genetically lower intelligence—although they think they have.

Q. Throughout, you have been saying that Negro performance in school is below that of whites. Are you sure of that?

A. Let me quote from a study by Herbert Wey and John Corey: "There are some top Negro students, some mediocre ones, and some quite retarded. This is also true of white children. However, the proportion of slow learners is greater among the Negroes. Differences are not as apparent in kindergarten and first grade as in the upper grades and high schools."[3] These data are generally accepted. The disagreement is on the causes—environmental or genetic—of the difference in performance.

Jensen and Coleman

Q. How have the writings of Arthur Jensen influenced your views?[4]

A. My views were first published in 1956 and have not changed much since. They are logical inferences from the known facts. Professor Jensen has confirmed and enlarged our knowledge of the genetic nature of intelligence differences. His monograph is a magisterial exposition of what science knows on the topic. His analysis is trenchant, lucid, and careful. I think his procedures are models of scientific methodology.

Q. But hasn't his work been attacked by many colleagues?

A. Certainly. The vehemence of the attack was in inverse ratio to the relevance—let alone cogency—of the arguments used. Professor Jensen has had no trouble in defending his conclusions. Against name calling there is no defense, of course.

Q. What, then, does Jensen say?

A. He has proved that most of the tested differences in intelligence among various groups are genetic—rather than effects of life experience (environment) ; and that on the average the genetically inherited intelligence of American Negroes is below that of whites.

Q. This seems inconsistent with the belief that all group inequalities must be attributed to the environment, and can be changed—equalized—by changing it; that inherited intelligence either does not exist or is irrelevant, or, finally, equally distributed among all groups; and with the idea that there are no real limitations to what can be done by manipulating the environment.

A. It is. And these are the reasons why Jensen has met so much opposition motivated by passionate and generous ideological convictions—but not supported by much else.

Q. Can you give some of the more rational arguments used against his views?

A. I can list but a few. Let me start with a semi-rational argument to which I replied in the following letter:

> The response by the Council of the Society for the Psychological Study of Social Issues to Arthur R. Jensen's article 'draws attention' among other things to Jensen's use of a 'social definition of race' for the population tested for intelligence. The tests led Jensen to conclude that there are probably genetic differences of intelligence among races and that the average inherited intelligence of American Negroes is below that of whites. The SPSSI Council's response points out that 'conclusions about the basis for racial differences are obviously dependent on the accuracy of the definition of race employed'; and that 'the genetic definition' would be 'more rigorous.' (Did Jensen neglect major intelligence testing done on genetically defined American Negroes? How typical would genetically defined Negroes be for the school population? Does anyone object to the 'social definition' if the conclusion is popular?)

> If the result of intelligence tests is, as SPSSI believes, largely the effect of social factors, then a 'social definition of race' suffices, and a genetic definition is irrelevant, since genetic factors are. If, however, Jensen should be right, and genetic factors are important, then the

fact that they have some white genes, can only mean one thing: Jensen understated the genetic difference between white and Negro intelligence, since the Negroes he tested were partly white. I am not sure that the authors of the response intended this conclusion but it seems the most plausible inference from their objection to Jensen's definition—unless the admixture of white genes is assumed not to affect Negro intelligence (in which case the Council's objection is unintelligible) or to decrease it, which seems implausible.[5]

Another frequent argument is that the tests considered by Jensen do not take account of the cultural deprivation of Negro children, or, of cultural differences that may cause them to perform less well than whites on these tests, which are said to reflect white culture. Yet blacks perform better on the more culture-bound verbal tests than on the others. More salient, on tests specifically designed to take account of the "ghetto subculture," whites outperform blacks just as much as on the others.[6] Moreover, Julian C. Stanley has shown that the usual IQ tests predict academic performance just as well for blacks as for whites.[7] Finally, most of the more sophisticated tests are reasonably culture-free.

Q. Couldn't one attribute the differences in tested intelligence to early childhood experiences and even intrauterine ones rather than genetic factors?

A. Undoubtedly that explanation works in some cases, but not on the average. Otherwise we would not find that the children of Indians—no less deprived than Negroes, and no more accepted in American culture—have, on the average, higher IQs than those of Negroes. Nor that Negro children test below white children when parental social class is the same.

Q. How great is the average IQ difference that you think is genetic?

A. Between 15–20 points.

Q. Is that enough to make a difference?

A. Yes. Remember that averages don't tell the whole story. Thus we find that at the upper end of this distribution only 11 percent of blacks have an IQ above 100—while 50 percent of whites do. Or, when we exclude, or at least minimize, the influence of deprivation and "culture" by comparing the children of blacks of high socioeconomic status with white children of the same socio-economic status, we find that 13.6 times as many black children have an IQ below 75 than do white children. In short, far more blacks test low, far fewer high, on intelligence than do whites.[8]

Q. What is the role of the Coleman Report in all this?

A. James A. Coleman, *et al.*, wrote a major statistical investigation of the quality of schooling available to minority and majority groups and of the effects that differences in schooling may have.[9] They surveyed 3,000 public schools.

Q. What were the major findings?

A. They concluded that "schools bring little influence to bear on a child's achievement that is independent of his background and general social context"—i.e., (1) schools are not all that different between white and black, and (2) what differences there are make no significant difference in the scholastic achievement of whites and blacks.

Q. This is surprising.

A. It is. But it seems true, though Bowles and Levin seem right in pointing out that the method of the study may have resulted in some degree of underestimation of the correlation between pupil achievement and school quality.[10]

Q. Is that the only finding?

A. There are many more. Those who took the Warren Court's ideas seriously may have been comforted by the finding "there is a small positive effect of school integration on the reading and mathematics achievements of Negro pupils after differences in socioeconomic background are accounted for"—the only positive effect of school integration on the achievement of the minority group.

Q. That would argue for integration.

A. Not necessarily. And note "small." Moreover, Bowles and Levin find that "the conclusions that Negro achievement is positively associated with the proportion of fellow students who are white, once other influences are taken into account, is not supported by the evidence presented in the report. Further, Wilson's findings independently support Bowles and Levin—and contradict Coleman.[11]

Q. Did Coleman consider genetic differences?

A. No. And, because he found differences in schooling, could not account for the difference in scholastic achievement, he attributed them to the home environment.

Q. Does that seem reasonable?

A. There is no question in my mind that such differences can, and probably do play a role. But unlike Coleman, I am now inclined to think that the preponderance of evidence supports the view that genetic factors account for most of the difference. Jensen's great merit lies in having made this clear.

Q. Then you think that nothing can be done to improve the education of Negroes?

A. On the contrary. What is given most weight in IQ tests is abstract thinking and reasoning—a highly heritable ability of which Negroes on the average have less than whites. But Negroes are usually superior in the ability to learn "associatively," which, in most life situations is as important, and more important in many. Thus, what should be done is to capitalize on the average Negro child's capacity for associative learning—both to maximize what can be learned that way, and to utilize it to learn as much conceptual thinking as possible.

Separation by Ability

Q. Then would you separate black and white children?

A. It is interesting to note that the answer here would be the same regardless of whether the differences are genetic or environmental. In the latter case my solution might, in time, be changed; in either case it would hold as long as the performance differences do.

Mixed education now impairs the education of Negro and of white children. For optimum education the white children obviously require maximum utilization of their present performance abilities. The Negro children require whatever can be done to increase their performance in view of the deficient environment of the past—regardless of whether there are genetic factors involved as well. And they require maximal utilization of their associative learning ability. Hence, at least for the time being, the needs of Negro children would be met best—that is, to their advantage and without disadvantage to others—by separate education geared to meet the obstacles presented by lack of opportunity and unfavorable environment and by genetic and subcultural differences. I am all in favor of improving the quality of education for all. But this can be done only if pupils are separated according to ability (whatever determines it). And this means very largely according to race—even if the criterion is learning ability as it should be, and not race.

The Gifted Child

Q. What about those Negro children who perform well? Should they not be transferred to white schools?

A. I think this might demoralize the remaining Negro children and could be hard also on the transferred child. Nonetheless, if both the white and Negro children (and/or parents) desire it, this objection would be greatly weakened. (If the gifted Negro child is transferred into a hostile white school environment, I doubt that there would be an educational advantage.)

But the main issue has little to do with the transfer of a few gifted Nego children. The learning ability of Negro children *on the average* is not as responsive as that of white children to the stimulation and the methods of average white schools. We don't know whether it will ever be. (Poor original environment may cause this, as may inherent factors. Desegregation is neither necessary nor sufficient to eliminate these disadvantages; and it would not help the average pupil of either group.) Therefore, Negroes and whites should be educated separately—unless there is evidence in specific cases that the learning of neither group suffers from congregation and that neither group objects. Instruction in schools for Negroes should attempt to remedy the disadvantages suffered by students coming from a culturally deprived home environment. This cannot be done except by separate education. Nor can different genetic abilities be utilized otherwise.

These differences should be remedied by the time institutions of higher learning are entered. If they aren't the student is not college material. If they are, there is no reason for separate college education unless there are specific psychological reasons for it, such as mutual hostility.

Q. Would your educational argument be the only justification for separate schools?

A. It would certainly make them rational from an educational viewpoint. But the school question has all kinds of implications with regard to coercion, freedom of association, psychic damage, effects on prejudice, and so on, into which we cannot go now.

Q. Your solution sounds educationally rational even without the arguments you don't want to go into. But some people assert that regardless of how good the educational facilities are, separate education is "inherently unequal" and that "modern authority" has shown that it inflicts psychic or educational injury on Negro children to the extent of depriving them of the "equal protection of the laws." This was the decision of the Supreme Court in *Brown v. Board of Education.*

A. I know. But if the Supreme Court allowed itself to be bamboozled by "modern authority" that in no way demonstrated what it persuaded the court it had demonstrated, we need not be as credulous.

Psychic Injury Unproved

Q. What do you mean?

A. I mean that there has been no demonstration whatsoever that separate education, when facilities and instruction are equalized, is "inherently unequal" or does psychic injury to Negroes. I have analyzed the allegations of "modern authority" in this respect on various occasions. Permit me to refer you to my "Social Science Testimony in the Desegregation Cases—A Reply to Professor Kenneth Clark," reprinted from the *Villanova Law Review.* I don't want to repeat myself.

Q. Do you mean to say the Supreme Court was wrong in the facts on which its judgment is based, and should reverse itself?

A. Professor Philip Kurland, of the Law School of the University of Chicago, wrote that "Dr. Clark's study was utilized by the Supreme Court to provide a factual base on which to rest its conclusion [in the *Brown* case]."[12] I myself cannot see how without the "facts" asserted by "modern authority" the court could have reached its decision. But the evidence for these "facts"—mainly but not exclusively Clark's—has been clearly shown to be wrong. Thus the Court if it follows the actual evidence of "modern authority," ought to reverse itself. I think it will happen, though possibly with more deliberation than speed.

Q. Forgive me for being so unsystematic, but I am bothered now by this question: suppose the average native intelligence of Negroes is inferior to that of whites, would that mean that Negroes are inferior to whites?

A. One may regard others as inferior to oneself, or to one's group, on the basis of any criterion, such as mating, eating, drinking, or language habits, religious practices, or competence in sports, business, politics, art, or finally, by preferring one's own type, quality or degree of intelligence, skin or hair color and so forth.

By selecting appropriate criteria each group can establish the inferiority of others, and its own superiority. This can be and is done by Texans, Democrats, workers, Yale alumni, Frenchmen, extremists, moderates, Chinese, and "liberals." The selection of criteria for superiority or inferiority is arbitrary, of course. The judgment of inferiority applied to others thus remains a value judgment, even if the qualities judged to render people inferior are actual characteristics of the group so judged. I do not believe that intelligence is any more relevant to judgments of inferiority than, say, skin color is.

If Negroes on the average turn out to have a genetically lower learning ability than whites in some respects—for example, the manipulation of abstract symbols—and if one chooses this ability as the ranking criterion, it would make Negroes on the average inferior to some whites and superior to others. Suppose four-fifths of Negroes fall into the lower half of intelligence distribution. Chances are that, say, one-third of the whites will too. Hence, if intelligence is the criterion, the four-fifths of the Negro group would be no more "inferior" than the one-third of the white group. (It seems clear that some degree of overlap would exist, regardless of what we will ever learn about native intelligence.)

Judgments of inferiority among whites are rarely based solely on intelligence. There certainly are many people who do not rank high on intelligence tests but are, nonetheless, preferable, and preferred, to others who do. I know of no one who selects his associates—let alone friends—purely in terms of intelligence. God knows, we certainly do not elect to political office those who are most intelligent. I would conclude that whatever we may find out about Negro intelligence would not entail any judgment about general inferiority anymore than anything we might find out about average native musical ability would. Why should either be of importance for general judgments of inferiority, superiority or equality than the other? Such judgments should evaluate the whole person individually. And they are necessarily subjective—although the facts evaluated are objectively determinable.

Moral Disadvantage

Q. What about the lower cultural performance of Negroes in their native habitat?

A. It is neither necessary nor useful to avoid value judgments in intercultural comparisons, as long as one keeps in mind that, like all value judgments, they are—as far as science is concerned—but more or less widely shared preferences. Thus one may evaluate the culture of primitive African tribes, Australian bushmen, or North American Indians *in toto* as inferior, equal or superior to Western culture in its various phases. Such judgments depend on one's value standards (ultimate preferences). If these are postulated, the judgment can be logically and empirically justified, though the standard on which it rests cannot.

If one uses as explicit criteria certain achievements such as the invention of a written language, or of the wheel, the creation of a literature, of arts and humanities, of mathematics, the rule of law, or medical progress, etc., then the cultural achievements of Negroes *in loco* compare unfavorably with those of Caucasians, Chinese, Near and Far Eastern groups, and others. This would constitute a disadvantage; it does not involve a moral inferiority unless the disadvantage is judged to be a moral one—a judgment not inherent in its description. (And of course one may also prefer the primitive to our own style of life, or discover special virtues in it that we lack.)

Neither the African environment nor subjugation in any form explains the lack of cultural achievement measured by these standards. (Note, however, that African historiography is in its infancy.) It does not follow that a bio-genetic explanation is correct: a hypothesis is not proven correct simply because other hypotheses do not explain the phenomenon at issue. But I see no reason—other than fashion—to discard the possibility of differential genetic distribution of talents among ethnic groups as a possible partial explanation. (If such a hypothesis should prove correct, it would be quite consistent with the aforementioned high intelligence of some Negroes, and with the ability of all to improve their performance under propitious circumstances.) There is no reason to believe that God ever was an egalitarian (the biblical God certainly was not). I don't think that He has read Professor Tumin since, or J. J. Rouseau. Nor that He has been sufficiently impressed by the U.S. Supreme Court to readjust reality and been persuaded to become one. It is entirely possible, then, that the differential performance of cultures must be explained, in part, by differential genetic distribution of aptitudes.

If we were to prove genetic differences of the relevant kind among ethnic groups, it would not necessarily follow that they are permanent and irreversible. However, genetic differences cannot be removed by education of the individuals involved, however much their effect may be mitigated. We do not know at present to what extent genetic inheritance may be influenced by various factors that can be brought to bear.

Q. Do you have any general conclusions?

A. None, but perhaps one thing deserves mention. Fifty years ago many social scientists were busy demonstrating "scientifically" the inferiority of Negroes to whites. As many are as busy now proving "scientifically" that there are no innate psychological differences whatever among ethnic groups, and that, unless children grow up in compulsory togetherness, they are unfree, and suffer psychological injury. The evidence for these contentions is as "scientific" as the evidence for the ideology fashionable fifty years ago. The fashion has changed but social scientists have remained its servants. They are all too well intentioned; but truth—and science, therefore—does not depend on intention. They obstinately refuse to act as scientists, committed as they are to various "causes" more than to the cause of science; yet they yearn passionately for the trappings and the prestige of science. For scientists moderation in the pursuit of truth is a fatal vice not offset by extremism in the pursuit of egalitarian ideologies.

References

1. H. G. Eysenck, *Encounter* (June 1964), p. 53. Italics added.
2. L. E. Tyler, *The Psychology of Human Differences* (New York, 1956), p. 453. Italics added.
3. "Action Patterns in School Desegregation," a Phi Beta Kappa Commission Project, p. 212.
4. Arthur R. Jensen, "How Much Can We Boost I.Q. and Scholastic Achievement?", *Harvard Educational Review* (1969), vol. 39, pp. 1–123.
5. Published in the *American Psychologist* (November 1969). The same issue also contains Jensen's own able reply to many other arguments.
6. See H. J. Butcher, *Human Intelligence* (London, 1968), p. 264.
7. In a recent article in *Science*.
8. These data are taken from Professor Robert A. Gordon's letter to the editor of *Scientific American* (October 27, 1970).
9. *Equality of Opportunity* (Washington, D.C.: U.S. Office of Education, 1966).
10. *Journal of Human Resources* (Winter 1968).
11. *Educational Consequences of Segregation in a California Community* (Washington, D.C.: U.S. Commission on Civil Rights, 1967), vol. 11, p. 185.
12. See Kenneth Clark, *Prejudice and Your Child* (Boston, 1963), p. 143.

Structures of Northern Racism

IRA KATZNELSON

Echoing DuBois, the late A. J. Muste once asserted that the world was divided most fundamentally between peoples who had rarely known humiliation as a national, communal, experience, and those who had. The vast majority of white Americans have belonged to the unhumiliated world, the overwhelming majority of blacks in the United States to the systematically humiliated, as slaves, and later, as semi-colonized, often brutalized citizens.

Indeed, the Constitution made the precise extent of the chasm between white and black Americans concrete, quantifying the humiliation: one black $= \frac{3}{5}$ of a man. This manifest expression of racism (which I would define, with Blauner, as "a principle of social domination by which a group seen as inferior or different in terms of alleged biological characteristics is exploited, controlled, and oppressed socially and psychically by a superordinate group"[1]) has been followed by countless others, including cultural deracination, horrible lynchings, and pseudo-scientific "academic" attempts to somehow justify pervasive patterns of discrimination by "proving" innate black inferiority.[2]

A litany of indictments is not the purpose of this essay. Those with any lingering doubts about the country's chilling racial past should read Elkins on slavery, Malcolm X's autobiography, or listen to the blues. To overcome the present, we must confront the past, of course, transcending the mystical history of happiness, a history of a people of plenty that white Americans taught their children for gen-

Ira Katznelson (Ph.D., Cambridge University) is Assistant Professor of Political Science at Columbia University and editor of *Politics and Society*. He is the author of *Race and the Politics of Incorporation*.

erations, a telling of the past that could not and usually did not deal fully with the country's troublesome black presence. But the most critical issue for the 1970s is not the necessary understanding of a racist past, but a sufficient comprehension of the contemporary complex relationship between structural arrangements, limitations on choice, cultural patterns, and the destruction of psyches. As Harold Cruse has put it:

> to say that America is a racist society is not enough—there is more to it than that. If American racism created the institutions, it is now the institutions themselves which legitimize the racist behavior of those who are the products of the institutions. The problem, then, is how to deal *structurally* with these institutions—how to alter them, eradicate them, or build new and better ones.[3]

Much academic work on race by well-meaning social scientists that focuses preeminently on black behavior misses the point that the identification and analysis of structure—those sets of relationships that limit and shape choice possibilities *differentially* for different groups and individuals—logically precedes the study of how men choose. One approach to race studies now in vogue, urban ethnography (the attempt to apply the field techniques of the anthropologist to racial minority groups in complex industrial societies) makes precisely this error. Many, though not all, urban ethnographers have focused on what Oscar Lewis called the culture of poverty, or the cultural and personality problems of the poor.[4] The policy implications of this position direct attention to proposed modifications in black behavior that, it is often argued, must be changed so that blacks can take advantage of what is assumed to be an open existing opportunity structure. Political scientists like Daniel Moynihan, who urged in his 1965 report that national policy be directed at correcting "distortions" in the black family, and Edward Banfield, who, in *The Unheavenly City*,[5] argues that the major cause of poverty is the attitude cluster of the poor, have vulgarized the ethnographers' work, and in so doing have revealed its repressive political implications.

For those concerned with accurate understanding, and with equality and liberation, the Moynihan-Banfield analytical and policy priorities must be reversed: the analysis of objective structural variables must precede the analysis of behavior. Identification and analysis of those constraints is the first step in undermining them and in providing the means to define and attain the new. It is in this sense that race relations research that pinpoints the institutional constraints on racial justice can contribute to concrete social change and transformation.

With these considerations in mind, let us explore, first, the historical roots of structured racial political inequality in the North, utilizing New York City as our case locale, and, secondly, contemporary patterns of urban dominance.

Historical Roots

In the history of American blacks, the period 1900–1930 stands out as a key structural period. In 1900 American racial contacts were limited largely to the South. There were 7,922,969 blacks, by federal government count, living in the South; only 902,025 Afro-Americans resided in all the other regions of the country combined. Though the percentage of America's blacks who lived in the South had declined from 90.6 to 89.7 in 1900, most Americans, at the turn of the century, were convinced that blacks would remain a fixed element, socially, as well as demographically, in Southern society.[6]

By the outbreak of World War I, however, this assumption had to be reassessed. Approximately 150,000 blacks left the South for the metropolitan areas of the North in the first fifteen years of the century. The movement, which came to be known as the Great Migration, rapidly accelerated during the War. By conservative estimate, almost 500,000 blacks migrated to the North in wartime. In the 1920s, well over 550,000 left the South. The black population of the Middle Atlantic states alone in this decade increased (as a result of natural increase and migration) by 868,000. By 1930 the percentage of America's blacks in the South had declined dramatically to 78.7.[7]

It is difficult to overstate the impact of this migration on the North and on the course of black history in America; it was, as August Meier has put it, "after Emancipation . . . the great watershed in American Negro history."[8] With the exception of Chicago, no city felt the impact of the migration more than New York. In 1890 there were 36,617 black New Yorkers (including those in the yet unconsolidated boroughs): in 1930 the figure had grown to 327,706. In 1890 one person in seventy in Manhattan, where most of New York's blacks lived, were black; in 1930, one in nine. In 1890 Harlem was a semirural, all-white upperclass community; in 1930 James Weldon Johnson correctly described Harlem as "*the* Negro metropolis" in America.[9]

In this critical and fluid period of migration, key structural-political decisions were made concerning the incorporation of the black population into the city's political structure. In the most widely respected history of this period, *Harlem: The Making of a Ghetto*, Gilbert Osofsky entitled the chapter on black ward policies, "A Taste of Honey," arguing that:

> while the urbanization of the Negro obviously caused great difficulties, it also provided the base for significant political power—political power unprecedented in the political history of the North. As the Negro population increased in numbers, the cynical and apathetic attitudes that typified the reactions of politicians in the later nineteenth century came to an end . . . Although the Negro's political progress in New York City was not an unqualified success, there obviously was greater advance in this sphere of community activity than in all the others. While the social and economic position of the city's Negroes tended to remain stable, or, with the Great Depression, even retrogressed, there was significant political mobility. In the 1890's Negroes were an almost powerless minority group in the metropolis. Their role, if any, was on the periphery of municipal affairs. Within the next generation, the generation that settled in Harlem, Negroes became an integral part of city government and politics—and politics proved a wedge for economic advancement.[10]

The statement is internally inconsistent, arguing on one hand that blacks were not socially and economically upwardly mobile, and on the other that success at ward politics translated into economic gains for New York's blacks. More significant, however, as I hope to show below, is Osofsky's dual confusion of group with individual mobility and of ethnic recognition with ethnic decision-making power, confusions that are the product of examining the behavior of a small number of leading black politicians without first having examined the structural arrangements that shaped and limited their actions. Because he did not ask the appropriate structural questions, Osofsky was misled by evidence of individual success. Black political power-lessness was the norm for the generation that settled Harlem; political progress was not a wedge for economic advance because in this period neither occurred.

I agree with Osofsky's implicit assumption that political mobility *may* translate into social and economic mobility as well. Thus, it can be argued that as a *result* of their political powerlessness, institutionalized in structured political linkages, the social and political problems of the city's blacks grew to unmanageable proportions. An extended discussion of black politics in this period is not possible here. A brief exploration of black-Tammany structural relationships compared to the usual group-Tammany Hall (Democratic party) pattern, however, is, I think, quite revealing.

The key structural decision made by Tammany in this period was the decision to link the city's blacks to the machine *indirectly* through a city-wide organization called the United Colored Democracy of Tammany Hall. On paper, the organization controlled all political and patronage matters concerning the city's blacks and the Democratic party. In fact, it was a powerless segregated institution whose primary tasks were winning for Tammany and isolating blacks from positions of real political influence.

The UCD was a city-wide organization; thus blacks were unable to compete for political power on the district or ward level, and under the machine it was district political control that mattered. As a result, as John Morsell has noted, the UCD's leaders "may, from time to time, have been listened to when central decisions were made on matters affecting them—or their community's—interests, but this never approximated the system of consultation and solicitation which is dictated by custom and practicality in the case of leaders of clubs which are on a footing of recognition by the county leadership."[11] While white ethnic immigrant political leaders emerged from their neighborhood political clubs in largely homogeneous neighborhoods to bargain with other ethnic political leaders with similar territorial bases, black politicians were selected by Tammany's white leadership, and had no community organizational base (there were no black Democratic party district leaders in Harlem before 1935 though the area was over 90 percent black by 1930). Thus black leaders and the United Colored Democracy acted as buffers in linking blacks to the Tammany machine. The mass of the black population was, as a result, largely isolated from the urban political system.

An analysis of the composition of the UCD leadership, its aims and achievements, which cannot be detailed here for lack of space, reveals that it was neither representative, responsive nor efficacious. Distinguishing between class position and political power, the contrast between the white immigrant and migrant black experiences in terms of mobility is striking. For European immigrants, economic mobility was the consequence of political advance, whereas for the black migrants, as Furniss has recently demonstrated, political mobility for individuals usually came after considerable economic and social mobility.[12]

In short, attention to structural questions—in this case, the creation of the UCD and its consequences—leads in turn to a concern with the character and performance of black political leaders *in this context*, to a comparative analysis of black and white ethnic situations, and to a focus on the relationship of political, social and economic mobility. All of these concerns have been overlooked in the analysis of this period in the past (of which Osofsky's work is the leading example), a neglect that has produced conclusions about political success based on the study of the behavior of individual leaders that are illusory and misleading.

Contemporary Patterns of Urban Dominance

Today's politics of racial confrontation, resistance, and counter-resistance in the Northern cities of the United States underscores the enormity of the failure to establish just racial political structures in the fluid period of migration. In New York City, rule by a native-born Protestant elite gave way to the politics of machine control in the late nineteenth century. After World War I, the machines slowly began to disintegrate. The process rapidly accelerated with the election of a reform mayor, Fiorello LaGuardia in 1933, and with the national welfare programs of the New Deal. The politics of New York, and most other large northern cities, entered a new phase marked by increasingly fragmented, relatively impotent, party organizations, and the development of independent, but not apolitical, bureaucracies that have become new centers of power. Though political forms have changed, for the black community *the central structural fact remains the same*: the community has continued to be controlled and administered politically from the outside.

In the machine period, when the party organizations provided the best access routes to positions of political control and mobility, blacks were on the periphery of party affairs. Indeed, between 1900 and 1950, only one black in New York City, Adam Clayton Powell, Jr., was elected to a first-rank decision-making post. To date, in municipal elections for the city's three leading offices of mayor, comptroller, and president of the city council, blacks have yet to be even nominated by either of the major parties.

Ironically, with the demise of New York City's political machines, blacks have begun to win a more equitable share of lower and middle level party positions. One black, J. Raymond Jones, even became the leader of Tammany Hall (1964), while others have served as borough president of Manhattan. By 1960 blacks controlled 21 percent of the borough's district leaderships, though only 14 percent of Manhattan's population was black. It is significant that only *after* the traditional party machines lost their primary position of influence were blacks permitted to participate on terms of near equality. "The unfortunate thing," Cornwell notes, "is that American parties have decayed as organizations to the point that they can make far less contribution to this process of adjustment than they could and did in the past."[13] The new foci of power are the centralized, over-institutionalized bureaucracies, and there the city's blacks remain essentially without power.

This shift in the locus of political power affects in a fundamental way the structured distribution of choice possibilities. With the demise of most American party machines, city governments have become, paradoxically, overinstitutionalized at the central bureaucratic level but under-institutionalized at the community or neighborhood level. As one consequence, those without access to and control of the bureaucratic structures are left without substantive political representation, thus becoming the objects of policy, rather than subject-participants in the making of policy. The contradiction between levels of urban institutionalization has been exposed in the past decade with the intensification of urban racial conflicts and with the demands by many blacks for functional and territorial control of ghetto institutions, demands that reflect accurate perceptions of bureaucratic remoteness, unresponsiveness, and political impotence, and the ironic fact that as blacks began to achieve some political power in party organizations, the traditional mechanisms were in disarray and no longer offered the traditional rewards of patronage, protection, and political contracts that had gone to other ethnic groups in the past.

Thus, both in relation to the machine politics of the early decades of the century and to the bureaucratic arrangements that followed, blacks have structurally been a politically subject population with "very little influence on the power structure and institutions of the larger metropolis, despite the fact that in numerical terms, Blacks tend to be the most sizeable of the various interest groups."[14] The structural situation of American blacks can thus realistically (not merely rhetorically) be likened to classic colonial patterns since the very essence of colonialism is the one-directional nature of power relations, linking those with and without power in structured institutionalized patterns.

For a variety of reasons, white liberal and Marxist scholars have had enormous difficulty in coming to terms with this patterned reality and its consequences, as have government studies. Even the Kerner Commission's *Report of the National Advisory Commission on Civil Disorders* that dramatically indicted "white racism" (a statement whose impact was heightened by the moderate conservative tinge of its membership) failed to come to terms with the colonial-like structured condition of American blacks. The commission's report is almost wholly without specific institutional criticisms. The organizational ties of the commission membership (including legislators, a union leader, the chairman of a corporation board, a mayor and a police chief) made it difficult, perhaps impossible, to explore the structural context and expression of the "white racism" so central to the commission's findings. As a result, despite its tone, the policy proposals of the report focused almost exclusively on the ghetto poor, on altering their behavior. Absent here, as in the work of the ethnographers and their political vulgarizers, was the sense that the life cycle of the ghetto poor can most accurately be seen as a cluster of related adaptations to structural-situational factors that limit the chance to choose. Thus, if society is conceptualized in terms of a hierarchy of choice possibilities, the ghetto poor are at the bottom with the fewest choices. To miss this point is to accept an oppressor's definition of the black condition.

Black Response

The two most important racial political developments of the late 1960s and early 1970s have been the violent ghetto rebellions that occasioned the Kerner Commission and the development of an identifiable movement, with varying strains, for black community control of the institutions that impinge most directly on the lives of the cities' black populations: school systems, social service and welfare bureaucracies, health care organizations, public housing agencies, and most dramatically, the police. These developments can not be understood without a recognition of the colonial-like structural reality discussed above.

If, broadly, politics is about "who gets what, how," it is also about who gets left out and how. Political bargains reached by competing groups in all likelihood are made at the expense of the relatively powerless. Thus structural arrangements—organized relationships of power—predispose particular policy outcomes.

There is a two-directional relationship between the extent to which a group trusts the political system and the means it employs to influence outcomes. Thus Gamson hypothesizes that while "a confident solidary group will tend to rely on persuasion as a means of influence . . . an alienated solidary group will tend to rely on constraints as a means of influence."[15] Where authorities are perceived as sharing the group's basic orientation and interests, their commitments are mobilized through friendly contacts, the presentation of information, and the like. At the other end of the continuum, where groups perceive authorities as being fundamentally hostile to their interests, they seek to alter outcomes by imposing sanctions on authorities.

The absence of radically-just political structures continues to make violence a highly possible outcome. As Lewis Coser has written:

The assertion of interest can ordinarily proceed on a non-violent basis in these social systems in which channels for such assertions have been legitimized. But where this is not the case, the chances are high that violence will be one of the ways in which interest is being asserted.[16]

Indeed, in his comprehensive overview of collective violence in European perspective, Tilly suggests that the most persuasive interpretation of collective violence is a political one: "Far from being mere side effects of urbanization, industrialization, and other large structural changes, violent protests seem to grow most directly from the struggle for established places in the structure of power."[17] Seen in these terms, the collective racial violence of the 1960s reflected the development of a riot ideology that viewed violence as a legitimate means of influencing a distant authority structure that only permitted token and powerless participation. For those who participated, the ghetto rebellions were the product of structural arrangements that limited choice possibilities to this alternative; for the violent actor, there is little or nothing to lose.

Thus the political arrangements of the period of the Great Migration, and the quasi-colonial bureaucratic patterns that followed, promoted the transformation of the black population from a collectivity "in" to a collectivity "for" itself. The parallel institutions created for the newcomers contributed directly to the groups; institutional enclosure, and the terms of these institutions insured a high degree of control by white authorities over the group's access to scarce class, status, and power resources.

Paraphrasing Michels, this kind of issue can not possibly be decided by the passage of individual molecules from one side to the other. The life chances of the individual black have been and continue to be bound up with the position of the group as a whole. At the wrong end of colonial-type relationships, the colonized, as Memmi has brilliantly shown, in internal as well as external colonies, have only two options: individual or collective solutions. Individual solutions, however, are ultimately untenable; the price is too high, it cannot be paid:

> He soon discovers that, even if he agrees to everything, he would not be saved. In order to be assimilated, it is not enough to leave one's

group, but one must enter another; now he meets with the colonizer's rejection. . . . [It is clear,] on the other hand, that a collective drama will never be settled through individual solutions. The individual disappears in his lineage and the group drama goes on. In order for assimilation of the colonized to have purpose and meaning, it would have to affect an entire people; *i.e.*, that the whole colonial condition be changed. However, the colonial condition cannot be changed *except by doing away with the colonial relationship.*[18]

Because the colonized cannot benefit collectively from racial political structural arrangements that they do not control or share in controlling, a classic Marxian "two-class" stratification dynamic emerges whereby subordinates and superordinates come into structural conflict with fundamentally contradictory interests, "an interest in the preservation of existing power relationships or the destruction of existing power relationships."[19]

The political content of black demands in the 1960s has increasingly shifted away from the Civil Rights Movement's search for inclusion in existing structural arrangements to an insistence on structural reorganization and a redistribution of power. The critical question for the Civil Rights Movement was one of participation, for the anti-colonial community control movement it is one of the structural *terms* of participation. From the perspective of the black colonized, community control of community institutions is a decolonizing, resource-and-power-building demand. And it is for this reason that these demands have been resisted, blunted, and co-opted by conservative and liberal political establishments.

Strategies for Change

To state explicitly what should be obvious: however benevolent the intention, whites have no role to play in resolving *internal* black community disputes, no role to play in directing black organizations, no role to play in drawing up black political programs and platforms. However, they *do* have a responsibility for overcoming those tendencies of cultural imperialism that are the product of historical and contemporary patterns of dominance.

The path toward racial justice in America will be eased by *precise* knowledge of the impact of particular structural arrangements on behavioral possibilities, to which whites can make a contribution. Identifying these structures and their implications is, of course, no substitute for action, but unthinking action will not do either. Once identified, those structural arrangements can best be combated by a double strategy that includes political mobilization through direct action from outside the system. Hence the outsiders, blacks, are the essential planners, organizers and implementers. This must be complemented by a reform strategy to alter structures from within, which is the point at which whites also have a role to play in bringing about change. It is the latter part of this dual recipe that is often disparaged by my fellow radicals, but this disparagement ignores a crucial distinction made by André Gorz, among others, between "reformist" and system-overcoming reforms:

A reformist reform is one which *subordinates* its *objectives* to the criteria of *rationality* and *practicability* of a given system and policy. Reformism rejects those objectives and demands—however deep the need for them—which are incompatible with the preservation of the system.

On the other hand, a not necessarily reformist reform is one which is conceived not in terms of what is possible within the framework of a given system and administration, but in view of what should be made possible in terms of human needs and demands.[20]

Reforms that seek to redistribute power democratically, like the demand for community control of education, challenge the system on its own terms, utilizing its rhetoric. They are therefore system-overcoming reforms in the sense that Gorz described. Radicals who reject such reformism ignore the fact that it *is* a viable strategy in America, precisely because, as Benjamin Barber has recently noted:

The true establishment, such as it is, is in fact vulnerable. Having adopted the rhetoric of democracy in tribute to its own ability to manipulate the majority, it is publicly committed to the principles of democracy. If its control is weakened, it must nevertheless continue to pay lip service to them . . . It is thus compelled to wage its battle against the re-creation of democracy covertly—forever in danger of being exposed.[21]

The dual aspects of the strategy of mobilization plus reform are mutually reinforcing, in that *together*, direct action and system-overcoming reform continually test the limits of what is possible, to turn the "not yet" into the "now," in the unremitting process of domestic decolonization.

References

1. Robert Blauner, "Internal Colonialism and Ghetto Revolt," *Social Problems*, XVI (Spring 1969), p. 396.
2. *The Harvard Educational Review* has recently reprinted, in two volumes, the responses it published to Arthur Jensen's Winter 1969 article, "How Much Can We Boost IQ and Scholastic Achievement?" Taken together, the responses by some of the most eminent social psychologists in the field indicate how utterly barren the Jensen argument is of academic cogency, consistency, and reliability, in spite of its superficial appearance of unimpeachable scholarly appropriateness. Nevertheless, it is not surprising that many on the right in America have gleefully seized on Jensen's arguments to lend credence to their racist thought and practice. See *Harvard Educational Review*, reprints numbers 2 and 4 "Environment, Heredity and Intelligence," and "Science, Heritability and IQ," issued in 1970 and 1971 respectively.
3. Harold Cruse, "The Fire This Time"?*The New York Review of Books* (May 8, 1969), p. 18.
4. For a discussion of the culture of poverty, see Oscar Lewis, *La Vida* (New York: Random House, 1966), pp. xlii–lii. A good anthology of urban ethnography that at least partially transcends the limitations discussed is Norman Whitten and John Szwed, *Afro-American Anthropology* (New York: The Free Press, 1970).
5. Edward Banfield, *The Unheavenly City* (Boston: Little Brown, 1970).
6. U.S. Department of Commerce, *Negroes in the United States* (Washington, D.C.: Bureau of the Census, 1935), pp. 7, 9.
7. *Ibid.*
8. August Meier, *Negro Thought in America* (Ann Arbor, Mich.: University of Michigan Press, 1963), p. 170.
9. For an overview, see Seth Scheiner, *Negro Mecca* (New York: New York University Press, 1965).

10. Gilbert Osofsky, *Harlem: The Making of a Ghetto* (New York: Harper & Row, 1963), pp. 159, 177.
11. John Morsell, "The Political Behavior of Negroes in New York City," (unpublished Ph.D. dissertation, Columbia University, 1951), pp. 28–31.
12. George Furniss, "The Political Assimilation of Negroes in New York City," (unpublished Ph.D. dissertation, Columbia University, 1969), pp. 386, 391, 413, 109.
13. Elmer E. Cornwell, Jr. "Bosses, Machines, and Ethnic Groups," in Lawrence Fuchs, ed., *American Ethnic Politics* (New York; 1968), p. 213.
14. Blauner, *op. cit.* p. 389.
15. William Gamson, *Power and Discontent* (Homewood, Ill.: Dorsey Press, 1968), pp. 164–169.
16. Lewis Coser, *Continuities in the Study of Social Conflict* (New York: Free Press, 1967), p. 196.
17. Charles Tilly, "Collective Violence in European Perspective," in Ted Gurr and Hugh Graham, *Violence in America: Historical and Comparative Perspective* (New York: Bantam Books, 1969), p. 10.
18. Albert Memmi, *The Colonizer and the Colonized* (Boston: Beacon Books, 1965), pp. 124, 126. Italics added.
19. Isaac Balbus, "Ruling Elite Theory vs. Marxist Class Analysis," *Monthly Review*, XXIII (May 1971), p. 38.
20. André Gorz, *Strategy for Labor* (Boston: Beacon Press, 1965), pp. 19ff. Italics added.
21. Benjamin R. Barber, *Superman and Common Men: Freedom, Anarchy, and the Revolution* (New York: Praeger, 1971), p. 123.

Urban Policy

The "Lower Class"

EDWARD C. BANFIELD

The tangle of social pathologies that people mainly have in mind when they speak of "the urban crisis" arises principally from the presence in the inner districts of the central cities and of their larger, older suburbs of a small "lower class" the defining feature of which is its inability (or at any rate failure) to take account of the future and to control impulses.

From *The Unheavenly City* by Edward C. Banfield. Reprinted by permission from Little Brown and Company. Copyright © 1968, 1970 by Edward C. Banfield. Edward C. Banfield (Ph.D., Harvard University) is Professor of Political Science at Harvard University, co-author of several books, and the author of several articles and books including *The Unheavenly City*, and *Moral Basis of a Backward Society*.

The lower (as opposed to working) class person never sacrifices any present satisfaction for the sake of a larger future one. He lives from moment to moment. This is to say, he does not discipline himself to acquire an occupational or other skill, to hold down a regular job, to maintain stable family ties, or to stay out of trouble with the law. His bodily needs (especially for sex) and his taste for "action" take precedence over everything else. The slum is his natural habitat. He does not care how dirty and dilapidated his housing is, and he does not notice or care about the deficiencies of public facilities like schools, parks, and libraries. Indeed, the very qualities that make the slum repellent to others make it attractive to him. He likes the feeling that something violent is about to happen and he likes the opportunities to buy or sell illicit commodities and to find concealment from the police.

For obvious reasons, "lower class" people are always unskilled and usually low income. However, the great majority of the unskilled and the low income—indeed, the great majority of slum dwellers—are not "lower class." It cannot be too strongly emphasized that being "lower class" is a matter of outlook and life style, not one of schooling, income, or social status.

Nor is it one of race. For historical reasons that are familiar to everyone the proportion of Negroes who are "lower class" is relatively large as compared to whites. This has little or nothing to do with race, however. Until a few decades ago the urban lower class was almost entirely white; every ethnic group, including the Anglo-Saxon Protestant one, contributed to it, and its outlook and style of life were strikingly similar to those of the present Negro lower class.

Now that relatively few whites are lower class, it is all too easy for whites (including, unfortunately, many teachers and policemen) to make the mistake of assuming that a poorly dressed and poorly spoken Negro must be "lower class." This would be an unsafe assumption in dealing with whites but it is a highly implausible one in dealing with Negroes, many of whom have had little or no opportunity to acquire the outward marks of working or middle class culture. Because of their failure to look beyond externals, many whites classify as "Negro" behavior what they should classify as "lower class." Similarly, some of the behavior by whites that Negroes assume to be "racially prejudiced" is in fact "class prejudiced."

It is impossible to tell from Census or other existing data just how many lower class people there are in the cities. To make a count one would first have to decide where to draw the line between the lower and the not-lower classes, and of course any decision about this would have to be more or less arbitrary. Depending on where the line was drawn, it is likely that between 5 and 15 percent of the population of the large central cities would be "lower class."

The size and importance of the problems that the "lower class" presents to the city are not at all well indicated by those figures, however. In St. Paul, Minnesota, a survey showed that 6 percent of the city's families absorbed 77 percent of its public assistance, 51 percent of its public health services, and 56 percent of its mental health and correction casework services. Studies in other cities have shown that a very small part of the population is responsible for most of the crimes of violence.

So long as the city contains a sizable "lower class" nothing basic can be done about its most serious problems. Good jobs may be offered to all, but some will remain chronically unemployed. Slums may be demolished, but if the housing that replaces them is occupied by the "lower class" it will shortly be turned into new slums. Welfare payments may be doubled or tripled and a negative income tax instituted, but some persons will continue to live in squalor and misery. New schools may be built, new curricula devised, and the teacher-pupil ratio cut in half, but if the children who attend these schools come from lower-class homes, the schools will be turned into blackboard jungles and those who graduate from them or drop out of them will in most cases be functionally illiterate. The streets may be filled with armies of policemen, but violent crime and civil disorder will decrease very little.

If, however, the "lower class" were to disappear—if, say, its members were overnight to acquire the attitudes, motivations, and habits of the working class—the most serious and intractable problems of the city would disappear with it.

If the problems of the city arise more from class cultural than from racial factors, not to recognize that fact may be a tragic error. Misplaced emphasis upon "white racism" is likely to make matters worse both by directing the attention of policy-makers away from matters that should be grappled with and by causing Negroes to see even more prejudice than actually exists.

Many social scientists are confident that people who live for the moment would soon begin to take account of the future if they were placed in a situation where it would be advantageous for them (in terms of the values that they themselves hold) to do so.

The "lower class" is present-oriented, these social scientists think, because conditions like racial discrimination have made it impossible, or nearly impossible, for them to improve their position by work and sacrifice. Society in effect tells the "lower class" person that he will not be allowed to get ahead no matter what he does.

Very likely there are people who feel, with more or less basis in fact, that any effort to get ahead would be effort wasted. It may be indicative of this that Negro boys are much more likely to drop out of high school than are Negro girls: most of the boys will get the same (poor) jobs whether they graduate or not whereas girls who graduate can count on good office jobs.

To the extent that present-orientedness is a rational response to real or fancied lack of opportunity, the way to eliminate it is surely to open opportunities that are unmistakably good. This is easier said than done however. How is it possible to offer a "really good" job to someone who has no occupational skill and no inclination to learn one and who perhaps very much prefers the excitement of street life to high salaried boredom? Unfortunately, the really-good-job treatment can be given only to those who do not have the disease that it is supposed to cure.

Even if the individual cannot be given a good job he can be given money, and some social scientists think that if his income is raised very dramatically this of itself will cause him to change his style of life. Perhaps it will in some cases. But it seems likely that in a very much larger number of cases the effect of very high welfare payment levels would be to induce people to be more present-oriented than ever.

It may be that in general "lower class" ways are not so much a response to lack of opportunity as they are deeply ingrained habits of the individual or the group. An adult who has been lazy and improvident all of his life is not going to change very much no matter what happens. If he learned in infancy and childhood to perceive, feel, and think in the manner of the "lower class" (as, for example, a Hopi child learns to perceive, feel, and think in the Hopi manner) he may suffer from a kind of psychological blind spot that will persist in later life and prevent him from seeing whatever opportunities are offered him. Insofar as this is the case, the effort of policy should be to protect society from him and him from it.

If "lower class" ways constitute a culture (strictly speaking, a sub-culture) that is learned in childhood, it would seem that the only way to eliminate it is to prevent children from being brought up in it. This means taking the child from his "lower class" parents at an early age and either giving him to adoptive parents who are not "lower class" or putting him in an orphanage. Of course there are obvious objections to this. One is that it is no crime to be "lower class" and a country which values human rights cannot deprive parents of their children on any such grounds. Other objections (if others are needed) are that it is doubtful whether enough orphanages and adoptive homes could be provided and that even if they could be the children might be more severely damaged by being taken from their natural parents than by being allowed to grow up in the "lower class" culture.

The number of adoptions might be increased by permitting the sale of children to persons of good character. This would not involve any violation of parents' rights but it would, if the bidding were active, offer them sizable inducements to hand the children over to persons who are better qualified to bring them up. That a child was offered for sale would be proof positive that its parents were not fit to have it.

Boarding schools and day nurseries are a somewhat more practicable possibility. These might be located in or near slum neighborhoods and staffed with working class women and girls. Even if attendance were free it is doubtful if many "lower class" parents would make use of them; the "lower class" mother sees nothing wrong with the way she brings up her children and she is apt to be very suspicious of social workers, teachers and their likes.

Perhaps it would be possible to bribe her to send the child to school with an increase of welfare payments but this would be very expensive since the increase would have to go to all welfare recipients who sent their children, not merely to the relatively small number of "lower class" ones who did. Even if ways were found of getting the "lower class" children to the schools it is not at all sure that their being there would do them much good. In an experimental project in Boston, 21 children aged two and one-half to six, all of them from "lower class" families, spent two to three mornings a week in a nursery that was generously staffed with highly trained personnel. After from one to three years of attendance there were some noticeable improvements in the children but these were not such as to offer much hope that the course of their lives would be drastically altered by the experience.

The Cities Are Ours

PAUL J. PICCARD

Introduction

A funny thing happened to the liberal reformers of the early twentieth century on their way to a modern, improved city: the strategic bombers wiped out Hamburg and much of Coventry. Out of the ashes of those tragedies came more effective urban renewal than the American democracy has provided in any metropolitan area. Hamburg and Coventry proved that the job of restructuring could be done; they suggested that it might be done with much less anguish and expense than has been customary in America. Before an old city was torn down, people could be evacuated; selected valuables could be salvaged. But even wanton devastation and killing achieved more effective results than those produced by all of the reform literature of the century.

Paul J. Piccard (Ph.D., University of Texas) is Professor of Political Science at the Florida State University, the author of numerous articles, and has edited a book, *Science and Policy Issues.* He has been President of the Florida Conference of the American Association of University Professors, and is currently the book review editor of *The Journal of Politics.*

Any large city in the United States today could be greatly improved by a World War II style air raid and fire storm. The whole nation, and possibly much of mankind elsewhere, would mourn the dead and rush aid to the survivors. The disaster area would be rebuilt as a showcase. Its old physical problems would be solved and the simplest planning would postpone the development of new ones. The cost could be defrayed by postponing "progress" elsewhere in the land: fewer trees cut for vacation cabins, less iron mined for superfluous and super-effluent automobiles, fewer video-telephones, less machine power for such household chores as shaving, brushing teeth, opening cans, crushing ice, blending cocktails, and other onerous aspects of life with the advertisers—in short, less pollution and more human involvement. The apparent sacrifices of reconstruction would be quickly repaid as an investment in our environment and our self-esteem.

To acknowledge the advantages of destroying our old cities is not to advocate a wholesale, indiscriminate purge. The point is simpler: we built these cities and we know how to rebuild them. Our problem is one of will, not of means. We seem to lack the will not out of failure to admit the problems—not out of a lack of disgust for the filth and corruption of our cities—but rather because of our reluctance to redistribute the costs and benefits of rehabilitating the cities.

The problems of the cities, moreover, are not just physical. We lack grace in our relationships with each other. We give each other a hard time. We cramp each other's style and space. We fight, rape, rob, and humiliate each other. We foul the nest. We are insensitive to the condition of life—unfeeling about others, unperceptive about ourselves. Like the physical problems of the cities, these too are of our own making and we know how to alleviate them. Again the problem is one of will, not of means. Just as in the physical case, we seem to lack the will not out of failure to admit the problems, not out of lack of shame for our misdeeds, but rather because of fear of the uncertainties that would follow if we genuinely tried love. Most of us most of the time seem to prefer seduction to coercion, generosity to selfishness, words to blows, and ballots to bullets. That we run our cities contrary to these preferences is a sad commentary upon our ineffectiveness. We have the vision. We know the means. But practically, we are inept. How ironic that we blush at our idealism and indulge a false pride in our "practicality"!

This critique says nothing about human nature and so cannot be undermined by the right-wingers' tired old lament that "You can't change human nature." We are considering human behavior—what we do to each other in the city—and we know that not only can we change our conduct but that it inevitably changes. Our nature tells us that we have the capacity for both sacrificial love and selfish alienation; our intelligence tells us that we direct the proportions of these basic qualities as they erupt in our social relations. However evil or virtuous we are by nature, we no longer burn witches, pillory adulterers, or march off to reclaim the Holy Land for Christendom. Our land was bare and we set the city on it; we shaped the city and regardless of our nature, we shall reshape it. The question is not *whether* but *how?* And likewise with costs and benefits, the question is not whether some people will get helped and others hurt—that is inevitable—but who will get what?

Is this a "rightest" or "leftist" perspective on man in the metropolis? Before proceeding with more specific subtopics, let us stipulate a definition of terms. Everyone is entitled to use and to explain the language; the effort here is meant only to clarify what follows, not to preempt words commonly used by others. The few authors represented in this volume, even with the help of our editor, do not share a precise agreement on the meaning of "left" and "right." Surprisingly, however, much of the vagueness of the terms is superficial. Behind many variations of the\explanations a unifying concept can be discerned. Perhaps more than anything else, and certainly as used in this chapter, the variable on the left-right scale is degrees of equality-privilege.

Sometimes this same basic idea is represented as a matter of change-stability, with the left accused of (or given credit for) advocating change while the right is identified with stability. This is compatible with the equality-privilege variable whenever the long-run trend of change is toward more political equality but it produces some peculiar results when the fictional "pendulum" is swung backwards and the rightists find change and the prospects of change pleasing. Thus with the central city turning "too black" as whites move to the periphery, the rightists yearning for white domination may produce a change in the city limits—perhaps even the dramatic change of city-county consolidation—while the leftists prefer to hold the line.

Another attempted usage identifies big government with the left and individual independence with the right. This is also congruent with the equality-privilege scheme whenever the big government is committed to equality but it breaks down whenever the fascists run the State—their right-wing government is as big and far-reaching as they can make it. The appearance that only the left favors government, moreover, is easier to maintain by ignoring the government functions favored by the right or assuming that these are somehow basic to society and not really governmental. The full panoply of traditional governmental interference in personal relations is thus screened out of consideration: the definition and protection of private property, police power, military operations, monetary controls, marriage and other contractual obligations, old-fashioned regressive taxes, promotion of domestic industries, the prescription of master-servant relations, the adjudication of disputes, and the like are all overlooked. These are all "big government" to the controlled people if not to the favored ones. Thus in the eighteenth century, leftists opposed the entrenched big government of the rightist elites. Since then the vocabulary has shifted but the basic issue remains the kind of government, not its size. In the twentieth century, leftists in Bedford-Stuyvesant, New York, favored neighborhood schools and rightists in Bradenton, Florida, had a similar preference but if both voiced opposition to remote, big government, each apparently had something else in mind.

The alleged distinction between centralized and decentralized government is just the same. Advocates of urban renewal, for example, will favor either centralized or decentralized government, depending not on left-right rhetoric but on whether the central or more-local government will promote their preference. The rightist position in one federation might favor national solutions while the leftists were preaching community control; in a different federation the tables might be reversed. If leftists in the United States have recently looked to the national Capitol rather than to the state houses, it is because the central government has been more sympathetic, not because centralization is, per se, left-wing. Again, ask Franco. Or contrast the politics of Atlanta under its liberal mayors with the appeal of the higher-level government of the State of Georgia under Governors Griffin and Maddox. Milwaukee once stood far to the left of both Wisconsin and the nation so that leftists there favored local policy-making.

Thus some apparently conflicting definitions of "left" and "right" result simply from local, timely perceptions. In the United States change and political growth seem to be liberalizing and the central government seems more liberal than many of the states. Within this context, people using avowedly different definitions are actually agreeing on a common, if hidden, variable: equality-privilege.

Another word: "equality" does not mean "sameness." Likewise, privilege is not the only route to individuality or diversity. The review that follows urges political and social equality; it does not seek uniformity, conformity, loss of identity, an ant heap, or a bee hive. Cities are for people—unique and equal human beings. If city schools, for example, provide equal education, they will graduate a great variety of merchants, artists, doctors, lawyers, priests, butchers, bakers, and candlestick makers, not robots.

Finally on definitions: "left" does not mean "extreme left" and "right" does not mean "extreme right." A convenient distinction between extremes and moderate positions can be based on methods employed: a commitment to the democratic process toward the center versus dictatorship at the extremes. Both extremes finally have their impact as totalitarian dictatorships, replete with secret police, goose-stepping elite guards, hierarchical order with authority running down and accountability running up, and a rigid prescription of status. The left-leaning liberal has no more identity with or responsibility for the left-wing dictatorships than the right-leaning conservative has with or for right-wing dictators. Lots of room for serious disagreement remains along the democratic portion of the spectrum with some rightists using democratic methods to persuade the public to preserve privileges for the few, and some leftists, equally democratic, advocating more and more economic and political equality. They have different visions of the city but each can admit the legitimacy, if not the desirability, of the other view.

Now let us carry this approach into some substantive political aspects of contemporary urban life in the United States. First we can examine cities as civilization. Then we can turn our attention to pollution. From that to the general appearance and utility of the urban landscape will be an easy step. Along the way we can look for signs of who governs our cities and how. More traditionally, the texts set up separate sections on the charter forms of municipal government: mayor-council, commission, city manager, and their variations. Here we shall attempt to relate these organizational forms to substantive issues rather than treating them in isolation. This chapter omits perhaps the most critical urban policy issues—poverty and race relations—because those are better covered by Susan and Norman Fainstein, elsewhere in this volume. Even so, the study of the issues and forms included here leads to a conclusion already anticipated by the introduction: the city is a mixed bag, all screwed up and yet a very hopeful, human creation.

The City as Civilization

If we could lift a man out of Babylon from the year 2029 B.C. and set him down today on the palisades of New Jersey overlooking Manhattan, we might well hear him give a low whistle and say (loosely translated), "That's the damnedest city I ever saw." The point is that all civilized men, for roughly four thousand years, have known of cities and have been able to recognize them at a glance. Approached from downstream or downwind, cities can be anticipated. Approached from any direction on land they signal their presence by the convergence and improvement of the trails. They are, in Boulding's phrase, "the prime mark of civilization."[1]

The language here is almost circular: cities are the chief characteristic of civilization and civilization is chiefly characterized by cities. Such an observation does no harm because, like the ancient Babylonian, we recognize cities by their adjacent buildings, their population density, and their officials, not by bookish analogies. The virtual tautology identifying cities and civilization is useful in focusing attention on the age, distribution, and function of urban places. All of our "civilizing" material possessions are at least indirectly the products of urban specialization and most of them come directly from cities as a result of decisions made in city banks and business offices. Likewise a great range of modern services are possible only in cities. Education, medical care, entertainment, the press, organized religion, and such matters are primarily urban achievements. Even wilderness recreation is now enjoyed with city-generated transportation and equipment. We have already noted, on the other hand, that city life has also created some monumental pain for its participants.

In contrast to urban existence, uncivilized men, nomadic tribes, primitive people of all sorts have known neither the blessings nor the curse of cities. Which kind of society has been better than the other is one of those useless conjectures that idle speculators can indulge. Mankind never had a choice—it all happened too gradually and with completely unimaginable variables—and individuals have either been spoiled by the cities so that their judgment is biased or they have no perception of cities to evaluate at all. We cannot simply assume that civilization is desirable but it is probably easier for a city dweller to denounce his culture and to dream of an idyllic pastoral life, or to contemplate wistfully a South Seas paradise, than for a primitive man to question the apparent advantage of knowing ahead of time, in the civilized manner, how to survive the next winter and the next pregnancy. Henry David Thoreau was a fraud—or at least the symbol into which he has been transformed is fraudulent—because he borrowed an axe, he kept his books, and he depended on his education. He took his civilization with him; he tried to have it both ways. Not many of us can have such an opportunity for it depends on surplus productivity. For mankind the combination of the city's products with Thoreau's Walden setting is absolutely impossible. A judgmental approach to the contrast between primitive and civilized society, therefore, is pointless.

To see that for better or worse, our civilization and our cities are locked together does not answer the harder questions: who gains and who loses from our urban institutions? Do they promote or retard the development of equality? We do not know enough about status and privilege in precivilized societies to answer the question historically and we do not have good enough predictive powers to respond in terms of the potential evolution of cities into a postcivilized world. What we can see is that cities and the middle class grew with specialization. Men freed from hunting and tilling the soil could sit in judgment on disputes between others, they could explain and cajole the gods, they could practice healing and teaching arts, they could manufacture goods, and they could grow rich through barter. If the politicians, priests, physicians, professors, and plutocrats were then "superior" to other men of different skills, their superiority was not intrinsic in their specialties. It resulted from claims and acceptance—from personal relations.

We see in all civilized societies—in all cities—some "men at the top," as Presthus called them, and others subordinated, but that is a corruption of insecure men, a consequence of scarcity, and a product of an inept economy. The various roles performed by the city's elite could as well be accomplished by equals with a variety of talents. In an army, the mess sergeant and the communications sergeant have different jobs but equal rank; likewise with the players of different instruments in a band, faculty members in diverse departments, firemen and policemen, and the superintendent of sewers as well as his counterpart in the parks department.

We find the notion of equality harder to imagine as between the sergeants and their officers, the band members and their leader, the faculty and the deans, the public safety officers and their captains, the department heads and the city manager, the councilmen and work crews, the mayor and the librarian, "Mr. Big" and John Q. Public. Our experience tells us that these specialized roles cannot be played by equals. Our experience is an inadequate teacher. It has never given us any material progress and we cannot rely on it for civic progress either. If we had waited to put on the Moon a man experienced at walking on that dismal satellite, we would never have landed anyone there. Experience can only tell us how we have lived in the past— what our cities were like, not what they can become.

Insofar as cities do demand inequality (assuming that the argument for equality fails), to that extent leftists must be discontented with urban civilization. Leftists have no basis for assuming that they can win their way and if governors must be superior to the governed, cities will always be unsatisfactory communities in the eyes of left-leaning critics. Even if cities inherently produce inequality, however, both they and their critics can survive with legitimate, if irreconcilable, goals. Problems, after all, are to be lived with and hopefully alleviated. They do not have to be solved. Even if urban civilization and equality are incompatible, the effort to reconcile them may be worthwhile. Socrates, Jesus, and our more recent martyres, Abraham, Martin, and John teach us that trying is enough.

The leftist view of cities in the United States is that too few people are getting too much out of them while too many people are not getting enough. The challenge is to give direction to reforms so that the benefits and burdens of life in close proximity to masses of fellow men may be more evenly distributed. By seeing the cities as civilization and by understanding that neither automatically provides for taming our savagery— that neither guarantees a gentle spirit or what is casually and erroneously called a "civilized" life—is to grasp the immense complexity of our problems. If Boulding is right that the meaning of the twentieth century is that it marks the transition from a civilized to a postcivilized society, then our task is to reshape life in the cities to justify the new label for surely we shall take our cities with us, or be taken by them, into the new era. With this much comprehension of the interrelationship between cities and civilization or postcivilization we can turn to some narrower problems that are peculiarly produced by urban populations. The first of these is pollution.

Metropolitan Pollution

The view of pollution presented here is not technically sophisticated; it is, rather, policy oriented. Chemists can identify the pollutants, engineers can design control devices, statisticians can calculate the consequences for life expectancy, and so on. Laymen can respond esthetically to what they see and smell and they can harken to the reports of the experts. Past policy has been established by default; new directions in overt policy can be established now only through conscious effort. If the experts do not convince enough laymen, no new decisions will be made and the tacit ones of laissez-faire will prevail, but the experts have an ally that will eventually persuade even the stubborn and the greedy: death. The London smog apparently killed over 4,000 people in 1952 and the British did something about it.[2] When that many immediate deaths are attributed to pollution in a city of the United States, that city, too, will finally take effective action. In the meantime, the influential people think it is not going to get them in their air-conditioned offices or outlying homes.

Pollution is intrinsically an urban problem. When fewer people living further apart using "natural" rather than manmade synthetic goods dumped their wastes, the natural processes of decay and absorption could digest the refuse and people could move away from the temporary excess. Pollution illustrates the basic, intrinsic problem of cities: when the family of Og moved close to the family of Moog they had not only all of the problems which they had had individually before but they also had all of the new problems generated by the friction at the points of contact between them. Neither much genius nor formal education is required to grasp the point that a river can carry away sewerage with no problems until someone tries to draw drinking water downstream. The air, likewise, can carry away exhausts without complications if nobody lives downwind.

When one family's outhouse started draining into another family's well, the city policy moved to public, mandatory sewers and a potable water system. As we come to see what we are doing to each other with more complicated chemical pollutants, we shall make the same adjustment. If people in the United States cared as much about deaths in London as about life closer to home, we would have gone on the ecology kick a decade earlier than we finally have.

Pollution illustrates eight basic, important things about city policy.

1. Policy is unavoidable. The only possible choice is what policy to have, not whether to have one or not. Cities will either tolerate or combat pollution to some degree and in that sense, no middle ground is possible.

2. The policy prevailing affects some people differently than others. Short-run benefits accrue to certain "dirty" industries from laissez-faire but only at the expense of other interests. As we regulate pollution, we shift the distribution of rewards and burdens.

3. Policy evolves; it can neither stand still nor do a complete about face. Policy must change incrementally. We slowly cleaned up household wastes in middle class residential neighborhoods and we can move on to tackle the most obtrusive forms of pollution next, but each new antipollution program can only attack part of the problem.

4. The policy controls only some people, only a "marginal

middle." Some people anticipate a policy and behave accordingly on a voluntary, individual basis; other people continue to violate a policy even after it is promulgated; only the remainder in the middle are controlled by the policy. Some ecologically sensitive beer drinkers have returned to returnable bottles; other clods still heave their cans out despite laws against littering.

5. Policy is adopted according to what people possessing political power prefer and like everyone else these people reach their preferences through some process of weighing advantages and disadvantages, not merely by applying general principles or political slogans. In the past these people have permitted pollution probably without fully appreciating the costs but as they learn a new calculus of consequences they will want cleaner air and purer water.

6. Policy is useful for obtaining commonly desired results that are not produced by individual action. One city gains nothing from treating its own sewerage if the city upstream is polluting the river, but by agreeing to a general policy, everyone can gain. One person cannot breathe clean air by abandoning the family car or installing an exhaust control device, but a general policy to that effect can do the job.

7. Policy is found in practice, not in intent. The gap between municipal ordinance or political pronouncement and performance is often abysmal but it is the latter that counts. Despite alleged efforts to the contrary, municipal policy generally tolerates the full range of environmental pollution.

8. People possessing political power prefer to preserve the prevailing patterns. Many people have so much at stake in the establishment that any change is threatening to them. Eventually policy evolves but in the meantime the people who get on top under existing conditions are loathe to experiment with reforms. The profit in making paper will probably be increased as more people live longer to use more paper but in the meantime the papermill operator, his banker, and his employees would rather not absorb the immediate costs of cleaning up waste byproducts. They can be pushed to new preferences by the threat of worse and more visible consequences.

If everyone possessed equal political power, leftists would have no quarrel with city policy toward pollution or anything else. In the unlikely event of such equality, nobody would have any reason to be a leftist. But with power unevenly distributed we can realize that the costs of pollution weigh more heavily on powerless people than on the powerful. A life-style sheltered from the obnoxious effects of pollution is easier for the wealthy than for the poor. Amphibious airplanes to isolated Canadian fishing lakes and electrostatic air conditioning filter systems at the office and at home are not yet the mark of blue collar employment. Once living at the city's edge upwind from the packing house, or upstream from the shipping channels, was enough protection. Then the central city tenements and water-front could be damned without serious involvement. Now that the problems are not so easily escaped even middle class college students and newspaper staffs are getting a public conscience. The middle class used to be amused by pictures of the Dead End kids actually swim-ming in the filthy river but now that their own lakes, and even their air, are health hazards, reform seems more likely.

What we have noted here about pollution policy is as true for other municipal policies as well. In some cases the sensitivity to the problem developed long ago. When business and the Army wanted literate employees, the cities and rural districts discovered that the workers' and farmers' offspring could learn to read and we got public schools in the nineteenth century. Some of the descendants of the original beneficiaries of that timely step towards equality now seem to regard that reform as the last legitimate one. Other problems remain, how-ever, although they do not yet concern many influential people so that they will remain unsolved and not even attacked by municipal authority for some time yet to come. Pollution is a good illustration because even young people are old enough to have witnessed the early transition of official response and to appreciate the desirability of further action.

Pollution policy is a good illustration for another reason: it clearly involves intergovernmental relations. Not only is it one of the func-tional areas in which federal, state, and local whirls are intertwined in Grodzins' marble cake,[3] but it is also a matter of international con-cern and action. For the United States, pollution along the Rio Grande involves Mexico, the resuscitation of Lake Erie depends on joint efforts with Canada, and preservation of life in the oceans will require multilateral cooperation. Even if John Donne had not been right before ("No man is an island . . .")[4] the threat of urban pollution would be enough to make his observation critical for our survival.

In none of this has a consideration of charter forms of government been relevant. Whether the city elects a stronger mayor, obfuscates the policy process with a weak mayor or a commission of semi-autonomous department heads, or pretends by hiding behind an appointed city manager that local problems are matters of engineering and expertise rather than politics, these observations about policy on pollution and the dominance of the people possessing political power are equally valid or invalid.

The charter form of city government, however, may influence the composition of the power structure and it will certainly channel political participation. Whether the city is run by the Ball family as the Lynds thought Muncie was, by a pyramidal business elite as Hunter believed Atlanta to be, or by the likes of a more democratic shifting pattern of interested parties (depending on the issue) that Dahl identified in New Haven, some influential people will play according to the appropriate rules in order to obtain results that they think will be satisfactory. Few of them would be overly concerned with whether they had to work with a mayor, commission, or manager. This is not to agree completely with Alexander Pope: "For forms of government let fools contest; Whate'er is best administer'd is best."[5] The way to get to a city manager differs from the technique for influencing a strong mayor and only fools would ignore the distinctions. Perhaps only different people can succeed under different forms. All forms, however, get some job done in response to some politically powerful people.

Political scientists do not know, and in principle cannot discover, who governs the cities of the United States or how. Any obscure neophyte instructor of municipal government can cut up Dahl, the big man from Yale and past-president of the American Political Science Association. Dahl found out more about who governs New Haven than most people would want to know, and he made his discoveries more scientifically than many of his critics, but both the conspiracy theory and the doctrine of unique cases permit disbelievers to reject his findings. The conspiracy theory holds that behind everything that Dahl thought he saw was a hidden power. All of Dahl's evidence to the contrary then becomes confirmation of the secret power's effectiveness—even more clever than we suspected. The doctrine of unique cases dismisses Dahl's New Haven as irrelevant for other cities and as out of date even for itself. Each city must be studied anew each day according to these purists. This inability to know who governs or how then becomes an excuse for ducking the issue and going on to measure the measurable that nobody else has bothered to measure before. The looser set of eight generalizations presented here, however, does not depend on such data collections or on ultimate answers. They can be argued regardless of who governs. For these purposes, then, pollution helps clear the air.

The City Scene

We have already noted that cities, even beheld for the first time, are identifiable as cities. Approached from lower ground, they have a distinctive profile; viewed from on high, they are laid out as nothing else; seen from an airplane at night, they identify themselves with fairy-tale illumination. From any angle they can be spotted by the pollution seeping out from their centers. Standing in the midst of a city, or trying to travel against the flow of peak-load traffic, is claustrophobic. Seeking decent housing in proximity to friends, work, education, and creation is frustrating. Security against the hazards of accidents or, less likely, criminals is expensive and uncertain. In all these respects, the appearance of our cities testifies to the privileged status of the select few at the expense of the deprived mass.

Many of the privileged people achieved their status through hard work, driven by a deep, personal, antisocial ambition; others inherited their position and regard it as proper but not as anything to be questioned. Few, if any, of the people who enjoy the benefits of urban civilization are privy to a considered plot of exploitation. Even the bigots among them can be decent grandparents, jovial club members, active volunteer workers for charities, devout members of a religious congregation—insensitive, perhaps, in some respects, but nevertheless somebody's best friends. We do not have to attribute evil to the people on top, and we would be terribly naïve to assign virtue to the ones at the bottom, but the inequalities of city life are undeniable. The concentric circles moving outward from central city decay to suburban affluence are so commonly observed that they tend to become invisible. The presence downtown of opulent islands serves to emphasize the basic pattern by sharpening the contrast between the rich and the poor. That the rich live or work there only part time and educate their children elsewhere further exaggerates the uneven distribution of urban amenities. That some of these islands were created by urban renewal projects is not comforting because the poor people were merely dispersed so that they would be less obtrusive, but still deprived.

A generation ago life in the cities was so dismal that we sought to alleviate it by enlisting the federal government in a housing program. When we first said we intended and what, with hindsight, we see we actually accomplished illustrate beautifully the second generalization formulated in our consideration of pollution policies: policy affects some people differently than others. The National Housing Act of 1934 created the Federal Housing Administration. It was originally entitled an act "to improve Nationwide housing standards . . ." and other purposes.[6] Fair enough. A nation with a housing problem in the midst of a terrible depression might want such a policy.

The first Federal Housing Administrator, James A. Moffett, soon gave his program a somewhat more precise objective. Addressing the Advertising Clubs of New York he made the goal seem to be the promotion of year-round advertising in place of "seasonal advertising." Moffett told his audience:

> Those who have kept so closely in touch with the program know how easy and convenient it is for the owner of a home or business property to finance the modernization of his holdings. Anybody who is a property owner, reliable, and receiving an income that will enable him to repay his loan in monthly installments can borrow the money.[7]

In other words, help was available to just "anybody" at all who happened to be well off at a time when 16 million people, approximately one-third of the labor force, were unemployed.[8] Sixteen million people were looking for jobs rather than for home-improvement loans. Although this housing story is old, it is worth recalling because the policy seemed so enlightened at the time and its consequences in terms of central-city decline and suburban sprawl were so poorly anticipated.

The first annual report of the FHA, shortly after Moffett's talk to the advertisers, provided a clue as to the effective (rather than avowed) direction of his program. The report identified "the duty of encouraging improvement in housing standards and conditions by making improved credit facilities available to the owners and prospective owners of homes and other property."[9] Enter the money-changers. *Congressional Digest* put it more bluntly: "The principal aim of the Act was to make home financing, on reasonable terms to the borrower, safe and attractive to private capital."[10] The FHA was finally equally candid in its fourth annual Report:

> [Before the 1938 amendments, FHA] was authorized to insure mort-gages on rental projects only where the purpose was "to provide housing for persons of low income." . . . this language could be con-strued only to mean multifamily structures or groups of houses built at the lowest possible cost for rent to persons of "relatively" low in-comes. There could be no pretense that private capital, even with mutual mortgage insurance, could provide adequate new housing for slum dwellers or others comprising the lowest income groups.[11]

"There could be no pretense" of providing for slum dwellers. Screw them! And a generation later the people brought up with the help of such New Deal programs for their families and for their economic ideology have the unmitigated gall to act as though they had achieved their superior status alone and that the miserable life of the slums is merely the just desert for moral defects of character. The Good News according to Matthew made the point that seems to be the motto of these New Deal beneficiaries:

> For the man who has will always be given more, till he has enough to spare; and the man who has not will forfeit even what he has. Fling the useless servant out into the dark, the place of wailing and grinding of teeth.[12]

Fling out 16 million unemployed and to those who have jobs and property give public support until they have enough and to spare. This is the kind of crap that gives organized religion such a bad reputation. Surely the spirit of charity that might yet alleviate some of the torment of the cities is better portrayed in other scriptures but the FHA never pretended to represent the best of those teachings.

In addition to the contrast between the appearance of the ghetto and the suburbs, another visible illustration of the uneven impact of city policies is portrayed by the superhighway fracturing poor neighborhoods in order to facilitate the free flow of private automobiles from beyond the slum, through it unseeing and undisturbed, to offices of the wealthy. First, those who are able move beyond the city's taxing jurisdiction, then they pressure the city to widen its main thoroughfares at the expense of other people's trees and front yards. Next the commuters expect the city to cut new direct routes through the heart of old neighborhoods. These new expressways consume block-wide swaths at the cost of millions of dollars per mile but property owners, not residents, are bought out. Even when a relocation program is attempted, a family grocery or a neighborhood tavern cannot take its customers with it. The prosperous and influential suburbanites who have caused the disintegration of social patterns in the lives of poorer people sometimes pass a moral judgment on the dislocated people and drive their own children to pot.

We are told that building streets is not a political matter—it is neither Republican nor Democratic—and therefore we are urged to leave the city manager unmolested as he makes sound engineering decisions. The manager form is a technique for insulating these allocations of costs and benefits from popular influence. It is not a way of avoiding the allocations. Nor does it avoid influence. Any drive through any city will demonstrate that some neighborhoods are better served by streets and sidewalks than others, and almost by definition the already "better" neighborhoods get the best public service.

Just as with pollution and housing, urban highways are intergovernmental programs. State road departments and federal interstate highway funds are involved. The ability of the city government to provide alternate forms of mass transit is hobbled by the legal framework and financial limitations imposed on the cities by nineteenth-century principles of state government. As explained by Dillon's Rule, the cities have the authority neither to administer nor to finance projects not authorized by their "parent" state governments.[13] Not even so-called "home rule" solves the problems of these restraints. Otherwise the kind of vigorous political leadership possible with a partisan strong mayor might innovate modes of transportation as well as easing other popularly perceived problems. Where these new policies require engineering or other expertise, the politically responsible mayor is as capable of employing the experts as would be an insulated city manager. The mayor, however, makes himself visible to take the credit or blame for the effect of the program.

The appearance of cities is also changed by the visibility and type of law enforcement. The contrast is sharpest between London police, unarmed, inconspicuously keeping traffic flowing and maintaining the good reputation of Scotland Yard on the one hand and on the other a city under military occupation, with obscenely armed patrols imposing curfews and other arbitrary forms of order. Most cities of the United States are usually somewhere between these extremes as their problems of order are typically greater than in Britain but generally less than during a riot.

Law enforcement not only changes the appearance of city life but like all other municipal policies it is not neutral as it impinges on personal behavior. The selective quality of law enforcement comes first in its statement of what behavior is formally sanctioned and what officially proscribed. Further differences of impact result from the uneven carrying out of the formal directives. One of the chief marks of civilization is that we have outlawed the physical means of settling private disputes and given the advantage to the clever, the articulate, and the wealthy rather than to the strong. Weaklings for thousands of years have used the law to impose their preferences on men more skilled in combat. This may be highly desirable but it is not neutral.

Regardless of the written law, however, the law in practice is something else. Not even Hitler could penetrate every Bavarian hamlet with his clearly dictated laws regarding Jews and taxes. While judges do interpret the law, as we were taught by uninterested junior high school civics teachers, the policeman's interpretation is much more relevant for life in the city. The crap shooter drinking rot-gut whiskey is more likely to be considered in violation of the municipal antigambling code than the poker player across town genteelly sipping superb scotch. Certain kind of bumper stickers seem to influence the patrolman's sense of the driver's ability to observe traffic laws. Perhaps the most glaring travesty is the selective enforcement of vagrancy laws—laws so bad on their face that they seem designed to legalize arbitrary discrimination. More routinely, city magistrates ran the vagrancy laws a close second in making poverty a crime. First in setting bail and then in imposing sentences that permitted anyone with money to buy his way out of jail ("30 days or $60"), the municipal courts guaranteed that the poor would get poorer while the more prosperous offender went back to his job virtually unscathed. And in this case as in others, the beneficiaries of the system liked to regard the victims as immoral.

The city scene changes with a lot of other variables. Where are the parks? What are the recreation programs? Are the streets cleaned? How are households and businesses served by the city? What is the impact of zoning ordinances, if any? Where the ratio of jobs to population is skewed, what provisions are made for redressing the balance? Are utilities abusing their right-of-way privileges? Is the city burning? In all of these matters, the advocate of equality is dissatisfied with the appearance of the city and hopes for remedial reforms.

Conclusion

Why is the hope for more equality in the city resisted so bitterly? All but the princes among us owe our status to the movements toward equality that elevated previously deprived people, and even the princes are better off today than their forebears.

In the short run the leftist seems always to lose. Cities respond to the preferences of elites. Sometimes, to be sure, the elite is a numerical majority of the voters. Whenever a question is submitted to a referendum (fluoridation? charter amendment?) the preference of the larger number prevails over that of the smaller. That is democratic whenever the plurality decision does not trample on a minority right essential to democracy, but democracy does not necessarily give leftists the degree of equality they seek. In some cities, the elite includes a politically well organized labor movement, but even that is not enough where a significant percentage of the local population is unemployed or unemployable. Nowhere have the leftists ever won equality and that is why they seem always to lose.

In the longer run, however, the aspirations of the leftists seem to fare better. They have gotten many of us where we are today. They keep winning reforms that are gradually absorbed into the conservative creed. The current generation of right-leaning elitists is always defending programs opposed by its ideological predecessors. The reason the egalitarians seem nevertheless to lose, then, is that they are never satisfied to rest with the achievements of their ideological antecedents. They can always see additional evidence of unwarranted privilege to oppose. They can never achieve their ultimate goal so they will always be frustrated.

The final irony of the city is that it has given us so much in tangible results and in our vision of what might be that we despair at its failures. The deep bitterness of Al Capp is understandable if pathetic.[14] He sees the city as a jungle and he is alienated from the trouble-makers roaming its streets victimizing innocent people. But a real jungle is worse, the frontier was worse with its vigilantes, the boss-ridden cities were worse, and the cities run by Greek and Cuban military regimes are worse. The virtuous middle class was produced by the specialization of civilization. The cities gave us our middle class. The middle class developed in the cities not through any deterioration in the status of the privileged elite but rather through the promotion of what had theretofore been regarded as inherently (or divinely) inferior subordinates. If this middle class and our cities will now be open to the further extension of this process of elevation —of bringing outsiders in, of sharing power and resources equally— then our cities can survive and we with them.

In a sense all of this chapter has been a leftist critique of the cities. In a more profound sense, however, it has been a defense of the system. It says that if more reform is achieved, the revolution will be unnecessary in order to reach the legitimate aspirations of a people yearning to be free—a people dedicated to the proposition that all men are created equal.

> The cities are ours and we made them.
> Our hands poured the concrete
>   and raised one story upon another unto the sky.

We invented electric elevators
   and raced them through the long shafts.
We darkened our own paths
   and crowded ourselves into our own canyons
   without a sense of direction.
We burrowed through our own tunnels
   and air conditioned our buildings
   that we might shut out the atmosphere
That we had polluted.

In the cities we knew not each other
   yet yearned for our own humanity
   lost among many.
We closed our eyes to each other
   that our problems would multiply,
Then looked upon the problems
   and said they were too big
   and they staggered us,
And we pretended that we had not done it ourselves
   and so could not undo it.
And some have resigned.
But the city mixes its problems with challenge
   and delivers dreams out of its dreariness.
The city is ours,
   and, like us, inconsistent.
It is bright in the darkness
   and warm in the cold.

Our wealth pours forth from the city
   and we relish it.
It is an oasis of our own design
   that we may have diversion and refreshment.
Joy and hope are massed in the city;
   children and lovers sleep under its mantle.
Our fellows cry out for our compassion
   in all the streets
That we inhabit together.

We behold the art of the city
   and are enraptured by its symphony.

We read its press and hear its voices
  that we may glimpse our own futures.
The city is home to our schools and our churches;
  its museums store up our civilization;
  our philosophers dwell in its towers.
From the city comes change for all the land,
  and out of change, progress
That we can direct.

What man has put together
  he can take apart
  and put back together again.
We live in the city
  and with the city,
But we are not its prisoners,
We can admit things to do
  and do them.
We can reach out for each other
  and make contact.
We can walk in our own darkness
  because we are not alone,
And we have light.

P.J.P.

Selected Readings

Banfield, Edward C., and James Q. Wilson. *City Politics.* Cambridge: Harvard University Press and The M.I.T. Press, 1963.

Bartlett, John. *Familiar Quotations.* 13th ed. Boston: Little, Brown, 1955.

Boulding, Kenneth E. *The Meaning of the Twentieth Century: The Great Transition.* New York: Harper & Row, 1964.

Bridgwater, William and Seymour Kurtz (eds.). *The Columbia Encyclopedia.* 3rd ed. New York: Columbia University Press, 1963.

Capp, Al. "Introduction," in Harold Gray, *Arf: The Life and Hard Times of Little Orphan Annie, 1935–45.* New Rochelle, N.Y.: Arlington House, 1970.

Dahl, Robert A. *Who Governs? Democracy and Power in an American City.* New Haven: Yale University Press, 1961.

Grodzins, Morton. "The Federal System," ch. 12 in *Goals for Americans.* Englewood Cliffs, N.J.: Prentice-Hall, 1960.

Hunter, Floyd. *Community Power Structure: A Study of Decision Makers.* Chapel Hill: University of North Carolina Press, 1953.

Lynd, Robert S., and Helen Merrell Lynd. *Middletown in Transition: A Study in Cultural Conflicts.* New York: Harcourt Brace Jovanovich, 1937.

Moffett, James A. "F.H.A.," *Congressional Digest,* 14 (January, 1935), 17.

Presthus, Robert. *Men at the Top: A Study in Community Power.* New York: Oxford University Press, 1964.

"Status of 'F.H.A.,'" *Congressional Digest,* 14 (January, 1935), 11.

U.S. Congress, *Congressional Record,* 73rd Cong., 2nd sess., 1934, 78, pt. 11.

U.S. Federal Housing Administration, *Annual Reports,* 1934, 1937, U.S. Government Printing Office.

References

1. Boulding, p. 3.
2. Bridgwater, p. 1979.
3. Grodzins, p. 265.
4. Bartlett, p. 215.
5. *Ibid.,* p. 317.
6. *Congressional Record* (May 14, 1934), p. 8814.
7. Moffett, p. 17.
8. Bridgwater, p. 862.
9. FHA Report, p. 3.
10. "Status of FHA," p. 11.
11. FHA 4th *Annual Report,* p. 19.
12. *The New English Bible.*
13. Banfield, p. 64.
14. Capp, p. 2.

Poverty

Things Are Getting Better All the Time

ROSE D. FRIEDMAN

In the eighteenth and early nineteenth centuries, getting enough to eat—that is, enough calories to eliminate hunger— was the major problem of the populace in almost the entire world, with the possible exception of Great Britain and North America. A family that had enough bread was considered in easy circumstances. It did not occur to students of living standards of that day that the working class might have essential needs over and above subsistence.

From *Poverty: Definition and Perspective* by Rose D. Friedman. Reprinted by permission of the American Enterprise Institute for Public Policy Research. Rose D. Friedman has been on the staff of the National Resources Committee, the Federal Deposit Insurance Corporation, and the Bureau of Home Economics. She is currently engaged in research on the economics of consumption.

The level of living per capita and per day of a working-class family "varied between a maximum of about two and a half to three pounds of wheat during the best years and an extremely low minimum which, as late as the eighteenth century, often fell below a single pound of bread a day." The subsistence minimum, an income that allowed the purchase of three pounds of wheat per capita per day—the equivalent of 3,500 calories—"did not represent a realizable possibility but *an ideal* whose attainment would solve every social problem." In the eighteenth century, this minimum was attained in France in only one out of four years.

As economic conditions improved, sociologists modified the concept of minimum subsistence by calculating the physiological minimum more and more generously. They paid increasing attention to the type of nutrition as well as number of calories. In addition, the minimum began to include some expenditure for things other than food, such as lighting, heat, and clothing.

Half the people of the world today still get less than 2,250 calories per day, and live on a diet primarily of cereal in the form of millet, wheat, or rice. Another 20 percent get less than 2,750 calories per person per day. For this vast multitude, getting enough to eat is still the major problem. Only the well-to-do three-tenths of the human race today get more than 2,750 calories as well as a varied diet which provides the calories that not only satisfy hunger but also maintain a healthy body. Considerably fewer than three-tenths of the human race have a level of living at which expenditures on food absorb less than half the budget. The inhabitants of the United States are among these fortunate few.

It is admitted by all that the average level of living in the United States today is among the highest in the world, and that it has risen greatly over the past century. But, some complain, many Americans have been left behind and have not shared in this rising level of living. Are they right? In every society and at all times there are wide variations among people in the standard of living. These wide variations exist today in the United States. But does that mean that a segment of the population has been excluded from the benefits of a rising standard of living? Has progress brought gains primarily to those at the top of the heap? Or to those at the bottom as well? Or primarily to those at the bottom?

Let us look at what has been happening to the level of living of the people at the lower end of the income distribution, the relatively poor. First, some general observations, and then some statistical evidence.

Technological change and industrial progress have wrought many changes in the basket of goods available to American consumers. In many respects, however, this progress has been far more important to the persons at the bottom of the income pyramid than to those at the top. To take just a few examples. Radio and television have brought news and entertainment into the homes of people at all income levels. But surely, at least as an entertainment medium, these innovations have meant far more to the poor than to the rich—as did the phonograph and the movies when they were developed. Concerts, theaters, dances, and lectures were always available to the rich—either through public performances, or in a still earlier era, by live performances in the home. For the masses, first the phonograph, then the movies, and now TV and radio provide opportunities for cultural enrichment that were once almost the exclusive privilege of the well-to-do. And the masses have availed themselves of the opportunity with abandon, as the ubiquitous TV aerial vividly documents. According to David Caplovitz in *The Poor Pay More*:

> 95 percent of the families—all but 25 of the 464 interviewed—own at least one television set. Sixty-three percent have a phonograph— about half owning one separate from their TV set, and another 12 percent owning a television-phonograph console. . . . The 95 percent of set-owners among these families which include a substantial proportion in the lower-income range of the working-class, is about the same as that found among samples of working-class families in the country at large, these including many skilled workers and home-owners. . . . As much as any statistics, these figures reflect the style of life of these young families. There is an accent on entertainment brought into the home by modern technology.

On a more practical level, electricity, running water, central heating, indoor toilets, telephones, automobiles, all of which we take for granted today, have changed the pattern of living available to the majority of American consumers even in the past 35 years. Says Herman Miller, in *Rich Man—Poor Man*:

Today electricity in the home is taken for granted as a more or less inalienable right of every American. Practically every home—on the farm as well as in the city—is electrified. Even on southern farms, ninety-eight out of every hundred homes have electricity. In 1930, nine out of every ten farm homes were without this "necessity." And the country was much more rural then than now.

The poor in rural areas have benefited especially from technological improvements. For them, even more than for the poor in metropolitan areas access to communication by means of telephone, to urban centers by means of the automobile, and to entertainment and education by means of radio and television have meant a great improvement in the social level of living.

Inside plumbing and central heating that are today part of the specifications for an "adequate" level of living were unavailable to all but the very rich in this country less than a century ago—and are unavailable to most people in the world today. Again, these improvements brought a far greater change to the life of the masses than of the classes. Servants could always provide the rich with the conveniences that water systems and central heating have for the first time now made available to the masses—and the same economic progress that has made these available to the masses has made servants scarcer for the classes.

These are all general and non-quantitative indicators of the changes that have occurred in the standard of life of the ordinary family. What of the quantitative evidence?

First, nutrition, the basic need of humanity: how far we have moved from the situation of earlier centuries or from the situation that prevails in most of the world today can be seen by the almost complete neglect of calorie requirements in judging the adequacy of the diets in this country. In terms of simple calorie requirements, the problem for the American people today is too many, not too few calories. In evaluating the diets reported by families in the Household Food Consumption Survey, 1955, of the U.S. Department of Agriculture, one report states, "Calorie averages, in partciular, were high." Even if a generous deduction were made for waste in the kitchen and at the table, the food consumed probably still would provide more calories than actually needed. The prevalence of overweight in the population is an indication of over-eating.

As the quantity and quality of food available in the more advanced countries increased, attention shifted from getting enough to eat to eating the right food, from number of calories to the importance of other nutrients. . . .

One report from the Household Food Consumption Survey, 1955, summarizes the improvement in nutrition as follows: "Diets in the United States have improved markedly since the 1930's. In 1936 when a large-scale household food consumption survey was made, a third of the diets were classed as 'poor.' When we apply the same standards to diets of the households surveyed in 1955, only a little over a tenth (13 percent) may be considered 'poor.' "

As to how the poor fared relative to the rich, this same report says, "Diets of families in the lowest income showed much greater improvement between 1936 and 1942 and 1948 than did diets of families in the upper income third. Between 1948 and 1955 all of the income groups shared fairly equally in the moderate changes."

If a healthy body is the first need, a healthy mind is the second. Schooling is another example of the far greater significance to the masses than to the classes of the improvement that has occurred in the standard of living of the American people. Less than a century ago (1870), only 57 percent of all children between 5 and 17 years of age attended school. By the turn of the century, this had risen to 76 percent, by 1920, to 82 percent, and by 1960 to 89 percent. It was this low in 1960 only because children were starting school at 6 years of age instead of at 5. Nearly 97 percent of all children between 7 and 17 years of age were in school in 1960. Even more dramatic are the figures on schooling at a higher level. In 1870, only 2 percent of the relevant age group graduated from high school. This tripled to 6 percent by 1900, tripled again to 17 percent by 1920, and again to 50 percent by 1940. It had reached 62 percent by 1956. Enrolled in institutions of higher education—junior colleges, and universities—was less than 2 percent of the relevant age group in 1870, and more than 30 percent in 1960. There is still scope for improvement, but much the greater part of this particular road has already been traveled.

To go from the specifics of food and schooling to the level of living as a whole, we can use income per family as a rough index of level of living—though as we shall see later it has many defects as a precise measure. Just 35 years ago, more than half of the people in this country would have been labeled "poor" by the poverty line of $3,000 income so popular today; 20 years ago, 30 percent; today 21 percent—and these statements are based on statistics that allow fully for change in the price level. In 1929, a year of great prosperity, about 11 million American families and individuals had incomes below $2,000 compared with 7 million in 1962. Despite a 63 percent rise in the total number of families and individuals from 1929 to 1962, the number with incomes below $2,000 actually fell by 32 percent.

By almost any yardstick, there surely has been a major reduction in the number of families with low income in this country over the past three decades. It simply is not true that any large segment of the American people has been left behind and has failed to share in the country's economic progress. If the trend in growth of real income of the past 35 years were to continue, the fraction of the population below the currently popular poverty line of $3,000 per family would become negligible before the end of the century. Of course, if the growth in real income continues, one of its manifestations will be a rise in what is regarded as the standard of poverty so that the poor will continue to be with us. All groups will continue to share in economic progress and the people then labeled poor will have a higher standard of living than many labeled poor today. How much poverty there is now or will be then depends on the yardstick used to define poverty.

American Social Policy: Beyond Progressive Analysis

SUSAN S. FAINSTEIN and NORMAN I. FAINSTEIN

Since the latter part of the nineteenth century American reformers have pressed for the eradication of poverty and the full participation of all citizens in the bounty of American productivity. Yet, the vision of a country without extremes of wealth and poverty seems little closer to realization now than it did one hundred years ago. In 1967 nearly 11 percent of all familes and 31 percent of nonwhite families were, by conservative government estimates, below the poverty level. More than 25 percent of all families and 48 percent of nonwhite families had yearly incomes below $5,000. Moreover, the lowest fifth of the population in 1967 received only 5.4 percent of the total national income, while the top fifth received 41.2 percent.[1]

The welfare state is less developed in the United States than in any of the other advanced capitalist societies. The American government has not—comparatively speaking—acted as the guarantor of what T. H. Marshall calls the "social element of citizenship": "By

Susan S. Fainstein (Ph.D., Massachusetts Institute of Technology) is Assistant Professor of Urban Studies at Livingston College, Rutgers University and a Research Associate of the Center for Policy Research.

Norman I. Fainstein (Ph.D., Massachusetts Institute of Technology) is Assistant Professor of Sociology at Columbia University and a Research Associate of the Center for Policy Research.

[this] . . . I mean the whole range from the right to a modicum of economic welfare and security to the right to share to the full in the social heritage and to live the life of a civilized being according to the standards prevailing in the society."[2] The "underdevelopment" of the American state in addressing itself to the social question (as it used to be called) has not been appreciably eliminated despite recurring thrusts of Progressive reformism. Like many a technologically backward society, the gap between ourselves and those nations more advanced in providing for the social welfare of their populations has not been narrowing. We can in part explain the halting progress of social improvement by the existence of widespread opposition to reformist aims. But we must also look at the limitations of the reform movement itself.

In a number of respects reform in America has remained strikingly constant throughout this century. During the sixties there was a new awareness among influential citizens and governmental policymakers of the continuing presence of a deprived, self-perpetuating lower class. Recent attempts at ameliorating the condition of the poor, however, have been essentially similar to the programs of earlier periods. The social programs inaugurated by the Kennedy and Johnson Administrations have differed little in their substance, in their rationales, and in the social composition of their supporters from those established during the Progressive period. In this essay we will attempt to reveal the roots of present American policy toward the poor in the Progressive tradition, to expose the limitations of Progressive analysis, and to consider the possibilities of significant social change in the interest of the poor.

The Progressive Tradition

The efforts of the 1960s at improving services for the poor have their roots in the social meliorism of the turn of the century. American public policy in relation to the indigent was not born out of the political power of a strong working class movement; rather it evolved from the charitable endeavors of a segment of the upper class, moved partly by genuine humanitarianism and partly by a desire to avert the threat to social stability presented by the immigrant lower classes.

The movement for city planning, new building codes, vocational education, settlement houses, and public recreational facilities did not emanate from those social classes that would be their beneficiaries. Instead, these movements were led by upper and middle class civic leaders who asserted that the measures they proposed were in the interest of the entire public.

The Progressives, refusing to admit that civic leaders could have interests antithetical to those of the deprived, argued that the power to make public policy should be reserved in the fields of both education and general government to those who had no particular or immediate stake in the outcomes. Thus, as Sol Cohen notes in comparing the educational Progressives with other Progressive reformers:

> The PEA's [Public Education Association's] leaders see themselves
> as wholly divorced from any special interest. The PEA presents itself
> to the public as an altruistic group of citizens who "have no axe to
> grind . . . no vested interest," who have "only one goal—to see that
> the best possible education is offered to the youth of the City of New
> York."[3]

But, as Cohen recognizes:

> The bulk of the evidence says otherwise. It [the PEA] has represented
> a single class interest. Over the years the PEA has taken its tone from
> a small, relatively homogeneous inner core leadership of wealthy,
> upperclass, well educated Yankee Protestants and German Jews. . . .
> The PEA's main concern . . . has been the preservation of social
> order and social stability.[4]

The bourgeois social basis of the Progressive movement and the tying of all reform to a general concept of the public interest meant that reform measures had to be justified not in terms of their benefits to a single group—the poor—but in terms of their rewards for the whole society. Thus, improving the lot of the poor was not interpreted to mean increasing their power or wealth at the expense of the power and wealth of other members of society. The idea that improvements in social welfare could lead to measures antagonistic to the interests of the bourgeoisie was either inconceivable to or not countenanced by the Progressives. Programs that *exclusively* benefited the poor could not be in the public interest and thus were unacceptable.

The Progressives defined the public interest in terms of assimilation, individual mobility, and equal opportunity. They did not consider equality of condition—that is, the equal participation of all classes in wealth and power—to be part of that public interest, nor did they question the possibility of achieving genuine equal opportunity given an initial condition of social inequality. The association of social policy with class interests that so dominated European social thought within the corresponding period, could be evaded in the United States through the reduction of social questions to problems of the public interest and through the substitution of equality of opportunity as a goal for equality of condition.

The Policy Goals of Progressivism

Reliance on the standard of the public interest as the measure of social welfare programs led to an immense stress on education as the instrument for bettering the lot of the lower classes. Educating the poor would not diminish the position of the better off; it would merely increase the sum of opportunity in the society and teach the offspring of the immigrants to give up the strange and threatening ways of their parents. The educational system would serve the multiple purposes of assimilation, of providing a path of upward mobility for the deserving, and of teaching practical skills to the majority. Progressive schools, directed by professional educators who in turn were responsible to public-spirited citizens, would provide the means through which the poor could realize the American dream of equal opportunity.

Similarly, the social service agencies and settlement houses aimed at providing slumdwellers with alternative models of life-styles. Social workers acted as socializing agents on behalf of middle class society, offering opportunities for mobility to those able to take advantage of them. Genteel, educated young people would live among the poor, thereby showing their own essential faith in the innate humanity of slumdwellers and also permitting these unfortunates to emulate their superior habits. While social workers were personally active in pressing for governmental reforms such as improved housing, parks, recreation, and public services, they did not envision themselves as political organizers of the poor. Rather, their role as political missionaries was to break poor people of their dependence on the political machine and to proselytize the middle class, "good government" political ethos to them. The Progressives were indeed the left wing of the bourgeoisie; but they were nonetheless respectful of bourgeois modes. While they rebelled against the selfishness and narrowmindedness of their class, they did not possess a political consciousness that might have led them to foment revolution in the slums.

Progressivism as a political philosophy emphasized increased democratization of public decision making, and the improvement of governmental operations through application of the norms of economy and efficiency. While the growth in professionalism and the increased power of the expert implied by the second objective seem to contradict the first, the two aims nonetheless fit together. In light of the doctrine of the public interest, they explain how Progressives could avoid the issue of giving political power to the poor while simultaneously advocating greater democracy.

Progressive political thought assumed a sharp separation between policymaking and administrative functions. For example, the proposals for the council-manager form of city government assumed that these two functions could be easily dissociated, and the city could be spared having untrained citizens making administrative decisions and unrepresentative bureaucrats making political choices.[5] The combination of greater democratization of policymaking and greater professionalization of administration meant that government would be subservient to the public will in both its policymaking and implementation aspects. Organization of the lower class would be dysfunctional to these objectives because prior to their socialization into middle class behavior patterns, the political activities of the poor would tend to be selfish, and thus antagonistic to the public interest. Therefore, the proper way of bringing the poor into the political system was through education. Once the schools and social agencies had succeeded in their objectives, poor people would naturally participate in political life. Their politicization, however, should occur only after proper preparation.

Progressivism did not recognize the interests of the poor *as a class*; its political and social objectives were based on the premise that poor people could rise, as individuals, from their unwholesome condition. The policies recommended by the Progressives, that have come to be embodied in many of our most familiar social institutions, make it possible for the potentially mobile to find opportunities for rising above the station of their parents. They do not, however, contribute to the elimination of the lower class as an enduring element in American life. As we argue in the next sections, recent reforms are squarely within the Progressive tradition and are no more likely to do away with relative deprivation.

Progressive Reform: Old and New

The Progressive movement arose out of a heightened sensitivity among a segment of the privileged classes to the distress of the poor, and from an awareness that poverty threatened social stability. Likewise, the reform program of the sixties can be traced both to a growing consciousness among some members of the upper strata of the extent of poverty and their perception of the danger to social stability presented by the Civil Rights Movement and black nationalist groups. While the impetus to recent policy can be traced partly to pressures exerted by black leaders, its content was framed by college professors, foundation executives, and federal officials. Thus, we see the model for the War on Poverty and Model Cities in the programs of the President's Committee on Juvenile Delinquency and the Ford Foundation's Gray Areas Program.[6] Similarly, Title 1 of the Elementary and Secondary Education Act (ESEA), which provided extra funds for schools in impoverished areas, derived from certain emphases in these programs, and found its support among advisers to President Johnson who viewed improved education as essential to bettering the lot of the poor:

> It is important to understand that the reform [Title 1 of ESEA] was not a response to public pressure. Unlike the great national programs passed during the New Deal, Title 1 did not arise from public demand. The poor were unorganized and had made no demands for such legislation.[7]

As in the earlier period, reform has been *brought to* "the people" rather than arising in response to their demands. The preface to a recent book on the settlement house movement, itself reflecting the general Progressive ethos, manifests the extent to which *noblesse oblige* still dominates, even among the more radical reformers:

> Despite differences between the two generations of reformers [Progressive and modern], they have much in common in spirit and tactics. The settlement worker who went to live in a working-class neighborhood in the 1890's, the peace corpsman who settled in an African village, the SNCC member who moved into a Mississippi hamlet, the Southern Christian Leadership Conference worker who lived in a slum tenement in Chicago in the 1960's all began their reform efforts from the inside: *they went to the people*, to the neighborhood, and started there.[8]

Because the program of reform has originated not among the poor or their direct representatives but among well-meaning upper-middle class leaders, it continues to reflect the same biases as did the program of the Progressive era. Federal policy toward the poor is the Progressive definition of the public interest as assimilation, individual mobility, and equal opportunity. The policy goal of the modern reformers, like that of the Progressives, is an *increase in the sum of social opportunity*, achieved through the provision of education and services, rather than a redistribution of income and power. In the light of this assertion, it becomes interesting to understand two apparent exceptions to the Progressive tradition—Aid to Dependent Children (ADC) and Maximum Feasible Participation—and to see how even they arise out of the prevailing Progressive ideology.

Two Seeming Aberrations

The federal welfare program was conceived during the Depression and was viewed as a temporary measure. The program's supporters argued that the need for welfare would fade away as old people came to be covered by Social Security and a return to prosperity relieved society of those reduced to indigence by adverse economic conditions. During the Depression the poor included such a large proportion of the population as to be no longer ostracized as alien nor identified as foreign or black; moreover, demands for assistance were being pressed forcefully by members of the needy group itself. There was no recognition at that time that ADC would become the largest component of welfare and that it would turn into a costly program of direct transfer payments to the poor. Subsequent reform proposals, including the Nixon Administration's family assistance plan, have all been addressed at ultimately reducing the cost of welfare by "getting families off the relief rolls." As Gilbert Steiner notes in discussing the 1962 welfare reform proposals:

> It took 27 years for the great reexamination of public assistance to occur. When that reexamination took place in 1962, it tended to concentrate on ways to achieve long-run reduction in cost, although it has yet to be demonstrated either that there is any adequate substitute for money in relief or that money payments in relief have ever been adequate.[9]

The major government program for income redistribution was enacted as a stopgap measure during the Depression and continues on barest sufferance. The program has never been justified as a redistributive measure, but rather as a necessary means of keeping the neediest from starvation and exposure. The Nixon Administration's plans for reform are aimed not at increasing the income going to the poor, but at building incentives into the program such that individual mobility through employment is not discouraged.

As was the case for ADC, framers of the Poverty Act did not fully recognize the significance of maximum feasible participation of the poor at the time of passage of enabling legislation.[10] This aspect of the war on poverty, which required participation of members of the affected community in policymaking bodies, was interpreted by community activists as providing the basis for power. As such, it provoked strong opposition from mayors and other established political authorities, with the result that the potential of Maximum Feasible Participation as a basis for mobilizing the poor into a counterforce against established power rapidly diminished. As Moynihan has succinctly put it, "It might be said that the CAP's [Community Action Programs] most closely controlled by City Hall were disappointing, and that the ones most antagonistic were destroyed."[11]

The fact that such legislation passed at all can be explained in the light of Progressive thought as it has evolved during the course of the century. The two old aims of assimilation and equality of opportunity and the continuing view of the poor as "different" developed, in their modern forms, into the goals of participation and broadening the opportunity structure within the context of a culture of poverty. Participation in community councils was intended as a means for making target groups feel integrated into the system, not as a method for promoting radical consciousness and providing power resources. There is little reason to doubt that participation of the poor, like the settlement house of old, was intended to be a cooptative device for assimilating the poor into the system. As Philip Selznick, in analyzing an earlier government program to foster "participation" comments:

> It is easy enough for administrative imperatives which call for decentralization to be given a halo; that becomes especially useful in countries which prize the symbols of democracy. But a critical analysis cannot overlook that pattern which simply transforms an unorganized citizenry into a reliable instrument for the achievement of administrative goals, and calls it "democracy."[12]

The optimistic notion that the poor could participate in program formulation without coming into severe conflict with established power rested on an assumption that there were slack resources in the system. Thus, poor people would both participate more and receive more benefits through the mobilization of additional resources rather than through depriving some other social group of its accustomed prerogatives. That poor people had so far not been active and not received benefits proportionate to their numbers was attributed to a "vicious cycle" of poverty, whereby the narrowness of the opportunity structure led to apathetic and anomic behavior, which in turn diminished the resources available to the poor. Thus, participation became an instrument for breaking into the culture of poverty. Rather than forming a locus for the development of opposition to middle class dominance, poor people's councils were to broaden the opportunity structure, thus facilitating middle class styles of behavior on the part of the poor.

Beyond Progressive Analysis

The effectiveness of Progressive reform has partly been limited by the social class of the reformers. The Progressive tradition has typically been associated with elements of the upper social strata, and the interests of the Progressives as opposed, perhaps, to their sentiments, have been in the maintenance of the basic structure of the political and economic system, a system in which they have a large stake. But the limited effectiveness of Progressive reform cannot be attributed only to the selfish interest of the reformers. One must also consider the extent to which reform efforts have been impeded by the faulty social analysis (and associated strategies) of the Progressives, who have acted according to their own ideology of what ails the social system and how change can and does occur. In doing so they have failed to recognize sufficiently their own social biases in terms of interest and power, the limited possibilities of entirely integrative (i.e., nonconflict) strategies, and the extent to which fundamental social change requires the mobilization of relatively deprived groups. This is true of the Progressives whether they be the muckrakers and educators of the turn of the century, the Ford Foundation of the Gray Areas Program, the originators of "Maximum Feasible Participation," or the contemporary liberal reformers associated with the Democratic left.

In order to perceive alternatives to the Progressive analysis it is necessary to consider a number of aspects of the socio-political system. These may be described in the following terms:

1. Inequitable distribution of scarce resources across the social structure;
2. The structural basis of group interests;
3. The range of societal debate and the existence of a dominant ideology; and
4. The position of government and the process of change to the advantage of deprived groups.

Social Structure and Inequality

Progressives have always sought the elimination of poverty as a *social* phenomenon through increasing total wealth, and the elimination of poverty as an *individual* pathology by providing equality of opportunity. The social argument rests on an absolute definition of poverty, rather than on a relative one that would evaluate the condition of deprived groups in terms of standards of decency prevailing at a particular historical period.[13]

There is, however, little reason to believe that poverty as a social problem will disappear so long as a large proportion of the population remains extremely disadvantaged in relation to the remainder.[14] Various of the miseries associated with being poor—bad health, low educational achievement, inadequate housing—seem to arise less out of absolute deprivation than from inequality itself.[15] For good health, education, and housing can be defined only in terms of what those who are best off are receiving. This has important consequences for the possibility of eradicating poverty through the cooperation of the upper social strata, for it means that members of these strata must be willing to accept a decline in their position relative to those at the bottom. In the absence of considerable political pressure from deprived groups, and a concomitant threat to the stability of the social order, the likelihood of such benevolence is small.

The second and perhaps dominant strand of Progressive thought on eliminating poverty emphasizes the importance of creating "genuine" equality of opportunity. But doing so ultimately implies that the social position that a child attains can be made to depend only on his biological characteristics and not on any attributes that are socially transmitted. Because, however, the resources children acquire with which to make their way in the world depend crucially upon the social stratum in which they are raised (even IQ has been shown to be related to social class, race, and ethnicity),[16] short of the dissolution of the family as we know it, genuine equality of opportunity is not likely to come about until our society is characterized by much greater equality of condition. This is not to say that much progress cannot be made in reducing the liability of low social origin, but only that there are some rather severe limits on how far an inegalitarian society can actually go in this direction.[17] After all, if those at the bottom are to have the opportunity to rise, those at the top must have an opportunity to fall.[18] Thus the Progressive goal of equality of opportunity for all remains at least as much a myth that functions to mask the real issues of social inequality, as a worthy end for social reform.

The fact of social inequality as a pervasive phenomenon becomes doubly important once it is recognized that interests are associated with different strata, and that, to a large extent, these interests conflict. At some risk of oversimplification, we may assume that the well-off have a stake in maintaining their privileged position. Those who are the comparative winners in the process of the allocation of scarce values (income, power, prestige) have an interest in supporting the institutional mechanisms that place them on top. This holds true whether we consider only allocation in the economic system, or broaden our focus to include institutions such as government bureaucracies, universities, and labor unions as these affect the distribution of values. The occupants of positions in organizational and institutional structures to which privilege accrues have a vested interest in maintaining the basis of their privilege. We need not assume that privileged groups (i.e., elites) conspire with one another or are homogeneous in terms of their interests,[19] but only that for the most part there is a conflict of interest between those at the top and those at the bottom of society.

There is a high degree of association between the distribution of income, wealth, and (to a lesser degree) prestige on the one hand, and power on the other.[20] Although the mass always has its numbers to employ as a political resource during elections, other resources are, on the whole, more easily and efficiently converted into social power. Such resources are, for example, money, control of jobs, official office, control over the media. Societal elites by definition have disproportionate power in comparison to their numbers. Broadly speaking, then, the interests of privileged strata are likely to be better defended than are those of the deprived. This is especially true if we define the latter as the poor, roughly the bottom 20 percent of American income earners. Accordingly, the Progressive optimism in the possibility of attacking poverty through appeals to reason and the compassion of the upper strata seems unwarranted.

Interests and Interest Groups

Progressivism has always accepted the Lockean belief that on the one hand intelligent, well-meaning men share common interests (the public interest), and that, on the other, interests are derived primarily from moral commitments rather than from positions in the social structure. It is for this reason that interest groups have rarely been given a social basis in liberal analyses of American political activity. Rather, it has been assumed by such political scientists as David Truman, V. O. Key and Robert Dahl, that an overall good (the public interest) results from the interplay of various organized interests, and, significantly, that nearly all important social interests are effectively represented in the political arena.

An alternative analysis would argue that most organized interests are those of the relatively privileged strata.[21] Moreover, when there are interest groups representing the needs of the deprived, these groups tend to be relatively powerless. Thus, it has only been in the last few years that poor urban tenants or welfare recipients could create any kind of organizational infrastructure. Both tenant and welfare-recipient interest groups are, however, much less powerful politically than their respective antagonists of landlords (realty boards, city housing agencies) and welfare bureaucrats (the allocators of welfare payments in the state and national governments). Even when the poor can overcome the manifold obstacles to organization, their meager resources require, as Michael Lipsky shows,[22] the intervention of "third parties" on their behalf. Such third parties of the relatively powerful, however, typically have interests at odds with forceful support of the causes of those at the bottom.

Although the difficulties of mobilizing those at the bottom of society into effective action groups are great, they may not be insurmountable. The creation of an effective trade union movement is one example of successful mobilization. Whether the poor have enough in common with one another both objectively and subjectively to form the basis for collective action is an open question. It may be that a relatively homogeneous segment of those in poverty— say urban blacks in the North—may eventually comprise a single interest group or party. Perhaps more likely, we will see a coalition of "functionally specific" interest groups; welfare mothers, rent strikers, advocates of community control of schools, and the police might either form an overall coalition or act independently, but have the total impact of their separate efforts lead to changes for the benefit of the urban poor. The important point is that significant improvement in the relative position of the poor will depend upon their own collective action, that such action will advance interests antagonistic in large degree to those of the well off, and that social change may not occur in the absence of conflict.

The Meaning of the Dominant American Ideology

The social, economic, and political *status quo* in the United States is supported by the presence of a dominant political ideology— Lockean liberalism,[23] of which Progressive thought forms one stand. The dominant ideology functions in several ways to prevent significant change to the advantage of the lower strata. First, its very dominance contributes to its invisibility, making "ideology" (i.e., alternative ideologies) politically suspect, even un-American; while at the same time artificially magnifying the comparatively narrow spectrum of political diagnoses available in the United States. Thus, the difference between the political formulations of the Democratic and Republican parties appears much greater than it would if, for example, the two platforms were placed within a European spectrum that ranged from the clerical, elitist, and conservative parties on the right to the socialists, communists, and syndicalists on the left. The absence of significantly different ideologies, particularly those of the left, makes it difficult for members of the lower strata to develop political diagnoses that would permit them to mobilize into coherent action groups or parties whose mission is fundamentally to alter the *status quo*.

Second, to the extent that we have had social reform it has been Progressive reform, with the inherent limitations therein. Yet because most members of the American upper strata think neither in terms of the European conservatives of old, nor in those of the modern technocrats, their willingness to engage in social and economic planning, to be indeed the implementers of Progressive measures, is severely circumscribed. So as a nation we have not gone very far at all toward implementing even the Progressive answer to the social question.

Third, the working class and the trade union movement are basically anti-socialistic; American politics is marked not only by the absence of a socialist party, but by the absence of socialist ideas. The result is that we have not had a major thrust from the bottom toward a more egalitarian society (at least not on the order of other industrial societies) nor the conflict strategy for social change typically advanced by the socialist movement. Appeals for group action, solidarity, and social advancement through collective action —such as, to cite a recent example, black power—are viewed by most Americans as illegitimate, and are rejected by a majority of the deprived themselves on the same grounds.

Ideological Homogeneity

It is typical for Americans to view their politics as nonideological, indeed, to pride themselves on the fact. Celebrations of American pragmatism fail however to recognize the extent to which our national political thought is circumscribed by a *single* ideology: Lockean liberalism. The central assumptions of liberalism[24] thus can be felt to be "given" as Daniel Boorstin has described it. Robert Lane puts this well in talking about the latency of our ideological assumptions:

> The common unchallenged assumptions about government derive from the almost universal acceptance of the same Lockean model, as Louis Hartz has pointed out. One consequence of this latency is that the American finds it difficult to argue about political principles, and there is little doubt that one reason why Americans become so furious over the arguments of the Communists is that their own political principles are hard to tear from their native bed in the unconscious.[25]

The bounds of the Lockean ideology define for the American mass the limits of legitimate debate, of conceivable alternatives. Symbols associated with the European left—"class solidarity, socialism, income redistribution"—are normatively proscribed within American political culture. Moreover, because counter-ideologies are not presented in the normal channels of political communication, the likelihood of significant change in consciousness within the lower class and thus the growth of solidarity and organization is significantly reduced. Yet without such organization the poor are in a weak position forcefully to advance counter-diagnoses, to broaden the range of debate and thereby to make greater mobilization possible. A circle of increasing radicalization is replaced by one of inertia, apathy, and powerlessness.

The dominance of Lockean liberalism is supported by the hegemony of the major political parties. Two parties contending for power provide the appearance of genuine choice, while their established power makes it difficult for new parties to arise and legitimate deviant modes of thought. Thus, while we have witnessed in recent years the growth of deviant ideologies associated with new left, black and Spanish militant movements, there has not been a concomitant development of national organizational strength outside of the two parties. The platforms of the Republicans and Democrats were not noticeably more divergent in 1968 than in 1960 or during the fifties. The noise of a minority of dissenters has obscured the fact that in the last two decades we have failed to see "non-Lockean" parties with even the strength of the Socialists of World War I, the Communists of the Depression, or the Wallace Progressives of the forties. Ironically, the increasing acrimony of debate in the political arena has not indicated a broadening in the range of institutionalized political alternatives.

The Business Class

The meaning of a dominant ideology in the United States is clearer when one looks at two social strata that have been involved in social reform in other industrial societies: the modern upper class of the industrial bourgeoisie; and the proletariat. First, consider the business class. The absence of an American aristocracy has also meant that conservative solutions to the social problem, in the European mode of Disraeli or Bismarck, have not been advanced by a segment of the upper class with its roots in the *ancien régime*. We have had no *ancien régime*. And we have had little class conscious aristocratic concern for the poor, a concern that in Europe was later to be adopted in the technocratic ideal of the *parvenu* industrial rich. Progressive reform, with all of its evasions and limitations, became the ideology of only a small minority of the bourgeoisie.

The dominant ideology of the business class during the early part of this century was laissez-faire liberalism, not Progressivism. Technocratic thought, with its emphasis upon a strong governmental role, upon elitism and the social duty of the upper strata of the wealthy and educated, has never taken root in the American business class.[26]

The American business class eschews planning and big government.[27] Rather, it celebrates the market (albeit a regulated one), equality of opportunity for those with the pluck and luck of the Alger hero, and, above all, limited government. "At its core," comments Robert Heilbroner, "the business ideology as a spiritual creed or as an historic beacon is vitiated by something that is missing—I cannot but think fatally missing—from its deepest conception. What it lacks is a grandiose image of human possibilities cast in a larger mold than is offered by today's institutions."[28] An upper class like that of American business with no "grandiose image," no sense of historical mission, is not likely to provide the power with which fully to implement even the nonradical social reform of Progressivism. This was true in 1910 as it remains today.

The Failure of Socialism

The relative lack of concern of the American upper strata with providing *their own* solution to the social problems of the industrial era must be juxtaposed to the absence of an alternative solution from the bottom. The business class was able to adhere to its Lockean principles precisely because there was no counter-formula of socialism. The failure of socialism to take root in the American proletariat thus functioned to remove the radical threat that would have made the moderate reformism of the Progressives (old and new) more palatable to the societal elites. At the same time, it eliminated an independent force for social reform emanating from the working class, a force needed to fully implement Progressive programs.

The pervasiveness of Lockean ideology, of liberal values and beliefs, has been perhaps the most significant factor contributing to the failure of socialist ideas to gain acceptance in the American proletariat.[29]

The focus on [liberal] equalitarianism and individual opportunity has . . . prevented the emergence of class consciousness among the lower classes. The absence of a socialist or labor party, and the historic weakness of American trade-unionism, appear to attest to the strength of values which depreciated a concern with class.[30]

The conservative consciousness of American workers and the avoidance of even quasi-socialist goals by labor unions means that the lower class, the *lumpenproletariat* that comprises the bottom 20 percent, have not been the beneficiaries of major reforms intended to appease the organized working class. Were labor unions—not to mention a working class party—advancing demands for the fully developed welfare state, we could expect a number of basic changes in the provision of public services, in the incidence of taxation, and in the role of the state in guaranteeing social security. These reforms, while not in themselves the product of a social movement of the poor, would undoubtedly be of great benefit to that group. But as the situation now stands, there is no socialist movement with which the poorest of our citizens could become allied.

Indeed, there is good reason to think that the working class as a whole is quite hostile to those beneath them. To a significant extent this phenomenon of class antagonism directed below rather than above may be explained by the working class belief in Algerism, by its Lockean consciousness. So, for example, Robert Lane described the beliefs about the poor of the working class men he studied:

> The rationale for [the condition of the poor] . . . turns chiefly on two things: their lack of education . . . and their general indifference. It is particularly this "not caring" that seems so salient in the upper-working-class mind. This is consonant with the general view that success is a triumph of the will and a reflection of ability. Poverty is for lazy people just as middle status is for struggling people. Thus, Ruggiero, a building maintenance man, accounts for poverty by saying, "There's laziness, you'll always have lazy people." . . . By and large these [workers] . . . believe that the field is open and that merit will tell. . . . They tend to believe that each person's status is in some way deserved.[31]

If a worker focuses on individuals within the fluid social structure depicted by American political mythology, he tends to maintain his own cognitive balance by deciding on the one hand that those above him must deserve their positions (otherwise how could he tolerate his) and on the other that those below must be less deserving than he himself is (lest his own status not be earned or justified).[32]

The lack of sympathy by the working class toward the poor is exacerbated by the common image of the poor as black. Racism is as much a part of the American political tradition as is the Lockean ideology. The antagonism between whites and blacks today deters the formation of a working-class-poor-people's alliance, just as ethnic divisions deterred the growth of working class identification fifty years ago. So long as the poor are associated with the nonwhite— which is indeed what they most frequently are in just those places where the union movement is strongest—we cannot expect much in the way of coalition between the *lumpenproletariat* and the more powerful groups above it.

To sum up, then, there is no socialist movement from which the poor could benefit. Moreover, the members of the "solid" working class are often more antagonistic toward the poor than toward their bosses. Social reform to the advantage of the lower strata accordingly has taken place primarily through the action of a minority of the upper strata. The form of such meliorism throughout this century has been Progressivism. But the bounds of even Progressive reform have been circumscribed both by the Lockean vision of the Progressives, and by the inability of Progressive reformers to have their programs fully implemented.

In a society dominated by the ideology of Lockean liberalism, reform itself is liberal, and thereby doubly weakened. First, it is weakened by an inability to recognize the structure of the sociopolitical system with which it is dealing, a structure that would have been more readily visible were Americans able to break out of the bonds of their omnipresent ideology. However, without a socialist— indeed, without even a conservative—alternative, this does not occur. Second, the same missing socialist movement that fails to provide a radical, deviant vision, does not create the threat from the bottom that must be answered by the dominant strata. Without a mobilized working class marching in the streets, the genteel Progressives in the drawing rooms appear unrealistic, almost radical themselves, rather than as enlightened defenders of the social order. The kind of reforms advanced by the Ford Foundation, or the President's Committee on Juvenile Delinquency or OEO can be viewed by most of the upper strata as utopian at best, or subversive at worst. Progressive reform is thus limited by the modesty of its own vision, and by the weakness of the social force by which it can be implemented.

Can significant reform in the direction of greater equality occur in the United States? In order to address this question one must consider the role of the national government in effecting reform, and the origin of the social force necessary for redirecting governmental policy.

Governmental Action and the Possibilities of Change

Progressive thought defined the proper role of government as one of supreme disinterest—government should act as the neutral, Lockean arbiter. In Hofstadter's words:

> [The State] must be severely neutral among all the specific interests in society, subordinating each to the common interest and dealing out even-handed justice to all. It would be for neither the rich man nor the poor man, for labor nor capital, but for the just and honest and law-abiding man of whatever class. It would stand, in fact, where the middle class felt itself to be standing—in the middle, on neutral ground among self-seeking interests of all kinds.[33]

There was a recurring failure to recognize that any action or non-action of government must necessarily serve some interests, and that government would only come to serve the poor when those in power identified the interests of the poor as coincident with their own objectives.

During this century the most powerful force for change at the local level has arisen not from the pressure of local forces on subsidiary governments but out of the impact of national policies. During the Depression for example, municipalities did not respond to the crisis of indigence until federal programs provided funding. In the Lynds' depiction of Middletown:

> Middletown has long had many of the ideas that are now being embodied in relief projects. . . . Also, there have always been men unemployed and wanting work. . . . [But] in a culture so patterned,

the likelihood of the emergence of forthright civic social change through the city's elected and appointed administrators is curtailed almost to the vanishing point. In good times things inch along; in bad times the city takes in sail. . . . Then suddenly, in 1933 the city shifted over, with the interjection of Federal planning into the local scene, and began to move in a non-Euclidian world in which the old civic axioms were suspended and the city was asked to state its civic desires positively, to frame a new series of axioms, and to go ahead and act on them.[34]

Similarly, the federal poverty program of the sixties forced local governments to dispense both material benefits and power to the poor. Thus, Bachrach and Baratz argue that:

what seems to be *the* major contributing factor to the process of political change has been the establishment in the city of federally financed programs designed to eliminate poverty. Without the federal grants-in-aid for its programs, Baltimore's anti-poverty effort would hardly deserve the name. Much more importantly in the present context, the anti-poverty agencies have been political catalysts in the city, chiefly because they have provided the black poor with a necessary means to organize for political action and to gain access to key decision-making centers.[35]

The crucial element for change in the treatment of the poor is thus an alliance between disadvantaged groups and a segment of the national elite, directed at a change in national policy. Such an alliance has two possible forms: an important segment of the ruling elite must, either for ideological reasons or in response to threat, form a coalition with lower class groups; or representatives of the poor must themselves become part of the ruling stratum. The latter case seems unprecedented in American experience, where even the labor movement, despite its great success in forging links with the Democratic party, has virtually no direct representation in government.

The former case, that of a coalition between the lower class and members of the ruling elite, is more likely, and may indeed represent a national response on the part of elite members. While the precondition for such an alliance is a militant consciousness and organized activity on the part of lower class elements, nonetheless "at critical historical points, the consequences of social change are met by political elites recruited only in part, if at all, from groups that reflect or embody the emerging future."[36]

There are two elements that may contribute to making social change a rational goal for elite members. First, and most obvious, is a perception that the continued existence of extreme social inequality creates a potential for social disorder sufficiently severe as to make change a desirable alternative. Second is the possibility for certain segments of the elite to benefit indirectly from improving the condition of the poor. These are politicians who can seize the poor as their constituency (according to the model of Robert Kennedy or John Lindsay) and bureaucrats whose job is to serve the poor, and who benefit proportionately from increases in funds to the poor.

Effective pressure from the bottom requires a consciousness among disadvantaged groups that the prevailing system is biased against them and a willingness to take risks in order to change that system. The most effective redistributive force would probably be a white working-class movement that felt itself more subject to exploitation by those above it than those below it in the social hierarchy. But, as we have discussed earlier, the American working class is oriented toward individual mobility rather than class solidarity, thus eliminating the possibility of a socialist force that, in demanding benefits for itself, would also divert benefits to those beneath it. In the absence of a socialist movement of this sort, one must look to organized urban blacks as the most likely source of pressure.

We have, in the last decade, witnessed a striking increase in black militance, as evidenced in ghetto riots, the rise of avowedly radical black groups, and the activity of organized client groups making demands on school systems, hospitals, welfare and other social service agencies. The localism of most black organizations makes coalescence into a unified national force unlikely. Nonetheless, they may present a sufficient threat and a sufficient potential for profit as to precipitate a response within segments of the political and administrative elite.

Reform, however, will remain within the limits of the Progressive tradition unless the forces at the bottom are able to dominate their representatives at the top. Barrington Moore identifies three preconditions for revolution: a social group with revolutionary demands; a split within the ruling elite; and defection of the army.[37] The first two of these are also the preconditions of reform. But radical (as opposed to Progressive) reform will only occur when those who stand to benefit from redistribution are the captors rather than the captives of governmental policymakers. This requires both a consciousness among the poor that their interests are fundamentally antagonistic to those of the well-off and the mobilization of resources at the bottom such that the lower classes are able to control their political representatives. While such a change in consciousness seems to be happening among urban blacks, the possibility of their acquiring resources sufficient to exercise control over national governmental decisions that affect them is extremely small. Given this situation, we can at best expect policy to continue in the Progressive mold, shaped by the sentiments and interests of bureaucrats and politicians who are for the poor but not of them.

References

1. U.S. Bureau of the Census, *Pocket Data Book, USA, 1969* (Washington, D.C.: U.S. Government Printing Office, 1969), pp. 198, 201. These income distribution figures represented only a miniscule change from 1947, when the lowest fifth received 5.0 percent of national income and the highest got 43.0 percent.
2. T. H. Marshall, *Class, Citizenship and Social Development* (New York: Anchor, 1964), p. 78.
3. Sol Cohen, *Progressives and Urban School Reform* (New York: Bureau of Publications, Teachers College, Columbia University, 1963), pp. 218–219.
4. *Ibid.*
5. Edward Banfield and James Q. Wilson, *City Politics* (Cambridge: Harvard and M.I.T. Press, 1963), pp. 138–151.
6. See Daniel P. Moynihan, *Maximum Feasible Misunderstanding* (New York: Free Press, 1969); James L. Sundquist, "Origins of the War on Poverty," in James L. Sundquist (ed.), *On Fighting Poverty* (New York: Basic Books, 1969), pp. 6–33; Peter Marris and Martin Rein, *The Dilemmas of Social Reform* (New York: Atherton, 1967).
7. Jerome T. Murphy, "Title 1 of ESEA: The Politics of Implementing Federal Education Reform," *Harvard Educational Review*, 41 (February 1971), p. 37. Moynihan makes exactly the same argu-

ment about the Economic Opportunity Act: "The war on poverty was not declared at the behest of the poor: it was declared in their interest by persons confident of their own judgment in such matters." (Moynihan, *op. cit.*, p. 25.)

8. Allen F. Davis, *Spearheads for Reform* (New York: Oxford University Press, 1967), p. xiv. Italics added.

9. Gilbert Y. Steiner, *Social Insecurity* (Chicago: Rand McNally, 1966), p. 34.

10. See John C. Donovan, *The Politics of Poverty* (New York: Pegasus, 1967), p. 40; Sanford Kravitz, "The Community Action Program—Past, Present, and Its Future?" in Sundquist, *op. cit.*, p. 60; Lillian B. Rubin, "Maximum Feasible Participation; The Origins, Implications, and Present Status," *The Annals*, 385 (September 1969), pp. 15–29.

11. Moynihan, *op. cit.*, p. 131.

12. Philip Selznick, *TVA and the Grass Roots* (New York: Harper and Row, 1966), p. 220.

13. An argument for the relative conception of poverty is advanced by S. M. Miller and Pamela Roby in their *Future of Inequality* (New York: Basic Books, 1970). So-called absolute conceptions of poverty have, moreover, been shown to reflect changes in the overall standard of living when such changes are viewed over long periods. Thus, Fourastie shows that the "poverty line" based on minimum diet, housing and clothing for French workers rose during the period of three centuries in proportion to changes in the *overall* wealth of French Society. See *Causes of Wealth* (New York: Free Press, 1960).

14. If the U.S. Government's absolute definition of a "poverty line" of roughly $3,000 (1965 dollars) for a family is used, there has been a dramatic decrease in the percentage of families in poverty during the years 1947 through 1965. The percentage of families poor *by this standard* dropped from 30 percent in 1947 to 24 percent in 1955 and, finally, to 17 percent by 1965. The significance of this decrease is limited, however, by data that show median family income rising rapidly during this period: $4,275 in 1947; $5,223 in 1955; $6,882 in 1965 (all expressed in constant 1965 dollars).

If poverty is defined as a level of income equal to one half of median income, there has been no change for the better in the percentage of families in poverty: 19 percent in 1947; 20 percent in 1955; and 20 percent in 1965. Victor R. Fuchs, "Redefining

Poverty and Redistributing Income," *The Public Interest*, No. 7 (Summer 1967), p. 90. Moreover, data on the share on national personal income received by those at the very bottom (the lowest tenth of the population) indicate that there has actually been a considerable increase of economic inequality during this century. Kolko estimates that the lowest tenth of income earners received 3.4 percent of all personal income in 1910; 1.0 percent in 1937; 1.3 percent in 1957; and 1.1 percent in 1959. Gabriel Kolko, *Wealth and Power in America* (New York: Praeger, 1962), p. 14. Even if the figure for 1910 is rejected as unreliable, we still conclude that the relative share of income going to the lowest tenth has not increased over the last several decades. This conclusion is accepted by Robin Williams, a sociologist not generally associated with the political left, who also finds no evidence that the situation has changed in the sixties. Robin Williams, *American Society*, 3rd ed. (New York: Knopf, 1970.)

15. See Nathan Glazer, "Paradoxes of Health Care," *The Public Interest*, No. 22 (Winter 1971), pp. 66–71; David Cohen, "Children and their Primary Schools," *Harvard Educational Review* (Spring 1968), pp. 329–340; Nathan Glazer, "Housing Problems and Housing Policies," *The Public Interest*, No. 7 (Spring 1967), pp. 21–27.

16. Cf. Patricia Cayo Sexton, *The American School* (Englewood Cliffs, N.J.: Prentice-Hall, 1967), pp. 58–62.

17. The argument for equality of opportunity is essentially the same as that for high social mobility. Recent sociological studies do indicate that children of blue-collar fathers have opportunities for upward mobility in the United States. However, it has also been found that blacks are in a highly disadvantaged position in their occupational attainment vis-a-vis whites of similar parental background, and, significantly, that when education is held constant, the relative position of blacks does not improve. In fact, as Blau and Duncan conclude, "Education does not produce the same benefits for Negroes as for whites, whether benefits are measured in terms of occupational achievement or mobility. The difference between mean occupational status of whites and nonwhites *increases* with higher educational levels." Peter M. Blau and Otis Dudley Duncan, *The American Occupational Structure* (New York: Wiley, 1967), p. 210. Italics added.

18. S. M. Miller has found, in this regard, that the rate of downward mobility from elite occupational positions (managers, officials,

owners of large enterprises, etc.) is lower in the United States than in a number of other non-socialist industrial societies (S. M. Miller, "Comparative Social Mobility," *Current Sociology*, 9 (1960), pp. 1–89).

19. In large industrial societies we can assume *a priori* that there will be at least some conflict of interest among different elites. Nonetheless, all societal elites will typically share some fundamental interests that are opposed to the interests of nonelites, and particularly to those of the most deprived strata.

20. Lenski concludes, after an extensive examination of stratification in different societies and varying stages of economic development, "if privilege is defined as possession or control of a portion of the surplus produced by a society, then it follows that *privilege is largely a function of power and to a very limited degree, a function of altruism.* This means that to explain most of the distribution of privilege in a society, we have but to determine the distribution of power." Gerhard E. Lenski, *Power and Privilege* (New York: McGraw-Hill), 1966), p. 45, ital. in original. Lenski's analysis is more subtle and complex than this statement taken out of context would indicate. His overall direction of "causation," however, runs counter to other "conflict" theorists who similarly emphasize the importance of power in creating and sustaining economic inequality, *i.e.*, the inequitable distribution of "the surplus." Marx, to cite the obvious example, sees property and the means of production in capitalist society as the ultimate basis for power. Thus, he can conclude that the state is a "superstructural" or epiphenomenon. While the precise nature of the relationship between the variables of power and privilege is a question that goes to the heart of social theory, the fact that a strong relationship exists, which is all we are asserting here, seems beyond dispute.

21. See Isaac D. Balbus, "The Concept of Interest in Pluralist and Marxian Analysis," *Politics and Society*, 2 (February 1971), pp. 165–172.

22. Michael Lipsky, "Protest as a Political Resource," *American Political Science Review*, 62 (December 1968), pp. 1144–1159.

23. Cf. Louis Hartz, *The Liberal Tradition in America* (New York: Harcourt, Brace, 1955), esp. pp. 3–19; also, Daniel Boorstin, *The Genius of American Politics* (Chicago: University of Chicago Press, 1953).

24. For example, that society is the product of autonomous individuals

whose wants are fundamental; that conflicting interests do not derive from alternative positions on a hierarchical and stable social structure; that government can act as a "neutral" party or judge in the "public interest"; that social change is the result of good winning out in a marketplace. . . .

25. Robert E. Lane, *Political Ideology* (New York: Free Press, 1962), pp. 349–350.

26. Cf. Robert L. Heilbroner, *The Limits of American Capitalism* (New York: Harper Torchbook, 1966), pp. 76–100.

27. See Andrew Shonfield, *Modern Capitalism* (New York: Oxford University Press, 1965), pp. 298–330.

28. Robert L. Heilbroner, "The View from the Top: Reflection on a Changing Business Ideology" in Earl F. Cheit (ed.), *The Business Establishment* (New York: Wiley, 1964), pp. 1–37.

29. For differing interpretations of the failure of American socialism see S. M. Lipset, *The First New Nation* (New York: Basic Books, 1963), pp. 170–204; Daniel Bell, "The Failure of American Socialism" in *The End of Ideology* (New York: Collier, 1962), pp. 275–299; James Weinstein, *The Decline of Socialism in America* (New York: Vintage, 1967).

30. Lipset, *op. cit.*, p. 171.

31. Robert Lane, *op. cit.*, pp. 72–73.

32. Turner's ideal type of "contest mobility" and of the contest ideology surrounding American education and pervading our social thought fits well with this syndrome. Ralph H. Turner, "Modes of Social Ascent through Education" in Reinhard Bendix and Seymour Martin Lipset (eds.), *Class, Status, and Power* (New York: Free Press, 1966), pp. 449–458.

33. Richard Hofstadter, *The Age of Reform* (New York: Vintage, 1955), p. 234.

34. Robert S. Lynd and Helen Merrell Lynd, *Middletown in Transition* (New York: Harvest, 1937), pp. 123, 125.

35. Peter Bachrach and Morton S. Baratz, *Power and Poverty* (New York: Oxford University Press, 1970), pp. 97–98.

36. Allan Silver, "Social and Ideological Bases of British Elite Reactions to Domestic Crisis in 1829–1832," *Politics and Society*, 1 (February 1971), p. 179.

37. Barrington Moore, Jr., "Revolution in America?" *New York Review of Books*, (January 30, 1969), pp. 6–11.

Environment

Reason and Ecology

ROBERT POOLE, JR.

The ecology issue is a perfect illustration of some
of the salient facts of American political life. First of all, it illumi-
nates the incredible ineptitude of a purely political approach to
formulating and solving social problems. Secondly, it illustrates the
tendency of the groups dotting the political landscape to react to an
issue—any issue—in terms of a standard "line," modified only
slightly to fit the particulars at hand. Finally, the ecology issue makes

Reprinted by permission of the author and *Reason*. Robert Poole, Jr. (M.S.,
Massachusetts Institute of Technology) is currently employed as a systems
engineer with General Research in Santa Barbara, and is editor of *Reason*.
He is a member of several professional organizations and the Society for
Individual Liberty.

clear the fundamental difference between the kind of limited-liability "state capitalism" that dominates our present mixed economy, and the libertarian ideal of a completely laissez-faire, full-liability system.

Despite the publicity and interest focused on ecological concerns of late, large segments of the *status-quo* right wing, primarily in the business establishment, still tend to soft-pedal the whole issue, charging the ecology buffs with exaggeration, emotionalism, and just plain animosity. Unfortunately, however, it is no longer possible to ignore the very real harm, to persons and property, resulting from damage to the ecosystem:

In the U.S. every year, some 72 million tons of carbon monoxide, 26 million tons of sulfur oxides, 13 million tons of nitrogen oxides, 19 million tons of hydrocarbons, and 11 million tons of carbon particles are poured into the air by factories, homes, and automobiles.[1] Automobiles also discharge 250 million pounds of lead into the air each year.[2]

"Killer smogs" have resulted in deaths in Donora, Pa. in 1948, London in 1952 and 1962, and New York in 1953 and 1966. The 1952 London smog was responsible for 4000 deaths.[3]

Rising acidity of rain and snow, due to sulfur oxides from German and British smokestacks, is leading to destructive changes in trees and fish life in Norway.[4] Los Angeles' smog is killing trees in San Bernardino, 80 miles to the east.

Annual U.S. property damage from air pollution is estimated at $12 billion by a group at MIT.[5]

A million tons of oil are released into the oceans every year, both accidentally and on purpose, from oil tankers. The Sargasso Sea now contains a permanent oil slick covering several hundred square miles.[6] Petroleum constituents are entering the oceanic food chain and could eventually reach human tables.

Over one billion pounds of active DDT still exist, either in the soil or in rivers, lakes, and the ocean.[7] As it moves up the food chain, DDT is progressively concentrated—the amount found in nursing mothers' milk is often two to six times greater than that allowed in milk for commercial sale.

The Political Response

Unfortunately, the response of the politicians to such events is distressingly predictable. Politicans have been turning handsprings in their eagerness to latch onto an issue that appears to be as safe as the flag and apple pie. As with any other issue, the politicians have proceeded to do only what they know best how to do: creating programs and bureaus and appropriating tax money to finance them. Thus, Nixon's 1970 State of the Union message promised "the most comprehensive and costly program in the nation's history," spearheaded by a "muscled, direct-action agency." To which Senator Muskie replied, "We [the politicans] must spend much more [of the taxpayers'] money."[8] Over 1200 measures affecting water resources alone were introduced into the 1969–70 session of Congress; 12 Senate committees and 13 House committees vied for the ecology spotlight.

How well do the government programs work? Several examples will illustrate the drawbacks inherent in politicizing environmental problems. One difficulty already much in evidence is that more than one government wants to get in on the action, leading to conflicting regulations and legal hassles. Inter-governmental disputes are of minor consequence, however, compared with the defects inherent in government regulatory agencies. As Ralph Nader and others are painfully discovering, there seems to be a regular pattern in the history of such agencies; they invariably come to represent and serve the special interests of the established companies in the industry being regulated. The ICC (Interstate Commerce Commission), the FTC (Federal Trade Commission), the FDA (Food and Drug Administration)—all have been investigated by Nader's Raiders over the last few years and the same pattern has appeared in each. The main function of the agency has turned out to be protecting the regulated industry from competition, while giving the government the appearance of protecting the consumer from the industry. All of which works out nicely for the Congressmen passing the regulations (who can pose as champions of the people), the industry leaders (who can get by with far less effort and uncertainty) and the regulatory agency bureaucrats (who can look forward to fat retirement jobs on the boards of directors of the regulated industries).

Those advocating the regulatory agency approach to environmental problems have given no reasons for thinking that the behavior of *new* agencies would turn out to be any different. Indeed, although the National Air Pollution Control Agency is only a few years old, there is already evidence of the same process in action. An Associated Press story disclosed that between 70 and 80 percent of all new cars coming off the assembly lines in 1970 did not meet the NAPCA exhaust emission standards, even though this was required by the Air Quality Act of 1967.[9] Rep. Paul Rogers disclosed ". . . what's more amazing is that the NAPCA knows this and *has known this.*" What has been going on is simple: the auto manufacturers submitted hand-tuned *prototype* automobiles to NAPCA for testing; NAPCA obligingly assumed that because the prototypes met the standards, the production models would too, hence, they never bothered to check the production models!

In a similar vein, former Secretary of the Interior Hickel blasted Chevron Oil for not meeting Interior Department regulations regarding safety valves on the offshore rig that leaked tons of oil into the Gulf of Mexico. The U.S. Geological Survey stated that Chevron had committed *347* violations of federal drilling regulations.[10] It would appear that years of living with government regulations and placating officials have led the oil industry into the usual relationship with its regulators. The normal emphasis, rather than being on protecting the environment, is on getting away with as much as possible, with the tacit approval of the friendly regulators. Given the thoroughly politicized nature of the situation, incidents like the Santa Barbara and Gulf Coast oil spills are inevitable. Although proposals for new agencies and stronger regulations continue to be advanced, it seems highly unlikely that they will accomplish much more than creating many new government jobs, winning votes for pollution-conscious legislators, and reducing competition in still more industries.

Several liberal Senators have been trying a somewhat different approach. Senator Gaylord Nelson has introduced a Constitutional amendment asserting "the right of every American to a decent environment."[11] Senator Henry Jackson's proposed amendment (defeated) to the 1969 National Environmental Policy Act included an "Environmental Bill of Rights" asserting that "each person has a fundamental and inalienable right to a healthful environment." One can sympathize with the Senators' realization that a fundamental change in the legal system is required, but unfortunately, the facts cannot be changed by mere legislative whim. There can be no such thing as a *right* to a "healthful environment"—could we eliminate the flu or malaria by declaring them illegal? Nor can there be a right to a "decent" environment, since that term can mean different legitimate ends to different people. To some environmentalists, a decent environment would be one without freeways, power lines, and subdivisions. To pass Senator Nelson's amendment would be to abandon any pretext of objective law, in favor of an orgy of subjectivism and interest-group warfare, as each group sought to exert control over everyone else, to ensure that *its* version of a "decent environment" was enforced.

Some Other Ominous Responses

As bad as the political proposals are, they are but a sample of the sloppy thinking running rampant outside the strictly political arena. Perhaps because the problems of the environment are so large and complex, many otherwise reasonable people seem unable or unwilling to deal rationally with them; since we've never faced such problems before, they appear to be saying, our past experience is irrelevant. Economists, and even businessmen are lamenting the "fact" that the mechanism cannot deal with pollution—not that it has so far failed to do so, but that it is inherently *incapable* of doing so.

Thus, we find David Kiefer, Senior Editor of *Chemical and Engineering News* writing that:

> The classical concept that an economy's resources are allocated most efficiently through the free interplay in the market place of supply and demand, prices and utility, may prove less meaningful in the future. The time-honored theory that a market economy works best when buyers and sellers are permitted to act unhampered in their own interests through countless individual transactions will seem less in touch with reality.[12]

At last year's American Economic Association meeting in New York, Harvard economist Kenneth J. Arrow pointed out that pollution is evidence of a wide divergence between the "private costs" and "social costs" of goods, the latter including environmental effects. Arrow considers the price system to be incapable of handling such "externalities," and claims that "society would be better off if it developed some 'nonmarket mechanisms' for allocating resources where private costs and social costs were substantially different."[13] At the same meeting John Kenneth Galbraith, after blaming pollution on the "sovereign" producer's careless pursuit of consumer satisfaction, called for " 'the replacement of the sovereign producer with the sovereign state' in determining society's pattern of consumption." Galbraith elsewhere has attacked the concept of economic growth, as indicated by a rising GNP. Likewise, Kenneth Boulding states that GNP is a measure appropriate to the "cowboy economy" of the frontier, in which production and consumption ("throughput") are considered good by definition.[14] However, in the "spaceman economy" foreseen by him, the concern will not be with *growth,* but rather with the efficiency by which a *fixed* level of activity is maintained. In this static economy, throughput will be minimized, not maximized.

Although Galbraith and Boulding are taking fairly radical views for economists, they sound conservative compared to the gung-ho environmentalists, some of whom are denouncing technology, *as such,* as the cause of pollution. Microbiologist Barry Commoner, in a *Time* cover story, called for a "complete overhaul of our progress through technology ethic."[15] One of the classic papers developing this rationale is the 1967 *Science* article by UCLA historian Lynn White entitled "The Historic Roots of Our Ecological Crisis."[16] White searches the history of Western thought and finds that the dominant view has always been that man should have dominion over nature. This view, White admits, helped pave the way for Western man's technological developments, from water power to agricultural mechanization to the steam engine; similarly, in the nineteenth century this view of man helped to foster the marriage of the scientific approach to knowledge with rapidly-developing practical technology, leading to the massive technological achievements of the twentieth century. All of this does not seem to impress White very much; focusing on the side effects of this technology, he argues that more science and technology are not going to prevent a "disastrous ecological backlash" and that what *is* needed is to "find a new religion, or rethink our old one." White recommends giving up the man-against-nature view, in favor of the ideals of St. Francis of Assisi and Zen Buddhism.

The New Left, needless to say, has picked up on this line of thought with a vengeance. A recent Los Angeles *Free Press* article exemplifies this viewpoint:

> The Greek rationalism of Aristotle, the Roman engineering mentality, the biblical anthropomorphic injunction to "have dominion over the land and subdue every creeping thing," the post-Enlightenment notions of growth and progress, the present technical corporate economic systems motivated by competition—all dominate the Western mentality of man against nature. Where nature works toward harmony, cooperation, and interdependence, advanced industrial society works toward growth, competition, and independence. The advanced nation state works in direct opposition to those basic life-giving *instincts* which have nourished our billion-year evolution. To repeat: *the domination of man by man and man over nature are two sides of the same coin.*[17]

Such self-serving "analyses" suggest that serious thinking remains to be done, to determine the true nature of the problems, their causes, and possible solutions.

Defining the Problem

What is really going on out there in the environment? What are the relevant facts, what are the problems, and what should be done about them? The most obvious fact is that there is a real and increasingly serious pollution problem. *Pollution may be defined as the transfer of harmful matter or energy to the person or property of another, without the latter's consent.* Thus, oil spilled on a beach, soot falling on a house, sulfur dioxide impinging on a man's lungs—all are cases in which the by-product of some sort of legitimate productive activity is carelessly discarded from the producer's property (factory, automobile, etc.) causing harm to the person or property of someone else.

Why do we have such serious amounts of pollution in a country supposedly based firmly on the right to life and property? The first reason is that, for the most part, serious pollution is a fairly recent phenomenon. It *used* to be true, as the engineering textbooks blithely state, that the air or a river or the ocean was an "infinite sink," i.e., a body whose mass is so great that its essential properties are unchanged by the miniscule additions that man could make, in the form of smoke or chemicals or sewage. (Norman Mailer summed it up in his campaign for mayor of New York, "Remember when you were a kid and they said that air is invisible . . . and it was?") For centuries, pollution existed only in specific locations (like factory towns), from which one was always free to leave if bothered by the pollution.

Only in mid-twentieth century did the combination of accelerating population and a rapidly-raising standard of living produce widespread pollution of such a magnitude that large numbers of people were aware of definite harm to themselves or their property. Unfortunately, our slow-moving, mixed-premise legal system has been extremely negligent in providing people with full protection. As Murray Rothbard recently pointed out,[18] when the courts have been confronted with cases of industrial polluters vs. injured citizens, the courts have generally ruled in favor of industry, considering pollution to be a "necessary evil." Thus, the absence in the law of a clear-cut, consistent definition of rights has allowed the present situation to develop.

The level of pollution would be nowhere near as great if the population were not expanding so rapidly, giving rise to more and more cars, power plants, sewage, etc. Thus, a second fact of central importance is that population is growing rapidly all over the world, greatly affecting any consideration of pollution, conservation and use of resources, or economic growth. In this regard, there is an important lesson to be learned from the population problems of the underdeveloped countries.

Experts in population biology, such as Dr. Paul Ehrlich of Stanford, warn that in most of these countries the rate of population growth is rapidly outstripping the growth in food supply, to the point where famines can be expected within five to ten years. How has this situation come about? The single most important cause has been governmental. Acting in accordance with their collectivist philosophies, the governments of these countries, aided by the U.S., enacted massive public health programs aimed at wiping out many diseases that had previously taken a heavy toll. As a result, the death rate dropped very substantially. The birth rate of the now-larger population remained the same, however, as people continued having the large numbers of children that they had traditionally needed to have in order to offset the high infant mortality rate. Oblivious to economic reality, the governments of these countries removed the "feedback" of increased costs of food, shelter, education, etc. that normally accompany a larger family size, by attempting to supply these services for "free." When combined with the people's ignorance of and/or hostility toward birth control, such policies guaranteed famine, given the primitive state of these countries' pre-capitalist economies.

Welfare programs have much the same effect on people in developed countries like the U.S.—destroying the link between family size and economic reality by relieving people of the responsibility for their own lives and actions. The consequences have not been as severe in the U.S. because the percentage of the population affected is fairly small. Nevertheless the population explosion does pose significant problems for this country. First of all, as population growth increases the demand for electricity, automobiles, and manufactured goods (all of which pose pollution problems) will increase. Even now the effectiveness of automotive pollution-control devices has been largely offset by the increased number of cars on the road. Today's new power plants are ten times the size of those of a decade ago, and nuclear power plants posing even greater environmental hazards are being pushed as the only way to keep pace with the demand for electricity. Most sewage systems are overloaded, and water shortages are beginning to occur. In addition, increased population means the conversion of more and more wilderness land into subdivisions, parking lots, etc., making escape from crowded urban areas less and less feasible. A more serious result is that changes occur in ecological cycles that could have serious long-term consequences.

The third major factor, then, is that ecology can no longer be ignored as an ivory-tower science. The most important legitimate point that Barry Commoner and Paul Ehrlich are making is that one's actions can have far-reaching consequences on other people's lives. "Pollution," as defined previously, refers to rather direct and obvious actions—the direct transfer of matter or energy to an unwilling victim's person or property. Ecology deals with actions that are much less direct. When a farmer uses DDT to kill insects in his field, most of it eventually winds up in the ocean, where it is concentrated by algae. DDT reduces both the respiration and reproduction rates of algae; thus, since algae serve as a major oxygen producer and as the base of the oceanic food chain, DDT in algae threatens both man's air and his food supply. The seemingly innocent actions of thousands of farmers can thereby have disastrous consequences for others.

Large-scale destruction of forests has similarly widespread effects. The production of oxygen from photosynthesis is reduced, the bird population is reduced (allowing insects and rodents to get out of hand), and the danger of erosion and flooding is increased. Building a large dam changes many biological cycles, due to the flooding of a river; in addition, seismic disturbances can result, due to the changed loading of the earth's crust.[19] The point of all this is to demonstrate that ecology, by determining the large-scale, indirect effects of man's actions on the life-support system of the earth, is revealing many facts that until now have scarcely been noticed. Neither our legal system nor political philosophy have dealt adequately with such facts, to date.

A Libertarian Analysis

Essentially, the problem boils down to the following: a continually-expanding population poses increasingly serious problems of direct (pollution) and indirect (ecological) disturbance of the natural environment. Such disturbances can, and often do, threaten the lives and property of large numbers of people. Politicians want to deal with such problems in political fashion—by erecting ever-greater forests of regulation and investing bureaucracies with ever more power to control people's lives. Romanticists, including some economists, ecologists, and New Leftists, want to force people back to the simpler things, so that their demand for electricity, automobiles, etc., will be reduced, thereby reducing pollution. When rising population causes even this simple life to lead to pollution, they would forcibly restrict population growth. The common denominator of all these solutions is *force,* and their frequent concomitant is a profound distrust of technology.

The libertarian, by contrast, argues that the key element in any just solution is the individual—both the individually-responsible polluter and the individually-harmed victim. A libertarian analysis, therefore, can provide two results: it can demonstrate that force, of the type practiced by governments, has been inappropriate in dealing with ecological problems; and it can point the way to solutions consistent with all the relevant aspects of the problem, not the least of which is human liberty.

As pointed out earlier, the single most important reason for the existence of a pollution problem is that government has failed to protect people's lives and property from assaults by pollutants. Oystermen have their livelihood destroyed by chemicals or heated water or sewage dumped into a lake or river—and *no one is held liable.* Homeowners can have their houses damaged by soot or sulfur oxides —and *no one is liable.* Motorists can drive around in cars spewing forth carcinogenic exhaust products—and *no one is liable* for the resulting respiratory disease and deaths. The government, supposedly the protector of our lives and property, has been so busy building bureaucratic empires and making volumes of regulations that it has failed to establish full liability for the actions of polluters. This failing, alone, makes government the primary culprit.

But there are also innumerable instances in which the government has encouraged pollution by its positive actions. Government action is, by definition, coercive. This means, in general, that the projects engaged in by the State are carried out differently from projects carried out by individuals or companies. In the absence of coercive power, private parties must rely on economic means for accomplishing things; hence, they are concerned with long-term efficiency, in order to maximize long-term profits. The automobile, the source of 50 to 75 percent of all smog, has become our dominant mode of transportation partly because of massive governmental subsidies over the years, in the form of highways financed by tax money, on rights-of-way acquired by the coercive power of eminent domain. In a completely free market, the number of privately-purchased rights-of-way devoted to inefficient modes of transportation like automobiles would be far less than at present. The entrepreneur seeking to maximize his profits would attempt to move the maximum number of people over his right-of-way, with the minimum expenditure of energy (fuel). The throughput (people moved per hour) of rapid transit trains is from ten to twenty times greater than that of automobiles.[20] Thus, in a completely free market, where the cost of automobile transportation would reflect the road owner's "opportunity cost" for alternative uses for his right-of-way, automobile transportation would be much less popular than at present. Many right-of-way owners would find rapid transit systems the most profitable, resulting in less overall air pollution, due to the latter's greater efficiency.

Other government-induced distortions of the economy come readily to mind. The State often asserts ownership of scarce resources such as beaches and scenic mountain areas, in order to preserve them for the benefit of all. To carry out this objective, the State allows virtually unlimited access to everyone, resulting in the familiar "tragedy of the commons" discussed by Garrett Hardin.[21] Since none of the users owns the land, he has no qualms about using it, overusing it, and abusing it; each man's additional use causes him more gain than loss, so additional users keep crowding in. Hence, we have filthy, overcrowded beaches, smog in Yosemite Valley, etc. In a free market, by contrast, the owners of such scarce resources would charge a price sufficiently high to ration out the supply among those most willing to pay; this way the resources could be preserved, rather than being slowly destroyed.

In addition to its negligence in defining pollution liability, and its pollution-inducing distortions of the economy, the government destroys the environment in yet another way—directly. The Army Corps of Engineers has a well-deserved reputation for creating classic public works boondoggles, at the expense of the environment. "Operating with virtual impunity, it continues to wreak ecological havoc across the land," writes Justice William O. Douglas.[22] The Corps, like government agencies in general, is liable to no one. Similarly without liability for the land it destroys is the Agriculture Department's Forest Service, which runs the National Forests. Although private industry has long been blamed for wholesale destruction of forests, the fact is that most such destruction has been on National Forest lands, for which the Forest Service bureaucrats grant cutting rights. Since the companies do not own the land, they have no long-term stake in conserving any particular plot; hence, they have sometimes leveled them to the ground. Forests owned by large lumber producers like Georgia-Pacific and U.S. Plywood are nationally managed, with the emphasis on long-range profitability. These forests are scientifically cut and reforested to assure a continuing supply of trees into the future. The Atomic Energy Commission persuaded Congress to pass a law (the Price-Anderson Act) exempting power companies from liability for damages in the event of a nuclear reactor disaster. The AEC is a law unto itself, being charged by law with promoting the use of atomic power, while at the same time being the sole judge and enforcer of radiation standards. Such conflicts of interest and perversions of liability exist throughout the bureaucratic structure.

In short, the preceding examples have pointed out how the government allows, encourages, and accomplishes the destruction of the environment. Such government coercion is obviously not going to *solve* the ecology problem. Yet government exists, and will continue to loom as a major factor in any solution. Given this fact, what sort of actions does a libertarian view suggest?

A Pollution Solution

For pollution, the best solution has been pointed out by economist Murray Rothbard, among others.[23] No programs, no bureaus, no tax dollars are required; all that is needed is that the courts recognize that all polluters must bear *full liability* for any and all harm caused by their pollution products. Once this principle is firmly established in law, companies will find it in their interest to spend large sums of money installing pollution-control equipment, rather than being constantly involved in lawsuits and paying out damages to thousands of people. The costs of pollution control, of course, would ultimately be borne by the consumers of the firms' products, i.e., by those who *choose* to associate with the firm, rather than being passed on to innocent third parties in the form of pollution (or as taxes). Thus, the market mechanism is the only truly *just* way of allocating the costs of pollution control, of internalizing the externalities.

Given the full-liability principle, the problem is reduced primarily to a technological one of determining what levels of various pollutants cause what sort of damage. Automobile pollution is somewhat complicated by the fact that there are many thousands of individual sources, each contributing only a small fraction of the total. Yet it is a fact that once the quantity of a particular exhaust product (e.g., carbon monoxide) in a given locality reaches the level at which human health is endangered, then the right to emit such an exhaust product ceases to exist. Such a product has then become, literally, a poison. At that point, vehicles emitting that exhaust product can no longer be allowed in that locality.

Some conservative economists are fond of stating that the air is being polluted because we have treated it as a free good when it is really a scarce resource. They then suggest *pricing* the use of air by means of "pollution licenses" or an "effluent tax." On the surface, this solution may appear reasonable, despite the possibly grotesque world it might lead to. Unfortunately, it is an example of the most serious failing of the conservative economists: nowhere in the proposal is there any mention of *rights*. This is the same failing that has undercut advocates of capitalism for 200 years. Even today, the term "laissez-faire" is apt to bring forth images of eighteenth century English factory towns engulfed in smoke and grimy with soot. The early capitalists agreed with the courts that smoke and soot were the "price" that must be paid for the benefits of industry, i.e., that the "public interest" required the sacrifice of somebody's property rights in order that all could enjoy manufactured products. Yet laissez-faire without rights is a contradiction in terms; the laissez-faire position is based on and derived from man's rights, and can endure only when rights are held inviolable. Now, in an age of increasing awareness of the environment, this old contradiction is coming back to haunt capitalism.

It is *true* that air is a scarce resource, but one must then ask *why* it is scarce. If it is scarce because of a systematic violation of rights, then the solution is not to raise the price of the status quo, thereby sanctioning the rights-violations, but to assert the rights and demand that they be protected. The air, after all, is only a medium through which various molecules move. When a factory discharges a great quantity of sulfur dioxide molecules that enter someone's lungs and cause pulmonary edema, the factory owners have aggressed against him as much as if they had broken his leg. This point must be emphasized because it is vital to the libertarian laissez-faire position. A laissez-faire polluter is a contradiction in terms and must be identified as such. A libertarian society would be a *full-liability* society, where everyone is fully responsible for his actions and any harmful consequences they might cause. Only then will the market mechanism operate with prices that include the *full* costs of all products—there will be no externalities to pass on to innocent third parties.

A Population Solution

How does this libertarian view deal with the population problem? Essentially, it recognizes that there cannot be a population problem once there is full liability—i.e., where everyone is fully responsible for his own life and actions. The "problem" comes about when government, by action or inaction, separates actions from their consequences. How this has worked in the underdeveloped countries has already been described. The upcoming famines in parts of the world will provide an eloquent, if gruesome, demonstration of the evil consequences of the State's attempt to remove from people the full responsibility for their own lives.

But what of the United States? Is there a population problem here? To answer this question requires the realization that we do not presently live in a full-liability society. If we did, then the decision to have children and the costs of their upbringing would be entirely the responsibility of the parents involved. In such circumstances, the birth of another child would not impose any direct costs on a third party. Hence although one might not *like* a crowded country, one could not complain that the increased population was actually a threat.

Contrast this with our present society. Every child born to people on welfare is a direct economic threat to innocent third parties, since the child's existence will increase their taxes. Similarly, every child born in this country is a threat to every non-parent who is forced to pay local, state, and federal taxes to support public schools. The public school system constitutes a vast subsidy from everyone else to those who are parents of school-age children, encouraging these parents to have and raise children without having to bear the full costs of their education. Hence, not only does the system violate rights in the present, it also provides a continuing incentive for more and more people to have more and more children, secure in the knowledge that they will only have to pay a small portion of the cost of educating them. The vast extent of this subsidy makes the $600 tax exemption for each child look almost negligible.

Beyond such direct costs of increased population, until such time as full liability is required of all polluters, any increase in population will result in increased pollution (more cars, more factories, more detergents, more pesticides, more sewage), with the resulting harm to persons and property. Since full liability is not likely to come about soon, an expanding U.S. population will continue to pose a pollution threat to life and property for many years.

Given that such is the case, what position should the government take? To say that government should just do nothing (since having children is an individual concern) misses the point that we live in a society in which government is *already* actively encouraging and subsidizing the increased production of children. For the government to actually do "nothing," it will have to stop doing a host of things that it presently does. The first thing it should do would be to repeal all laws regulating sex and marriage. State governments currently restrict the sale and advertising of contraceptives and prohibit entirely the free use of abortion (except for a few states). The government also enforces traditional monogamous marriage, which has the effect of encouraging people's life-styles to fall into the typical nuclear family pattern. Other possible life-styles, such as group marriages with a few children raised by several couples, and homosexual marriages are illegal because they are "against public policy," which is presumably the maximization of child-rearing by the nuclear family. By allowing and encouraging people to choose whatever life-style they desire, the social pressure to conform and have three children like everyone else would be reduced.

In addition to these changes, all tax discrimination between single people, married people, and parents should be abolished, such that there are no longer any tax incentives favoring one life-style over another. Following these changes, the government should begin phasing out the public school system, perhaps at first by means of the education voucher system, but with the ultimate goal of returning educational expenses to where they belong—to the parents of school-age children. Finally, the government should work toward eliminating all forms of welfare, recognizing the incentives provided by the Welfare State for increasing population.

An Ecological Solution

Finally, what does a libertarian view imply for ecology? The basic principle is again full liability for one's actions. The major contribution of the ecologists is to discover the facts inherent in the complex cycles that take place in the earth's life-support system. That many of these facts are new and unfamiliar does not mean they are any less real. If everyone continues to dump DDT and other chlorinated hydrocarbons into the earth's water supply, for example, we will eventually end up short of food and oxygen. Ecology can tell us what the consequences of certain actions will be, so that we can evaluate them hopefully in advance of their causing serious harm. Clearly, the result of *some* such evaluations will be the conclusion that certain actions, if continued or engaged in, will cause demonstrable harm to human life, because of the resulting changes in the ecosystem. Such actions may legitimately be prevented, by force if necessary, since if carried out, those actions would be aggression against some or all of humanity.

This is not to say that any time an "ecologist" asserts that he doesn't like a certain factory or dam or farm or other enterprise, that it must be shut down. Ecologists don't have any magic abilities not possessed by others; the same need for rigorous, logical thinking required in any science is required by ecology. Since the epistemological principles are universal, ecologists can and must demonstrate to non-ecologists *what* facts they are concerned about, *how* they know what the implications are for action (or ceasing of action), and *why* this action is required. Unfortunately, in our less-than-rational society, this is no easy task for ecologists. For this reason, perhaps, one should not yet be hypercritical of the Ehrlichs and Commoners when they dramatize the possibilities of "eco-catastrophes." Perhaps such tactics are necessary to awaken our legislators and jurists to the need for an enlarged concept of liability.

At the same time, however, there is no excuse for tolerating an ecologist's irrational feelings about economics or technology, just because he is an expert on ecology. Thus, when Commoner calls for over-hauling our "progress through technology" ethic, it is up to rational technologists to set the record straight. This is even more necessary when non-ecologist laymen start making pronouncements about halting the "irreversible depletion of resources" or ceasing to "exploit" nature. As the preceding analysis has shown, it has been man's faulty conception of rights and responsibilities that has led to the present pollution/population/ecology crisis. Technology, to be sure, has provided various tools that man can use, but the existence of technology does not guarantee that man will use it rationally. This is determined by man's philosophical premises, particularly by his political philosophy.

Although technology can be used wisely or unwisely, it cannot really be considered neutral. Technology is inherently life-supporting in that it seeks to apply man's understanding of the facts of nature, to enable him to live on earth (or in space) more effectively. For most of recorded history, men were imprisoned by a subsistence economy in which so much effort was required merely to stay alive that there was little or nothing left for improving their physical well-being. This was the world described by Malthus, in which the size of the "economic pie" is fixed, such that one man's gain can only be procured by another man's loss. But the free market, by providing an atmosphere in which technology can flourish, can change all that. The size of the pie increases, such that everyone who participates gains.

Buckminster Fuller is one of the few people who seems fully to appreciate this significance of technology. He points out that at the turn of the century, less than 1 percent of the world's population was participating in the benefits of industrialization; by 1914 this had risen to 6 percent, by 1940 to 20 percent, and by the 1960's to 44 percent of humanity. How has this been possible, given the fixed amount of resources that the eco-fans are so worried about "depleting"? Fuller writes:

> As the percentage increased from one to 44, it meant that total organized world tonnage of metallic and metabolic resource utilization was supplying only 1%, then 6%, then 44%. During this half century of industrialization, the world's population has been increasing at a faster rate than additional resources have been discovered. That is, the ratio of world copper, mined or unmined, or of iron, mined or unmined, per capita, has been continually decreasing. Therefore this increase in numbers served has not been the result of the addition of more resources, but the consequence of scientifically-designed multiplication of the performance per unit of invested resources. Transferring communications from wire to wireless is a typical means of doing more with less.[24]

This is the essential nature of technology—finding ways of doing more with less and less use of resources, per unit of accomplishment. The supply of raw materials on "space-ship earth" is fixed; true, some can be used up in their present form (such as oil), but the law of conservation of mass states that matter is never used up—it merely changes its form. The basic chemical elements remain, available for man's ingenuity to put to better use:

> Science continually does more with less each time it obsoletes and scraps old innovations. Scrap is resolved to some part of the inventory of the 92 regenerative chemical elements. Interim improvement in technical measurement of performance makes possible an ever higher magnitude of new performance by reuse of the same quantity of the original inventory of the chemical elements.[25]

Nor is there a real need to despair over our use of energy; again, the law of conservation of energy states that energy can neither be created nor destroyed (except by a nuclear reaction, when matter is converted to energy). At present, the earth is living off of easily obtained stored-up energy (savings) such as oil and coal, yet the earth also receives daily income in the form of solar energy, at present virtually untapped. Thermonuclear fusion is a likely future development, probably before the end of this century, providing virtually unlimited energy from hydrogen, the simplest of all elements.

Thus, far from being a threat to mankind's survival, technology provides the means for enabling all of mankind to enjoy a better life, participating in the "industrial equation," by means of increasing the usefulness of our supply of resources. Technology produces real wealth, in the form of the increased capability of man to do things, per unit of matter or energy expended. Redistributing the existing wealth provides no net gain. Wealth must be produced, and technology is the means by which this is accomplished.

But only in an atmosphere of full-liability freedom, true laissez-faire, can mankind have both ecological awareness *and* technological progress. Those who cry that we must choose between a technology that destroys the environment or a simplified, static, no-growth society misunderstand both technology and ecology. *Nature, to be commanded, must be obeyed;* to have dominion over the earth, man must understand *all* the facts and must act accordingly. A full-liability society, having learned this lesson, can have its cake and eat it too.

References

1. Thomas K. Sherwood, "Must We Breathe Sulfur Oxides?" *Technology Review* (January 1970), pp. 25–31.
2. "Lead Concentration in City Air Increases," *Chemical & Engineering News* (March 9, 1970), p. 42.
3. Sherwood, *op. cit.*
4. "Pollution Defies Europe's Borders," *The New York Times* (Jan. 10, 1970), p. 24.
5. "Smog's Four Horsemen," *Technology Review* (Jan. 1970), p. 72.
6. "Oil Called Peril to Food Supply in Sea," *The New York Times* (Jan. 16, 1970).
7. Steven H. Wodka, "Pesticides Since *Silent Spring*," *The Environmental Handbook* (New York: Ballantine Books, 1970), p. 77.
8. "Nixon Plans Massive Attack on Pollution," *Chemical & Engineering News* (February 2, 1970), p. 24.
9. "Many Assembly Line Autos Flunk Air Pollution Tests," *Associated Press* (April 3, 1970).
10. "The Crackdown on Water Polluters," *Business Week* (April 4, 1970), p. 28.

11. "Senator Nelson to Ask for Antipollution Measure," *The New York Times* (January 20, 1970).
12. "The Changing Ground Rules of Business Economics," *Chemical & Engineering News* (January 26, 1970), p. 25.
13. "Who Will Foot the Cleanup Bill?" *Business Week* (January 3, 1970), p. 64.
14. Kenneth Boulding, "The Economics of the Coming Spaceship Earth," *The Environmental Handbook, op. cit.*
15. "Economic Growth: New Doubts About an Old Ideal," *Time* (March 2, 1970), p. 74.
16. Lynn White, Jr., "The Historical Roots of Our Ecological Crisis," *Science* (March 10, 1967), pp. 1203–1207.
17. Barry Weisberg, "Politics of Ecology," *Los Angeles Free Press* (March 20, 1970), pp. 34–35. Italics added.
18. Murray N. Rothbard, "The Great Ecology Issue: Conservation and the Free Market," *The Individualist* (February, 1970), pp. 1–6.
19. Gordon J. F. MacDonald, "The Modification of Planet Earth by Man," *Technology Review* (October–November 1969), pp. 27–35.
20. William W. Hay, *Introduction to Transportation Engineering* (New York: Wiley, 1961), pp. 271–279.
21. Garrett Hardin, "The Tragedy of the Commons," *Science,* Vol. 162 (December 13, 1968), pp. 1243–1248.
22. Justice William O. Douglas, "The Public Be Damned," *Playboy* (July 1969), p. 143.
23. Rothbard, *op. cit.*
24. Buckminster R. Fuller, *Ideas and Integrities,* (Englewood Cliffs, N.J.: Prentice-Hall, 1963), pp. 251–252.
25. *Ibid.,* p. 142.

On Promoting the General Welfare

CLIFFORD HUMPHREY

In the last few years scores of books and hundreds of articles have been written about ecology. The vast majority of these publications reflect the present lack of understanding about the ecological perspective. Part of the reason for this is that the word "ecology" has been interpreted and used in various ways. It is being defined in some dictionaries as "the relationship of an organism to its environment," while contemporary writers refer to its two Greek roots from which we obtain the meaning "household knowledge." This concept is much more accurate and forces upon us a very integrated and complete way of thinking about our basic situation. The notion of household implies a tranquil process that requires the proper workings of many parts and processes to function. Such a view admits to the possibility of upsetting the household by knocking one or more of the parts or processes off balance. Therefore, ecology is not something new or separate from social issues. All social problems are clearly related to the mismanagement of the common household. Maintenance of our present society is dependent on the exploitation of people and the destruction of our life-support system. This is a vital point and its importance has been missed by scientists, writers, commentators, politicians, activists and other citizens.

A social group's success or failure at promoting its own welfare is related to two major factors: the adequacy and relevance of the

Clifford Humphrey is Director of the Ecology Action Educational Institute. He was the founder of Ecology Action and is the author of numerous articles on ecology and a book, *What's Ecology?*

information base upon which priorities are developed and decisions made; and the quality and equity of the administration of these priorities and decisions. The ecological perspective is a new vantage point from which to determine what constitutes adequate and relevant information, and by what parameters its administration should be evaluated. This perspective is constructed from a new synthesis of data about ourselves and our physical and social environment. It recognizes the entire surface of the planet and all life thereon as a single integrated household. This recognition denotes a process that is an ongoing interplay between the three components of this common household. They are the house itself (natural habitats and various constructed dwellings), the occupants (all forms of life), and the various relationships that exist between the two. These relationships are of two types: between the household and occupants, and among the occupants themselves.

The continuity of human societies within this household is threatened from three directions, reflecting these basic household components. The first is "natural disasters" such as droughts, earthquakes, and severe storms. These are household fluctuations and are related to such things as solar storms, orbit of the moon and earth, and the shifting of the earth's crust, which are irregular but relatively cyclic. Sometimes several such factors combine to produce household disaster. For example, an unusually high tide, a function of the closeness of lunar orbit, and unusual solar storm activity, which may change the course of the jet stream across North America allowing warm rain to fall on the snow peaks in the Sierra, could combine to bring about disastrous floods in the delta area of central California.

The second danger to household continuity and tranquility is a breakdown of relationships between its members. The social fabric tears until the needs of its individual members are no longer being met and the purpose of the group is not accomplished.

The third danger is that relationships between occupants and household will result in cumulative and/or irreparable damage to household occupants. This household is also the common life-support system composed of the natural physical environment and the processes that nourish it—rainfall, sunshine, and decomposition. Man's activities have become so pervasive that it is hard to find any portion of the earth's surface or process that has not been altered by our actions. These alterations are seriously threatening the life support system upon which we are dependent. This occurrence is something that we never consciously decided to do, but now we are faced with recognizing its implications. Our actions are not only undermining our own support but are degrading the habitats and food supply of many other animals, all of which play a part in maintaining the fitness of the common household.

Any government that is mandated by its people to provide for their welfare and security in perpetuity is obligated to actively prevent the occurrence of these dangers. The situation we face today as a survival crisis is a complex mixture of all these dangers. The crisis is unprecedented in both magnitude and scope. Many of our cities are built in almost total disregard of flood plain and earthquake dangers. Reserves of food as security against drought and blight are almost nonexistent.

Social inequities have become so numerous and serious that their immediate demands and our reacting to their various social manifestations is consuming time and resources that should be applied to long range solutions through eradication of the conditions of scarcity and racism that spawn them.

The general welfare has been badly damaged by practices developed in the short history of this country, and the speed with which it can be repaired has been unnecessarily retarded by the incomplete understanding of the ecological perspective. Many who have suffered and bled because of long standing abuses are today opposed to the ecology movement. People within the ecology movement claim that they do not understand how this could be, but the truth is that this movement has misrepresented itself—not so much because of intent but because the time has not been taken to study and think and work out the implications of this perspective.

Household knowledge provides a basic frame of reference that can show us how we can go about our activities without destroying our physical surroundings or exploiting each other. But to do this, we have to understand how the household functions and acquire the knowledge that we have not realized that we needed.

Our cultural aspirations and biological requirements are fulfilled at great cost to other people and the household parts and processes. It has been fashionable to blame technology, but the fault lies primarily with the misapplication of science through a naïve economic system. Traditional market economics have forced and led us into a situation that rewards us for jeopardizing our future welfare.

A *"New"* Land and an Old Culture

Our country started with a vision about increased freedom, security, and welfare, followed by frustration and a revolution. But as we look around us today, we find that only the patterns and instruments of exploitation have changed. Those who responded to Thomas Paine's *Common Sense* knew that they could do better for themselves and their families than be taxed and governed by the country they had left. The settlers made a move to be on their own, but they were only equipped with the culture and information that eighteenth-century Europe had given them.

The vastness of America and its plentiful resources provided the illusion that the republic was new and different and had solved many of the problems that were plaguing European cities and countryside. The colonies and the adjacent lands had not been previously depleted or exploited by the development of the culture and technology recently imported and applied to the land. This illusion was so total that a false pride was generated. The thrust of "manifest destiny" squashed Indian nations, and displaced many people in the interest of an uncluttered map. History has recorded the difficulties of felling the forests and wrenching stumps and boulders from the land; of the miners overcoming tremendous obstacles as they gathered minerals from the earth. But the factory towns of nineteenth-century America were similar to the slums of industrial Europe. Public health problems became severe, wages were low, and the hours long. The activities of "settling" the "new" world set the pace for our present single-minded approach to security and welfare.

National security and family well being was a matter of economics, a function of an expanding commerce that consumed ever-increasing amounts of raw materials. Such things were not seen as a threat to the general welfare. Rather, they were thought to enhance it.

Our government was impaneled without having an adequate information base or procedural outline with which to carry out their charge. The government in which we placed our trust to carry out the vision of increased security and welfare has been overseeing the destruction of the lands within the republic and the people upon them. This understanding is not so much an indictment, as it is proof that our government has been operating without enough relevant information, and that past administrative policies have thereby created social inequities and perpetuated environmental degradation. Man's conception of his basic surroundings has been that of a collection of nation-states separated by oceans and barren land areas. While cultural groups of each of these nation-states speak of the people's well-being in governmental and religious documents, few, if any, have taken the necessary steps to assure the well being of their citizens throughout time. Relationships between these nation-states have for the most part been a function of avaricious foreign trade programs. In the past, the price was the only concern—not, for example, that a fishery was endangered by silt from a logging operation that yielded timber for export. As we institutionalized our economic processes, the long-range impact on the earth's life-support system was not imagined or sought by its propagators.

While the ecological perspective offers a new vantage point for criticism of and comment upon all of man's past actions, its greatest potential lies in helping us to look ahead. As cultural man learns more about the ecosphere and his impact upon it, he will, if he is to survive, establish strict conditions for the satiation of his needs and the satisfaction of his wants. The slow movement toward automobile emission standards is part of the beginning of this process. However, such standards will prove to be inadequate because they only deal with poisons per car, or per unit of exhaust, instead of total poisons added to a particular air basin. This is a way of making the smog legal, just as a small fine for industrial pollution actually constitutes a small application fee for a license to pollute. Pollution abatement by itself cannot promote the general welfare.

We have not been in the habit of thinking in terms of absolutes— the existence of only so much water, only so much topsoil, and that only a limited amount of any foreign substance can enter an ecosystem without disrupting or damaging it. When our country was founded, the general welfare had to do with commerce, defense, and personal freedom. Our constitution reflects these beliefs. However, the pursuit of these beliefs without ecological constraints has yielded a way of life whereby we now have a vested interest in our own destruction. Not only have we already seriously degraded our surroundings and perturbed many ecosystem functions, but we have initiated damaging practices upon whose continuance our institutions are themselves dependent. Our economy grows as capital is created. It is created unto itself with no consideration for ecosystem function. To increase the availability of capital we have organized the concept of credit. This extension of credit takes for granted the continued destructive practices that can turn the profit expected. Not only is the practice fundamentally naïve, but it is disastrously self-correcting. The practice will stop when we have wrung the earth dry.

This concept of credit is linked to the concept of land ownership. In terms of life-support system dependence there is no difference between land and sky. But one is easier to fence than the other. As our numbers increase it becomes essential that each portion of the earth's surface be used at its optimum potential function in this finite system. Land ownership is now perceived as permission, even an obligation, to produce a profit for its owners and so benefit the economy. Do we live to support an economy that is devouring us? Or do we facilitate an economy that serves the general welfare?

Preoccupation with pollution abatement at the federal level is not an adequate stance in the face of the present dangers. It may be understood that our situation is unprecedented, but as yet we are not actively searching for unprecedented solutions. A look at the impacts we are precipitating will help clarify the task before us.

Basic Household Impacts

It makes little difference if soil is mismanaged in Africa or Iceland, the result is that the planet becomes less able to support life. Automobiles mix lead into the common air supply wherever they are driven. We know of many such examples of pollution and environmental destruction from the reports in our newspapers, magazines, etc. These can be classified as four basic kinds of impact: *energy inequity, open cycles, household contamination, and surface destruction.*

Energy inequity: It would be a pleasant experience to be able to put a hundred dollars into a savings account and withdraw a thousand. An even wilder fantasy would be to imagine perpetuating the situation. Unfortunately, in real life one rarely gets something for nothing. The process of life on earth is powered by solar radiation. This simple realization leads us to the most insidious of the impacts on our life support system. Mankind in general and Western man in particular, depend upon the availability of more energy than is currently being supplied by the sun. We rely on petroleum fuels to plant our crops, harvest them, prepare and deliver food to the stores, or bring the food to our homes. The same applies to building our houses, lighting them, heating them, and cooling them.

This energy inequity is dangerous in three ways. First, as the fossil fuels (petroleum, natural gas, and coal) are consumed, surplus heat is produced and radiated out into space. Geophysicists are alarmed that we may be in danger of warming the earth's atmosphere enough to upset the self-regulating systems that maintain a constant temperature range in our household. It is conceivable that these systems have a threshold tolerance and a slight excess beyond that unknown point may precipitate a rapid, unknown and unexpected result. Knowledge of such a theoretical threshold without knowledge of a specific tolerance for handling non-solar heat calls for extreme caution. Such considerations have led to the prediction of an inevitable return to muscle power. (Both human and animal labor stem from the utilization of our daily solar energy ration.) Dr. Harrison Brown at the California Institute of Technology in Pasadena has pointed out that the heating of homes, offices, and plants could be done directly with solar heat. This process could also help to reduce the amount of heat unnaturally reflected from manmade surfaces in urban areas.

Rather than only finding alternate energy sources such as solar or atomic energy for our present needs, it is likely that we will also have to find ways to lower our present energy needs through technology and social reorganization. Alternatives to our present style of life must be considered as the supply of fossil fuel diminishes.

The second danger is that the combustion of fossil fuels results in tremendous quantities of carbon dioxide being added to the atmosphere. All of the effects of its addition and subsequent displacement of other gases is not known. On people the effect of additional CO_2 is similar to living at a higher elevation with less oxygen available per breath. It is a richer mixture for plants as they require carbon dioxide for their metabolism. Aside from the metabolic effects of increases in carbon dioxide it appears that carbon dioxide may also restrict or retard the radiation of heat leaving the biosphere. If this is the case, we are creating a greenhouse effect by continued use of fossil fuels. As more CO_2 is released into the air, heat is trapped, causing a gradual increase in global temperature.

The last way this energy inequity dependence is dangerous relates to the artificial and temporary life style it may foster. If a human population of fixed number discovered coal, oil, and gas and switched over to them for as long as they lasted, and *did not* increase their population size, they could probably switch back to forest resources (recent and renewable solar energy) when the fossil fuels were exhausted. However, if the possibilities of fossil fuels were seen as a means to reorganize the society, and resulted in increased numbers, because "production" could be increased, dependence on a finite resource could be disastrous.

Open cycles: This refers both to natural organic cycles that man has interrupted and to nonorganic extractions that man could make into a complete, though unnatural cycle. In a "natural" situation, leaves, fruit, and nuts will fall to the ground and return to the soil. Man takes many crops from the fields, forests and sea without returning any organic material to the ground. The wasted organic materials from food harvesting and processing, kitchen scraps and sewage contain trace mineral elements that are necessary for proper plant growth and human nutrition. Because these elements are not being recycled (returned to the soil) our food is losing its nutritional value and plants are losing their vitality. The U.S. Department of Public Health points out that bread made in 1947 had twice the nutritional value of bread today. The reason is primarily the nature of our culture. Expedient merchandising practices allow the wheat germ, the most valuable part of wheat, to be taken off in order to keep insects out of the flour in storage.

The second type of cycle could be represented by the tin can. Tin and steel ores are both finite yet we do not extend ourselves to preserve these resources.

Types of Open Cycles

   A. Organic material, interrupted natural cycles
      1 Sewage
      2 Food processing scraps
      3 Garbage
      4 Paper and wood
      5 Human skeletons
   B. Inorganic material, man-created open cycles
      1 Aluminum cans
      2 Tin cans
      3 Glass containers
      4 Metal objects

Household contamination: This type of impact is more commonly referred to as pollution, but that term is rather vague and could describe various specific impacts under all of the headings. This impact factor is the most diverse and presents the very difficult problem of trying to assign a relative value to these varied forms of contamination. That is to say, would it be "better" to have three units of heat and one unit of radiation contamination from a nuclear power than the chemical contamination (SO_2) from a coal fired generating plant?

Types of Household Contamination

   A. Chemical
      1 Placed on the environment purposely: pesticides, herbicides.
      2 Placed in the environment without purpose: flume gases, tire wear, automobile exhausts.

B. Heat
  1 Solar heat reflected from man-made surfaces.
  2 Heat generated by man at the earth's surface, atomic fission, burning of fossil fuels.
C. Psychological
  1 Conflict over desire for goods and services and ability to obtain (use) these goods and services.
  2 Over-stimulation through too many visual, audible, and other sensory inputs.
  3 Cultural stress through an obvious conflict between reality and culturally prescribed behavior.
  4 Social stress from population density.
D. Noise
  1 People in crowded areas
  2 Industrial operations
  3 Household activities (dwelling place)
  4 Operation of vehicles, trains, planes
E. Nonbiodegradable material
  1 Plastics
  2 Detergents
  3 Concrete
  4 Glass
F. Radiation
  1 X-ray machines
  2 Bomb testing and manufacture
  3 Nuclear excavations and gas field activation
  4 Nuclear power plant
  5 Uranium mine dumps
  6 Stored and discarded waste or by-products

Surface destruction: This category includes any damage caused by humans to the surface of our life support system. Clearing the land to make room for different types of construction projects is a relatively straightforward case of obliteration; such things as logging, open pit mining, tailing dumps, and settlement ponds are also straightforward and easy to classify. In terms of production on a year-to-year basis, the earth is now producing food of different types, and total production for all forms of life has decreased. In other words, people food has displaced animal food; one species displacing many others. Agricultural practices have also increased soil and wind erosion of farmlands and have damaged some soils by salination. This results from the evaporation of large quantities of irrigation water which leaves residues in the soil.

Other agricultural areas have seemingly become more fertile because of careful methods. It is possible for a farm to be producing well now, but actually losing topsoil every year. Soils are also damaged by compaction from farm equipment. In most cases these kinds of agricultural impacts depend on local conditions and are not as straightforward as an open pit mine or a parking lot.

Types of Surface Destruction

A. Direct obliteration
   1 Highways
   2 Roads
   3 Parking lots
   4 Railroads
   5 Airports
   6 Asphalt and concrete surfaces
   7 Surface space for all buildings except greenhouses
B. Indirect destruct on
   1 Mining activities
   2 Logging activities
   3 Man-precipitated disasters such as mud slides, forest fires, floods
   4 Agricultural impacts

The Survival Crisis

Before this crisis can be clearly understood one more point remains to be made about the ecosphere. The life process itself provides a buffer between its biological needs and the unfiltered harshness of the sun and the cold bleakness of space. The atmosphere moderates the temperature, and the soil moderates water availability. This buffer also includes storehouses of needed nutrients. Millions of years of experience with cyclic climatic changes have established these requirements. The common climatic changes are annual but meteorologists are now sure that many others have a ten, twenty-five, and even one hundred year cycle. Seeds lying dormant for years in deserts waiting for a rain, a cover of topsoil that can withstand a long dry period, and many more examples comprise these reserves. We are now mining the buffer required for the continuity of life, the very system that supports us and other life forms.

Agricultural experts proclaim to the world that food production is increasing, and that is true. But no one is talking about the long-range effects of such exploitive practices on the quantity or quality of the planet's soils. Our wells are going deeper and deeper into the earth, sucking up its waters. The poisons required to maintain our very precariously balanced mono-agricultural techniques are toxic to soil organisms and are poisonous to many animals. Bee populations have been decimated in many growing areas forcing farmers and orchidists to hire bees annually for proper pollination. It has been learned that usage of the SST may bring about the rapid deterioration of stratospheric ozone, thus letting in blinding or even fatal ultraviolet radiation. Some of the things we have done in ignorance of household functions have in effect set a trap for ourselves. Mercury from industrial operations has resulted in a few known cases of acute mercury poisoning of people. These industrial operations are usually adjacent to waters that exit to the sea through a very busy harbor. Because of increased erosion upstream, sedimentation is increased, which requires more dredging. Sizes and numbers of ships are increasing, requiring an expansion of port facilities. The most common method of dredge spoils removal is to dump them at sea, in deep water and/or in a swift current. Any mercury, cadmium, arsenic, lead, and other toxic compounds or substances will be released in relatively large volume into the marine life in our coastal waters.

Man's stay on this planet is no longer a function of the fitness or compatibility of his genetic information with his surroundings, but is a function of how quickly he can learn about his environment and bring his affairs into alignment with this knowledge. But even though our survival is a function of cultural evolution, we are still ultimately dependent on biological evolution. Only this process is capable of maintaining the overall fitness of the common life-support system. The biosphere is constantly changing. The earth's surface is composed of scale-like plates that are slowly moving. Mountains are rising and falling, and the attitude of the earth in space is not constant. All these changes are compensated for without man's knowledge. The dynamics of evolution and ecological succession are constantly adjusting the interdependent relationships of the life processes. When the activities of man lead to the extinction of plant or animal, these processes have been deprived of essential information. Options for future adaptations and expansions are forever lost.

The four household impacts and the perturbances of the evolutionary processes have precipitated an unprecedented survival crisis. Figure one is a conceptual tool that depicts the expansion of human activities and the resulting impact on the life support system. The graph depicts this relationship from several thousand years ago, through the resolution of present problems, to a few hundred years into the future.

The bottom line is similar to the population curve, but it represents the combined magnitude of three parameters. First, the number of people; second, what they take from the environment; third, how harshly these things are gathered. The conceptual tool is applicable

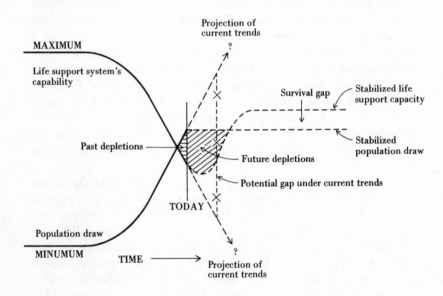

Figure I: *Survival Crisis Graph*

to the pressure of users on Yosemite Valley as well as harvest pressure on fisheries in Malaysia. These three parameters could be identified in any specific case as well as in the scale of variations for a total global overview.

The top line depicts the combined effect of both physical and social parameters on the general fitness of the life-support system. Because humans have nutritional, social, and psychological needs, "life-support systems" include everything required for a healthy and tranquil life. The decline in the top line represents everything from topsoil depletion and degradation to an increasing suicide rate. Any factor or the various factors contributing to a decline in the top line (e.g., household deterioration or disfunction such as eco-system simplification, ozone deterioration, mining of ground water, etc.) may or may not be interdependent. Because such diverse indicators are strictly accumulative only in terms of total resources needed to repair and reclaim original or maximum household fitness, it is possible that some combinations of impacts or malfunctions will be self-perpetuating or self-destructive. This top line reflects diverse parameters in a slightly different manner than the bottom line. The elements of the rising bottom line represent the complete human requirements on the life-support system.

The crossover of these two lines depicts the most fundamental change in man's relationship to his environment since his emergence on earth. He has now become dependent on depleting the household's fertility. He is now actually mining the life-support system itself rather than harvesting a sustained yield from that system. He is destroying what he breathes, poisoning what he eats and drinks, degrading the soils, and perturbing the many complex systems that control ecosphere functions. How long can the investor deplete his capital with a hope of re-establishing the original interest return rate? As the distance of disparity between population draw and life-support system capability increases, the cost of recovery also increases. The sobering possibility exists that we may run up such a debt that we may not have enough resources, man hours, metallic and nonmetallic energy and organic materials left on earth to bring about an uncrossing of these lines and to establish a sustained relationship with the capabilities of the life-support system.

The dotted lines after the vertical line, "today," represent the task before us. Population draw must be stabilized, perhaps even reduced, life support system fitness must be reclaimed. The separation between fitness and draw, after sustained yield or a steady state is reached, is a cushion against potential wholesale household disasters of the three basic types: natural disasters, social deterioration, or another era of life-support systems depletion. The shaded area, shown on the graph as existing and future depletions, represents depletions of the system's capabilities. Because the ecosphere and its reserves are finite, the existence of such depletions means that the system is running at a continual and threatening loss. We do not know how great a loss the household can sustain. To further cloud man's future, the dynamics of recovery are complicated. For example, watersheds need water to recover, but if towns and cities need all the water from that area to fill their reservoirs, the watershed will never fully recover to its original water monitoring capacity. It will also be necessary to temporarily expand even greater amounts of energy and resources as we construct a society that is capable of a sustained yield relationship with its environment. Soil reclamation plants, smaller agricultural units, recycling systems, adequate health, nutrition and housing for all, relevant educational programs, a major shift in the energy base from depletable to renewable and so on—an era of construction on the way to an enhanced general welfare.

While it may be true that government has facilitated the systematic exploitation of land and people, government facilitation is the only way a sustained yield relationship will ever be achieved.

The education, planning, and coordination required to accomplish this task are unprecedented in human affairs. Local, state, and federal governments all have many responsibilities, as does each person in securing a future for ourselves and our children. Allocation of resources (how much oil out of the earth for what purposes) can only be done at the national and international level, while farm land, acre by acre, can only be protected at the local level. If such massive transformations of our affairs are not to be as traumatic for everyone as today's "rat race," an unprecedented educational program is required for our entire society. Such a program can only be funded at the federal level and administered locally. The participation of everyone and every institution is required. Survival cannot be bought, legislated, or enforced; it has to be lived. But living it, at least requires permission, if not active facilitation.

At this point in time our government is not taking adequate steps to extricate us from the existing extremely dangerous situation. It should be expected that as the condition and parameters of human existence change the nature of surveillance, monitoring, and reclamation chores will also change. Such things are simply not being done on an adequate scale or level of integration. In short, we have never formally defined in relation to what we know about ourselves, the household and how it functions, the general welfare or what its promotion entails—even though its promotion in perpetuity is the basic task for which we annually give our government billions of dollars.

Foreign and Military Policy

United States Foreign Policy: The Last Quarter-Century

ANTHONY T. BOUSCAREN

On November 23, 1970, a Lithuanian seaman aboard the trawler *Sovetskaya Litva* jumped from his ship to the U.S. Coast Guard cutter *Vigilant*, seeking asylum. The Soviets demanded that he be returned. The *Vigilant*'s skipper, Commander Ralph Eustis, called Boston Coast Guard District Admiral William B. Ellis for instructions. Eustis was told to hand the seaman, Simas

Anthony T. Bouscaren (Ph.D., University of California) is Professor of Political Science at Le Moyne College, and was formerly associated with The National War College. He is the author of numerous books on national and international politics, and serves on the editorial boards of the *Intercollegiate Review*, *Ukranian Quarterly*, and the *International Migration Review*. In 1968 he was central New York chairman of the Citizens for Nixon-Agnew.

Kudirka, back. When Eustis replied that he was afraid the Russians would hurt Kudirka, Admiral Ellis declared: "I don't think that will happen. They are not barbarians." The Russians came to get Kudirka, beat him repeatedly, and with Coast Guard cooperation, returned him to the Soviet ship.

In mid-1941, when President Franklin Roosevelt had made up his mind to help the Soviet Union following the German invasion, his foreign policy advisor William Bullitt recalled Stalin's crimes against humanity and the Soviet record of treaty violations. Bullitt recommended some *quid pro quo* to insure that the Soviets not replace the Nazis as overlords for Eastern and Central Europe. Roosevelt replied: "Bill, I just have a hunch that Stalin is not that kind of a man, and that if we give him everything he asks for, *noblesse oblige*, and demand nothing in return, that he will work with us for a world of peace and democracy."

Maybe Stalin and his successors are not barbarians, and maybe Hitler wasn't either, but they make good substitutes. Even Khrushchev admitted Stalin's crimes, and the Soviet record in the Katyn Forest massacre, the rape of Poland, Czechoslovakia, and Hungary, and the Cuban missile crisis is there for all to see. Perhaps history is not Admiral Ellis' strong point. Roosevelt admitted he knew little about communism or the Soviet Union. Our civilian and military leaders, more often than not, have failed to do their homework. General Eisenhower failed to see anything wrong in letting the Russians take Berlin in the spring of 1945, even though the Allies could easily have gotten there first.

It has been argued by Herbert Feis and others that had Roosevelt lived longer, he would have dealt more realistically with the Soviets than did Truman (who agreed to forcible repatriation of refugees and escapees from the Communist world in Germany). I am inclined to accept this thesis, as the evidence is clear that Roosevelt, a week before his death, realized that he had been taken in the Yalta agreement about Poland. But this is small consolation for the Poles, who trusted in the Anglo-American commitments made in the Atlantic Charter.

It was not until 1947 that President Truman came to recognize the stark fact that the Soviets were not only not reciprocating our concessions and effusively emotional good will, but that Stalin was deliberately expanding the areas of Soviet domination as part of a new conflict, euphemistically called by some the "cold war." Truman resolved a crisis in his administration by firing Henry Wallace (who favored more concessions to Stalin), and by supporting Secretary of State James Byrnes (whose experiences with the Soviets in Germany led him to recognize the stark realities of the situation). The upshot was the Truman Doctrine and the beginning of containment, a bipartisan foreign policy that remains in effect today (although not always successful, as witness the take-over of Cuba in 1958).

The United States did not seek a conflict with the Soviet Union, as our concessions made at Teheran, Yalta, and Potsdam demonstrate. After the war, we withdrew our forces from Europe and China, hoping for a return to peace, and convinced that with the defeat of Germany and Japan no serious obstacle lay in the path of peace. It was not until the Communists threatened Greece and Turkey and Berlin, and took over in Prague in 1948 (not content with a coalition government) that we even began to react. The take-over in China did not elicit the same response that Japan's earlier invasion of China did. Indeed Truman and Marshall sought to force a coalition government on Chiang Kai-shek, and even went to the length of placing an embargo on all arms shipments to Nationalist China (June 1946 to June 1947) in a vain attempt to twist Chiang's arm.

Revisionist historians have tried to suggest that somehow we, not the Soviets, started the cold war. Their arguments are about as valid as the earlier historians who insinuated that we and the British were more responsible for starting World War II than the Japanese and the Germans. I remember a political scientist at Yale seriously telling my class that Finland, not Russia, was guilty of threats to the peace in 1939 and 1940.

There are more revisionists now than then, because of the leftist bias that social scientists have exhibited over the years. Thus in 1938 hundreds of prominent American intellectuals defended the Stalin purge trials, and described the Stalin Constitution as "democratic." Late in 1969 the Carnegie Commission on Higher Education released the tabulations of a survey of 60,448 faculty members in American universities: 58 percent of the political scientists described themselves as "liberal," 13.8 percent "left," and 16.2 percent "middle-of-the-road." Only 8.4 percent considered themselves "moderately conservative" and a mere 0.7 percent "strongly conservative"; of the historians, 68.7 percent were either liberal or leftist.

The above may help to explain why, at this late date in history, educated Americans like Admiral Ellis still do not regard the Soviets as being anywhere near in the same category as the Nazis. As one who has been active in captive nations work in this country, I can testify that there are many steelworkers, miners, janitors, and other humble folk of Central and Eastern European extraction who have a far better understanding of what we are up against than most Ph.D.s in the social sciences. There is much wisdom in William F. Buckley's observation to a Syracuse, New York audience in 1961 that he would rather have the country run by the first 800 people in the Syracuse phone book than 800 professors at Harvard.

But the prospects are not all bleak. There are many liberals today who, through bitter experience, recognize the reality of the Communist challenge. They include Dean Acheson, Walt Rostow, Sidney Hook, Dean Rusk, and George Meany, among others. Unreconstructed liberals at the Massachusetts Institute of Technology refused to take Rostow back after government service, and it was a long time before Dean Rusk found a job.

Indeed, in many ways, the internal dialogue (to use the current polite word) on foreign policy is no longer between liberals and conservatives; rather it is between leftists, on the one side, and liberals and conservatives on the other. Liberal Democrats in the Senate like Jackson of Washington and McGee of Wyoming have received as many brickbats from the left as conservative Republicans, perhaps even more. During the 1968 presidential campaign, Hubert Humphrey and his supporters were often heckled unmercifully, and even were the targets of physical violence. Toward the end of the Johnson-Rusk Administration, our leaders were afraid to accept speaking engagements due to the demonstrated hooliganism of the Left.

Many liberals and most conservatives support Israel against the Egyptian-Soviet build-up following the seven-day war of 1967. Somewhat the same coalition supports collective security in Europe (NATO), in Asia (SEATO), and in the Caribbean (Cuba 1962 and Dominican Republic 1965). In a more general way, and noting the decline that set in during the Kennedy Administration (in a vain effort to induce the Soviets to reciprocate our national security restraint) a coalition of liberals and conservatives has supported the concept of deterring the Soviets from adventurism through a nuclear power that is both formidable and credible. On each of these issues the Left is implacably hostile to United States foreign policy; indeed some of its shrillest voices favor enemy victory on one or several fronts.

For better or worse, most liberals and now many conservatives accept, as a matter of practical politics, the "no-win" policy of containment, from Truman through Nixon. Eisenhower endorsed it in Korea, as did Kennedy during the missile confrontation when we agreed not to invade Cuba if Russia withdrew its missiles. Although we did at one time liberate North Korea before the Chinese intervention in Korea, we have refused to liberate North Vietnam, under three administrations. Indeed, there was no bombing of North Vietnam for ten years after the Communists crossed the 17th parallel in 1955, and then only of secondary targets. United States foreign policy is gradually becoming more and more restrained, more and more defensive. A 1969 paper produced by R. G. Shreffer and W. S. Bennett of the Los Angeles Scientific Laboratory states categorically:

> Military victory, like concepts of 'unconditional surrender,' has been recognized as obsolete since World War II. We must structure our policies accordingly. . . . Our military goals should not be victory but deliberate stalemate. . . . The role of our military services must be to support a national strategy of diplomatic deterrence; failing that, they must merely seek an early stalemate, not defeat of enemy forces.

This is an exceedingly mature and restrained approach, but it is enormously handicapped in international relationships by the fact that our adversaries refuse to limit their own strategy. Both Hanoi and Peking are formally and openly committed to the idea of victory, not standoff, in Vietnam. *The Peking Review* commends "the 34 million [Communist] Vietnamese people who have the firm resolve to fight and win." We have become accustomed to such exhortations and have been inclined to shrug them off, while analyzing deeds, not words, hoping thereby to produce the basis for American withdrawal and a *de facto* settlement in Vietnam. But we have not become accustomed at all to the idea that powerful forces in Soviet Communism are equally unwilling to tolerate the thought of compromise, whether in the Middle East, Hungary, or Czechoslavakia. In October 1970 there appeared in the Czech military journal *Lidova Armada* an article by Lt. Col. Josef Sedlar, entitled "Education in Hatred of the Enemy." Sedlar is close to high ranking Soviet officers, whose views he reflects:

> Concepts like struggle, hostility, hatred of the enemy have, in the terminology of the Communist movement a just and humane meaning. . . . Those who wage this struggle [for communism] have a truly historical right to . . . preach hatred against a social system [capitalism] . . . Education in hatred of the enemy is greater in the armed forces than in any other social organism.

Thus in the case of Soviet Communism, instruction is advocated in hating an ideological opponent with whom there is not any war and with whom vital negotiations such as the SALT talks are proceeding. The gap between an increasing moderation of thought in the West (together with its concrete application) and the revival of extreme military chauvinism in the East is increasingly evident. It is hard to conceive of the possibility of any enduring accord between the two in any vital area so long as one side develops a strategy postulated on compromise and the other side pursues a strategy of victory fanned deliberately by inculcated hatred.

Having established our frame of reference, we can proceed to examine the application of United States foreign policy in the indicated major areas: Middle East, Europe and NATO, East Asia, the Caribbean, and the strategic confrontation. With the partial exception of the Middle East (the period 1947–1955), these areas must be considered within the framework of the war that the Soviets thrust upon us, beginning with the threat to Greece and Turkey. The battles of this war have included: Greece (1944 and 1947–1949), Berlin (1948 and 1961), Czechoslovakia (1948 and 1968), Hungary (1956), Iran (1946), Lebanon and Iraq (1958), the seven-day Middle East conflict (June 1967), the China war (1945–1949), Quemoy-Matsu (1958), Tibet (1951), Korea (1950–1953), Indo-China (1955–present), Philippine Hukbalahap insurgency (1947–1957), Malaya

(1947–1957), The Congo (Belgium) (1960–1964), Cuba (1958, 1961, 1962), Guatemala (1947–1954) and the Dominican Republic (1965).

The East Asia battles largely stem from the Yalta decisions that strengthened the USSR in the Far East (as well as in Poland), the continuing Soviet assistance to the Chinese Communists (notably 1945–1949) and the refusal of the United States to render similar aid to the Chinese Nationalists. The Communist take-over of mainland China led to the Korean war, the conquest of Tibet, and the Communist challenge to Southeast Asia. U.S. liberal policy toward Syngman Rhee of Korea was similar to our policy *vis à vis* Chiang Kai-shek (the attempt to disengage from hard-line anti-Communist conservatives, based on alleged fear of confrontation with the USSR). In January 1950, Secretary of State Acheson, speaking for President Truman, announced that henceforth Taiwan and South Korea would be excluded from the U.S. defensive perimeter in the Pacific. Shortly thereafter Soviet Marshal Malinovsky began to train North Koreans and Chinese for the invasion of South Korea. Using the liberal argument that communism was primarily an economic question (people "go" Communist because they are hungry), the Truman Administration embarked on a program of economic aid to South Korea, while withholding military aid beyond that required for a constabulary force. The Communist invasion of June 25, 1960 pitted T–34 tanks against automatic pistols and carbines.

Once the Communists crossed the 38th parallel, the United States (together with token United Nations forces) decided to help defend South Korea. For the first time in history a fairly sizeable element of American society vigorously opposed the efforts of Truman and Eisenhower to save South Korea. This leftist fall-out from the Wallace-Communist crusade of 1948 organized into "peace councils" that made contact with Communist authorities in Pyongyang to exploit American prisoners of war and their families (by inducing them to sign "peace petitions"). This same phenomenon occurred, on a much larger scale, during the war in Vietnam.

After the retreat to the Pusan perimeter, General MacArthur landed behind the enemy lines at Inchon, liberated Seoul, and in accord with the United Nations General Assembly resolution of October 7, 1950, liberated North Korea. This was rather significant, considering the inhibitions of containment; it was not repeated in the Vietnam war. The Chinese Communist invasion of Korea in December 1950, coming on the heels of the liberation of North Korea, led to a United States backing-down. First, the Truman Administration refused to retaliate against the enemy base in Manchuria, and even severely restricted bombing the Yalu river bridges (while ruling out attacks against the Korean rail center at Racin— 40 miles from the Soviet frontier); secondly, the United States abandoned the liberation of North Korea. Refusal to bomb the enemy effectively led to severe casualties during the Allied retreat to east coast evacuation ports, and to the second Communist capture of Seoul.

Although the United Nations Charter specifically calls for sanctions, including naval blockade in cases of aggression, there were no military sanctions applied against the territory of Red China or the seas bordering that country. Chapter 7, articles 41 and 42 of the Charter remain unenforced to this day. Following the firing of General MacArthur, a limited Allied offensive led by General Van Fleet liberated Seoul and pushed into North Korea again (although not with the intent of liberating the entire North). The enemy forces were in full flight, when Soviet diplomat Jacob Malik, on the first anniversary of the Communist invasion, called for negotiations. The Truman administration stopped the successful offensive, and there followed two years of talks first at Kaesong, then Panmunjom, while men died on the stalemated battlefield. As chief negotiator Admiral C. Turner Joy recounts it in his book *How Communists Negotiate*, the United States made the major concessions on truce supervision and inspection and the prisoner of war issues. The Panmunjom settlement of July 1953 was hardly America's finest hour; General Mark Clark later said that he was ashamed to sign the agreement that allowed the Communists (named by the United Nations as the aggressor) to remain in North Korea, undefeated and unpunished. The Chinese Communists began, with some justification, to refer to the United States as a "paper tiger," and the Pyongyang regime has, since 1953, engaged in a series of provocations, including the Pueblo incident and the attempt to murder President Park of the Republic of Korea.

Even though the Communist world was weak and divided during

1953 (Stalin's death and the uprising in East Berlin), the West did nothing to take advantage of the opportunities that existed. We, not the Communists, were in a position to negotiate from a position of strength in 1953. Taking advantage of our timid policy of defensive containment, the Peking regime began to demand the Chinese Nationalist offshore islands, beginning with the Tachens. After much clamor, the Eisenhower Administration forced the Chineses Nationalists to evacuate the Tachens, to the consternation of the authorities in Taipei. Following a visit to the Far East by Secretary of State Dulles, Congress passed the Defend Formosa resolution, that provided for the U.S. defense of Formosa (Taiwan) and such offshore island positions as were considered vital to that defense. In 1958 when the Communists attacked Quemoy and Matsu, the Eisenhower Administration, after some hesitation and ambiguity, supported the successful Chinese Nationalist defense of the strategic islands.

The involvement of the United States in Southeast Asia, as in Northeast Asia and China, stems from prior Communist action. After World War II, Communist elements in the Philippines, Dutch East Indies (later Indonesia), Malaya, Indo-China, Thailand and Burma engaged in acts of violence against the governments of these countries. In most cases (except Burma and Malaya which were in the British sphere of influence), the United States came to the assistance of the threatened governments. Previously our government pressured the Netherlands and France to grant self government to Indonesia, Vietnam, Laos, and Cambodia. The Southeast Asia Treaty of 1954 included Thailand and the Philippines, together with Vietnam, Laos, and Cambodia as protocol states. After the 1954 Geneva Conference on Indo-China and the French withdrawal, the United States became more involved, in response to the Vietminh threat to the State of Vietnam (shortly thereafter the Republic of Vietnam), Laos, and later on (1970) Cambodia.

Both the United States and the State of Vietnam (South Vietnam) refused to sign the Geneva Agreement because the French and the British made too many concessions to the Communist Vietminh (notably handing over Hanoi and Haiphong), and because the Communists rejected the United States–South Vietnamese insistence on free elections for all Vietnam under United Nations supervision. The Eisenhower Administration, together with leading Democrats like

Senators Kennedy and Mansfield, were pleased with the accession to power of the Vietnamese nationalist leader Ngo Dinh Diem in Saigon, and extended military and economic aid to his government.

Diem, with our support, defeated the rebel Cao Dai and Hoa Hao and their French supporters, resettled almost one million refugees from North Vietnam, while seeking to make South Vietnam more secure from the Vietminh attacks. He was reasonably successful until 1962. That was the year that the Kennedy Administration tried to compromise the crisis in Laos by forcing the resignation of the anti-Communist leader Phoumi Nosavan, while bringing to power a coalition government including the Communists. This more or less legalized the Communist control of one-third of Laos, including land adjacent to South Vietnam along which the Vietminh soon built the Ho Chi Minh Trail. The changed situation in Laos made the defense of South Vietnam more difficult. Then Sihanouk, in Cambodia, having lost confidence in the United States, decided to accommodate himself with the Communists, who soon began using his country as a privileged sanctuary from which to attack South Vietnam.

To compound his problems, a neutralist and pro-Vietminh Buddhist clique, led by Thich Tri Quang, began to engage in acts of violence against the Diem Government. Half of Diem's cabinet members were Buddhists, and there was no truly religious problem. From Diem's point of view there did exist a treasonous clique hell-bent on accommodation with Hanoi. But when he moved against Thich Tri Quang, his enemies (in Vietnam and in the United States) accused him of repressing Buddhism. Averill Harriman and Roger Hilsman, in the Kennedy Administration, persuaded the President to encourage anti-Diem forces in Vietnam. This led to the uprising on November 1, 1963, and to the death of Diem and two of his brothers (some members of the Kennedy Administration accused Diem of "government by family"). The immediate post-Diem period was characterized by coups and counter-coups, all set in motion by the original anti-Diem uprising. It was not until the advent of the Thieu-Ky Government, based on the elections of 1966, that stability returned to South Vietnam.

In the wake of the Tonkin Gulf incident and the general escalation of the ground war by the Communists, the Johnson Administration decided at long last to engage in air strikes against secondary targets in North Vietnam. But the airfield at Hanoi was never touched, nor was there any interdiction of the supplies coming in to Hanoi (in 1943 the United States mined that port to deny its use to the Japanese). The bombing, limited as it was, took some of the pressure off the U.S. and South Vietnamese forces, and certainly complicated for the Communists the problem of transporting supplies from North to South Vietnam. However, in response to much clamor by leftist groups in the United States, President Johnson unilaterally stopped the bombing in 1968. Senate "doves" assured us that this would lead to fruitful negotiations with Hanoi.

The Nixon Administration decided to turn over more responsibility to the South Vietnamese armed forces (ARVN) and began a unilateral withdrawal of U.S. forces from South Vietnam. This was further facilitated by the successful though limited operation of May 1970, which cleaned out the privileged sanctuary of the Vietminh in Cambodia. The 1970 elections in the United States retired such vociferous opponents of collective security as Senators Goodell, Gore, and Tydings, and Congressman Lowenstein, which seemed to indicate public acceptance of the Nixon policies in Southeast Asia. But so long as a hostile and aggressive Communist regime remains in Hanoi, some U.S. forces will have to remain in South Vietnam, as they do in South Korea and western Europe.

The United States commitment to Israel, beginning in 1947, led to a gradually increasing U.S. involvement in Middle East affairs. Meantime we did act to shore up governments in Iran and Lebanon that were threatened by the U.S.S.R. and/or internal leftist forces. In 1955 the Eisenhower Administration abandoned plans to help finance the Aswan High Dam project in Egypt, when it learned that Nasser had concluded a secret arms deal with the U.S.S.R. The Soviets, taking advantage of our pro-Israel position, decided in 1955 to espouse the cause of the Arabs, notably in Egypt. In 1956 we blocked a joint Israeli-French-British invasion of Egypt (which was triggered by Nasser's blocking the Suez Canal and seizing the International Suez Company that operated the Canal). The reasoning was that we could not condone this, any more than we could condone the Soviet invasion of Hungary. The difference was that we did nothing at all to stop or even deter the Soviets from acting in Hungary. We did not even recognize the regime of Imre Nagy.

By the spring of 1967 the Soviet arms build-up in Egypt and Syria had reached alarming proportions, with Israel calling for help from the United States, Britain, and France. Fortunately for the West, Israel was able to gain a complete and convincing victory in the June war of 1967, by engaging in a devastating preemptive air strike against the Soviet tanks and planes employed by Egypt and Syria. But neither Nasser nor Brezhnev accepted their defeat as final, and soon the flow of Soviet military aid to Egypt was resumed, while Cairo called for a war of revenge.

The United States sought to encourage negotiations that might cool off the combatants, negotiations that might induce the Soviets to stop aiding Egypt, so that we might be able to slow down or stop aid to Israel. But neither Egypt nor the U.S.S.R. seem to be much interested in ceasing and desisting.

The Middle East conflict has led to some most interesting domestic political ramifications. Vietnam "doves" become "hawks" when the question of defending Israel comes up. Senators who advocated withdrawal and negotiations in Southeast Asia demanded blockade of Egyptian ports and, if necessary, U.S. military involvement to defend Israel. Generally speaking, liberals and conservatives have supported collective security in the Middle East, whereas the American left has taken a pro-Soviet and anti-Israeli position.

The Middle East problem has, since 1955, become "Sovietized," thus leading to a greater U.S. involvement. The latter has also been occasioned by the Soviet naval build-up in the Mediterranean, and the change of government in Libya (now pro-Egyptian). The United States gradually took over Britain's role of guardian of the eastern Mediterranean after World War II. The commitment grew first with the Baghdad Pact and then, in 1958 (when the enemy took Baghdad) the Central Treaty Organization. The long standing commitment to Israel then took on new proportions when the Soviet Union became a Middle East power and egged Cairo on to greater adventurism.

As for Western Europe, many Americans believed that with the defeat of Germany in 1945, the United States could withdraw its influence and return to business as usual. But postwar economic problems in Europe plus Soviet belligerency and the crises of 1948 in Czechoslovakia and Berlin forced us to become involved, first, with the Marshall Plan, and then a year later (1949) with the North

Atlantic Treaty Organization. NATO, reinforced by the nuclear deterrent, was supposed to cool off the Soviets. It succeeded, with respect to western Europe, but not with respect to Berlin, Hungary or Czechoslovakia. And as the Soviets developed their own nuclear capability, they felt free to engage in adventures as far abroad as Vietnam, Laos and Cuba.

In 1961 the Kennedy Administration decided to soften the nuclear deterrent first by a slow down in its development (do not build "offensive" weapons that might antagonize the Soviets), and finally by a complete cessation of the construction of ICBMs and nuclear submarines. More than this, President Kennedy announced that in the event of a Soviet attack on Western Europe or the United States, there would be a "pause" rather than an automatic nuclear response. This was hardly reassuring to our European allies; France especially was unwilling to consign its fate to the whims and fancies of an American president. Under De Gaulle's leadership, France then proceeded to develop its own *force de frappe*. The defection of France from NATO weakened the organization, and forced the moving of headquarters to Belgium.

It was Kennedy's hope that if we unilaterally limited our own strategic arms program, the Soviet might reciprocate. Kennedy's gamble did not pay off, and the Western world is less safe today as a result. First the Soviets caught up to us in deliverable megatonnage, then they caught up to us in total numbers of ICBMs. In addition they developed an ABM system.

Berlin has been subjected to a series of Soviet pressures, largely due to the fact that the Truman Administration in 1945 was afraid of insisting on a strip of land connecting West Berlin and West Germany, or iron-clad guarantees of access to the city. Our response to the 1948 blockade was the immensely costly airlift, instead of sending in a tank column (we still possessed a monopoly of nuclear weapons at the time). In 1953 we stood by and did nothing during the East Berlin uprising. Indeed the Eisenhower Administration shut off the RIAS Radio so as not to spread the news of the uprising to East Germany. And in 1961 the Soviets began to build the ugly wall right through the city, in flagrant violation of the Occupation Statute, while we did nothing.

There was some speculation that Khrushchev put the missiles in

Cuba in order to be able to blackmail us in Berlin. In any event the Soviet and Communist success in Cuba in 1958 marked a turning point of great portent—the breaching of the Monroe Doctrine for the first time in history. The advent of Castro to power reflects credit not only to his friends in Moscow but also to some Americans who were so obsessed with the evil of Batista as to conclude that any change would be for the better. Herbert Matthews of *The New York Times*, in particular, portrayed Castro as a sort of modern Robin Hood. Castro's public relations men could scarcely have improved on Matthew's "news" stories.

By early spring 1961, leading liberals, as well as conservatives, recognized the threat that Castro and his sponsors presented not only to the Americas, but to the Cuban people. President Kennedy decided to go ahead with the plan, originally launched by the Eisenhower Administration, to help Cuban exiles overthrow Castro. Unfortunately for the Cuban people, however, timidity and a guilt complex so enveloped advisers such as Adlai Stevenson, that key elements in the liberation attempt were eliminated, notably the final air strike against Castro's air force. Had this strike been carried out, it is most likely that the landing at the Bay of Pigs could have been effected without interdiction by Castro's war planes. The defeat of the Cuban exiles was even more a U.S. defeat, and a defeat for the Cuban people.

During the summer of 1962, Cuban exiles warned the Kennedy Administration that offensive Soviet missiles were being installed in Cuba. It was not until October 14, 1962, that the Administration believed the warnings. On that day a U-2 plane took photographs of several MRBM and IRBM sites under construction. The purpose of the Cuban installations was revealed to President Kennedy on October 18, when Soviet Foreign Minister Gromyko informed him that the Soviet Union would conclude a separate peace treaty with East Germany, immediately after the Congressional elections of November 6, 1962. This was approximately the date by which the Cuban missile bases would become operational. At a critical point in urgent negotiations on Berlin, Khrushchev would then be able to disclose that he now had a formidable fire-power deployed on America's very doorstep.

Our response to the Soviet build-up was a show of naval strength (but not a blockade). There ensued secret negotiations resulting in an agreement whereby the Soviets promised to withdraw the missiles if the United States would promise to block Cuban exile efforts to overthrow Castro. In addition, the United States dismantled IRBMs in Turkey and Italy. It was quite a price to pay.

Castro remains as a thorn in the side of the Americas, repressing his own people as they were never repressed even under Bastista, exporting revolution to the Americas (including the United States), and threatening the security of the Caribbean with Soviet submarine activity centered at Cienfuegos (see Bouscaren, "Soviet Global Naval Strategy," *Washington Report*, December 7, 1970).

In 1965 leftist forces inside and outside the Dominican Republic sought to overthrow the government of that country. One of the ring-leaders was Juan Bosch, former Dominican President and the darling of many American liberals and leftists. U.S. troops were sent to the area when President Johnson disclosed that the threat of another Castro takeover existed. The Organization of American States (OAS) then established an inter-American military force to protect an interim government until elections could be held, and U.S. forces withdrew. The interim government was the result of U.S. pressures to force the resignation of General Wessin y Wessin and other conservatives considered distasteful in liberal circles. Subsequent elections brought to power moderate conservative President Balaguer, and the situation became stabilized.

The bipartisan policy of containment has more or less succeeded in East Asia (once it was applied *after* the Communist success on mainland China) and in Western Europe. In the Middle East Soviet influence has expanded into Egypt, Syria, Yemen, Libya, and Algeria. In Eastern Europe Soviet control has been reestablished in Poland, Hungary and Czechoslovakia, as "national Communism" seems to have gone up in smoke (Yugoslavia excepted). In the Caribbean, and Latin America generally, Soviet and Communist influence are on the rise. One can hardly speak of containment, in fact, when there is no front. This is also true of Indo-China. And it is in the nature of the dynamics and of the Western-Communist confrontation that the defender refuses to cross the fifty yard line. Only the attacker can score.

As suggested above, most conservatives and many liberals support containment. The policy was, in fact, launched by liberals, George

Kennan among them. The major alternative to containment is general withdrawal, based on certain isolationist assumptions of the past. This alternative is presented in its radical form by the leftists, and in its moderate form by an element of the liberal movement that for the most part has no governmental experience (in the Executive Branch) and appears to be motivated at least in part by the political objective of overthrowing the Establishment of the Democratic party.

I submit, however, that some conservatives and even a few liberals believe that containment can be improved on. Several years ago there appeared a learned treatise entitled *A Forward Strategy for America*, written by Robert Strausz-Hupe and William Kintner of the University of Pennsylvania, and Stefan Possony of Stanford. It contained many suggestions for the improvement of U.S. foreign policy that would not leave all the initiative to the other side.

We have, of course, undertaken some initiatives, as in Guatemala (1954), Iran (1951), Dominican Republic (1965), Cambodia (1970) and perhaps some others of which I am unaware. Yet even in these cases our action was precipitated by prior Soviet action. Only in the case of Guatemala was there a *bona fide* recovery of territory previously controlled by the other side. There have been other "successes" of sorts: the change of governments in Indonesia (Suharto replacing Sukarno), in Cambodia (Lon Nol replacing Sihanouk) and in Ghana (the overthrow of Nkrumah). But many students of strategy believe that the Free World performance can be improved upon, utilizing something of the "active defense" concept employed by Israel, extending even, as it did in 1967, to preemptive strikes. Possibly our Cambodian venture could be compared to this example.

A forward strategy for America and its allies would be based on the proposition that if the Soviets, the Red Chinese and their proxies persist in their efforts to extend Communist tyranny outside the boundaries of the USSR and Red China, then the Free World can (as it did during World War II and part of the Korean War) react by, in selected cases, liberating territories taken by the Communists. We are not talking now of countries like Bulgaria or Rumania, but rather of peripheral areas such as North Vietnam, Albania, and Cuba. The emphasis, practically speaking, would be on eroding away pockets of Communist power, through a comprehensive strategy of political, economic and psychological warfare, combined with counter-guerrilla operations. Wherever possible, indigenous rather than U.S. forces would be utilized. For example any operation aimed at upsetting the Communist apple cart in Haiphong (such as mining the harbor) would be undertaken by ARVN units. In the present situation in Cambodia these units, rather than U.S. forces, are being utilized.

In the case of Cuba, our naval power can prevent any future Soviet attempt to re-install missiles. Meantime we can quietly encourage and even assist the efforts of Cuban exiles to harass Castro in every possible way. Such a new program would offer some hope to the Cuban people. A forward strategy would also further impede if not stop altogether Castro's training of leftists from the Americas (including U.S. citizens).

The concept indicated would tie our cause to that of the nations captive under Communist rule—would identify the United States with the hopes and aspirations of the 95 percent of the population of these countries which are non-Communist. Captive Nations Week would become Captive Nations Year; exiles, refugees, and escapees from Communist rule would be given the opportunity to serve in NATO, SEATO, and other allied units under their own colors. We would actively encourage defections, and make clearer than we have to date that the United States welcomes those who seek to escape tyranny, whether it be Nazi, Fascist, or Communist.

Because of the realities of today's nuclear age, there are many situations that greatly inhibit our freedom of action. Unfortunately, thus far, we have limited our own freedom of action far more than the other side. In the case of the Hungarian uprising of 1956, for example, we could easily have recognized the Imre Nagy Government; our Ambassador in Vienna, together with other allied ambassadors, could have gone to Budapest after Nagy came to power, to demonstrate our solidarity with his cause, thus constituting a sort of international presence that might well have deterred the Soviets from re-invasion.

Our entire cultural exchange and trade relationships with Communist countries would be re-examined to ascertain their worth within the framework of the proposed forward strategy. The idea of the "pause" after an initial Soviet attack would be abandoned. We would make it very clear that any such attack would result in automatic counter-attack either against Soviet missile and air bases or, if too late, against Soviet cities. We would proceed with a full ABM program, never again to engage in unilateral limitations of arms program, research, and development.

In the case of Vietnam, we would continue troop withdrawals only if and when there are comparable withdrawals of Vietminh from South Vietnam, Laos, and Cambodia. We would, at the same time, encourage our South Vietnamese allies to take such action as they saw fit to interdict the port of Haiphong. The Nixon-Laird policy of "protective reaction" by air strikes would be enlarged, so long as the Communists persist in acts of violence outside the territory of North Vietnam.

I cannot say whether such a program would be politically feasible in the United States. But it could be sold, as President Roosevelt sold the policy of internationalism after his famous Quarantine Speech of 1937. Emphasis would be on protective reaction, as practiced by Israel. It could be sold not necessarily as a new policy, but as an extension and improvement of present policy—in order to *more effectively* secure threatened areas of the free world, and to save lives. We would no longer, in short, wait every time until the other side attacked.

In his remarkable book *The War of the Innocents,* Charles Bacelen Flood notes that most of his writer, publisher, and professor friends oppose the defense of Southeast Asia (although not of Israel).

> They wanted the entire effort liquidated, but to this desire they added a corollary . . . If they could not have it cease altogether, they wanted it limited, held to minimum of provocative activity. . . . I thought of the face of that dead boy when they carried him past at Polei Djereng. What were we supposed to say to him? Sorry, son, that weapon that killed you might have been destroyed some six hundred miles north of here, but there were policy considerations. The policy considerations, the untested notion that bombing a port in North Vietnam would substantially widen the war, was not going to do that boy any good—he was dead as he was ever going to be, and we went on letting his brother draftees be attacked from a sanctuary in Cambodia that outflanked South Vietnam.

The spirit of a forward strategy is also reflected in these words of Flood:

The inescapable fact was that if we were not going to do more to put North Vietnam out of action, then we were allowing ourselves to be confronted by a situation in which the struggle between a mighty and indecisive nation and a small and determined one came down to small groups of armed men hunting each other in the jungle. The least we could do was to put in more hunting parties than the other side had, which it was certainly clear that we could do on a population basis alone; but we were not doing it. When we were not trying to hit a mosquito with a hammer . . . we were playing six-man touch against an eleven-man tackle team on the ground.

The American Crisis

HANS J. MORGENTHAU

It would be comforting if one could assume that what is wrong with America at home and abroad could be remedied with relative ease by passing some more legislative enactments, by reorganizing once more the Federal government, by electing once more a different president, preferably from the party in opposition. Time was when such remedies might have sufficed. The issues that impinge upon us today are not isolated malfunctions within an otherwise sound system but organic defects of the system itself. In consequence, the remedies, in order to be appropriate to the issues, must seek to reform the system itself.

"What Ails America," reprinted by permission of *The New Republic*. Copyright © 1967, Harrison-Blaine of New Jersey, Inc. "The Impotence of American Power," reprinted by permission of *Commentary*. Copyright © 1963 by the American Jewish Congress. Hans J. Morgenthau (J.U.D., University of Frankfort) is Albert A. Michelson Distinguished Service Professor of Political Science and Modern History at the University of Chicago, and Leonard Davis Distinguished Service Professor of Political Science at City College of the City University of New York. He is the author of numerous articles and books, of which the most recent is *Truth and Power*.

To cite here only two examples—more will be discussed later on —our military intervention in Indochina does not result from the miscalculations of a particular administration, that a different administration could easily remedy. Rather that intervention stems from a profound misunderstanding of the nature of the contemporary world and America's place within it, a misunderstanding that is not the failing of a particular administration but of a whole political civilization and that will call forth other—perhaps even graver—miscalculations if we do not narrow the gap between our understanding and the nature of the real world.

Domestically, our economic and environmental difficulties, not only destroying the enjoyment of life but threatening life itself, can in good measure be attributed to a wastefulness in the production, distribution, and use of economic resources, that in the long run will bankrupt even the richest nation. Paradoxically, this waste is produced under the conditions of potential economic abundance by a system whose institutions and modes of operation derive from the traditional conditions of economic scarcity. Here too, our modes of thought and action concerning the contemporary world must be drastically revised in view of the nature of that world.

What Ails America

Contemplating the American scene today—the disarray of foreign and domestic policies, the violence from above and below, the decline of the public institutions, the disengagement of the citizens from the purposes of the government, the decomposition of those ties of trust and loyalty that link citizen to citizen and the citizens to the government—one is reminded of the other two great crises that similarly put into question the very identity of America; the crisis of the 1860's and that of the 1930's. However, a comparison among these three crises puts the peculiar gravity of the present one into stark relief.

The Civil War was a conflict between the two geographically defined, incompatible conceptions of the nature of American government and society, strengthened within their respective geographic areas by the very fact of conflict. That conflict, manifesting itself in military terms, could be, and was, settled by force of arms. The victory of the North restored and strengthened beyond challenge the unitary character of American government and established in legal terms the equality and freedom of all American citizens. Yet it is the measure of the failure of Reconstruction that in actual terms the drastic inequality that it was one of the purposes of the Civil War to confine, if not eliminate, was preserved and even accentuated in its aftermath. While Lincoln proclaimed that this nation could not endure half free and half slave, that is exactly as it has endured.

The crisis of the 1930's was similar to the present one in that it threatened to tear asunder the very fabric of American society. It was a crisis of the American purpose; it challenged the assumption of the uniqueness of America and suggested the failure of the American experiment. However, there were two escapes from the despair the crisis engendered: Marxism, which drew the logical conclusion from the denial of American uniqueness and the apparent failure of the American experiment by promoting the class struggle that was expected to transform the United States in the image of an equalitarian and libertarian utopia; and the New Deal, which affirmed the American promise through radical reform and creative reconstruction.

It is the distinctive and ominous mark of the present crisis that it has produced no remedy consonant with the ideals of America. It could not have produced one, for the inability to do so is an element of the crisis itself. The democratic state is in a blind alley, and so is American democracy. America, then, suffers from two types of ailments: those it has in common with the other major democracies, and those that are peculiarly its own.

The general crisis of democracy is the result of three factors: the shift of effective material power from the people to the government, the shift of the effective power of decision from the people to the government, and the ability of the government to destroy its citizens in the process of defending them.

Throughout history, the ultimate safeguard of the interests and rights of the people vis-a-vis the government has been the ability of the people to overthrow the government by force, that is, to make a revolution. This ability was a result of an approximately equal distribution of the means of physical violence between the government and the people. Before the beginning of the century, roughly speaking, the government met the people, barring superior organization and training, on a footing of approximate equality. Numbers, morale, and leadership then decided the issue.

This approximately equal distribution of military power between government and people has in our age been transformed into the unchallengeable superiority of the government. The government has today a monopoly of the most destructive weapons of warfare, and because of its centralization, the government can acquire instantly a monopoly of the most effective means of transportation and communications as well. Against such a monopolistic concentration of superior power, the people can demonstrate, protest, and petition, but they cannot overthrow it through revolution. Thus, as long as a democratic government can count upon the loyalty of the armed forces, it need not fear the wrath of the people, exploding in revolution. What it must guard against is to be voted out of office.

However, the voting process, both in the legislatures and in popular elections, has lost much of the bearing it formerly had upon the substantive decisions of the government. For the most important decisions that government must render today, in contrast to the past, are far removed both from the life experiences and the understanding of the man in the street. A century ago, the issue of slavery was susceptible to the judgment of all; today the issue of integrating the descendants of the slaves into American society presents itself as an intricate complex of technical problems, to which the man in the street may react emotionally but with which only experts in education, housing, urban affairs, welfare, and so forth can competently deal. Thirty years ago, the American people and their elected representatives could still have a competent voice in determining the military policy of the United States; today, Congress passes the $70 billion budget of the Department of Defense with essentially ritualistic scrutiny, giving the experts the benefit of the doubt. The great issues of nuclear strategy, for instance, cannot even be the object of meaningful debate, whether in Congress or among the people at large, because there can be no competent judgment without meaningful knowledge. (The ABM debate of 1969 was the exception that proved the rule.) Thus, the great national decisions of life and death are rendered by technological elites, and both the Congress and the people at large retain little more than the illusion of making the decisions that the theory of democracy supposes them to make.

The great decisions democratic governments are called upon to make are always justified in terms of the common good—that is, of the benefits that, at least in the long run, will accrue to the great mass of the citizens. Even where that justification obviously masked special interests or served as an ideology for a particular class identifying its interests with those of the community, the claim had in the past a certain plausibility. For even a democratic government that only served the pursuit of the happiness of some of its citizens sought to preserve the life and liberty of most of them. In the last analysis, the performance of this elementary and vital function established in the eyes of the citizens the moral legitimacy of government. The government had a claim upon the citizens' obedience and allegiance because, at the very least, it made it possible for them to live.

It is the distinctive characteristic of the nuclear age that this moral foundation upon which the legitimacy of democratic government has rested in the past is no longer as firm as it used to be. A government armed with nuclear, biological, and chemical weapons of mass destruction still intends to protect the life of its citizens against a government similarly armed. But in truth it cannot defend its citizens, it can only deter the prospective enemy from attacking them. If deterrence fails and he attacks, the citizens are doomed. Such a government, then, bears the two faces of Janus: Insofar as it is able to deter, it is still its citizens' protector; if it fails to deter, it becomes the source of their destruction.

This new quality of modern government, precariously poised at the edge of the abyss of self-destruction, is vaguely felt, rather than clearly understood, by the man in the street. He beholds with awe and without confidence that gigantic machine of mass destruction and he also wonders whether a government so constituted still deserves the obedience of loyalty it claims and once deserved. If it is true that *ubi bene, ibi patria*, where is his fatherland?

These ailments, from which all major democratic governments suffer, are reinforced by the ailments peculiar to America. It is not just that the latter must be added to the former, but the peculiar ailments of America provide specific instances of the general crisis, they make that crisis relevant to specific issues facing America; and they give those issues a general poignancy. Three such issues call for our attention: racial violence, Vietnam, and the Presidency.

What the citizen suspects of the government's performance of its function as his protector against the foreign enemy, he has empirical proof of in his relations with his fellow citizens: The government is no longer able to perform its elementary function of protecting the lives of its citizens. It is unable to protect the black American and his white sympathizer against the violence to which they are subjected by white racists and arbitrary law enforcement, and it is unable to protect the citizens from the violence that has erupted in the black ghettos and is likely to erupt again and spread. And it is unable to put into practice the imposing body of legislation enacted by Congress for the purpose of integrating the blacks into American society and the poor into the productive economy. A government possessed of unprecedented power appears to be impotent in the face of the threat of social disintegration and the promise of social justice.

I shall not here repeat the arguments I have advanced since 1961 against our involvement in Vietnam, first by warning against it and then by pointing to its political aimlessness, military uselessness and risks, and moral liabilities. I want only to reemphasize, and enlarge upon, two points.

The war is not only politically aimless and militarily unwinnable in terms of the Administration's professed aims, but it also violates the very principles upon which this nation was founded and for which it has stood both in the eyes of its own citizens and of the world. It is an antirevolutionary war fought by a revolutionary nation. It is Metternich's war fought by the nation of Jefferson and Lincoln. As the President and the Secretary of the General Synod of the Netherlands Reformed Church put it on July 24, 1967, in a letter addressed to the National Council of Churches of the United States:

> Hostilities in Vietnam have reached such proportions that the United States government's professed aim, *viz.* to stop the advance of communist influence in South East Asia and to establish a democratic

regime in Vietnam, seems remoter than ever before. This is all the more alarming since the nation in whose behalf the war is supposedly being fought is being slowly but surely brought to ruin by the subtlety of the chemical and conventional weapons used and by the complete social, cultural, and spiritual dissolution with which it is threatened. A nation's "liberation" is sealing its doom. If the United States really has the well-being of the people of Vietnam at heart, we are prompted to ask whether there is any point at all in continuing this war. . . .

We Dutchmen and Dutch Christians and Churches owe our liberation from the yoke of cruel, anti-Christian oppression partly to your nation's willingness to sacrifice lives and property. Since the war, too, the Dutch and other nations cherished great hopes of the United States' contribution to the organization of a new community of nations. In view of this it is all the more regrettable that we are compelled to point out to you that your nation is losing the confidence placed in it, since it is [casting doubt on] the sincerity of its pleas for freedom and justice. . . . For that reason alone the United States should stop the war in Vietnam without delay by taking new initiatives.

The United States is incapable of liquidating the war because of its faulty perception of reality and its unattainable goals. It acts upon the assumption that it is defending South Vietnam against aggression. If only North Vietnam left its neighbors alone, to quote Mr. Rusk's celebrated phrase, there would be no trouble in South Vietnam. However, fruitful negotiations with the government in Hanoi are impossible because we seek to gain at the conference table what we have been unable to achieve on the battlefield: The destruction of the Viet Cong as an organized political force. Even if the government of North Vietnam were willing to hand us that victory, it would be unable to do so without the cooperation of the Viet Cong. The test of our willingness to liquidate the war will be not the withdrawal of most of our combat troops, but the establishment of a civilian government in Saigon that will inevitably negotiate a settlement of the war with the Viet Cong.

The waging of a war that runs counter to the national ethos and the inability of the most powerful nation on earth either to win or to liquidate it has had a deleterious effect upon the prestige of the government and of the political system through which we are governed. If we had a parliamentary system, this Administration would not govern us today, and its place would have been taken by an Administration not compelled by its psychological needs to prove itself through military victory. As it is, the opponents of the war, within and outside Congress, can only raise their voices in warning and protest, they can collect signatures and table and even pass resolutions; but they know that they have no power to change the course of events. The only resort left to them is to work for a change in Administration through the next elections, and they must hope, but can by no means be confident, that another Administration will pursue a wiser course.

Thus, they cannot help but ask themselves what kind of democracy it is in which the will of the people and of their elected representatives counts for so little and in which a President and a few advisers, having acquired a vested psychological interest in the perpetuation of error, are allowed to persist in involving the nation in a disastrous war. We thought that this was the way absolute monarchies were run in times past. Thus, Talleyrand could say in 1808 to Czar Alexander I: "The Rhine, the Alps, and the Pyrenees are the conquests of France; the rest, of the Emperor; they mean nothing to France." We could say with equal right today: The integrity of the American territory and institutions, the Monroe Doctrine, the balance of power in Europe and Asia—those are the interests of America; the war in Vietnam is the President's; it means nothing to America.

However, the Administration must make it appear that our involvement in Vietnam is not the result of the errors in which a succession of Presidents and their advisers have persisted, but that it serves the vital interests of the nation. The obvious implausibility of such a representation has opened up what has come to be known as the "credibility gap." The people refuse to believe what the government tells them it is doing and plans to do. As they once credited Washington with not being able to tell a lie, so they almost take it for granted that his contemporary successors will not tell the truth. This lack of trust is not limited to official statements on Vietnam; it extends to all matters of public concern. For deception is being practiced not occasionally as a painful necessity dictated by the reason of state, but consistently as a kind of lighthearted sport through which the deceiver enjoys his power.

This withering away of the public's trust in the government might matter little to a totalitarian regime, which can afford to govern through terror and the manipulation of the mass media of communications. Yet a democratic government cannot rule effectively, and in the long run it cannot rule at all, if it is not sustained by at least a modicum of the freely given support of the people and their elected representatives. In the American system of government, in particular, the President, by constitutional arrangement and political tradition, is the molder of the national will, the educator of the people, the guardian of its interests, and the protagonist of its ideals. The President is the incarnation of the nation-in-action; when the nation wants to know what it is about, it looks to the President to find out.

In that noble and vital mission, recent presidents have completely failed. For a time, President Johnson triumphed in that sphere of action in which he is a past master: The manipulation of Congress in support of legislation. Yet even these legislative triumphs in large measure remained ineffectual; for President Johnson, seeking an unattainable consensus and bent upon avoiding inevitable conflict, was unable to marshal the popular energies necessary to implement the legislative enactments. And his failure as a national leader and the decline of his personal prestige made him ineffective even in his dealings with Congress.

This personal failure is not just an issue between this particular President and the American people. It affects the vitality of the democratic process itself. If his Administration could be neither influenced nor trusted, why should one hope to influence and trust another one? If this is what the democratic process leads to, how good is democracy?

The combined impact these two sets of critical issues—the general ones common to all major democratic nations and the peculiarly American ones—have had upon American society has resulted in the present crisis of American politics. In order to assess the nature of that crisis, it is first necessary to consider the uniqueness of the American body politic.

America is unique in that it owes its creation and continuing existence as a nation not to geographic proximity, ethnic identity, monarchical legitimacy, or a long historic tradition, but to an act of will repeated over and over again by successive waves of immigrants.

It was not natural or historical necessity that created America or Americans, but a conscious choice. This voluntary element in the American nationality accounts for a peculiar looseness in the social fabric of America, whose texture is subject to continuous change. In consequence, American society is singularly adaptable to changing circumstances. But it is also singularly vulnerable to disruption and disintegration.

Since America owes its existence to a series of successive choices, those who have chosen America are free to choose otherwise. That availability of choice is strikingly revealed in the emphasis of the Declaration of Independence upon the right to revolution as a universal principle and, more concretely and personally, in what Abraham Lincoln wrote to Joshua Speed on August 24, 1855: "When it comes to this [the Know-Nothings' getting control], I should prefer emigrating to some country where they make no pretence of loving liberty—to Russia, for instance, where despotism can be taken pure, and without the base alloy of hypocrisy." No other Western nation, with the exception of Spain, has since the French Revolution had to reaffirm its very existence as a nation through a bloody civil war.

It is, then, not surprising that the combined impact the critical issues discussed above have had upon American society has been both disruptive and disintegrative. The refusal of large groups of politically conscious blacks to participate in the life of white Americans amounts to the disruption of American society into two separate and hostile societies. The alienation of many intellectuals and the retreat of the more sensitive and morally committed youth from political life are indices of disintegration.

What these different movements have in common is a negative attitude toward American society and the American purpose that that society is supposed to serve. They do not work within American society in order to improve or transform it, or even to revolt against it. They offer no viable alternatives to the *status quo*, but only different ways of escaping from it. They have given up on American society and opted out of it. Theirs is a politics of despair, that is, no politics at all, for America. "Black Power" is a self-defeating futility born of such despair. Advocacy of an Afro-American society within an indigenous social, economic, and paramilitary framework substitutes for the American purpose of equality in freedom for all citizens the very segregation, albeit with a positive content, that that purpose has been trying to overcome. The "New Left," the refusal to bear arms or pay taxes, the hippie movement, are protests against the political and social order, reassertions of individual choice outside the political order, or anarchism and return to nature à la Thoreau, albeit without any positive moral orientation toward a new social order.

Nobody will underestimate the seriousness of the disruption of American society through black separatism and hostility. But there is a strong tendency, officially inspired, to dismiss as inconsequential the apolitical and antipolitical attempts at escaping from American society and politics altogether. Most of the individuals who thus try to escape are not predestined for that role; they are not, as it were, the congenital nonconformists and eccentrics. Quite to the contrary, they would have been, if they had been given a chance, the pillars of society, the experts, the reformers, the politicians and statesmen, that is, the elite—small in numbers but irreplaceable in quality—from which a society receives its ability to grow, renew itself, live up to its purpose. That some of her best children have turned their backs upon America, that the powers-that-be have reacted to that desertion with either equanimity or derision and vilification is a measure of the gravity of the American crisis.

A society threatened with disruption or disintegration can maintain itself in two ways: through a creative effort at reconstruction or through violent repression. The former is the democratic way, of which America and modern England provide examples. The other is the fascist way through which Germany, Italy, and Spain maintained themselves as integrated societies. Yet these examples show that the two choices are available only in the initial stages of the crisis, that is, when the powers-that-be are tempted to close their eyes to the potential seriousness of the crisis. Once the destructive results of disruption and disintegration have become obvious, it is likely to be too late for democratic remedies. There is, then, an element of tragedy in such a crisis of democratic society: When it could still be served by democratic measures of reconstruction, there appears to be no need for them, and when the need has become obvious, it is too late for them.

It would be rash indeed to try to predict the outcome of the present crisis of American society. Yet whatever the outcome, the present trend toward violence rather than creative reconstruction is unmistakable. The white man in the street appears to believe that too much has already been done for the blacks, and he is afraid and in an ugly mood. The politicians translate that mood into calls for war against "crime in the streets" and for the defense of "law and order," that is, violence in defense of the *status quo*. On a higher level of sophistication, we are lectured by Mr. Moynihan on the merits of "The Politics of Stability" for an existentially unstable society, and liberals are asked to make "much more effective alliances with political conservatives"—an echo of the *"union sacree"* through which the societies of Western Europe tried to save themselves in the interwar period.

On the highest level of authority and power, the trend toward violent repression rather than creative reconstruction coincided with President Johnson's consensus philosophy. That philosophy, untenable on both theoretical and practical grounds, was readily available as ideological justification and rationalization for the formation of a phalanx of all law-abiding citizens, protecting the established order from troublemakers of all sorts. Among them, the powers-that-be count not only the black rioters but also the opponents of our involvement in Vietnam. President Johnson and his supporters time and again accused the dissenters of giving aid and comfort to the enemy, thereby strengthening from above, and giving an official sanction of sorts to the trend toward disintegration operating on the individual level. If the powers-that-be have the courage of their convictions, they must sooner or later do openly what at times they have tried to do surreptitiously and what an organization ironically misnamed Freedom House has openly advocated: stifle the dissent that they equate with disloyalty or treason.

Finally, there exists indeed an organic relationship between the trend toward violence at home and our policies in Vietnam. For in Vietnam, too, we have had a choice between accepting as inevitable a national and social peasant revolution and destroying the revolutionaries through violent repression, and we have chosen to pound, thus far without decisive effect, an intractable problem into oblivion. In intellectual, moral, and practical terms, nothing is indeed easier and less ambiguous than to deal with a social problem by oppressing and getting rid of the human beings who pose it. It is not accidental that many congressional advocates of violent repression in Vietnam represent states whose societies could not exist without the violent oppression of large masses, sometimes the majority, of their populations. Nor is it by accident that a retired Air Force General was, according to the *Anaheim Bulletin* of August 12, 1967, loudly applauded when he told his audience of American Legionnaires: "Military takeover is a dirty word in this country, but if the professional politicians cannot keep law and order it is time we do so, by devious or direct means." The problems we are facing at home are infinitely more complex and resistant to creative manipulation than those we are facing in Vietnam. Thus *a fortiori* the powers-that-be must be tempted to deal with our domestic problems as they are dealing with the problem of Vietnam: through the violence of impotence.

This is an ominous prospect. It can be avoided only if it is faced in time. We cannot afford the policies of consensus and stability, which ought to be the result, not the condition, of sound substantive policies and can be imposed upon an unstable and warring society only through violence. We need a supreme effort at radical reform creating unity and stability out of that dissension and unrest that are inseparable from radical reform.

The Impotence of American Power

The United States has at its disposal the greatest concentration of material power existing in the world today; in terms of productive capacity and military strength, it is the most powerful nation on earth. Yet the government of that most powerful nation is incapable of making the actions of even the weakest of foreign governments conform to its desires. It is incapable of doing so even with regard to governments that owe their very existence to American support and could not survive for twenty-four hours were that support withdrawn.

South Vietnam, South Korea, and Taiwan are cases in point. None of these governments could exist without the economic and military support of the United States and without the American commitment to go to war in their defense. Yet we told the Government of South

Vietnam before our military intervention to change its policies and composition, and it changed neither. We told the Government of South Korea that it ought to respect at least a minimum of democratic rights, and we were rebuffed for our "intervention." We told the Government of Taiwan that it ought not to station some of its troops on the offshore islands, and these troops are still stationed there.

Within the traditional sphere of influence of the United States, Cuba has been transformed into a military base at the service of a hostile power and into the headquarters for the subversion of the Western Hemisphere, and we have been unable to put a stop to it. In many countries of Latin America, we are unable to forestall the threat to our interests implicit in the polarization of the politics in those nations between the defenders of the *status quo* and the revolutionaries.

The history of our foreign-aid policy is testimony to our inability to achieve our political purposes even with an abundance of material means. So is our economic policy *vis-a-vis* the Communist bloc; our attempts to wage the Cold War by economic means have been frustrated by the eagerness of our most prosperous allies to make economic gains at the risk of strengthening the common enemy. The Atlantic Alliance, the cornerstone of our foreign and military policies, is crumbling, and we stand watching the process of decay without being able to arrest it. Pakistan is our ally and has received billions in American aid, but we have been unable to dissuade it from making common cause with Communist China against India, a country that we support. We tried to transform the army of a neutralist Laos into an instrument of American policy, and Laotian Communism is today stronger and more threatening than before.

We are here in the presence not of isolated failures, which any foreign policy must take in its stride, but of a pattern of impotence that points to organic disabilities in our foreign policy. That so powerful a nation as the United States is so consistently unable to achieve what it sets out to achieve cannot be due to accidents or personal insufficiencies alone. The cause must be sought in certain impediments to the effective exercise of American power, which seem to paralyze even the best makers of policy. Three types of such impediments can be distinguished: the objective conditions under which contemporary foreign policy must be carried on; the moral and intellectual assumptions underlying the American approach to foreign policy; and the anti-Communist tenet of American foreign policy. No single one of these factors can explain the impotence of our power, but together they may well do so.

Two objective conditions of contemporary world politics limit our power, as they do the power of all major nations: the availability of nuclear weapons, and the moral stigma that attaches to colonialism and to the policies traditionally associated with it.

The availability of nuclear weapons limits the freedom of action of the nuclear powers even more than it does that of the non-nuclear ones. The latter may reason that they can afford to threaten another nation with conventional force or actually use force against it, for the risk that one of the nuclear powers will intervene with nuclear weapons on one or the other side is likely to be remote. Nuclear powers in this respect are in a much more precarious situation. If they face each other with the threat or the actuality of conventional force, escalation into nuclear violence is an ever present possibility whose realization depends upon accidents, miscalculations, and, above all, the importance of the stakes. The situation is only somewhat, and not necessarily much, less precarious if a nuclear power threatens force against a non-nuclear one to whose defense another nuclear power is committed.

Since nuclear war, in contrast to conventional force, is recognized by all concerned not as a rational instrument of national policy but as a suicidal absurdity, nuclear powers are extremely reluctant to use any kind of force in support of their respective national interests. Yet in a world of sovereign nations it is impossible to support national interests effectively without the ultimate resort to military force. Thus the impotence of American policy toward Cuba is matched by the impotence of Soviet policy with regard to Berlin.

The example of our policy toward Cuba also points to the other objective condition limiting the use of our power. Twenty years ago, it would still have been a simple matter to remove through the use of force the threat Castro's Cuba constitutes to our interests. The Marines did it before, and they could have done it again. Leaving the problem of nuclear war aside, it would not be impossible to do the same thing even today, but it would not be a simple matter, and for two connected reasons. This is the age of the emancipation of the weak nations from the control of the strong ones. It is not only former colonies that have been emancipated; legally sovereign but actually dependent nations have been emancipated as well. In dealing with these latter, the strong nations can no longer use their power at will without incurring moral reprobation and risking in consequence a loss of prestige and influence. A great power may take these risks if the interests at stake appear important enough. This is what the Soviet Union did when it sent its army against the Hungarian Revolution of 1956, and while the moral reprobation the Russians earned for this move is but an ineffectual memory, the political and military gains have proved to be lasting.

However, the change in the moral climate has also affected the military issue itself. Twenty years ago, the government of Cuba presided over a by and large inert mass of people; it was an old-style dictatorship and the military problem consisted in the main in removing it and replacing it with one favorable to the interests of the United States. Today, just as the weak nations have been emancipated from control by the strong ones, so have the populations of the weak nations been emancipated in differing degrees from passive submission to their respective governments. Some of these peoples have become active participants in the process of emancipation, and they now have governments that govern in their name and with their support. Thus, a strong nation intervening with military force may not accomplish its task by removing the government or even by conquering the country. It may also have to subdue the population at large, which may take up arms against it. While these possibilities do not rule out the use of force, they make the powerful nations think twice before resorting to it.

The United States has gone farther in abstaining from the use of its power than is justified by a correct assessment of these two objective factors. It has been paralyzed in the use of its power, military and other, by two moral principles which, it has persuaded itself, have governed its foreign policy in the past and must govern it in the future: equality and nonintervention. In its relations with its allies, the United States has been caught in a dilemma between its responsibilities as the most powerful member of an alliance and the principle of the equality of men and nations, which has guided its judgment, if not its actions, since the beginning of its history. The consistent application of superior American power would have reduced the allies to satellites and would thereby have defeated the very purpose for which these nations had become the allies of America. On the other hand, the successful conduct of an alliance on the basis of the equality of its members presupposes that the identity of interests among the allies and their awareness of this identity are so complete that they will pursue common interests with common measures through spontaneous cooperation. To the degree that reality falls short of this assumption, the alliance cannot operate.

Of these two alternatives, the United States has consistently chosen the latter. The United States has refused to bring its superior power to bear upon its alliances on behalf of common interests that were naturally inchoate and were competing with divergent ones. The result has been disintegration, of which NATO is the prime example, or else the exploitation of American resources by a weak but determined ally. Governments that govern only because the United States maintains them, such as those of Taiwan and South Vietnam, and governments that have no alternative to the American association, such as those of Pakistan in the 1950's and Spain, have been able to play a winning game in which the United States holds all the trumps.

The most potent of these trumps is intervention, through either the withholding of benefits or the inflicting of disadvantages. It is this trump that we have consistently refused to play on moral grounds. Yet regardless of one's moral evaluation of intervention, it is obvious that we are intervening massively and effectively all over the world and that what we have forsworn is not intervention *per se* but only certain kinds of intervention. This position is morally untenable and, as will be shown, politically self-defeating.

To cite the example of South Vietnam, which is but more flagrant and at present more acute than many others: We intervened by putting Diem into power and supplying him with the implements of power. He owed his authority and power to our continuous political, military, and economic intervention. We intervened by establishing and keeping him in power because we thought that such intervention was in our and his countries' interests. If this kind of intervention is morally justified, where is it written that it is morally indefensible to intervene in order to compel Diem to pursue the policies for the sake of which we installed and kept him in power, or to remove him from power when he has proved himself incapable of pursuing those policies? The Western tradition of political philosophy justifies revolution against a tyrannical government, and even tyrannicide. Intervention in support of such morally justified undertakings is by the same token morally justified.

The issue here is not really moral but intellectual, and the moral issue is raised only as justification and rationalization of an attitude that shrinks from certain kinds of intervention, not only in the domestic affairs of other nations but in the political *status quo* as such.

We are at home with political actions that are but a repetition of past action and whose results are likely to stabilize things as they are. Yet we dread unprecedented political action because we dread the uncertainties, the risks, and the unknown results that such action is likely to conjure up. Thus we prefer safe routines in support of the *status quo* to innovations that will disturb it. It is only when we are face to face with a clear and present military threat that we act with bold and innovating zeal. But when we are faced with a political crisis, actual or impending, we are incapable of the foresight, sureness of touch as regards means and ends, and manipulative skill that are the prerequisites of successful political action. We tend to make the political problem manageable again by redefining it in military terms; thus we can act once more with unambiguous simplicity and without regard for those complexities, uncertainties, and risks inherent in the political act. And as concerns the political problem, we wait for something to happen: for de Gaulle to disappear from the political scene, for the Diem regime to straighten itself out, for something to turn up in China. However, short of death and natural catastrophes, nothing can happen but the actions of others, filling the void our paralysis has left.

Hence, the crisis of the Atlantic Alliance, proclaimed but by no means created by de Gaulle in January, 1963, took Washington by surprise. Our government reacted with indignation but not with reflection and political action. Yet the Suez crisis of the fall of 1956 ought to have opened its eyes to the inevitable decline of our alliances due to radically altered objective conditions. Pointing to the forms this decline was likely to take, I wrote in 1957: "While these considerations are admittedly speculative from the vantage point of 1957, they may well reflect the actuality of 1960." However, faced with the actuality of the 1970's, our government has been able to think of only remedies of most dubious value.

Finally, our impotence is aggravated and rendered irreparable by our commitment to anti-Communism as the overriding objective of our foreign policy. For most of our allies, anti-Communism is at best incidental to concrete national objectives and at worst irrelevant to them, being a mere device to secure and keep American support. Thus the governments of Taiwan and South Vietnam are not so much anti-Communist on principle as competitors for power with governments that happen to be Communist. Pakistan has allied itself with us in order to be able to fight not Communism but India, and it turned to China as soon as we gave military support to India against the latter.

While the anti-Communism of these and others of our allies is a matter of expediency rather than principle, it is our commitment to an indiscriminate anti-Communism, neglectful of concrete national interests, that enables our allies to deprive us of our freedom of choice. They can counter every move of ours that displeases them with an argument supplied by us: "If you do that, we shall go Communist." And so we stand helplessly by while they have their way.

Our impotence in the fullness of our power is, then, in some measure the result of objective conditions over which we have no control and which restrict the power of other powerful nations as well. In good measure, however, the source of that impotence is in ourselves. We are paralyzed because our moral, intellectual, and political judgment has gone astray. Our judgment must be reformed before we can expect to recover the use of our power, and upon that recovery the improvement of our foreign policies must wait.

The National Security Managers and the National Interest

RICHARD J. BARNET

"Foreign policies are not built on abstractions. They are the result of practical conceptions of the national interest. . . ." Charles Evans Hughes once noted when he was Secretary of State.[1] The key word of course is *practical*. Like the flag, the national interest can mean many different things to different people. The term in itself is the classic abstraction. It has virtually no inherent meaning. It acquires meaning only through interpretation. Those who play the role of interpreting the national interest are the priests of the modern state. Their values, their analysis of events, and their faith in the future determine what is deemed to be in the nation's interest and how it is to respond to the world political environment.

This of course has always been so. In times past those who managed the affairs of a great nation invariably defined the national interest in terms of power and glory. Whatever accrued to the majesty of the state was in its interest. It mattered little how much the people had to be taxed for it or how many had to die. The realization that a leader's conception of the national interest may be self-serving or fallible lay behind the attempt in the American Constitution to subject the foreign relations power to some form of democratic control. As Abraham Lincoln put it at the time of the Mexican War:

Reprinted by permission of *Politics and Society*. Richard J. Barnet is co-director of the Institute for Policy Studies. He was formerly an official of the State Department and an adviser to the Department of Defense. He is the author of *Intervention and Revolution*, and *The Economy of Death*.

The provision of the Constitution giving the warmaking power to Congress, was dictated, as I understand it, by the following reasons: Kings had always been involving and impoverishing their people in wars, pretending generally, if not always, that the good of the people was the object. This, our Convention understood to be the most oppressive of all kingly oppressions: and they resolved to so frame the Constitution that no man should hold the power of bringing this oppression upon us.[2]

The Vietnam catastrophe has dramatized the reality that democratic control of foreign policy has failed. The executive has been given extraordinary powers to commit the United States to military intervention abroad and has simply taken others. Congressmen lack the information on which to make informed judgments about the national interest and they are not encouraged to obtain it. It has generally been assumed that there is no alternative to vesting life and death power over the society in the hands of a few men. For example, in the Cuban missile crisis of 1962 about ten individuals made the decisions which by their modest contemporary estimates beforehand could have resulted in 150,000,000 casualties. Their analysis of the national interest was the only guide. That fact is taken as an inevitable consequence of the nuclear age. Whether, indeed, the advent of nuclear weapons has rendered democratic control of foreign policy obsolete or merely made it more essential is beyond the argument of this paper.

The extraordinary concentration of power in the hands of the executive does, however, make the question of recruitment of the National Security Managers a particularly crucial one. These are the men who occupy the top foreign policy and national security positions (assistant secretary and higher) in the Departments of State, Defense, Army, Navy, Air Force, Central Intelligence Agency, Atomic Energy Commission, and the White House staff. It is their collective picture of the outside world which has formed the basis for official judgements of the national interest. Their job has been to simplify the kaleidoscopic experience of the last generation for the rest of us. They have defined the threats to the national interest, made the commitments that were supposed to meet the threats, and, in most cases, have been the sole judges of their own performance.

I have examined the backgrounds and careers of the 400 individuals who held these positions from 1940 to 1967. Certain patterns revealed by the study may help to explain why the United States has defined the national interest in the way that it has.

The men who have designed the bipartisan foreign policy have for the most part been without experience in the politics or administration of domestic affairs. They have been above electoral politics. Fewer than ten individuals of the group have held elective office of any kind. Only Harold Stassen, Chester Bowles, Averell Harriman, and G. Mennen Williams held high office. (It is noteworthy that the first three were the leading mavericks among the National Security Managers during the last generation. Stassen and Bowles both lost their high posts for bucking official orthodoxy.) Their skills have not been those of the politician who must at least give the appearance of solving problems or reconciling competing interests if he hopes to be reelected, but those of the crisis manipulator. Dean Rusk characterized his personal goal in office as Secretary of State as handing the Berlin Crisis over to his successor in no worse shape than he found it. This is the managerial or "keep the ball bouncing" view of statecraft characteristic of those who count on being somewhere else when the ball drops.

Since National Security Managers have been recruited outside the electoral process, they do not expect to have to defend their policies before the electorate. Public opinion therefore plays a marginal role in the formulation of their concept of the national interest.

Fewer than 10 percent of the top national security bureaucrats have held appointive positions in agencies that deal with domestic problems of American life. The lack of experience with public domestic problems characteristic of almost all National Security Managers has helped to perpetuate the artificial separation between the national security institutions and the rest of the government. A generation of National Security Managers have asserted that we can have a military machine "second to none" and do everything that needs to be done at the same time. This assertion, which rests on the premise that there is not much that needs doing in American society is an easy one for those without firsthand knowledge of America's domestic crises or responsibility for dealing with them. Thus, national priorities have become seriously distorted for two reasons. First, we have no institutional machinery for evaluating competing demands on the tax dollar from the Military Establishment, on the one hand, and from the rest of the country on the other. Second, we have put in charge of the national security bureaucracy for a generation men who by virtue of career, training and interests have little sensitivity to public problems in domestic society.

Since the National Security Managers are remarkably insulated from public opinion and are responsive to a far narrower range of domestic pressures than are the managers of the domestic agencies, the process by which they are recruited is particularly significant. During the last generation National Security Managers have been primarily recruited from the world of big business and high finance.

If we take a look at the men who have held the very top positions, the secretaries and undersecretaries of State and Defense, the secretaries of the three services, the chairman of the Atomic Energy Commission, and the director of the CIA, we find that out of ninety-one individuals who held these offices during the period 1940 to 1967, seventy of them came from major corporations and investment houses. This includes eight out of ten secretaries of Defense, seven out of eight secretaries of the Air Force, every secretary of the Navy, eight out of nine secretaries of the Army, every deputy secretary of Defense, three out of five directors of the CIA, and three out of five chairmen of the Atomic Energy Commission.

The historian Gabriel Kolko investigated 234 top foreign policy decision makers and found that "men who come from big business, investment and law held 59.6 percent of the posts."[3] The Brookings Institution volume *Men Who Govern*, a comprehensive study of the top federal bureaucracy from 1933 to 1965, reveals that before coming to work in the Pentagon 86 percent of the secretaries of the Army, Navy, and the Air Force were either businessmen or lawyers (usually with a business practice).[4] In the Kennedy Administraton 20 percent of all civilian executives in defense-related agencies came from defense contractors.[5] Defining the national interest and protecting national security have been deemed to be the proper province of business. Indeed, as President Coolidge used to say, the business of America is business.

The collection of investment bankers and legal advisors to big business who designed the national security bureaucracies and helped to run them for a generation came to Washington in 1940. Dr. New

Deal was dead, President Roosevelt announced, and Dr. Win the War had come to take his place. Two men, Henry L. Stimson, Hoover's secretary of state and a leading member of the Wall Street bar, and James V. Forrestal, president of Dillon Read Company, one of the biggest investment bankers, were responsible for recruiting many of their old friends and associates to run the war. In the formative postwar years of the Truman Administration when the essential elements of United States foreign and military policy were laid down, these recruits continued to act as the nation's top National Security Managers. Dean Acheson, James V. Forrestal, Robert Lovett, John McCloy, Averell Harriman, all of whom became acquainted with foreign policy through running a war, played the crucial roles in deciding how to use American's power in peace.

Once again it was quite natural to look to their own associates, each an American success story, to carry on with the management of the nation's military power. Thus, for example, Forrestal's firm, Dillon Read, contributed such key figures as Paul Nitze, who headed the State Department Policy Planning Staff in the Truman Administration and ran the Defense Department as deputy to Clark Clifford in the closing year of the Johnson Administration. William Draper, an architect of United States postwar policy towards Germany and Japan came from the same firm. In the Truman years twenty-two key posts in the State Department, ten in the Defense Department and five key national security positions in other agencies were held by bankers who were either Republicans or without party affiliation. As Professor Samuel Huntington has pointed out in his study, *The Soldier and the State*, "they possessed all the inherent and real conservatism of the banking breed."[6] Having built their business careers on their judicious management of risk, they now become expert in the management of crisis. Their interest lay in making the system function smoothly—conserving and expanding America's power. They were neither innovators nor problem solvers. Convinced from their encounter with Hitler that force is the only thing that pays off in international relations, they all operated on the assumption that the endless stockpiling of weapons was the price of safety.

The Eisenhower Administration tended to recruit its National Security Managers from the top manufacturing corporations rather than from the investment banking houses. To be sure, bankers were not exactly unwelcome in the Eisenhower years. Robert Cutler, twice the president's special assistant for national security affairs, was chairman of the board of the Old Colony Trust Company in Boston; Joseph Dodge, the influential director of the Bureau of the Budget, was a Detroit banker; Douglas Dillon, of Dillon Read, was undersecretary of state for Economic Affairs; Thomas Gates, the last Eisenhower secretary of defense, was a Philadelphia banker and subsequently head of the Morgan Guaranty Trust Company.

But most of the principal figures of the era were associated with the leading industrial corporations, either as chief executives or directors; many of these corporations ranked among the top 100 defense contractors. Eisenhower's first secretary of defense was Charles Wilson, president of General Motors; his second was Neil McElroy, a public relations specialist who became president of Proctor and Gamble. One deputy secretary of defense was Robert B. Anderson, a Texas oilman. Another was Roger Kyes, another General Motors executive, and a third was Donald Quarles of Westinghouse.

When President Kennedy was elected on his campaign promise to "get the country moving again," the first thing he did was to reach back eight years for advice on national security. Many of the men he appointed as top National Security Managers of the New Frontier were the old faces of the Truman Administration. In addition to Dean Rusk, a strong MacArthur supporter in the Korean war who wrote the memorandum urging the UN forces to cross the 38th Parallel in Korea, Kennedy's State Department appointments also included George McGhee, a successful oil prospector and principal architect of Truman's Middle East policy. Adolf Berle, Averell Harriman, Paul Nitze, John McCone, John McCloy, William C. Foster and other experienced hands from the national security world also made it clear that the new administration would follow familiar patterns.

The Kennedy Administration brought in a few new faces as well. The appointment of McGeorge Bundy as special assistant to the president for national security affairs inaugurated what has come to be a tradition of giving that crucial staff position to men holding academic chairs. Bundy, Rostow, and Kissinger are hardly typical professors nor were their appointments recognition of independent academic work. Each had been unofficial consultant or insider for years before his appointment. (In an interview Rostow once noted that he had not spent a year outside the government since 1946.) Each rose in the national security bureaucracy by becoming the protege of powerful men such as Acheson, Stimson, and Rockefeller or by working directly for the election of the presidential candidate. The other Kennedy innovation was to bring in a group of young economists from the Rand corporation to introduce systems analysis and cost effectiveness into the Pentagon. But with the exception of Bundy's, the principal positions were filled according to old specifications.

Robert McNamara was president of Ford instead of General Motors; Roswell Gilpatric, appointed deputy secretary of defense, was a partner of a leading Wall Street law firm. In career experience he differed from his immediate Republican predecessor, James Douglas, in three principal respects. His law office was in New York rather than Chicago. He had been under-secretary of the Air Force while Douglas had been secretary. He was director of Eastern Airlines instead of American Airlines.

The recruitment patterns in the key positions in the Department of Defense relating to procurement, research, development, and other contracting functions are particularly significant. Recently Senator William Proxmire brought up the case of Thomas Morris, the former assistant secretary of defense for procurement who became vice-president of Litton Industries. In his last year as procurement chief Litton contracts jumped from $180 million to $466 million, an increase of almost 250 percent. Senator Proxmire charged the firm with "buying influence with the Pentagon and plenty of it" through a "payoff."[7] Morris had indeed been "integrally and powerfully involved with every Pentagon decision" on procurement, as Proxmire charged, but his case was by no means unique. A generation of engineer-entrepreneurs, high level systems managers, and procurement specialists have been shuttling back and forth between defense contractors and strategic positions in the Department of Defense.

This trend began in the early 1950's, with the Korean rearmament and the beginning of the missile program. In 1950, William Burden, a partner of Brown Brothers, Harriman and a director of Lockheed Aircraft Company, was made special assistant for research and development to Air Force Secretary Finletter. A month after he resigned in 1952, one of his partners, James T. Hill, who later was active in Itek (a Rockefeller-financed defense corporation) became assistant secretary for management. Burden was followed in the research and development job by Trevor Gardner, president and majority stockholder of Hycon Corporation. Gardner, who had been put in charge of a committee "to eliminate inter-service competition in development of guided missiles," resigned in 1956 in protest over the Defense Department's refusal to give the Air Force exclusive control of the missile program. During his years in Washington, his company tripled its government contracts. His successor was Richard Horner, a career scientist who had worked for the military. In less than two years Horner managed to land a senior vice presidency with the Northrop Aircraft Company. His successor, Joseph V. Charyk, did even better. He came from Lockheed, and after four years of advising on what the Air Force should buy and build, became head of Ford's space technology division and later, after another stint at the Pentagon, president of the Communications Satellite Corporation. His three successors, Brockway McMillan, Courtland D. Perkins and Alexander Flax, managed to combine similar patriotic service with careers as managers or directors of the Bell Telephone Laboratories, Fairchild Stratosphere Corporation and Cornell Aeronautics Laboratory, all major defense contractors.

Many principal officials of the Air Force either had a home in the aircraft industry or found one on leaving office. Malcolm MacIntyre, under-secretary in the Eisenhower Administration, for example, was a Wall Street lawyer who moved up after his Pentagon service to the presidency of Eastern Airlines and later to a vice presidency of Martin Marietta, another leading contractor. Robert H. Charles, a Johnson appointee who handled the C-54 cargo plane and was prepared to pay Lockheed almost $2 billion more than the contract price, had been executive vice president of McDonnell Aircraft. Philip B. Taylor, appointed by Eisenhower to be assistant secretary in charge of material, had been with both Curtiss Wright and Pan American. Roger Lewis, another Eisenhower assistant secretary in charge of material, had also been a vice president of Pan American World Airways and finally president of General Dynamics. Another assistant secretary, Joseph Imirie, became yet another vice president of Litton Industries.

The principal officers in charge of research, development, and procurement for the Army have included William Martin (Bell

Labs), Finn Larsen (Minneapolis Honeywell), Willis M. Hawkins, Jr. (Lockheed), and Earl D. Johnson, who like Frank Pace, a former Secretary of the Army, climbed from the Pentagon into the presidency of General Dynamics. The Navy research and development officers, James Wakelin, Robert W. Morse, Albert Pratt, have been associated with such leading defense contractors as Itek, Chesapeake Instruments, Ryan Aeronautics, and Simplex Wire and Cable. From 1941 until 1959, the Navy had an assistant secretary in charge of its own separate air force. Two of them were Wall Street lawyers and directors of aviation corporations: Artemus Gates (Boeing); John L. Sullivan (Martin Marietta). Two others were connected with the airline industry: James H. Smith (Pan American) and Dan A. Kimball (Continental Airlines). Kimball later became president of Aerojet General.

Many of the most important decisions on research, development, and procurement have been made at the Defense Department level. Here also the recruitment patterns are the same: in the Eisenhower Administration, Frank Newbury (Westinghouse), Donald Quarles (Western Electric, Sandia Corp.), Clifford Furnas (Curtiss Wright), to give three examples. In the Kennedy and Johnson Administrations, John Rubel (Lockheed, Litton), Eugene Fubini (IBM, Airborne Instruments Laboratory), Harold Brown and John Foster (Livermore Laboratories).

Why are these recruitment patterns important? Why do they raise problems? There is a certain superficial plausibility in recruiting Pentagon managers from the weapons professionals in industry. But the practice builds into the operations of government a commitment to an escalating arms race. For the men who sustain the weapons research, development, and procurement process, service in the Pentagon is an essential element of career building. In virtually every case the individuals in charge of these functions have used their tenure at the Department of Defense to better themselves. Many have come as vice presidents and left as presidents. Quite apart from the question of conflict of interest, which is a serious one, there is the larger problem of biased judgement. In discussing the Morris case noted earlier Senator Proxmire pointed out that almost 90 percent of defense contracting is by negotiation and not by competitive bid. Thus "whether Litton or some other firm gets a particular contract will be determined very largely by the subjective attitude of Pentagon officials toward Litton officials."[8] The real problem however, is not so much a matter of corrupt practice as distorted perception. The men on the Litton Industries–Pentagon shuttle have no incentive to look for or to find an alternative to the arms race. Indeed, they need continued psychological assurance that there is no alternative to stockpiling instruments of death. When virtually the only people who make the crucial initial decisions whether new weapons systems are needed, whether they cost too much, or who should make them, are those men who directly and personally stand to gain from big defense budgets, a national policy of escalating military budgets has already been established.

However, the recruitment of the National Security Managers primarily from the world of business raises some larger issues that are even more significant. First, it should be said that this practice is typical of other great nations. The dominant interest group or class in a society normally takes control of its foreign relations. Since the business of America is business, what could be more natural than that businessmen should decide the national interest?

The first problem is that the homogenous backgrounds and virtually identical careers of the National Security Managers produce a standard way of looking at the world, a set of shared, unchallengeable assumptions. It has often been asked during the Vietnam War how almost everybody in the upper reaches of government could be so wrong about the underlying premises of United States policy. Most of the men who have set these assumptions and have operated over the last generation from them have been drawn from executive suites and law offices within shouting distance of each other in about fifteen city blocks in New York, Washington, Detroit, Chicago, and Boston. Their reference group for deciding the national interest is narrow. When planning a decision of national security policy they do not normally solicit the views of civil rights leaders, farmers, laborers, mayors, artists, or small businessmen. Nor do people from these areas of national life become National Security Managers. In almost thirty years there has been one woman and no Negro appointed to the top national security positions. Indeed, when Martin Luther King expressed opposition to the Vietnam War, he was told that it was "inappropriate" for someone in the civil rights movement to voice his views on foreign policy. The opinions that the National Security

Manager values are those of his friends and colleagues. They have power, which is often an acceptable substitute for judgement, and since they view the world much as he does, they must be right. They are also the men with whom he will most likely have to deal when he lays down the burdens of office. "What will my friends on Wall Street say?" the director of the Arms Control and Disarmament Agency once exclaimed when asked to endorse a disarmament proposal that would limit the future production of missiles.

There are of course differing policy views among the National Security Managers. There is rivalry among the military services and differing attitudes within bureaus of the State Department. But the consensus on premises and ends have been remarkably secure. Keeping ahead in the arms race is the key to security. The solution of urgent domestic problems must be deferred until some undetermined point at which ideal security will have been achieved. Given an imperfect world, the country is doing as well as can be expected in developing its own resources and in guiding the world to a stable order.

The National Security Manager is likely to be among the most shrewd, energetic and often engaging men in America, but he has little feel for what is happening or should happen in his country. When Charles Wilson, the former president of General Motors who became Eisenhower's secretary of defense blurted out his delightful aphorism, "What is good for General Motors is good for America and vice versa" he was merely restating the basic national security premise. Using national power, including military forces if necessary, to create a "good business climate" at home and abroad is more important than a good social climate in lower class or middle class America. An excited stock market rather than the depletion rate of the nation's human and natural resources is the index of America's progress. The National Security Manager sees this country from a rather special angle because, despite the thousands of miles he has logged, he is something of an emigré in his own society. The familiar itinerary takes him from one air-conditioned room to another across the continent, his office on Wall Street or LaSalle Street, his temporary office at the Pentagon or in the White House basement, a visit to a London or a Texas client, a dinner at the Council on Foreign Relations and so forth. The closest he ever comes to seeing a hungry

American is when his dinner companion is treated to bad service at one of Manhattan's declining French restaurants.

Under the stimulus of defense spending the American economy has boomed, but its benefits have not been equitably shared. The disparity between rich and poor in America has widened. The National Security Managers have not regarded the redistribution of wealth as a priority concern for they have had neither the experience nor the incentive to understand the problems of the poor. Their professional and personal interests are with the business and commercial interests whom they serve and with whom they identify.

By recruiting the National Security Managers from those who have been successful as conservators and managers in the booming domestic economy we have built into the system a powerful bias in favor of a dynamic *status quo*, i.e., preservation of America's preeminent economic and military position by the continually increasing and projecting American power abroad. Just as a corporation can stay in place only by moving ahead so a nation must expand its power. Again, this is hardly an exceptional philosophy for a great nation nor one limited to men from business backgrounds. The party bureaucrats who are the National Security Managers in the Soviet Union have a remarkably similar outlook as to the proper role of a great nation. The point is that a moment in history when technology has altered the meaning of national security fundamentally and the problems of human survival are utterly different from anything facing mankind before the men who define the American national interest are by virtue of temperament, background, and class interest those with the least incentive to make changes. Looking at the world from where they do, they see little urgency for radical alternative political and social solutions to the problems of how men live in their own country, much less in the outside world.

The National Security Managers have measured their triumphs and failures in terms of their ability to use national power to compel other governments to yield to America's will. Security they have defined as keeping open as many options as possible through the skillful manipulation of the political environment. But the purpose of this vast managerial effort has been lost. Skillful management leading to the acquisition of more power has become an end in itself.

We know that social organisms survive only if they are capable of learning from their experience and adapting to changing circumstances. As the nation prepares to enter the twenty-first century it is clear that we need a new definition of national interest. There can be no national security until international relations are seen not as a competitive games but as a strategy for creating a world environment in which the central question is not the acquisition of power but the use of power to make the world liveable for man. To do this we need radically different institutions for defining and implementing the national interest. And very different sorts of men, with different allegiances and interests, to manage the problem of survival.

References

1. Portions of this paper are excerpted from Richard J. Barnet, *The Economy of Death*, published by Atheneum Publishers, 1969.
2. Abraham Lincoln quoted in Roy P. Basler, *et al.*, eds., *The Collected Works of Abraham Lincoln*, vol. 1 (New Brunswick, N.J.: Rutgers University Press, 1953), pp. 451–452, and cited in Merlo J. Pusey, *The Way We Go To War* (Boston: Houghton-Mifflin, 1969), p. 61.
3. Gabriel Kolko, *The Roots of American Foreign Policy: An Analysis of Power and Purpose* (Boston: Beacon Press, 1969), p. 19.
4. David T. Stanley, *et al.*, *Men Who Govern* (Washington, D.C.: The Brookings Institution, 1967), p. 141.
5. *Ibid.*, p. 142.
6. Samuel Huntington, *The Soldier and the State* (Cambridge: Harvard University Press, Belknap Press, 1957), p. 380.
7. U.S. *Congressional Record* (May 5, 1969), p. S 4543.
8. *Ibid.*

Part III

How Can We Survive in an Age of Discontinuity— and Should We?

Introduction: Alternative Futures for America

The following articles are meant to be suggestive, not definitive, of the various alternative futures for America. For example, two alternatives that command significant followings, especially among the young, are missing. One is the total, violent destruction of the existing economic-social-political system, to be rebuilt upon radical principles. This concept is emphasized by several radical left groups such as the Weathermen. The contributor who had intended to be a spokesman for this position, however, was engaged in the Mayday protest in Washington, D.C. The resulting legal proceedings left him little leisure for writing.

Similarly, many individuals seek to avoid the frustrations of attempting to cope with reality, and instead choose to opt out of the whole system into a private world that is often based on the drug culture. The contributor who had intended to write an article on "freaking out" apparently took his research seriously. At any rate, he has not been heard from.

Nevertheless, the five articles here and several earlier ones do present varied alternatives that should stimulate their reader's independent thought.

Part III has been organized on the basis of a continuum from skepticism, pessimism, belief that some tentative changes may be possible, a concrete proposal for bringing about change, to a very optimistic vision of its immanence. Here, as in the introduction to Part II, the terms conservative, new left, libertarian, and socialist are being used in the sense in which they were defined in the introduction to Part I.

As has been suggested in that earlier introduction, Robert Booth Fowler's vision of the American future is that of a philosophic conservative, stressing the probability of gradual and evolutionary change and the improbability of human nature altering in the future any more than it has in the past. He rejects all futurist proposals on the ground that pessimistic prophets are elitists who seem to inflate today's problems and deflate the future's prospects, optimistic prophets seem to be lost in abstractions, and the vision of the prophets of a counter-culture is unclear, confused and undeveloped. He believes that change will occur, and on the whole is optimistic about its direction, but expects that change to evolve from the basic traditions of the society rather than coming from any radical revolution of values and institutions.

Michael Parenti would be skeptical of even this guarded degree of optimism. He does not anticipate any likelihood of restructuring human nature, or basic American political institutions. Thus, he believes that optimists are blind to the inescapability of interest and power. He maintains that in the future as in the past the major decisions about how the vast resources of our society are used will be made by the private sector of the economy. Because he maintains that the economic institutions of a capitalist society are rarely, if ever, held accountable for the enormous social costs of their profit system, he is quite pessimistic about the possibility of reform toward the new left goals of a more free and egalitarian society.

Henry S. Kariel maintains that although there are significant ideological and institutional impediments to such change, it *is* possible to establish some base line, some point of departure. He therefore stresses the value of experimental action, virtuosity and creativity. While defeat may be likely, he believes that the new left goals are worth the gamble.

Philip Brenner proposes a concrete experiment that he believes to be a fruitful starting point for change toward the same goals—a new education. He views the present educational system as one that fosters competition and one that denies self-fulfillment to children, thereby tending to incapacitate people from challenging the existing political order. Thus, he views the present educational structure as supportive of the competitive, inegalitarian, product orientation of a capitalist society. In its stead he suggests specific means to alter the existing educational structure toward one that could free people's critical faculties by assisting them to develop a meaning for themselves physically and enabling them to understand the societal barriers that constrain them. While he argues that such a change in the educational system cannot alone change society, it seems a useful beginning.

The final article in Part III presents an optimistic counter-culture argument. "The times they *are* achanging," claims Rod Manis, and they are moving inexorably in the direction of a libertarian society. He describes this new culture as "thinking for yourself," and believes that it will increasingly make the concepts of "right" and "left" irrelevant.

Several other articles in this volume also present alternative visions of the American future, and conceptions of the most effective means to bring about their preferred changes. For example, in discussing the environmental crisis in Part II, Robert Poole, Jr., and Clifford Humphrey present quite divergent alternatives. The socialist alternative is presented in articles by Hyman Lumer and Andrew McLaughlin.

A Skeptical Look at the American Future and Her Futurists

ROBERT BOOTH FOWLER

It is so noisy now that even the person genuinely concerned to discover how we can possibly live in our "age of discontinuity" and live well in the future must be annoyed. Who can hear himself thinking? The noise from the clatter and clashes of the multitude of prophets, soothsayers, and social scientists who propose

Robert Booth Fowler (Ph.D., Harvard University) is Assistant Professor of Political Science at the University of Wisconsin, has co-authored a reader on contemporary political thought and authored several articles. He is prouder, however, of having received an award for excellence in teaching from the University of Wisconsin.

to help us creates just too much din. Suddenly these prophets are everywhere. They relentlessly and noisily seize on the present and predict the future. They have made the question of "how to survive" in the future their business—often a profitable one—and they often boldly declare that they know the ways and the answers.

Alas, the prophets of our age disagree. They disagree from their first judgment; some see survival as doubtful; others see it as likely. They also disagree widely on the bases upon which they make their respective basic assessments of the future. The prophets and futurists contend endlessly with themselves and with us over just what is the greatest threat or the greatest hope regarding our survival. One can easily feel depressed at the lack of unity and single purpose in all the contemporary futurist debates.

Perhaps there is a better response in answer to the question of the American future than all the frenzied noise and clamor that the prophecy business today offers. This essay is partly an attempt to suggest outlines of this more adequate response. Mine is a quiet one in a noisy age. It is seemingly easy-going in an age of intense self-righteousness; it is relatively calm in the midst of the contemporary cries of alarm or salvation. There is no element of desperation.

I propose that we do three things in this age of discontinuity as we consider our future and our chances for survival. First, we need to get off the bandwagon of the alarmist or joyous futurists and prophets and generally ignore them. My essay will argue that a consideration of the most popular alternative futures predicted or proposed for America today shows that they deserve rejection. They either involve accepting values that ought not to be sanctioned or constitute mere speculation posing as firm prediction, or both.

Second, I propose that we doubt their master assumption that in one or another possibly important ways the future and future men promise to be different, either for better or worse. I suppose I am conservative because I am convinced that our new prophets cannot demonstrate that there will be fundamental change in the essentials of life. Certainly my view clashes directly with the fashionable liberalism or radicalism of the futurists of our day. Third, I propose that we act as men and women have always done: do what we can to make the world better, avoiding the dramatic despair of the pessimistic prophets and the radical optimism of many other futurists.

Pessimistic Prophets

We must begin by looking at the popular, pretentious world of prophesy today. To suggest its great inadequacies is our task. One immense camp of futurists is certain that our continued existence as a nation, or as human beings, is a highly doubtful matter. They usually see our national and world situation as bleak and desperate. These pessimists match their grim description of the present and visible future with radical prescription. For a desperate situation radical measures are suggested to halt the alarming trends of human and environmental destruction.

These pessimistic prophets stand out today for another reason. Besides the substance of their worried assessments and drastic proposals for change, they have a distinct personal style. They are both terribly earnest and terribly busy. After all, they believe they have to be this way—the message is too important and too serious for any other approach. They remind one of so many prophets of old who also had an idea that they had beheld in the present the frightening future.

Unfortunately, of course, these latter-day prophets of gloom and experts in doubtful futures are themselves flawed from the first in one crucial way: they are frequently far apart in their analyses about just what in the present appears to doom the future. Sometimes, to be sure, they see and passingly acknowledge competing analyses. One scarcely knows which to choose—if any.

Four explanations for the allegedly unfortunate shape of our future compete for dominance today. They appear to have unleashed a torrent of books and prophecies upon us, using the explanations of the population explosion, the ecological crisis, the technology menace and the political crisis.

Problems of race and racism appear to belong in the list no longer. Of course it is still mandatory today for all intellectuals to acknowledge both that the race problem is terribly crucial and that America is a racist country. The truth remains, however, that everybody knows the open secret that the glamor has gone out of the race issue for white intellectuals, prophets, and social scientists. Certainly blacks know. Part of the reason for the latest change in fashion here of course is that blacks proved uninterested in the prophecies of white intellectuals.

Indeed, blacks proved one of the most common assumptions of the once noisy racial pessimists wrong. Not so long ago all America was going to burn down in the fires of racial war, or so the pessimists said, so the reigning intellectual speculation asserted. It never happened. The pessimists' prophecy was flatly wrong.

There are lots of intellectual prophets today who have now moved on to new "crises," new outlets for their pessimism. Yet one wonders why it is that when they look back to their agitation about racial destruction they do not see how inaccurate their extreme pessimism was. What they should have realized is that people never like having their homes or stores burned down, or their communities in riot. Blacks in the ghettoes of course turned out to be little different than anybody else. Sadly, little has improved for many blacks except in terms of individual efforts and specific projects. Life did not end either, however, including the life of the American polity. There is a lesson for the professional pessimists and crisis-mongers of our time here.

The proponents of the population crisis make big claims as the reason for their pessimism for our future. They assert that future life itself is at stake. They say that very shortly overpopulation dooms us. Some say ten years are left, others prefer twenty-five, and some prefer a later date in time. But all are very anxious. None is now more famous (nor more successful) as a result of his crusade to save man from death by overpopulation than Paul Ehrlich. His book, *The Population Bomb*,[1] and his tireless, earnest, militant speeches have carried the message everywhere. He has company in a host of parallel prophets and organizations that are also involved in the cause.

What is at issue here is not the fact that world population is growing at a disturbing rate, nor is the fact that this rate needs control at issue. Few would dispute these points anymore. However, there are plenty of reasons for not joining the population crusade. First, its claims are too dramatic and sweeping. Where did it get the curious idea that human existence is not going to be able to deal with this problem without the elimination of all life? There is plenty of justification for thinking that nature is every bit as able to deal with human overpopulation as it does with deer overpopulation. The factors that Malthus described are still with us: if we overpopulate too greatly starvation, disease, and war will kill us off.

Now there is nothing attractive about this possibility; but even this grim possibility involves something much less drastic than the end of the human race. Moreover, abortion, birth control, smaller families, and increased food production will help. The history of population prediction has been notoriously and repeatedly wrong before, and is likely to be wrong again. In any case, the gloomy predictions are built upon present or alleged present trends. We should remember that prediction from such grounds is a doubtful business always.[2]

The great frustration for Ehrlich and the population crisis movement is that they cannot understand why people do not act as drastically as the movement demands. Therefore, they ascribe the reason to lack of education or political failure, or both. Perhaps this is a partial explanation, but certainly there is more. Clearly people do not care as much as Ehrlich and his associates do because they do not perceive the same threat. Contrary to the population crisis movement's view, this does not make people irrational or uneducated or misled. Instead, they are just more concretely focused—they care about life now and having children now. Perhaps too they are more confident of nature and life. Their life and life in general around them goes on. Ehrlich is an abstraction. The question of the extinction of the species is an abstraction. Why are popular perceptions to be so casually rejected in such an elitist way? Will the eventual path become an intense political and social authoritarianism and elitism as the means of dealing with the non-frightened masses? The actual and potential elitism of the population movement bothers one.

Certainly one ought to worry and wonder about population growth the world over. Certainly one ought to move ahead toward population control. As yet, however, I see no reason to view population growth as anything like the greatest future menace of our times endangering our very future. Certainly I see no reason for the desperate rhetoric of the population movement. Here the noise is loud, but it is still not convincing, nor are its elitist tones attractive. Assertions of pessimism do not constitute evidence, only scare tactics.

Many of the same points apply as well to the dogmas of the more alarmed futurists and prophets of the ecological crisis. Here again one should be clear. No one is going to deny that there are problems with our natural environment that are important for our future survival such as problems of air pollution, water pollution and preservation of natural resources. We all know, and have known for a long time, that these problems need attention and are not getting enough.

Yet this has nothing to do with the worried tone, the bleak predictions, and the drastic solutions that appear daily. The alarmist claims pronounced nightly by Walter Cronkite on his news programs are backed by such crisis-shaped books on specific areas as J. Esposito's *Vanishing Air*[3] and such vulgar political muckraking books as J. Ridgeway's *The Politics of Ecology*.[4] Indeed, there is no question for the ecology movement that the whole matter has come down to a situation wherein we literally need a broad *Agenda for Survival* as in the revealing title of a new book on the ecological crisis.[5]

The ecological situation may well be desperate. Some substantial questions need answering, however, before we turn our understanding of the future and our programs of the present over to the ecological pessimists. On one level these questions concern the actual seriousness of the situation. Who and what are really affected, how much, and in what ways? Who and what are going to be affected, how much, and in what ways? Much, much more needs to be known about these matters before anybody bows down to the fashionable eco-crisis mentality. Agitated assertions that life on earth is in doubt or already lost do not constitute detailed argument. There also should be a good deal more modesty on the part of the eco-prophets. They are wont to proclaim the future without much admission of what they know—that the future is never simply an extension of the present trend.

On another level, there is reason for serious exploration of the eco-crisis outlook's twin assumptions that are so central to its claim for universal attention and worry. The movement's members always argue that almost everyone in the world is in the crisis together. Militant ecologists feel that here is the issue that need not divide us and that ought not to divide us between the vast majority and the evil tiny minority of pollutors and destroyers. So the ecological movement appears to promise both a way of human unification and a minority to hate. Both offerings are nicely, and possibly necessarily, linked to each other.

It is actually unclear how much of the alleged present and future problems involve nearly hysterical reaction about pollution or depletion of areas or resources mostly relevant only to the life-style of the Western world's upper and upper-middle class. "Saving" remote wilderness regions, for instance, is hardly something that deeply involves all our futures. Meanwhile, to make everything pure enough for ecologists many businesses may be forced to cease operation, which sometimes involved very tangible costs.[6] Moreover, no one questions the suspiciously upper-middle and upper class base of the ecological movement. Are we to assume that members of these classes are wiser than other citizens?

Few ecologists doubt this assumption. The other side of their dubious self-confidence is their frequent assertion of the primacy of their crisis. Yet there is some question whether there are not other issues of as great or greater importance measured in terms of substantial effect on people. Among these issues may be racial problems, poverty, and, yes, population control. For most people in America much of the so-called ecological crisis is just too remote from their lives. They often do not have the time, or money, or both to worry about the long run. To the ecologist who usually does have the time, or money, or both this is incredibly short-sighted. It is not self-evident that he is right.

In addition, most people do not have time or money or interest either for the scarcely concealed nature-romanticism of the ecological futurists. Popular attitudes rarely include extensive celebrations of nature or the natural; more often, they involve a determination to use (sometimes foolishly) nature, bend it, and conquer it. In contrast some ecologists must appear to be simply naive nature-lovers; and, in fact, they rarely do explain what is so sacred about nature. As of yet, the ecological movement seems unable to show that many of its goals are essential to continued life or even decent life as opposed to indulging nature-romanticism. This should be their task if they wish to be taken seriously.

Finally, whenever this case is made, if it can be, one should insist on an honest accounting. One should always insist that the costs of any project of ecological "survival" appear fully and openly. Ecology costs money. It will cost lots more than it has already. We do not want, I trust, to have anyone fooled into thinking that the money spent on ecology could come from the air itself. It will have to come from somewhere. This source and the supposed benefits of the costs should be made clear in general and in every case.

The terrible sense that man is fundamentally a destroyer, a notion deeply implicit in the pessimism of the population and ecological futurists, is repeated by those whose attention is on man's technology as the great and growing enemy threatening men in the future. Sometimes, the technological pessimists see man as the despoiler of a precious nature through his use of technology; this describes the position of the more anarchic anti-technologists. Paul Goodman has often expressed this view and more recently Lewis Mumford has added his vigorous voice.[7] More often today, the view of the pessimistic technologists is that the problem with technology is that it is out of control, not bad in itself. Perhaps the most famous book of recent years expressing this idea was of course Herbert Marcuse's *One Dimensional Man*.[8] There the image of most people is unfailingly condescending and elitist. They cannot see that technology has them in its grips nor that it quickly turns out to be the tool of only a few and of benefit to only a few. The masses are fools.

This elitist view is ill-disguised in the outlook of all the futurist pessimists, whether their concern is primarily technology or not. In all cases they face a situation where their particular crisis is so evident to them and yet not very evident to most of those around them. This gap is most of the reason why these prophets despair of the future.

There appears to be a distinction, however, between the perspective of the population and ecological schools of worry and the technological one. The technology group is usually sharply more elitist— though Goodman is a very definite exception. These elitists like Marcuse see the masses as easily led and manipulated and have little confidence that they can be counted on for change. The population and ecology people generally hope (perhaps wistfully) that the problem is much more purely a matter of ignorance.

Technological pessimism is everywhere now. For example, it has played a large role in the current controversy over campaign advertisements in American mass media. McGinniss' *The Selling of the President 1968* recently provided a notorious, sensationalized, and sometimes implausible setting for the controversy.[9] The question posed is whether technology, in this case as slick ads and powerful mass media, has taken over politics in America. During the campaigns of 1970 the usual hue and cry of some intellectuals swelled up, a crisis was pronounced, the national news magazines rushed to get in step, and suddenly the whole democratic electoral system was about to die at the hands of technology and the money it served.[10]

Behind all the shouting lay not only the broader technology crisis scare but also the elitist assumption that voters can be sold anybody by fancy and elaborate media technology. Fortunately, this particular aspect of the great technology crisis is now relatively dormant. Perhaps the reason is that even the extreme alarmists could see that the 1970 election returns did not offer much evidence that technology had swept away voters' own judgments, reasonable or perverse. A lot of money and a fancy media technology just did not guarantee victory.

The issue is not whether there are problems with mass media technology in campaigns or with the rising influence of technology as a whole. The issue is whether there is any overwhelming crisis. Nobody has demonstrated that crisis, though it is fashionable in many intellectual circles to discuss it as a given. Moreover, attacking the rationality of most people because they disagree with one does not establish that they are being manipulated or controlled by technology or its putative managers. Nor does it establish any crisis.

The more frankly anti-technological views just have not yet grasped that they and most people in America are hopelessly far apart. They hate technology while most people love most of what it has brought. People love cars and want to drive them; they love television; they want dishwashers. There will be no voluntary going back. People have tasted the fruits of technology and want them. They prove this throughout the world when they have the chance and the money to do so.

These facts do not mean that there should be no checks to control for unwanted side results. They do mean that searches for societies that will not worship technology are probably futile, and one cannot help suspecting that opposition to technology sometimes actually constitutes a game played by those who are not in basic economic need and never have been. Technology promises enormous opportunities to raise people's living standards around the world. Those who would simply reject technology and its promise should not be confused with noble idealists in any realistic accounting.

A final crisis that has its eager but pessimistic prophets in America is the alleged crisis in our political system. The political system supposedly totters before collapse. Some charge that it has lost any legitimacy as a democratic system because it is ruled by a "military-industrial complex"; others claim that it is losing legitimacy because it has become too decentralized, having parceled away its power to political interests; still others, the most confused, seem to charge that both faults exist.

By far the most popular assertion in the Left today is that a rather tight elite rules, an elite that must be toppled by one means or another. The power elite thesis flows out of the earlier work of C. Wright Mills,[11] but it is now carried on by a host of social scientists including Domhoff in *Who Rules America?* and Dye and Ziegler in *The Irony of Democracy*.[12] It receives its most rhetorical and aggressive display in the speeches and writings of many in the contemporary New Left such as Tom Hayden.[13]

A much more accurate view is probably the minority anti-pluralist one. It claims that the problem is the opposite. There is too little elitism, too little government and authority. They have all been surrendered to private interests. Lowi's *The End of Liberalism* makes the most serious current attack along these lines.[14]

In any case, the political situation is often viewed as desperate. The power elite school is pessimistic for the future because of their genuine doubt about whether revolution can be achieved in America; their pessimism is not only about the political situation, but also about its future regeneration. The grim prognosis of the anti-pluralist outlook usually flows from a less radical stance, often nonrevolutionary. However, the despair for the future they too share is also only partially based on the present condition of the American political system; it too includes a doubting perspective on the chances to change it.

Neither outlook tells one much about why its vision of the future would be better than the present. Talk about socialism, liberation, or an end to "surplus repression" gets us nowhere very definite.[15] Lowi does no better; his book is revealingly split very unevenly between 283 pages on the evils of the American political system and values and a meager twenty-eight pages on his alternative future. This gap is terribly representative of the whole situation within the political crisis camp. Exceptions are rare.

Robert Paul Wolff stands out as the rare exception. In his works we can see actual attempts to go beyond rhetoric and be specific about the outline of his desired radical future. He does not get very far perhaps, but at least he earnestly tries.[16] Wolff also stands out because he notes with distaste the pall of elitism that hangs over much of the pessimistic left-wing futurist thinking today. He tellingly points out how implausible and elitist is the conventional radical claim that the government is an elite controlling a foolish mass. He sees that this is elitist scapegoating.[17] Lowi too may come very close to proposing an openly elitist solution, though he seeks to avoid this conclusion by insisting that his new elite have democratic authorizations.[18]

The strangest feature of all the writings of futurists who see a political crisis is that they never come to terms with the desparity between what they do not like and what is accepted in America except by making elitist dismissals of most people. Most of these thinkers talk a good deal about the alleged political crisis in America and about "unmet needs." Yet nobody actually ever shows that the political system is falling apart or that it has lost the consent of the overwhelming majority. None of the crisis people can do these things because the American political order has by no means collapsed nor have any signs appeared that it lacks popular consent. This reality is of course terribly inconvenient for those who want to convince us to see the desperate situation they do. One can certainly understand why they have given way to pessimism and elitism, but not why either is justified.

Perhaps there might be a saving grace for those who claim the crisis of our time is in our political institutions and for all of us if they could develop a sense of humor. Indeed, all varieties of pessimistic futurists need to learn how to laugh. We need to be suspicious of the unending and strident seriousness and worrying that lie behind the pessimistic futurists, never more sadly illusrtated than in Jason Epstein's grim-faced recent assault in *The New York Review of Books* on a book that dared to laugh somewhat at fashionable left-wing radicalism.[19]

Even if every particular pessimistic futurist could show that his special crisis was terrible indeed and that his doubts about the next decades had substantial justification, still room would be needed for some laughter and joy. Some of that laughter should be directed at themselves; we all need the perspective that laughter provides.

Perhaps too it might help our pessimistic futurists to escape the whole serious, desperate, and elitist tone of their movement. Do we have coming yet another version of the American puritan phenomenon? That possibility for the future is really something to be pessimistic about.

Optimistic Prophets

The trouble with the question of alternative futures for America is that you have gotten only half way through the miasma of alarm and conflicting claims when you have investigated the pessimistic prophets. They may seem shrill, but at least they are often attempting to get down to the level of concrete problems of today. Their fears of tomorrow make them do so. On the other hand, the optimistic prophets often are far away from the concrete, lost in abstractions about the future or personal dreams for the present. They so often appear to finesse today and today's troubles and struggles for futurism. This is why they ought to be largely ignored even as the pessimists ought to be ignored when they inflate today's problems and deflate the future's prospects.

The optimistic futurists are no more united than are the pessimists. They too engage in plenty of internal warfare over the precise keys to a better social or personal future. The most fundamental division exists between the technological optimists and the radical optimists. No two schools of contemporary thought could be as distinctly separated—except in their basic hope in the future.

The technological optimists are in vogue today. That the technological pessimists are also flourishing is not a paradox at all. The present success of both is simply a sign that you can count on a hearing these days if you are prepared to speak of the future, regardless of what you say.

Probably the three most famous of the technological optimists are Daniel Bell, Zbigniew Brzezinski, and Herman Kahn. All have turned increasingly to the prophesy business. In particular, their emphasis has been on technological progress and their prognosis for America and America's allied states is favorable. They lead the fashionable post-industrial, technological society analyses of the United States, Western Europe, and Japan, stressing the emergence of a new stage in human historical development. This post-industrial stage is characterized as one in which societies are highly technological, urban, affluent, educated, and nonideological. They are also claimed to be little concerned about matters of wealth distribution and class conflict.

Bell's recent work is explicitly concerned with this model and the future. He is chairman of the American Academy of Arts and Sciences' Commission on the Year 2,000, a giant (and one suspects, expensive) exercise in futuristic speculation for the technological optimists. Bell's writings in connection with his work with the commission and elsewhere indicate his substantial sympathy for the kind of technological, post-industrial society that he predicts will be more and more the shape of our future.[20]

Brzezinski is a more recent convert to technological futurology, but he is working hard to catch up. His major work in the field is *Between Two Ages: America's Role in the Technetronic Era*. It is a testament to Brzezinski's confidence in the technological future; indeed, at points it is as close to rhapsody as technological optimists get.[21]

Brzezinski is probably more widely known for his term for our new society to be, already partly in existence. He calls it the "technetronic" future. Bell's "post-industrial" term now has a competitor and Brzezinski's creation has helped establish him as a genuine technological futurist. It appears that it is mandatory for technological prophets to invent words, phrases, categories, or systems. Apparently, the idea is that new terms for new ages and futures are a positive good. One assumes that foundations and academies and others whose money is often naively passed out take these creations to be enlightening about the future in some way. It is hard to see why or how.

Herman Kahn's longtime devotion to futurism and his fervent praise of technology's potential is well known. More than almost any of his fellow predictors of the optimistic school, Kahn predicts with dramatic, torrential abandon.[22] His prolific suggestions and guesses may make him hard to take seriously, yet a good case can be made for him as one who freely admits that he is speculating. Moreover, his free (if often wild) speculations are often interesting and thought-provoking. The proper contrast here is with Bell and most of the rest of the technological prophets. They are so much less honest and free-spirited in their love of and practice of fantasy.

Kahn has another reputation, however. It is as the most arrogant man in the sometimes very arrogant and smug group of technological optimists. His recent book, *The Emerging Japanese Superstate*, reveals Kahn at his most dogmatic in the necessarily uncertain business of prediction.[23] Still, Kahn's intellectual confidence or arrogance has been overrated while the attractions of his mental playfulness have been grossly ignored.

Now that Brzezinski has taken up the fad of the post-industrial society Kahn will certainly seem less arrogant. Brzezinski sweeps groups of opponents into the ash can of history faster than even the crudest Marxist: the emerging technetronic society dooms all of its (or Brzezinski's?) opponents. Brzezinski, no more than Marx, considers it appropriate to reject what history promises. Therefore, of course Brzezinski does not admire those who set themselves against the technetronic future. They are dismissed.

Brzezinski is not alone here. Confidence in history among the enthusiasts of the future post-industrial world is general. It generally relieves them of any doubt that they will triumph and that their opposition will lose. So imperious is history, so commanding is history's rush to their model for the future that those who do not join in and in effect sanctify history's alleged movements are portrayed as reactionary pockets unable to adjust to the developing present and coming future. Why one should necessarily adjust to their future is never made evident by the technological optimists.

Despite their historical optimism, these men and the growing legions of others involved in the common task of predicting (and lauding) the post-industrial future are not to be misunderstood as naive optimists. They are optimists since the future is presented as mostly promise; but they explain that difficulties will be met only if technology is directed by those who know what is best, if things are planned well, and if irrational groups do not interfere.

John McDermott has argued what is clear enough: that elitism of the most egregious sort lurks everywhere in the affection the technological prophets have for the expert, the technocrat, and the skilled planner and predictor. The post-industrial optimists always deny that they are out of the democratic tradition. And the indications of intense elitism that McDermott recognizes do not at all eliminate a formal commitment to "democracy." McDermott may be and, indeed, is too polemical and he grinds too hard on his own left-wing axes. Nonetheless, his exposition of the elitism in the technological enthusiasm movement is convincing.[24]

McDermott is also sure that the elitism he sees is really deeply conservative in the sense of wishing to preserve "liberal" America. Certainly there is little doubt that optimistic post-industrial futurism attracts a significant and growing part of the liberal intellectual and academic establishment. One notes the array of men in this category involved in Bell's futurist project; one also notes that of the forty-two contributors to Bell's preliminary report almost all are forty years old or older, usually much older.[25]

No doubt, McDermott exaggerates the political bias of the technological enthusiasts. One wonders, however, if the middle-aged and self-confident liberals busy with post-industrial and technological society futurism speak for many of the intellectuals now developing; as later parts of this article suggest, optimism for the future may be found sometimes among younger thinkers, but rarely for reasons related to those of Bell and his associates. At best their attitude toward technology seem ambivalent. One suspects that there will be a growing gap between the Bells and the McDermotts.

My questions about the back-door elitism and virtual historical determinism present in our optimistic futurists represent only two reasons why one should have reservations about the whole movement. A much more obvious reason is that their prophecies and predictions may not be very accurate. This possibility deserves exploration.

For example, the truth is that some technological prophets' predictions of diminishing social conflict and ideological thinking in post-industrial societies were wrong.[26] This is a major error. Why should we assume that there will not inevitably be others? Moreover, why should we not assume that such very convenient mistakes (con-

venient given the liberal politics of nonconflict, consensus, and non-
ideology of many of our optimists) will not inevitably flaw their
prophecies hopelessly? One need not agree with the view that the
technological optimists erred in the past because they pretended that
classes and class conflict could or would go away to recognize the
essential failure of judgment and to wonder about their predicted
futures.[27]

Despite any past failure, I remain puzzled by the works of these
post-industrial and technological society prophets. They are predictions and of course much of what they say is simply clever and sometimes informed guessing. Such guessing is always fun to engage in.
I have been puzzled, however, over why it is often taken so seriously.
The answer appears when one understands that these prophets rarely
call themselves speculators.

Instead, the scientific and quasi-scientific claims made for predictions and guesses are on the upswing. Yet even from within the post-
industrial prophets' own house there is marked disagreement concerning the validity of much prediction.[28] From without this world
of optimism, the picture and estimations are much bleaker and much
less equivocal. There doubt reigns about assumptions that the past
or present are much of a guide to the future, that predictors can
possibly handle the new and as yet undiscovered (or chance), and
that past experience with prediction gives much hope.[29]

Counter-Culture Prophets

While the elitist, often overbearing, pretentious character of the
optimistic futurists of the liberal, technological, post-industrial school
makes them an unattractive guide to alternative futures for America,
their optimistic counterparts on the Left constitute no better guides.
Probably the greatest irony about the whole optimist camp is that it
consists of these two factions—that so thoroughly detest each other—
the optimist radicals and the optimist liberals.

Optimistic radical thought about America's future is largely
asocial, apolitical, and privatist and therefore worlds apart from
pessimistic radical thought. The optimists do not talk in terms of

political revolution or political action. They believe they have left all these notions behind. Instead, they concentrate on another variety of change: cultural revolution.

Their orientation permits optimism about the future now only because of their master assumption that people can be different in important ways and that they are even now transforming themselves in some cases in very hopeful directions. The nature of the specific cultural change or revolution that the various optimistic radicals seek varies of course, but they unite in applauding what they believe to be a developing new culture in America. It promises a new day.

Of course the new culture has its roots in the alleged subculture of American youth. Youth are presented as our new culture heroes; they have in mind a portion of that minority of American youth that is upper and upper-middle class and involved with the so-called counter-culture. The new style of life supposedly emphasizes the values of feeling, play, sincerity, community, timelessness, eroticism, and sometimes drugs. Just how all these values fit together, or ever will, is never clear in the writings of the prophets of the coming cultural revolution. These prophets, in fact, often take considerable offense at the idea that they ought to have well-delineated philosophies or programs now or for the years ahead. It is just such a non-spontaneous, overly rational outlook that they recoil from because it is allegedly incapable of achieving anything of deep value.

The most well-known commentator on the cultural revolution and its prophets for a brief time was T. Roszak and his often adulatory, *The Making of a Counter-Culture.*[30] However, so fickle—or intellectually insubstantial—is this movement that Roszak is now already falling from grace. The new star is Charles Reich. His book, *The Greening of America*, is a work full of all the endless ritual affirmations of the cultural revolution. It is so intellectually inferior to Roszak that one wonders why it has attracted so much attention. Apparently its vogue derives from Reich's attempt to create a crude typology of styles of human consciousness. Not surprisingly, Reich happily and easily predicts the future triumph of his favorite, that similar to Roszak's counter-culture that Reich calls "Consciousness III."[31]

Also part of the whole cultural optimism movement are more radical figures like Jerry Rubin and Abbie Hoffman, recently of the

Chicago Conspiracy Trial. Unlike Roszak or Reich, they do not make the slightest effort to be commentators on America and her future. They simply say "come with us and be the future."[32] They make Reich and Roszak look like subtle and profound theorists with systematic notions of society and history.

Another style of cultural optimism can be found in authors and works that explore particular parts of the new counter-culture. Many involve the characteristic sex-worship. Here Norman O. Brown's writings that preach "polymorphus" sex as the route to the new era are a landmark.[33] While his work tends to be difficult, obscure, and mystical, other works of sexual "liberation" such as Dr. David Reuben's *Everything You Always Wanted to Know About Sex* are available for the more practically oriented.[34]

Not all the cultural revolution optimists think sex is everything by any means. Some, for example, think the specific answer is in communal living or encounter groups and other forms of intimate living not explicitly or entirely sexual. Here too there is much to read if one is so inclined.[35]

In short, the prophets and the enthusiasms of the cultural revolution movement are really endless today. They fascinate one and the paperback book stores and shelves are inundated with their wares. Still, the various prophets of the counter-culture should be mostly ignored in the end. There are at least four reasons or sets of reasons for this conclusion.

First, nobody should rally around the counter-culture prophecy for the simple reason that it is just too unclear, confused, and undeveloped. What are the values it desires and predicts for the future? How well do they fit together? What is the order of the priority of these values? These are the most fundamental kinds of questions to ask of any ideal future. The answers to them cannot be located, however, in the writings of men like Roszak and Reich, much less Rubin and Hoffman, as their critics accurately and decisively complain.[36] Affirmations and rhetoric are never a substitute for disciplined analysis—especially when one proclaims the virtues of a special future.

Perhaps one might expect the counter-cultural futurists to express themselves better in the overwhelming part of their work that is negative in thrust. Unfortunately, all the denunciations of contemporary American society conceivable do not make the counter-culture prophesy lucid or even vaguely descipherable. Neither are denunciations a substitute for reasoned explication and argument. The sad part is that the counter-culturists miss a splendid opportunity to make their case by trying to come to terms with the present and other alternatives for the future.

In short, I am convinced that one just cannot locate any systematic rational theory and argument from the cultural revolution's celebrators. Eventually one concludes that there is little enough of a coherent vision to discover. Of course there are goals and many values in the counter-culture world. Certainly there is a vision in some loose sense. Unfortunately, it is best appreciated by feeling; and feeling is not, after all, a substitute for thought.

Some of these vague goals and values are the second reason why this optimistic approach to America's future is woefully unsatisfactory. For example, there is the familiar elitism we know by now to expect in each of our contemporary futurist outlooks. Many of the counter-culturists obviously despise those who disagree with them, a category that encompasses almost certainly the vast majority of America; moreover, the counter-culturists also obviously feel superior to most middle class Americans who are condemned as hostile to feeling, as hypocrites, as vulgar materialists, and so on. It all adds up to an attitude on the part of many who indulge in the counter-culture and wish it well for the future that is elitist and condescending toward most Americans. Obviously, such ideas are potentially enormously dangerous.[37]

A third set of objections directs itself to the questionable practicality of the discernable parts of the various counter-culture prophets' wishes. One aspect of the argument contends that all the cultural revolution talk about the present and future is so totally abstract that it is useless. Compared to the counter-culture futurists, the technological optimists are super-empiricists and thoroughly concrete. In short, there is little if any effort to offer serious empirical evidence that any of the counter-culture notions can succeed on a society-wide basis. Romantic enthusiasm and mysticism will not do when offered as a full substitute for empirical analysis.[38]

Another aspect of this argument questions whether the entire counter-culture fad will amount to anything practical that might make the world a little better. The talk is good—sometimes—but it is always vague and abstract. Meanwhile, the main focus is on cultural and personal transformation. Unfortunately, that promises to do nothing obvious for the poor, the black, or the environment. Nobody should make any mistake here.[39]

Of course there is nothing surprising about this gap between the counter-culture enthusiasm and the concrete social problems of our time, despite a lot of pleasant talk of the "idealism" of many in the counter-culture. The cultural revolution movement is composed of a section of very advantaged youth and their adult admirers. It is hardly a shock that they are far away in their concerns from the dramatically disadvantaged in our society. One should not pay any attention any longer, however, to the counter-culturists' ritualistic affirmations regarding the poor and the blacks. They do not mean much, as both the poor and blacks seem to realize.[40]

Finally, a fourth part of the convincing case against the counter-culture futurists and prophets centers around the frankly utopian nature of the desired and predicted future(s). So much happiness, unity, and transformation looms up as our future that huge amounts of skepticism are mandatory for anyone who is not breathlessly ignorant of human history and present human experience. For a while, making similar negative observations about counter-culture prophecies was considered somehow cynical and unpleasant, if true, in many intellectual circles. Today that is less and less the case. The contrast between the counter-culturists' upper-class utopia of "play" and "wholeness" and the ongoing reality of most people's lives of work, family, struggle, limited happiness, now receives pointed attention. Increasingly sympathies as well as views of reality shift toward the average life rather than the counter-culture fantasy. It is none too soon.[41]

Living

About the radical optimism of the counter-culturists as with the technological optimism school, there is no more reason to pay much attention to their prophecies about America's future than there is reason to pay attention to the prophecies of the several styles of pessimistic futurists. All of them make uncertain and dramatically conflicting claims about the future. Beyond that, all bring values that are noxious in the wake of their addiction to prophesy and prediction. Their common affinity toward elitism is especially troublesome.

The point is that the whole discussion about alternative futures for America now has become an intellectual fashion that has produced considerable miasma and more expensive and wasteful studies and grants than the subject deserves. There is nothing wrong with cautious planning—it is even essential. Futurism is another matter; and futurism is rife today.

Our best bet is to forget all about the question posed in this essay: how to survive in an age of discontinuity? For, despite all the noise, the rhetoric, and the studies, we can be sure that we and all people have a pretty good chance of surviving and, in any case, no study will alter those chances.[42] Our topic questions concede the very matter that is at stake: whether survival is suddenly an open question now and whether fundamental change is likely. I doubt both.

We cannot know, but I suspect that all the talk of the apocalypse or of beautific change in the future is to be only talk. People will go on loving and hating, sleeping and eating as best they can, expressing hope and fear, showing anxiety and friendship. They will struggle to get as much pleasure and avoid as much pain as possible. They will change as much as they have to, but mostly they will follow their habits. We are mundane beings and we will likely continue to be.

Of course we should do what we can to make our world and America better. Of course we should try and be decent. None of the camps of futurists have any monopoly on moral concern and action, despite what several of them seem to think. Still, while some futurists indulge in apocalyptic rage and call it reasoning and while other futurists speculate and call it prediction, most people will go on living, doing the best they can. They are not apathetic; they are not immoral. They simply have made their choice concrete, living the best way they can now, as opposed to the abstractions and elitism of the futurists swept up in agitation about alternative futures for America. It upsets all futurists intensely, but most people obviously expect America to survive and assume that in essentials she and we will be about the same. It is my view that nobody has shown these expectations to be false.

References

1. New York: Ballantine, 1968.
2. Rene Dubos, "The Despairing Optimist," *The American Scholar* (Winter 1970–71), pp. 16–20; Joseph W. Krutch, "What the Year 2,000 Won't Be Like," *Saturday Review* (January 20, 1968), p. 234.
3. 1970; this is edited by Esposito and is a "report" from the Nader organization.
4. New York: E. P. Dutton, 1970.
5. 1970.
6. *Wisconsin State Journal* (January 1971), p. 1.
7. Paul Goodman, *People or Personnel* and *Like a Conquered Province* (New York: Vintage, 1968), and L. Mumford, *The Myth of the Machine* (New York: Harcourt, Brace, 1970).
8. Boston: Beacon, 1964.
9. New York: Trident, 1969.
10. Both *Time* and *Newsweek* made a project before and after the 1970 election of booming this theme and worry.
11. C. Wright Mills, *The Power Elite* (New York: Oxford, 1959).
12. G. William Domhoff, *Who Rules America* (Englewood Cliffs, N.J.: Prentice Hall, 1967), and Thomas Dye and Harmon Ziegler, *The Irony of Democracy* (Belmont, California: Wadsworth, 1970).
13. Tom Hayden, *Trial* (New York: Holt, Rinehart & Winston, 1970); this is the latest work from Hayden.
14. Theodore Lowi, *The End of Liberalism* (New York: Norton, 1969).
15. Marcuse's many works illustrate the point as well as anybody's and more kindly than most would; of his *Essay on Liberation* (Boston: Beacon, 1969), or his *Eros and Civilization* (New York: Vintage, 1955).
16. Robert Paul Wolff, *In Defense of Anarchism* (New York: Harper & Row, 1970), and *The Poverty of Liberalism* (Boston: Beacon, 1968).
17. Wolff, *The Poverty of Liberalism, op. cit.,* ch. 3.
18. Lowi, *op. cit.,* ch. 10.
19. Epstein, "Journal du Voyeur," (December 17, 1970), pp. 3–6.
20. D. Bell, "The Year 2,000—the Trajectory of an Idea" in *Toward The Year 2,000 Work in Progress,* D. Bell, ed. (Boston: Houghton Mifflin, 1968), pp. 1–13; and D. Bell, "Notes on the Post-Indus-

trial Society," *Public Interest* (No. 6 & 7, 1967); D. Bell, *The End of Ideology* (New York: Collier, 1962).

21. New York: Viking, 1970.
22. For example, see "The Next Thirty-Three Years: A Framework for Speculation" by Herman Kahn and Anthony Wiener in Bell, ed., *Toward the Year 2,000, Work in Progress, op. cit.*, pp. 73–100.
23. Englewood Cliffs, N.J.: Prentice-Hall, 1970.
24. John McDermott, "Technology: The Opiate of the Intellectuals," *New York Review of Books* (July 31, 1969), pp. 25–35.
25. See the list in Bell, ed., *Toward the Year 2,000, Work in Progress, op. cit.*
26. Two leading cases in point are Daniel Bell and Seymour Martin Lipset.
27. F. Myers' "Social Class and Political Change," *Comparative Politics*, Vol. 2, No. 3 (1970), pp. 389–412.
28. See, for example, D. A. Schon, "Forecasting and Technological Forecasting" in Bell, *op. cit.*, pp. 127–146 and F. C. Ikle "Can Social Predictions Be Evaluated?" in Bell, ed., *op. cit.*, pp. 101–126 and L. J. Duhl, "Planning and Predicting," *ibid.*, pp. 147–156; also, cf. R. Dubos, *op. cit.*, p. 17.
29. Here see, for example, J. W. Krutch, *op. cit.*, pp. 232–237.
30. Garden City, N.Y.: Doubleday, 1969.
31. New York: Random House, 1970.
32. See Jerry Rubin, *Do It!* (New York: Simon & Schuster, 1970) and Abbie Hoffman, *Revolution For The Hell of It* (New York: Dial, 1970).
33. Especially see Brown's *Loves's Body* (New York: Vintage, 1966).
34. New York: McKay, 1969.
35. See for a sample of such work, Carl Rodgers, *Carl Rodgers on Encounter Groups.*
36. See R. Starr, "Consciousness III" in *Commentary* (December 1970), pp. 46–54; and "Lysergic Gotterdammerung" by D. L. Bromwich in *ibid.*, pp. 55–59.
37. N. Podhoretz, "The New Hypocrises" in *Commentary* (December 1970), pp. 5–6; and R. Nisbet, "An Epistle to the Americans" in *ibid.*, pp. 40–45.
38. J. Passmore, "Paradise Now" in *Encounter* (November 1970), pp. 3–21, and Starr, *op. cit.*
39. Bromwich, *op. cit.*, p. 59.

40. Nisbet, *op. cit.*, pp. 42–44.
41. Passmore, *op. cit.*, and Nisbet, *op. cit.*
42. Yes, atomic war is always a *possibility*.

The Possibilities for Political Change

MICHAEL PARENTI

A question pressing upon us with increasing urgency is, what are the possibilities for political change in America? More specifically, can the political system serve as a means for effecting the substantive reallocations needed to solve the enormous problems created within and by our economic system? What can we hope will be done about the continued plunder and pollution of our natural resources, the growth of a titanic military-industrial establishment, the massive concentration of corporate wealth and all its ensuing abuses, and the widespread infestations of rural and urban poverty? What kinds of solutions are in the offing, and, indeed, what kinds of definitions do we bring to the idea of "solution"?

Customary Approaches to Social Problems

Before considering the possibilities for political change, let us give some critical attention to the usual ways of approaching social problems. Social scientists and lay commentators alike have commonly assumed that solutions are arrived at by a process of system-

Reprinted by permission of *Politics and Society*. Michael Parenti (Ph.D., Yale University) is Associate Professor of Political Science at the University of Vermont, and the author of numerous articles and several books including *The Anti-Communist Impulse*, and *Power and the Powerless*.

atic investigation. By identifying all the salient variables and then constructing paradigms that unravel the complex interactions of these variables, we can equip ourselves with inventories of causes and resources and develop strategies for solution. The remaining task would be to convince the decision makers to push the buttons provided by the social scientists. It is expected that the human stupidity and inertia of political actors would deter the implementation of certain proposals, but decision makers are thought to be as hungry as anyone else for viable programs and sooner or later would not be unresponsive to the promises of science.

This scientistic, technocratic view of social problems presumes that decision makers are as immune to the pressures of power and interest as scientists are, or as scientists think they are. What is missing from this scientism is the essence of politics itself, an appreciation of the inescapability of *interest and power* in determining what solutions will be deemed suitable, what allocations will be thought supportable, and indeed, what variables will even be considered as interrelating and salient. The presumption that there is a scientifically discoverable "correct" solution to problems overlooks the fact that social problems involve conflicting ends and often irreconcilable value distributions; thus one man's "solution" is often another man's disaster. A "correct" proposal for some political actors may be one that resolves the threat of an opposing interest without causing any loss of profit or status to oneself. Hence the first instinct of established interests is so often toward half-hearted reform and whole-hearted repression ("law and order"). For other advocates, a "correct" program is one calling for nothing less than momentous reallocations in the substance and process of the entire productive system (a remedy that offers the kind of paradigm that usually escapes the serious attentions of most liberal middle-class social scientists).

The solutions to social problems cannot be treated except in the context of vested and conflicting interests that give vested and conflicting definitions to the problem. This is true whether the question is rebuilding the ghettos or withdrawing our troops from Vietnam: the solutions are potentially "at hand" or "nowhere in sight," depending on the ideological priorities and commitments of various proponents.

The scientistic approach presumes that problems exist because of the prevailing ignorance of the would-be problem solvers rather than because of the prevailing conditions of power among social groups. But social problems are never resolved by study but by action. Many of the social ills with which we live have been studied repeatedly, but since they have not yet been resolved it is assumed by the proponents of scientism that they need further study. Here we have an uncharacteristic instance of social scientists pretending to an *ignorance* they do not really possess. For the last thing some of our problems need is further study. Witness the hundreds of studies, reports, surveys and exposés done on Appalachia by a variety of commissions, committees, economists, and journalists, extending back more than half a century.[1] Neither history nor the historians have "bypassed" or "neglected" the people of Appalachia. The material forces of history, in this case the timber and mining companies that swindled the Appalachians of their lands, exploited their labor, and wrecked havoc with their lives, were all too attentive to the destinies of that region even though they were never held accountable for the social costs of their actions. The plunder and profit that is the history of the region has been duly documented; yet Appalachia is still treated today as a kind of historical mishap, an impersonal and presumably innocent development of "changing times," a "complex situation" needing our concerted attention.

Similarly, the plight of the urban poor in various Western industrial societies has been documented by official and unofficial sources for more than a century, and in recent decades we have traced the web of interests, the private and public forces, North and South, at the national and local levels, that have contributed to, and perpetuated, the black ghettos. The story is well known to us, but our discoveries have brought forth no solutions.

To be sure, the first step toward remedy is to investigate reality. But, eventually, if no second step is taken, no move toward action, then the call for "a study of the problem" is justifiably treated as nothing more than a symbolic response, an "appropriate reciprocal noise," designed to convey the impression that decision makers are fulfilling their responsibilities.[2] The commissioned "study" becomes an act that violates its own professed purpose: rather than inducing change, it is designed to mitigate the demands for change. Appearing before the Kerner Commission, the psychologist Kenneth B. Clark noted:

> I read that report . . . of the 1919 riot in Chicago, and it is as if I were reading the report of the investigating committee on the Harlem riot of '35, the report of the investigating committee on the Harlem riot of '43, the report of the McCone Commission on the Watts riot.
>
> I must again in candor say to you members of this Commission—it is a kind of Alice in Wonderland—with the same moving analysis, the same recommendations, and the same inaction.[3]

By incorporating Clark's admonition into its pages the Kerner Report may have achieved the ultimate in co-optation, for it, itself, is a prime example of that kind of official evasion and obfuscation designed to justify the very status quo about which Clark was complaining. The Kerner Report demands no changes in the way power and wealth are distributed among the classes; it never gets beyond its indictment of "white racism" to specify the forces in the political economy that brought the black man to riot; it treats the obviously abominable ghetto living conditions as "causes" of disturbance but never really inquires into the causes of the "causes." It does not deal, for instance, with the ruthless enclosure of Southern sharecroppers by big corporate farming interests, the subsequent mistreatment of the black migrant by Northern rent-gouging landlords, price-gouging merchants, urban "redevelopers," discriminating employers, insufficient schools, hospitals, and welfare, brutal police, hostile political machines and state legislators, and, finally, the whole system of values, material interests, and public power distributions from the state to the federal capitols that gives greater priority to "haves" than to "have-nots," servicing and subsidizing the interests of private corporations while neglecting the often desperate needs of the municipalities. The Kerner Report reflects the ideological cast of its sponsor, the Johnson administration, and in that sense is no better than the interests it served.[4]

To treat the *symptoms* of social dislocation (e.g., slum conditions) as the *causes* of social ills is an inversion not peculiar to the Kerner Report. Unable or unwilling to pursue the implications of our own data, we tend to see the effects of a problem as the problem itself.

The victims, rather than the victimizers, are defined as "the poverty problem." This is what might be described as the "VISTA approach" to economic maladies: a haphazard variety of public programs are initiated, focusing on the poor and ignoring the system of power, privilege, and profit that makes them poor. It is a little like blaming the corpse for the murder.

The Inescapability of Interest and Power

In looking to the political system as a means of rectifying the abuses and inequities of the socio-economic system we are confronted with the inescapable fact that any political system, including one that observes democratic forms, is a system of power. As such, it best serves those who have the wherewithal to make it serviceable to their interests,—those who own and control the resources of money, property, organization, jobs, social prestige, legitimacy, time and expertise, and who thereby command the attentive responses of political decision makers. Indeed, our political system works well for those large producer and corporate interests that control the various loci of power in the state and federal legislatures and bureaucracies. One can find no end to the instances in which public agencies have become the captives of private business interests.[5] Economic power is to political power as fuel is to fire, but in this instance the "fire" actually feeds back and adds to the fuel; for political power when properly harnessed becomes a valuable resource in expanding the prerogatives of those economic interests that control it. To think of government as nothing more than a broker or referee amid a vast array of competing groups (the latter presumably representing all the important and "countervailing" interests of the populace) is to forget that government best serves those who can best serve themselves.

But the material advantages of the owning classes are supposedly offset by the representative forms of a democratic system that make explicit and institutionalized provision for the power of numbers (and if the non-elites have nothing else they at least have their numbers). But numbers are not power unless they are organized and mobilized into forms of political action that can deliver some reward to or punishment to decision makers, and the mobilization of potential numerical strength requires the use of *antecedent* resources. Just as one needs the capital, so one needs the power to use power. This is especially true of the power of numbers, which, to be even sporadically effective, requires large outputs of time, manpower, publicity, organization, knowledgeability, legitimacy, and—the ingredient that often can determine the availability of these other resources—money. The power of numbers, then, like the power of our representative institutions, is highly qualified by material and class considerations.

Consider those agencies that are specifically intended to mobilize and register the power of numbers, the political parties. The image of the political party as an organization inclusive of and responsive to the interests of rank and file voters does not find ready confirmation in the experiences of dissenters who have sought entry into the party system. To be sure, new voters in both rural and urban counties are usually welcomed into the party roles, especially if they are white and if their loyalties promise to fit into the established spectrum of political choices, but new ideas and issues, new and potentially disruptive interests, are treated most unsympathetically by the county bosses and district captains whose overriding concern is to maintain their own position in the ongoing "equilibrium"; more often than not, the instinct of the local clubhouse, that "cogwheel of democracy," is to operate with exclusive rather than inclusive intent.[6]

In general, the two-party system throughout the local and national levels *avoids* rather than confronts many of the basic social problems of our society, or, when confrontation materializes, the electoral stances are usually reiterations of conventional formulas rather than invitations to heterodox ideas and choices. One need only recall how liberals and conservatives, Democrats and Republicans, spent twenty-five postwar years demonstrating their anti-Communist militancy on almost all domestic and foreign policy issues, thereby giving public debate on the question of "America's role in the world" to new levels of impoverishment. In an earlier work, I suggested that:

> The American political system has rarely been able to confront fundamental images, or serve as an instrument of creative discourse, or even engage in public discussion of heterodox alternatives. The two-party competition which supposedly is to provide for democratic

heterodoxy, in fact, has generated a competition for orthodoxy [on most important questions]. In politics, as in economics, competition is rarely a certain safeguard against monopoly and seldom a guarantee that the competitors will produce commodities which offer the consumer a substantive choice.[7]

Offering itself as the voice of the people, as a measure of the polyarchic will, the representative system becomes one of the greatest legitimating forces for the ongoing social order and all its class abuses. A closer study of the "eras of reform" seems to support rather than refute this view. If the political system has done anything in the nineteenth and twentieth centuries, it has kept the populace busy with symbolic struggles while manfully servicing the formidable appetites of the business community. To take one instance among countless ones: the legislation of 1887 marking Congress's "great" reform effort in transportation gave the people their railroad regulation law and gave the business magnates their railroads complete with risk-free investment capital (compliments of the U.S. taxpayer), free land, and many millions of dollars in profits.[8] Similarly, the history of who got what during the New Deal has still to be written. There yet may emerge an American historian who will spare us his description of the inspirational rhetoric, the colorful personalities, the electoral ballyhoo, the hundred days of legislative flurry, the Brain Trust, the court-packing fight, etc., and get down to a systematic and, I suspect, startling study of the New Deal's dealings with the political economy, revealing what classes carried the burdens of public finance, what ideologies prevailed at the operational level, what interests were left out and what interests actually got what magnitude of material outputs.[9] *Symbolic allocations to public sentiment and substantive allocations to private interests—such has been the overall performance of our political system even in times of so-called social reform.*

Speaking about the late nineteenth-century American political life, Matthew Josephson refers to the

> contradictions between ideology and interest, between 'eternal principles of truth and right' and class-economic necessities . . . between the mask and parade—the theatrical duelings of prejudice, associations of thought, patriotic sentiment, illusions—and the naked clash of different conditions of existence, different forms of property and economy.
> . . . Behind the marching songs and slogans of the Ins and the Outs

. . . We must grasp at the pecuniary objects, the genuine, concrete interests, the real stakes being played for, as in every historic social conflict.[10]

For Josephson, the captains of industry were the "men who spoke little and did much" in determining the shape of our society and the quality of our lives, while the political leaders were "men who, in effect, did as little as possible and spoke all too much."[11] Together, the "robber barons" and the "politicos" represented the difference between substantive and symbolic politics.

Indeed, one might better think of ours as a dual political system: first, there is the *symbolic* input-output system centering around electoral and representative activities including party conflicts, voter turnout, political personalities, public pronouncements, official role-playing and certain ambiguous presentations of some of the public issues that bestir presidents, governors, mayors and their respective legislatures.[12] Then there is the *substantive* input-output system, involving multibillion dollar contracts, tax write-offs, protections, rebates, grants, loss compensations, subsidies, leases, giveaways, and the whole vast process of budgeting, legislating, allocating, "regulating," protecting, and servicing major producer interests, now bending or ignoring the law on behalf of the powerful, now applying it with full punitive vigor against heretics and "troublemakers." The symbolic system is highly visible, taught in the schools, dissected by academicians, gossiped about by newsmen. The substantive system is seldom heard of or accounted for.

The have-nots who hope to win substantive outputs by working their way through the symbolic input-output system seldom see the light at the end of the tunnel. The crucial function of the electoral-representative process is to make people believe that there is a closer connection between the symbolic and the substantive than actually exists. But those dissidents and protestors who decide to make the long march through primaries, fund-raising, voter registration, rallies, canvassing, and campaigning soon discover the bottomless, endless qualities of electoral politics. They find out that the political system, or that visible portion of it that they experience, absorbs large quantities of their time, money, and energy while usually leaving them no closer to the forces that make the important substantive allocations of this society. On those infrequent occasions when reform candidates do win elections, they discover still other absorbant, deflective, and dilatory forces lying in wait. They find themselves relegated to obscure legislative tasks; they receive little cooperation from party leaders or from bureaucratic agencies. To achieve some degree of effectiveness in an institution whose dominant forces can easily outflank him, the newly arrived dissenter frequently decides that "for now" he must make his peace with the powers that be, holding his fire until some future day when he might attack from higher ground; thus begins the insidious process that lets a man believe that he is fighting the ongoing arrangements when in fact he has become a functional part of them. Many of the accounts of life in Congress are studies in the methods of co-optation, the ways would-be dissenters are socialized to the goals and priorities of a conservative leadership.[13]

There are, of course, less subtle instances of co-optation: reformers have been bought off with promotions and favors from those who hold the key to their advancement. Having tasted the spoils of victory, they may reverse their stance on essential issues and openly make common cause with the powers that be, much to the shock of their supporters.[14] Well-meaning electoral crusaders who promise to get things moving again by exercising executive leadership, upon accession to federal, state, or local executive office soon discover that most of the important options involving jobs, property, money, and taxes are dependent upon resources controlled by large corporations capable of exercising an influence extending well beyond the political realm as it is usually defined. When local, state, and federal officials contend that the problems they confront are of a magnitude far greater than the resources they command, we might suspect them of telling the truth, for in fact the *major* decisions about how the vast resources of our society are used are made by the *private* sector of the economy, and the economic institutions of a capitalist society are rarely, if ever, held accountable for the enormous social costs of their profit system.

What Do The Powerless Do?

Contrary to the gradualistic vision of America, things are getting worse, not better. As opposed to a decade ago, there are more, not less, people living in poverty today, more substandard housing, more environmental pollution and devastation, more deficiencies in our schools, hospitals, and systems of public transportation, more military dictatorships throughout the world feeding on the largesse and power of the Pentagon, more people from Thailand to Brazil to Greece to Chicago suffering the social oppression and political repression of an American-backed status quo. The long march through the American electoral-representative process has not saved the Vietnamese; it has not even saved the redwoods; nor, if our ecologists are correct, will it save the environment. Nor has it put a stop to the aggrandizements of American imperialism and its military-industrial complex. Nor has it brought us any closer to a real "war on poverty." Nor has there been any revision of priorities, any reallocations of resources away from the glut of a private commodity market and toward essential public needs and services. It is a small wonder that as social dissenters become increasingly aware of the limitations of debate, petition, and election for purposes of effecting substantive changes, they become less dedicated to election rituals and less attentive to the standard public dialogues heard within and without representative assemblies. For the same reason, those who *oppose* change become *more* dedicated to dialogue and symbolic politics, urging protestors to place their faith in reason, in free, open (and endless) discussion, and in the candidate of their choice.

In a system that responds only to power, what do the powerless do? Consider, once more, the problem of poverty: the people most needful of sociopolitical change, in this case, the poor, are by that very fact most deprived of the resources needed to mobilize political influence and least able to make effective use of whatever limited resources they do possess. If the poor controlled the values and goods needed to win substantive payoffs, they would not be poor and would have less need to struggle for outputs that the economic and political systems readily allocate to more favored groups. This is the dilemma of lower strata groups: their deprivation leaves them at the low end of any index of power and their relative powerlessness seems to ensure their continued deprivation.

Lacking control of the things that would make decision makers readily responsive to them, and therefore, lacking the specialized, organized, persistent, and well-financed forces of influence needed to function successfully in the *substantive* area of our dual political system, the dispossessed are left with the only resources they have: their voices, their bodies, their buying power and their labor; denunciations and demonstrations, sit-ins and scuffles, boycotts and strikes, the threat of disruption and actual disruption. The effectiveness of their protest actions, of course, is handicapped by the same scarcity of resources and consequent instabiliy of organization that limits their opportunities for standard political influence. Nevertheless, the last decade has witnessed a growing tendency among aggrieved groups to heed the old Populist dictum to "raise less corn and more hell," to embark upon actions that incovenience the normal arrangements of middle-class life and often upset middle-class sensibilities.

That is the idea—to inconvenience and upset. By increasing their nuisance value, the protestors hope to achieve a greater visibility for themselves and a greater sense of urgency in the public mind for the problems at hand. The nuisance and disruption caused by direct actions also become a leverage for those of little power, the withdrawal of the disruption being used as a negotiable resource. Thereby do dispossessed groups such as workers, blacks, students, and the poor attempt to induce through crude means a responsiveness from officialdom that the business community accomplishes through more effective and less strenuous channels.

But many of the' demands put forth by protestors might be described as "transitional revolutionary." That is, they are essentially reformist and non-revolutionary in appearance *yet they are impossible to effect within the present system if that system is to maintain itself*. Students demand, for instance, that the university cease performing indispensable services for the corporate-military economy, including various kinds of vital research and personnel training, and that it withdraw its investments in giant corporations and devote a substantial portion of its resources to the needs of the impoverished, many of whom live within a stone's throw of its ivy-covered walls. And they demand that the multibillion dollar system of domestic and international service and armed protection given to the corporate elites be ceased on behalf of a multibillion dollar public investment against domestic and international poverty (one that would preempt some important private producer interests at home and abroad). While sounding enough like the reformist, peaceful-change-within-the-system policies of the gradualist, these demands are essentially revolutionary in their effect in that they presuppose a dedication to interests that deny the essential interests and power of the prevailing elites.

It becomes understandable, then, why appeals to reason and good will do not bring reforms: quite simply, the problem of change is no easier for the haves than for the have-nots. Contrary to the admonitions of liberal critics, it is neither stupidity nor opaqueness that prevents those who own and control the property and the institutions of this society from satisfying the demand for change. To be sure, the established elites suffer from their share of self-righteous stubborness, but more often than not, meaningful changes are not embarked upon because they would literally undercut the security and survival of privileged interests, and it is in the nature of social elites that they show little inclination to commit class suicide.

In the early stages of particular social conflicts neither the haves nor the have-nots are fully appreciative of the systemic contradictions and limited options they face. An "Upward Bound" plan here, a "Head Start" program there, and an outpouring of rhetoric everywhere—such are the responses of the ruling interests, believing as they do that an abundance of symbolic outputs should sufficiently placate the malcontents. America was not built in a day, they remind us, and only time and patience will—through unspecified means—rectify our "remaining" social ills.

At the onset, protestors operate under somewhat similar assumptions about the basic viability of the system. There are "pockets" of poverty, "discrimination" against blacks and a "senseless" war in Southeast Asia: social problems are seen as aberrant offshoots of a basically good, if not great, society, rather than as endemic manifestations of the prevailing forms of social privilege, power, and property. The first soundings of dissent are accompanied by anticipations of change. There is often a kind of exhilaration when people, finally moved by that combination of anger and hope that is the stuff of protest, take to the streets: the handclapping, slogan shouting, the signs, the crowd are all encouraging evidence that many others share one's grievances. But, as time passes, as the symbolic dramatizations of protest produce little more than the symbolic responses of politicians (along with the free-swinging clubs, mace, tear gas, and guns of the police) dissent begins to escalate in tactics—from petitioning one's congressman to marching in the streets to "trashing" stores to the burning and bombing of draft boards, banks, and corporation offices, to sporadic armed encounters.

Just as significantly, dissent begins to escalate in the scope and level of its indictment. Increasingly convinced that the political system is not endowed with the responsible, responsive, creative, and inclusive virtues its supporters ascribe to it, dissenters begin to shift from incrementalist pleas to challenges against the fundamental legitimacy of the established economic and political elites. There is evidence of a growing militancy among deprived racial minorities, of a consciousness that begins with pleas for equal treatment in the ongoing society and soon evolves into a sweeping condemnation of white America's "power structure." A visible number of blacks, Mexican-Americans, Puerto Ricans, Indians, Orientals, and others have made the journey from civil rights "moderation" to radical militancy, from Thurgood Marshall and Roy Wilkins to Malcolm X and Eldridge Cleaver.

The white student movement has undergone similar transitions in both tactics and ideology. Many of those who pleaded for a cessation of the bombing of North Vietnam in 1966 were urging that we "bring the war home" in 1970; the V-sign of peace has been replaced by the clenched fist of resistance; "staying clean with Gene" has less appeal today than more direct and more radical forms of action. And in May 1970, the sporadic peace parades were replaced by a national student strike, the first of its kind in American history, affecting over four hundred college campuses and at least an equal number of high schools.

Even among those who are described as "the silent majority" one finds some signs of a leftward discontent. White workers suffering the deprivations of their class as laborers, taxpayers, and consumers have experienced the contagion of protest. More often than not, the experiences of their own oppression are expressed in resentment toward "pampered" and "subversive" students and an almost obsessive animosity toward blacks who are seen as "getting everything" while they, themselves, must bear the costs. Yet there are indications that this picture is oversimplified. Labor has not reacted toward the protestors with one voice. The Vietnam war, the tax burden, inflation, and other such things could not be blamed on students and blacks. Discontent with "the establishment" can be found among small but growing numbers of working whites and there is clear indication that important elements in the labor movement, especially in the ALA, look upon the national student strike and upon student militancy in general with something other than disfavor. There are indications, in places like Detroit with its "Black-Polish Alliance" and Chicago with its "Unity Coalition," that blacks and whites are beginning to join forces in protest action.[15] With increasing frequency students have been moving off campus, both individually and in organized moves, to join picket lines and to draw bonds of common action and interest with workers. Meanwhile, there has begun to emerge among the more literate segments of professional, middle-class America a spirit of protest that began as an antiwar expression and has since become an indictment against the whole quality of life in America. Finally, one should not overlook the increasingly widespread problems of morale and disaffection found in that most crucial of all power institutions, the U.S. Army, problems that, if they continue at the present rate, may have real revolutionary potential.

Yet neither should we overestimate the potential strength of radical protest nor underestimate the coercive, repressive, and preemptive capacities of the established politico-economic powers. From election laws to property laws, from city hall to federal bureaucracy, from taxation to welfare, government helps those who can best help themselves and this does not mean those wanting and needing fundamental changes in the class structure and in the ways in which the wealth of this nation is produced, distributed, controlled, and used. To deal with the protestors, the elites still have a variey of symbolic outputs as close at hand as the next election or the next press conference. Along with this they have the ability to discredit, obfuscate, delay, and "study" (what Richard Neustadt calls the "almost unlimited resources of the enormous power of sitting still").[16] Furthermore, elites are rarely hesitant to use the systemic rewards and punishments, the jobs, wealth, and institutions they control for the purpose of encouraging political conformity. And should all else fail, they have at their command that most decisive of political resources—the one the pluralists rarely talk about—the forces of obedient and violent repression: the clubbing, gassing, beating, shooting, arresting, imprisoning, rampaging forces of "law and order."

In sum, it is no longer a certainty that we will be able to solve our social ills by working with the same operational values and within the same systematic structures that have helped to create them. It does seem that we have seldom appreciated the extent to which the political system responds to, and indeed, represents, the dominant interests of the socio-economic system, and also how frequently political structures are simply bypassed by a corporate economy that significantly shapes the quality of our lives while in most respects remaining answerable to no one. A more realistic notion of how power is allocated and used in the United States should leave us less sanguine about the possibilities for political change. As of now we have no reason to hope that the "guardians of the public trust" will stop behaving like the servants of the dominant private interests, and no reason to presume that our political institutions will prove viable in treating the immense problems of this unhappy society.

Protest of a radical or potentially radical nature has arisen in a great many sectors of the American public. But the growth in protest has not brought forth a commensurate move toward needed changes from the powers that be, and the reason for this unresponsiveness, I have suggested, lies not in the technical nature of the problems but in the political nature of the conflicting interests, specifically in *the inability of the dominant politico-economic elites to satisfy the demands for structural changes while maximizing and maintaining their own interests.* Radical protest, then, is both a cause of and a response to the increasingly evident contradictions of the social system. Given the "Three R's" of politics—reform, repression, and revolution—it can no longer be taken as an article of faith that we are moving toward the first.

References

1. See Harry M. Caudill, *Night Comes to the Cumberlands* (Boston: Little, Brown, 1962), for the best recent study of Appalachia.
2. Murray Edelman, *The Symbolic Uses of Politics* (Urbana, Ill.:

University of Illinois Press, 1964), offers a most provocative discussion of the ritualistic and control functions of political acts.

3. Clark's testimony is quoted in the *Report of the National Advisory Commission on Civil Disorders* (the Kerner Report) (New York: Bantam Books, 1968), p. 29.

4. See Andrew Kopkind's excellent critique of the Kerner Commission "White on Black: The Riot Commission and the Rhetoric of Reform," *Hard Times*, 44 (September 15–22, 1969), pp. 1–4.

5. See Grant McConnell, *Private Power and American Democracy* (New York: Knopf, 1966), for a good discussion of the public powers of private interest groups.

6. For two studies of the ways local political parties work to defeat and exclude the dissident poor, see Philip Meranto, "Black Majorities and Political Power: This Defeat of an All-Black Ticket in East St. Louis," in Herbert Hill, ed., *The Revolt of the Powerless* (New York: Random House, 1970), and Michael Parenti, "Power and Pluralism, A View from the Bottom," in Marvin Surkin and Alan Wolfe, eds., *The Caucus Papers* (New York: Basic Books, 1970).

7. Michael Parenti, *The Anti-Communist Impulse* (New York: Random House, 1969), p. 101.

8. Many of the rail lines built were overextended and of dubious use to American communities, but pecuniary gain rather than public service was the primary consideration. See Matthew Josephson, *The Robber Barons* (New York: Harcourt, Brace & World, 1934), pp. 306–307.

9. At least one American historian, in a very brief study, does note how the New Deal serviced the corporate owning class while devoting its best rhetoric to the common man: see Paul K. Conkin, *The New Deal* (New York: Crowell, 1967). See Gabriel Kolko, *Wealth and Power in America* (New York: Praeger, 1962), pp. 30ff. for a discussion of New Deal taxation policy.

10. Matthew Josephson, *The Politicos, 1865–1896* (New York: Harcourt, Brace & World, 1938), pp. 8–9.

11. *Ibid.*, p. v.

12. See Edelman, *The Symbolic Uses of Politics*, for the best discussion of these components of the political system.

13. See Donald R. Matthews, *U.S. Senators and Their World* (Chapel Hill: University of North Carolina Press, 1960). For a discussion of how protest organizations and left-wing parties become co-opted into established parliamentary system, see Ralph Miliban,

The State in Capitalist Society, (New York: Basic Books, 1969), ch. 7.

14. This is a common enough occurrence in local politics but also not unknown at the national level where the symbolic appearances developed during the campaign soon collide with the substantive interests of the powers that be. Within four years, the American people elected two presidents who promised to end the war in Vietnam and who, once in office, continued to pursue that conflict with full force.

15. See William Greider, "Poles, Blacks Join Forces in Detroit," *Chicago Sun-Times* (October 12, 1969), p. 10.

16. Richard Neustadt, *Presidential Power* (New York: Wiley, 1960), p. 42.

Points of Departure

HENRY S. KARIEL

It is said that he had declined to be blindfolded and, what is more, that he had succeeded in persuading all of the condemned to decline likewise. They had lined up (or were being lined up) and he kept talking, describing what they all saw. He spoke rather vaguely at first, then became increasingly precise, and near the end, having time, he playfully tested his words to find the most telling. As he slowly kept turning their common experience into words, the others began to assent, correct, and elaborate, establishing connections and relating feelings they hardly knew they had. They recalled their past and found ways of leaving their mark for those who would follow. Thus they diverted themselves and lived out what

Henry S. Kariel (Ph.D., University of California at Berkeley) is Professor of Political Science at the University of Hawaii. He has edited several books and authored numerous articles and books of which the most recent was *Open Systems: Arenas for Public Action.* He is a member of the Caucus for a New Political Science, and serves on the Council of the American Political Science Association and on the editorial boards of several professional journals.

lives they had—minutes, days, years. While they let death come however it might, it took none by surprise. They all had flirted with it, but he more than the others. When he died, he was worn out, for he had added to his burden by making more of his world, his time, and himself than he had to, as much as his powers allowed. What he or any of them had actually said is not remembered, only the fact that they had somehow kept talking.

DANIEL RAYES

Professors do not renew a culture. The sources of renewal are no less irrational than the sources of revolutionary death sentences against it.

PHILIP RIEFF

Just short of surrender, which is where I happen to find myself, we may yet send out our signals, or even less assertively refer to such lifelines as we might discern among flotsam and jetsam at the outer edges of contemporary American politics. Implicated in social science, responsible because of mere association, we could do worse, I think, than use our words and symbols to represent marginal interests, making them visible at the center. We might at least attend to experience by talking, by learning to treat academic projects as if they were forms of action. To avoid frenzy or paralysis, we might rely on our imaginations and use them in practice, giving a positive voice to that majority among us that remains peripheral to the operations of our pluralist regime.[1] Disconcerted and perplexed, we might slowly begin to govern the forces governing us—the lonely, harried, aching, desperate figures in the American landscape and the fine-spun network that holds them in their place.

I realize how hard it is to act from the margin and clear space for maneuver. How can we possibly free ourselves from the manifest center—the insinuating efficiency of the prevailing machinery of control, the men and schedules that order our lives? How can we gain a perspective that discloses that whatever politics America has generated, it is less than the whole of imaginable reality? What alternative ideologies and institutions are conceivable?

A new perspective—an ideal transcending the actualities of American public life—is surely wanted. We crave more than a new consciousness, wanting nothing less than some wholesome theory of the good society, some standard to justify new public policies, to orient political action, to get hold of ourselves. We would surely be grateful for a comprehensive myth to make us move with more composure, more civility. But none seems available.

Still, a review of the ideological and institutional impediments for effective action may establish a base line, a point of departure. Explicitly confronting and naming our troubles may help us put them in their place, making clear that they are not the totality of being but something placeable and specific, merely parts of the whole misleadingly advertised as solutions. Were we to come to terms with that part of America that we experience as imposing and implacable, with its corporate technology and (as Louis Hartz aptly called it) its Lockean consensus, we may be able to delineate a point of view for legitimating practicable modes of action. I say that we may, for it is too late to be certain.

Ideological Impediments

Gently defeated at home, in school, in welfare bureaucracies, in professional groups, and ultimately in the political system, numbed by recurrent failures to make public policies respond to political action, we have become increasingly aware of the way in which we are deflected and consoled by the prevailing ideology. The opposition of a counter-culture has made ideological impediments increasingly easy to identify. A score of writers have noted the price we pay for the limitation of our politics, for the creed of individualism and privacy. Jules Henry's *Culture Against Man* (1963) and Philip Slater's *The Pursuit of Loneliness* (1970) are but counterparts to such films as "Midnight Cowboy," to the stream of novels that testify to the incompleteness of American lives, as well as to the innumerable empirical studies that disclose the welter of forms assumed by our alienation from politics. These various efforts to attach pictures and names and finally numbers to the unlived parts of our lives expose us as devoid of community, as deprived of political space, as cheated of opportunities for validating our experiences by sharing them.

The whole of politics would seem to be so defined as to keep what is best in us—our most generous impulses—outside, confined in nonpolitical private arenas. It is in fact so thoroughly an American convention to regard politics as a struggle for the power to allocate scarce material that an alternative conception is virtually unthinkable. Following the dominant ideology, we engage in political action so as to realize some quite definite, circumscribed objective, so as to make it yield something tangible. If we go into politics at all —and even casting a ballot is a partial entry—it is to reap some specific reward, something that, when all goes well, will serve to enrich our private life. We electioneer, vote, lobby, and even occupy public office in order to make the laws favor us, or at least to keep them from doing us harm. The rewards lie not in the process but in some calculable results. The process itself is no meaningful substitute for victory. It is but a means to an end.

Because most candidates and bills are defeated, the political process seems to consist of a succession of painful experiences. Only the few are said to be able to bear them. Nothing is gained, according to the prevailing conception, by someone who merely identifies new interests, publicly displays them, and succeeds in bringing them into a state of balance. Only future generations or invisible interests might be gratified by such balancing acts. There would seem to be so few rewards and pleasures in the *process* of politics that it seems incredible that anyone should aspire to engage in it at all. For Americans, as Sheldon Wolin and John Schaar have noted:

> Politics means bargaining and compromise between organized groups for limited and usually material prizes. To most citizens, it means periodically choosing between one or another moderate candidate and one or another blurred issue. Even though the stakes are limited, the rules of the game are many and confining. Hence, small novelties look like major violations. When new actors appear, *e.g.*, blacks or students, employing new tactics and language, and pursuing "ideal" goals, intense fear and hostility are aroused. Such departures are viewed as radical, not because they necessarily are, but because politics itself has been so narrowly conceived, so tightly drawn, that innovation appears as revolution. Americans have always been hospitable to economic innovation but in recent times they have become increasingly suspicious and fearful of creativity in the political.[2]

The texts and courses in American political science merely restate the familiar public expectations, offering little to make creditable a conception of politics as publicly creative activity. True, some political scientists have pointed to the expressive aspects of politics, recognizing political participation as symbolic, treating it as the most comprehensive of the performing arts.[3] But at the center of the discipline, politics is seen in "realistic" terms as a mode of behavior in which individuals—to the extent that they are rational—strive to maximize their power. In widely respected theory, the citizen remains the economic man who has learned from *Federalist No. 10* that he is driven by private ambition and that he will find it in his self-interest to enter the political marketplace, there to strike what bargains he must to extract what he can.

We assume—and there is not much in the professional literature to give us the lie—that in the liberal society we advance by individual effort, balancing our budgets, and pulling ourselves together.[4] We are convinced that we get out of life precisely what we put into it, and that what we give away is precisely what we no longer have. Life being a zero-sum game, affection must be rationed. There is a time and place for everything. Calculate. And when in trouble, remain attuned to reality: history offers clear lessons and the facts speak for themselves. In academic terms, everything (in the final analysis) is functional to some system whose parameters can be unambiguously specified. And in conventional terms we take college courses for grades, accumulate grades for the record, use the record to get a job, the job for money, and money for the kind of existence that enables us to watch the next generation repeat our earnest quest for results. Understandably, we like to persuade ourselves that the Sunday magazine section ads for retirement plans have it right: life's golden years, if they come at all, come at the end.

Of course a counter-culture has suddenly brought all this into relief. Further, the astringent individualism first given voice by Thomas Hobbes and Adam Smith has been opposed both by muckraking journalists and by dissidents in corporations, news magazines, law firms, and medical clinics. More often, however, it has been opposed simply by withdrawal from whatever is said to matter or by that arrogant indifference toward success and talent that Jack Nicholson portrayed in "Five Easy Pieces." And Charles Reich's celebration of Consciousness III in *The Greening of America* (1970), whatever its limits, has at least helped make distinct what the dominant modes of consciousness amount to. Yet while these reactions serve to delimit the prevailing ideology, they provide no foundation for moving beyond it. Fatigued or enraged—or both—we retain the great liberal formula.

Institutional Impediments

If the dominant ideological posture remains as a massive impediment to the designing and construcing of alternatives, so do existing institutional arrangements.[5] More than a generation of scholars has delineated the degree to which oligarchical rule blocks change and is nevertheless accepted as a matter of course in all large-scale public and private organizations. American government—including its informal, nonofficial components—is widely seen to have departed from the ideal of the eighteenth-century proponents of democracy. Today, no one minds acknowledging that elite-governed hierarchies of power have emerged as effective integrators of conflicting interests and as major determinants of man's opportunities to develop and establish his own potentialities. To be sure, theoretical adjustments have had to be made: elitism, it is said, fortunately furthers democracy. The so-called essentials of democracy may yet be upheld through the struggle of a plurality of organized interests. Business, labor, agricultural, religious, professional, and cultural groups, it is alleged, are in such wholesome competition with one another that sound public policy is the natural result of their interaction. Because all Americans belong to groups and can join and leave them at will, individual interests are thus ineluctably protected. In this analysis, the old theory of individualism is saved by the new one of pluralism. As sovereign individuals are replaced by sovereign groups, the self-regulating process of interest-group competition ostensibly makes everything come out well—if not now, at least in the end.

Against this consoling view, various critics have maintained that American pluralism can no longer deliver what it promises. Beginning with Herbert Croly's classic defense of Hamiltonian means to achieve Jeffersonian ends, countless studies have focused on the way in which private groups frustrate the further development of democracy in America. Our acquiescence in the ideology of pluralism, rather than guaranteeing the representative character of public policy, has had the practical effect of benefiting existing groups over those still struggling for recognition. The well organized are favored over those still trying to find their voice. And the governmental agencies that supposedly regulate the economy, in fact become the handmaidens of dominant interest groups. As a result, the elites of politically unrestrained groups—the leadership of DuPont, of the National Industrial Pollution Control Council, the Teamsters Union, the American Medical Association, or the Farm Bureau—formulate public policy as a matter of course. While the rank and file minds its own business, the leadership is free to determine the level and distribution of national income, to direct the allocation of resources, to decide the extent and the rate of technological, economic, medical, and educational development. Those sensitive to the needs of the corporate structure are moved to fix the level and the conditions of employment, the structure of wage rates, and the terms, tempo, and season of production not only for their own hierarchies but also for their smaller corporate neighbors who obligingly regard the policies of the big ones as models. The men at the top decide which labor markets and skills to use and which to reject, and control the quality of goods and services as well as the quantities and standards of consumption. As they engage in their diverse operations, they embrace—often with sincere tenderness—equity owners, employees, suppliers, distributors, and the mass of ostensibly sovereign consumers. Their task is less to advance the common cause of a homogeneous voluntary membership than to coordinate and adjust conflicting interests.

Insofar as the modern corporation is in possession of an actual surfeit of material and financial resources, its management understandably turns from profits to welfare, making not only economic policies but also political ones. Retaining earnings, it becomes free to be playful learning to engage in philanthropic, aesthetic, educational, and research activities whose costs and benefits can scarcely show up on financial balance sheets. Thus corporate managers act as stewards of the public interest, assuming the roles of political actors. They are free to act—to play—as if duly commissioned to form a more perfect union, to promote the general welfare, and to secure the blessing of liberty to ourselves and our posterity. They can feel summoned to move onto the public stage, there to define and supply the nation's cultural and spiritual goods. Responding to one another's cues, they are free to govern.

This situation is seen as acceptable because "private" governments have managed to seem beneficent. And it has been theoretically legitimate because we continue to think of our society as composed of an immense number of groups that we can voluntarily enter and leave. But here, too, it has been amply shown how difficult it is to practice one's trade outside the prevailing organizational hierarchies. The unaffiliated doctor is as effectively penalized as the unaffiliated truck driver. Furthermore, the evidence indicates that we do not really live up to the proverbial model of ourselves as a nation of joiners: we scarcely belong to anything genuinely ours even when we have been impelled to join. Are there many members of the PTA, the county medical association, or the Automobile Association of America who get a sense of inner satisfaction from participating in "their" groups, who experience the rewards promised by the advocates of pluralism? Since the recent advocacy of "revenue sharing," it has become doubly necessary to reaffirm that decentralization of government, far from giving "power to the people," delivers it to nationally organized interests; that "grass-roots democracy" reinforces power already centralized and consolidated under private auspices; that insofar as so-called private associations are neither private nor voluntary, their oligarchical structure smothers the individual just as effectively as any tyrannical state. In the absence of a revolutionary transformation of the organization of technological and economic power in America, it is but sentimental to assume that the dispersal of public power might promote self-government. The prevailing degradation of pluralist democracy is well documented.

Oliver Garceau writing on the AMA (to begin dropping names that every library card catalogue can link with titles), Philip Selznick on the Tennessee Valley Authority, Grant McConnell on the Farm Bureau, Robert Engler on the oil industry, Samuel Huntington on the Interstate Commerce Commission, Norman Kaiser and Phillip Foss on governmental advisory groups, Michael Reagan on what he has called "the managed economy," Hans Morgenthau on "the new feudalism," Arthur Selwyn Miller on the "techno-corporate state," Charles Reich on "the new property," David Riesman on "veto groups," C. Wright Mills on "the theory of balance," Ralph Miliband on "the state in capitalist society," William Domhoff on the ruling class, John Kenneth Galbraith on "the new industrial state," Seymour Melman on "Pentagon capitalism," Duane Lockhard on "the perverted priorities of American politics," Theodore Lowi on "interest-group liberalism"—all these have appealed to the facts to jeopardize the theory of America as pervasively heterogenous and pluralistic. And in his *Critique of Pure Tolerance* (1965), Robert Paul Wolff has carefully pulled some of these accounts together and unmasked the theory as ideology.[6] Calling attention to experiences behind the pluralistic facade, he has shown the vacuity of the central dogma of pluralism—the deceptive notion that personal freedom is likely to be extended when the government acts as a neutral umpire among the powerful and as administrator of the powerless.

These empirical studies have focused on the myriad ways in which the politics of organizational hierarchies restrict participation to the few who administer the rest, but they have scarcely examined how men act and feel *within* these organizations of power. Writing impressionistically, Mills attempted to break through, but few have followed him. True, there are some novels and films, as well as accounts by defectors from corporate crystal palaces. But so far, few have acknowledged that there are men at the top of our various establishments who willingly work overtime so as to play roles that are distinctively political. Such men simply do not seem to be "in politics." They would seem in earnest pursuit of profits, not pleasure.

So far, neither the spheres within which they play what seem to be merely economic games nor the policies they take pleasure in enacting have been perceived as *political*. Politics, we still assume, simply does not refer to the economic, seemingly private sector. Regarding the economy as nonpolitical, we are embarrassed to make political claims on it. We don't expect all individuals to be granted the same opportunities for development in the economy that they have won within the polity. In the polity, we think of the mass of men as incommensurable and irreducible, as not properly subject to externally imposed inequalities. But in the economy, the so-called private sector, we tolerate coercive organization, hierarchy, inequality, nonparticipation, and arrested personal development. Equalitarian, democratic aspirations are thus confined to the so-called public sector. Defining the polity narrowly in terms that do not refer to *all* power relationships, we leave the economy to itself—or rather to those with the power to run it. Ideally, their power is not to be restrained except, of course, by the free operations of the market-place. Political power, however, is restrained, as shown by the checks on governmenal action written into the Constitution. Democracy, narrowly conceived as related to the constitutional system but not to economic and industrial life, is therefore believed to be substantially achieved even though it fails to touch the center of the lives of most Americans.

Our double standard—freedom for the economy, restraint for the polity—might be more apparent if those who have commanded the economy had been self-conscious conspirators, or if they had never been philanthropic and sentimental, or if a steady stream of ever-improving goods and services had not been made possible by our natural wealth, or if Horatio Alger's story that we can succeed with diligence and good manners had been statistically tested, or if generations of apologists writing history books, movie scripts, and newspaper editorials had been less resourceful and corrupt. More-over, it might be less difficult to see the freedom of the economy and the restraints on the polity if the two were in fact neatly separated.

Of course, the power of the polity has steadily grown; yet it has been less used to extend the sphere of democratic politics than that of economics, disproportionately enlarging the range of discretion of those who exercise power in the economy. Thus, even while anti-trust legislation is passed or while holding companies are checked or while steel prices are rolled back, the polity is nevertheless put in the service of the economy. It is used to preserve industrial peace, to maintain an orderly market, to persist in research for "development," and to guarantee a dependable labor supply. There is little question, for example, that the exercise of power by the Interstate Commerce Commission pleases the railroads, that the state boards of health and the American Medical Association enjoy incestuous relations, that the work of licensing bodies and labor relations boards are sup-ported by the unions, and that Defense Department procurement officers and suppliers and military hardware share an interest in enlarging the defense budget without reference to patriotic senti-ments.

This would not be disquieting if the democratic practices we associate with the polity had been injected into the economy. But the fact is that we have hardly supported any democratization of economic and industrial life. Worse—as policies and candidates are merchandised it is the polity that increasingly is losing its democratic features, its very scale and complexity encouraging the replacement of politics by administration. Even at the municipal level experts either make the decisions or accept the momentum of past commitments. Having become sophisticated about such things, we suspect that demands for mass participation in political decision-making— whether in industrial production, education, medicine, or recreation —merely betray an unrealistic nostalgia for the simple life. Being what we call "realists," we expect society to be administered by public-private conglomerates ranging from the Communication Satellite Corporation to the Pharmaceutical Manufacturers' Association, from the Business Council to the National Association of Insurance Commissions. Believing that they legislate benevolently, we are grateful that they save the mass of men from the agonies of politics.[7] Thus we sustain the prevailing inequalities of participation, influence, and benefits. We know that the men governing the economy play their public roles in a manner that is neither despotical nor tyrannical. As Alexis de Tocqueville anticipated in 1840, they exercise tutelary power. And the nonplayers, de Tocqueville added, are:

> constantly circling around in pursuit of the petty and banal pleasures with which they glut their souls. Each one of them withdrawn into himself, is almost unaware of the fate of the rest. Mankind, for him, consists in his children and his personal friends. As for the rest of his fellow citizens, they are near enough, but he does not notice them. He touches them, but he feels nothing. He exists in and for himself, and though he still may have a family, one can at least say that he has not got a fatherland.
>
> Over this kind of man stands an immense, protective power which is alone responsible for securing their enjoyment and watching over their fate. That power is absolute, thoughtful of detail, orderly, provident, and gentle. It would resemble parental authority if, fatherlike, it tried to prepare its charges for a man's life, but on the contrary, it only tries to keep them in perpetual childhood. It likes to see the citizens enjoy themselves, provided that they think of nothing but enjoyment. It gladly works for their happiness but wants to be sole agent and

judge thereof. It provides for their security, foresees and supplies their necessities, facilitates their pleasure, manages their principal concerns, directs their industry, makes rules for their testaments, and divides their inheritances. Why should it not entirely relieve them from the trouble of thinking and all the cares of living?

Thus it daily makes the exercise of free choice less useful and rarer, restricts the activity of free will within a narrower compass, and little by little robs each citizen of the proper use of his own faculties.[8]

It is hard to stop quoting Tocqueville and easy to use him to overstate the argument. Admittedly, the dividing line between the actors within our establishments and the nonactors outside is more blurred than he implied. Experience is more tangled than social typology allows. Yet abstract types of the kind that Tocqueville delineated alert us to the undiscussed parts of contemporary reality, and useful ones are hard to come by.[9] What limits the usefulness of the available analytical models is that they tend to trace decisions made (and decisions not made) back to the individuals and groups who made them (or failed to make them). Hence we are led to perceive elites and their clients, actors and nonactors. Or we are led to perceive various clusters, aggregates, combinations, parties, coalitions, or even "the American people"—but all constituted, in the final analysis, by autonomous individuals, men in full command of themselves. The result is not an image that is wholly "wrong" but rather one that makes for endless disappointments. It certainly does not tend to inspire pessimism: after all, our defects are seen as corrigible. Men are in charge, or might yet be in charge. One is allowed to conclude that democracy is a precarious thing but that, given the will and some modification of the machinery of politics, men can make it work.

By focusing not on the men however, but on what Marx called the material conditions of our existence—the entire institutional context of our half-lived lives—the present might turn out to be more explicable and the future less surprising. That is, seeming incongruities—our wealth and our poverty, our idealism and our violence, our cleanliness and our filth—may emerge as quite congruent, as functioning well in relation to the given structure. But so far, we have hardly inquired about the nature of the structure, its specific shape, its momentum and logic. We hardly know what behavior patterns, from the point of view of the structure, must be designated as "necessary," "rational," "orderly," "progressive," "efficient," "legal," "peaceful"—that is, functional.

However heady the vision of the future provided by Reich's *The Greening of America*, he is right, I think, in assuming the usefulness of maintaining that the contemporary state has assumed an unprecedented form, that the totality is a self-generating and self-serving force of its own, that the whole is more than the sum of its parts, and that "the truth is in a whole, not the parts." Yet Reich, too, offers us no more than an anthology of our troubles. Like legions of critics, he too does not presume to confront the structure of our collective existence and defend a conception of political health that might give order to our mixed perceptions. Although descriptive accounts such as his merely feed our rage or contribute to our cynicism,[10] they can serve to expose the scope and the subtlety of the pressures of manifest reality, revealing that the best, too, are apt to become victims. If some reality is to be tested and reconstructed, they can help us locate it. Their words may fail to enlarge the future, but they can make us conscious of the miseries of the present. To be sure, we may not, in the end, have the intellectual energy to confront the whole of the prevailing structure. In that case, we might nonetheless seek to treat the details with special care, stating experiences so that the intensity of the light we bring to bear on them gives intimations of what remains to be seen by men with more nerve and greater vision.

Experimental Action

Perceiving America's dominant ideology and institutions as present base lines from which to depart, we understandably wish to know something about our final destination. Yet each of our efforts to spell out some new utopia turns into an embarrassment: when carefully thought out and elaborated, the ideal turns out to be exasperatingly familiar. The forms in which opposition is currently expressed—subversive manifestoes, songs, emblems, posters, films, uniforms—readily emerge as integrated components of the prevailing system, further advertising its benign rationality. Still, the very firmness of what is so incredibly fixed and absorbing at the center of our lives and our consciousness enables us to see what already exists to excess. The very density and intransigence of the center invites us at least not to look for more of the same. Thus in our search for some commanding myth, for some account of our destination, we might first note what the prevailing reality ought *not* to be—and then seek to build on this negative foundation with a measure of care and affection.

However various and accommodating the political system may be, clearly it is *not* easy to miss, *not* ready to dissolve, *not* playful and vulnerable. Were we to accept our ability to sustain a serious commitment to playfulness and vulnerability as a positive good, we would be prepared to authenticate whatever organization of life is playful and vulnerable, whatever forms are experimental, flirtatious, elusive, and equivocal, whether they find embodiment in institutions, life-styles, political practices, university departments, academic courses, or scholarly publications. Resolving to emerge in opposition and to move beyond the prevailing ideological and institutional closures, we would risk discontinuities, following Ovid rather than Virgil. We would have to support a form of action—a political science—designed to put our fixations and reifications into jeopardy. Our sole commitment would be to remaining precariously in process, to ongoing participation, to politics. Declining to stand for anything secure and dependable, we could merely assent to interminable flux—and, by implication, to whatever disciplines and structures help us maintain such a posture. We could offer no theory, but rather merely manifold disciplined expressions of man's will to keep his balance while in motion, to present himself in as many guises as he can bear. We would have to *contribute* to the reservoir of curses, gestures, and metaphors rebellious men and women have made up to cope with the unspeakable powers of elites that have all but become brute forces of nature. And as we would give public recognition to law-defying expressions, we would gradually learn to comprehend repressed, still disreputable parts of ourselves and of others, thereby helping marginal men and marginal interests merge. Our view would be one from the bottom up, as Michael Parenti has put it. Our focus, in his words, would be on "the active non-elites who attempt to overcome the social distance that separates the subject of politics from the object by trying to participate both in the creation of an issue-agenda and in issue-decisions."[11] Our focus would be on human figures gaining their distinctive voice as they defy the given natural order or the existing organization.

Once we see our present experience not as predestined and fated but rather as problematic, we may become at least ideologically free to engage in experimentation. We might then test alternatives vicariously in the manner of the novelist who places familiar experiences into unfamiliar contexts or we might test them direcly in such actual settings as neighborhoods, schools, places of employment, or universities—but, in any case, testing them always to determine the limits of our capacity to act as political beings. We would then pursue our interest in using practical demonstrations to accredit an ideal of society whose members are active participants in an interminable process—*and who do not mind such activity*. I know of no finer expression of this than Rousseau's vision of the human festival, a gathering of men that has no ulterior motive or transcendent purpose, an endlessly rewarding display of self:

> But what will be the object of these entertainments? What will be shown in them? Nothing, if you please. . . . Plant a stake crowned with flowers in the middle of a square, gather the people there, and you will have a festival. Do better yet: *let the spectators become an entertainment to themselves;* make them actors themselves.[12]

Surely any lesser state must arouse us, leading us to resist whatever conventions induce us to compromise. Thus whatever conditions may seem good enough for the moment, there would seem to be no reason to settle for anything that merely balances an inequalitarian process for arriving at decisions with an equalitarian one for remaining indecisive. Acknowledging that hierarchical structures are indeed necessary—imposed on us by forces we remain powerless to master —we may yet persist in working toward the equalitarian, participatory ideal.

Of course there is an understandable fear of mass participation and equality, a worry about the consequences of extending the reach of the institution of politics. Recent totalitarian movements have taught us to beware. As the fate of the Weimar Republic make clear, "politics" have repeatedly invaded and corrupted cultural enclaves within which men had been creatively at play. So-called political rulers have used the machinery of culture to satisfy messianic drives, fulfill inhuman norms, and build the most hideous of monuments. Culture, we know too well, has been forcefully subordinated to goal-oriented systems; it has been compelled to end-results—can we not welcome its extension and push toward equality, thereby activating individuals who are citizens in name only? True, social systems ruled by goal-oriented men have often destroyed cultural activities, usually in behalf of future generations that, so it was said, would not have to be driven so hard. The acceptance of discipline and the surrender of culture have been the well advertised price of progress. But must this price be paid in each specific case? Must we accept every case against the expansion of politics? Does it not have to be shown that we, here and now, cannot afford the kind of agonizing play that is politics at its most authentic?

To determine whether it is actually true that we are victims of ungovernable forces, we have no alternative but to engage in experimental probing. Such probing requires that we try whenever and wherever possible to inject politics into closed systems. As Nevitt Sanford has argued, "To induce a desirable change—toward further growth or developemnt or toward greater health—we have to think in terms of what would upset the existing equilibrium, produce instability, set in motion activity leading to stabilization on a higher level."[13] We must promote the social settings that allow us to discover and name our various desires. Moreover, we must be enabled to weigh and balance our desires without feeling overwhelmed by the task. What is required is the creation of environments sufficiently complex to make the playing of oddly new roles a genuinely inviting option.

The task of the individual involved in an action-oriented political science is here identical to that of the individual as responsible citizen. In either case, he is obliged to recognize that however developed a society may proclaim itself to be, it is always at least partially arrested in its development, not wholly capable of integrating new experiences, not fully articulate, suffering from shocks and expressions aggravated by checks and balances that retard action. Combining the roles of political scientist and citizen, he must act without assuming advance knowledge of the end of human development. Accordingly, he cannot presume to argue in principle for excluding anyone from participating in the process of determining his ends for himself. Nor can he ever claim to have found (in Seymour Martin Lipset's notorious words) "the good society itself in operation." There are no acceptable stopping places, only points of departure.

Devoted to further development, the political scientist must be continuously receptive to the experiments men perform on themselves to give meaning to their lives. Recognizing that experiments are transgressions—efforts to violate what is authoritatively said to be law— he cannot withhold his approval of eccentricity on abstract grounds. He must be open to the efforts of men to display and test themselves, accepting unspoken intimations and barely expressed needs, unseemly gestures and dirty words, grateful for each of them. At best, his openness will encourage whoever is at dead center to come to terms with seemingly infantile forms of behavior, with extremism and violence. By making our ambiguous fate public and vivid, by giving names to its qualities in term papers, research, books, films, lecture halls, or theaters, he helps men get their bearings. Like the individual psychologist, he provides specific occasions that impel violated and neglected groups to identify and govern themselves. Designing realities that encourage otherwise unrepresented groups to present themselves in public, he acts *for* them until they finally become inspired to act for themselves.

Insofar as he provides no prefigured end toward which he expects others to move, he unavoidably applies his energies to the perfecting of procedures that promote virtuosity and creativity. He must therefore be ready not only to keep departing from where he finds himself but also to accept the discontinuities entailed by this protean posture. Like Camus' Sysiphus, he is buoyed up by his awareness. He makes the most of his fate by welcoming whatever discipline makes him more conscious of it. There is certainly no other way in which the inevitability of one's defeat can yet give pleasure.

References

1. "The flaw in the pluralist heaven," E. E. Schattschneider has written, "is that the heavenly chorus sings with a strong upper class

accent. Probably 90% of the people cannot get into the pressure system." *The Semisovereign People* (New York: Holt, Rinehart & Winston, 1960), p. 35.

2. Sheldon S. Wolin and John H. Schaar, "Is a New Politics Possible?" *New York Review of Books* (September 3, 1970), p. 3.

3. See Hannah Arendt, *The Human Condition* (Chicago: University of Chicago Press, 1958); Murray Edelman, *The Symbolic Uses of Politics* (Urbana, Ill.: University of Illinois Press, 1964); and Robert J. Pranger, *The Eclipse of Citizenship* (New York: Holt, Rinehart & Winston, 1968).

4. It is hard to ground these impressions about the dominant American ideology in empirical studies. Nonetheless, the following are useful: Gunnar Myrdal, *An American Dilemma* (New York: Harper & Row, 1944), ch. 1; Robin M. Williams, Jr., *American Society: A Sociological Interpretation* (New York: Knopf, 1951), ch. 2; Francis X. Sutton et al., *The American Business Creed* (Cambridge, Mass.: Harvard University Press, 1956); Thomas V. Dibacco, "The Political Ideas of American Business: Recent Interpretations," *Review of Politics*, 30 (January 1968), 51–58; Elton E. Morison (ed.), *The American Style* (New York: Harper & Row, 1958); S. M. Lipset, *The First New Nation* (New York: Basic Books, 1963); John H. Bunzel, *The American Small Businessman* (New York: Knopf, 1962), ch. 3; Robert E. Lane, *Political Ideology* (New York: Free Press, 1962); Robert E. Agger et al., *The Rulers and the Ruled* (New York: Wiley, 1964), pp. 14–32.

5. I am here borrowing from chapter two of my *Open Systems: Arenas for Political Action* (Itasca, Ill.: F. E. Peacock, 1969); used by permission of the publisher.

6. Critiques of ideologically tainted scholarship are conveniently collected in William E. Connolly (ed.), *The Bias of Pluralism* (New York: Atherton, 1969); and a book edited by me, *Frontiers of Democratic Theory* (New York: Random House, 1970).

7. Peter Bachrach has noted that "most decisions are obeyed because they are regarded as authoritative, as being reasonable or potentially reasonable within the context of the value frame of those who obey." *The Theory of Democratic Elitism* (Boston: Little Brown, 1967), p. 69.

8. Alexis de Tocqueville, *Democracy in America* (New York: Harper & Row, 1966), pp. 666–667. Tocqueville went on to speculate (p. 708) about the possible consequences of the ascendancy of the

military and concluded that this would make little difference: "I am convinced that in such a case there would be a sort of fusion between the ways of clerks and soldiers. The administration would adopt something of the spirit of an army, and the army would take over some of the ways of civil administration."

9. Thus it is not astonishing that Tocqueville's model of pluralistic elitism should remain attractive. Yet it is worth considering (1) the leading metaphors of such writers as Henry Adams and Norman Mailer; (2) the efforts to use Marx's categories to come to terms with America; (3) William A. Gamson, "Stable Unrepresentation in American Society," *American Behavioral Scientist,* 12 (November–December 1968), 15–21; and (4) Zbigniew Brzezinski, *Between Two Ages: America's Role in the Technetronic Era* (New York: Viking, 1970).

10. They do so especially when they are as misleadingly judicious and balanced as Duane Lockard, *The Perverted Priorities of American Politics* (New York: Macmillan, 1971); or Thomas R. Dye and L. Harmon Ziegler, *The Irony of Democracy* (Belmont, Calif.: Wadsworth, 1970).

11. "Power and Pluralism: A View from the Bottom," *Journal of Politics,* 32 (August 1970), p. 507.

12. This passage is quoted (p. 215) in Marshall Berman, *The Politics of Authenticity: Radical Individualism and the Emergence of Modern Society* (New York: Atheneum, 1970), a fresh, masterful study of the roots of contemporary radicalism in Montesquieu and Rousseau. Their utopia should be seen as shared by Nietzsche and Wilde.

13. *Self and Society* (New York: Atherton, 1966), p. 37.

Children Without Walls: A New Political Education

PHILIP BRENNER

Introduction: The Politics of Education

An individual confronts two political barriers to personal development and self-fulfillment by being educated in the United States today. One barrier is psychic, the other is societal, and both involve the way in which the individual relates to our political structure. In a fundamental way, then, all of our education today is political education, and to change the educational process is a political act.

Psychically, a person is made to feel in school that he is a resource for the use of others. He is taught to give up control over his own life. Often we hear public officials talk about human resources for the society as if this were the measure of the worth of people. Children are rewarded and punished on the basis of how well they learn skills—teachers teach skills, not children. People are driven to perform so that they can reach the next step of a hierarchic order, be it high school, college, a white collar job, or an executive position.[1] Always the personal goal is created by an agency outside of the individual. Using his skills, the individual is taught to fit into a slot prepared by an outside agency. He is kept ignorant of the purposes of his education, only being told it will be good for him someday.

Philip Brenner (Ph.D. candidate, Johns Hopkins University) spent a year working in Congress as an American Political Science Association Congressional Fellow, and was co-director of the Washington Mini School. He is currently on the editorial board of *Politics and Society*.

People are trained to relate to each other in terms of social roles, and it is natural that we come to think of ourselves, that we define ourselves, in terms of our roles rather than in human terms.

The psychic barrier is manifestly political in the way it works to prevent opposition to the existing political order. The rulers of the order thus have an interest in maintaining those instruments that will engender such a psychic barrier.

The mechanism that relates a psychically unfulfilling educational process to the maintenance of the political order is social mobility. Higher paying jobs tend to be associated with the number of years of formal education a person has had, and so education is celebrated as the means to social mobility. We compete with each other to get up the education ladder so that we can get ahead, rise up, and be a "success."

However, in doing so we act out a deception. It is a deception for two reasons. First, studies now indicate that years of schooling is but an arbitrary yardstick in assigning people to jobs.[2] People do not need the level of education to perform most jobs that is required to be hired for these jobs. We require credentials for the most ordinary tasks, and thus differentiate people by their years of education, without consideration of individual ability.

Second, social mobility in our society is largely a myth. From the early part of this century to the present a very small percentage of the population has controlled the nation's resources, and received the bulk of the nation's wealth. The mass of the population has been relegated to the role of dividing the remaining resources and responding to those who exercise authority. In an expanding economy that fact has been obscured because incomes have risen. Therefore, an increasing number of people can raise their standard of living and appear to be independent. Nevertheless, although they tend to earn more than their parents had, their positions relative to each other remain essentially unchanged. To the extent that some people rise more than others, from the equivalent of a lower-middle class stratum, for example, to an upper-middle class one, there is some social mobility, but they still only receive a slightly larger piece of the pie that remains after the bulk has been cut away, and they share the plight of many a suburban executive, whose position in life is not his to control.

An emphasis on social mobility, then, serves to direct attention away from the gross inequality in our society, in terms of wealth, and power and authority. People endure the educational process in pursuit of a success defined by others that is not only a myth, but is often personally unsatisfying to them because it *is* defined by others. In the process, they deny their natural bond with people who are in the same objective circumstances, so that they challenge each other instead of the structures that promote inequality.

This is the classic ploy of divide and conquer. The beneficiaries of the inequality, through the machinery of the State, foster an educational process that promotes cleavages among the people by embodying the competitive spirit. And so it becomes difficult for people to see their common circumstances and to join in common force to change the existing order. The order persists.

It is not sufficient to attack the psychic barrier because there are societal barriers to self-fulfillment that also prevent it in a physical way. Not only does the State support an organization of society that rewards those who comply and punishes those who do not comply with the hierarchic, competitive order. The State has also brought us to a point where we may be prevented from living our own lives most literally. Ostensibly the State came into being to provide for our safety and protection, yet today our government endangers us by engaging in military adventures, it is unwilling to control the use of modern technology so that technology does not lead to chronic conditions, and it perpetuates conditions that enslave non-whites and contribute to their physical impairment.

In this regard, too, the educational system is so structured as to protect the existing political order from effective attack. Our education is divided into discrete units, each separate from the next. We learn in piecemeal so that we have great difficulty in confronting the existing order as a whole. We can either fit into it or drop out—it overwhelms us so that we cannot confront it effectively.

We may learn what a corporation is in the technical sense, but we are not educated to know how the corporate structure of General Motors, for example, may generate death on the highway. Both its bureaucratic features stymie efforts by those in lower ranks to introduce safety equipment into car design, and its sheer size commits many employees to a continuation of present company policies, and numerous small stockholders to a stable, high dividend return. Its predominance in the economy, and the increasing number of cars on the highway, is reinforced by the government when it avoids anti-trust suits against G.M., builds the highways, and finances the suburban homes that promote the use of cars. In turn, the government's tax returns increase in proportion to the sales volume of cars, and the volume depends on style changes instead of the incorporation of safety equipment and sturdiness. No one favors death on the highway, but by being taught to concentrate only on a narrow area of concern and not see connections, people at each joint of the corporate structure overlook how their activities might contribute to highway deaths.

In order to achieve self-fulfillment, then, both political barriers must be overcome—the psychic and the societal. This is a fundamental task we must undertake because self-fulfillment is an essential life force. This proposition was developed by Viktor Frankl, father of what is called the "Third Viennese School of Psychotherapy." Frankl observes that the "existential vacuum is a widespread phenomenon of the twentieth century."[3] By existential vacuum he means "a loss of the feeling that life is meaningful. This existential vacuum manifests itself mainly in the state of boredom."[4]

In his research Frankl found that it is the "striving to find a concrete meaning in personal existence" that underlies the activities of a person who has not become deadened, and that meaning is achieved when a person takes responsibility for his own life.[5] Frankl argues that we are very aware that life is transitory and that out of this awareness each person must fashion his own meaning. "At any moment," Frankl declares, "man must decide, for better or worse, what will be the monument of his existence."[6] The act of freely choosing a meaning in life is the essence of self-fulfillment.

That this is a significant educational concern is not a new proposition. In 1900 John Dewey wrote:

How many of the employed today are mere appendages to the machines which they operate! This may be due in part to the machine itself or the regime which lays so much stress upon the products of the machine; but it certainly is due in large part to the fact that the worker has had no opportunity to develop his imagination and his sympathetic insight as to the social and scientific values found in his work.[7]

In other words, the political implications of our educational system demand primary attention, because the political order has become central to our lives. To consider a new educational system is to look first at what political education it embodies, because the new educational system that we need is one that provides a new political education.

The political task of a new educational system must be to assist people to develop a meaning for themselves psychically. It must also enable them to understand the societal barriers that constrain them physically. As Frankl explains, an important precondition to personal meaning is that a person understand his circumstances.[8] It is important, then, to consider how meaning comes about, and how we can foster the meanings we desire.

Experience and Meaning

None of you really expect this chapter to be read by children. You anticipated before opening this book that I would have written on a "level" that you could understand, and that the concepts and perhaps the language would have little meaning for children. A child might recognize the words, but he would be like Alice at the tea party when "the Hatter's remark seemed to her to have no sort of meaning in it, and yet it was certainly English."

You will divine meaning here because of your tacit knowledge. This knowledge is more than vocabulary. The symbols I use have meaning for you because you have used them, and have seen them before in contexts that had meaning for you. What I am talking about is not primarily previous experience with them in politics or education. The relevant experience is academic, though it is the experience with education and politics that adds to the meaning of the words for you.

To know about politics—not the literature on politics—requires a different sort of experience than an academic one. As politics is more often intuitive than cognitive, and is bound up with values, not antiseptic formulae, so one cannot experience politics through books.[9] Knowledge derives from experience; what has meaning for us is that which we have experienced.[10]

New experiences build on old ones. We learn and acquire knowledge by making connections between related experiences, but we need not be able to articulate the past experiences for them to be meaningful. Articulated meaning may come only when all the pieces fit together. The past experiences form an unspoken tacit knowledge,[11] and we may not even be able to articulate what we know to be whole, though we can use it to proceed with our connections. For example, we might be able to pick out a face in the crowd and still be unable to describe adequately that particular face. Jerome Bruner describes the process of knowing general ideas this way: "It is often the case that the development of the general idea comes from a first round of experience with concrete embodiments of ideas that are close to a child's life."[12]

How then can we educate children about the political world in a meaningful way? Without experiencing the political world, reading about politics in school does not open up vistas; it merely continues children's old experiences with words, or creates meanings that are different from the real meaning of the political world. The structure of experience determines what meaning a child will derive from any new experience. And the central political fact about children's experiences today is that they occur in school.

These educational experiences are isolated from the "real world." Just that phrase, "real world," suggests that what happens in school is not real. And we all think about school that way. Children experience this isolation daily—what takes place in school is supposed to be different from what occurs elsewhere.

John Dewey proposed to resolve this dilemma by integrating into the curriculum real world work experiences such as carpentry.[13] In addition, he argued that the real world was a world in which the scientific approach was predominant. Thus he maintained that it was necessary to impart to children an experience with that approach.[14] Clearly, these proposals overlook the real world.

Some well-meaning modern day reformers have attempted to provide children with real world experiences by simulation. Games of diplomacy and democracy, games for all aspects of life have been introduced, but the games are not true to life. The experience of playing only tends to reinforce the worst in school—the denial of creativity and self-fulfillment.

With games, the players are assigned roles. Children learn to accept the rules of the game and then how to win or succeed in terms of this external agency. Most importantly, the game is not real. As Dewey contends, a genuinely educative experience is one in which the person cares what happens;[15] a child must feel what real consequences of his actions are, in a personal way. In a game the decisions are irrelevant to anything but the game. This fosters the notion that the problems involved are other people's problems, which they are not.

Other educational reformers propose to help children confront the political world by fostering their natural curiosity. They maintain that children can be trained to survive by learning to "detect crap," that is to question vigilantly.[16] Yet if a person does not experience the world until she leaves school, how will she know what questions to ask, which questions are important? If a child is kept isolated, how is she supposed to transfer what she experiences in a "safe" environment to the real world.

School itself, therefore, presents a dilemma in providing children with real world experiences from which they can develop a clear meaning of the world, because *schools isolate* children from the world. At the same time, *a school provides an experience of its own that is imbued with political meaning.*

In an authoritarian school, children learn submissiveness as well as mathematics if they are to "succeed." In most schools they learn to direct their energies to future goals that are defined by teachers rather than by their own interests. They often experience that the world is made up of right and wrong answers, and that those in authority always have the right answers. They learn that they can be reduced to a quantified equivalent, to a graded profile, and that the way to relate to people is by reference to their numerical summary. And they learn to ignore their feelings and to replace them with strategies of "faking"—in John Holt's terms—in order to receive acceptance and approval from authority.[17] This is a powerful political experience that has a significance I outlined a few pages back. Not only do schools teach children to deny themselves self-fulfillment, schools also tend to incapacitate people for challenge to the ongoing political order.

The course of my argument has led us to a position that we should abandon schools, because of the political consequences of placing children in schools. This might seem to be a preposterous suggestion, as one might conclude that I mean we should abandon the education of children. Rather, I mean that we too easily equate education with schools, and this equation is not a natural law.

We only began to educate the mass of children predominately through schools about a century ago. Prior to that time education occurred in the home, in apprentice programs, in church—that is, in more varied ways. Today we have placed the primary burden on one specialized institution that we call a school, although we still learn much that we consider to be important in other settings.

By making schools the focus of education, we create an institution that can then relate to other institutions in our society. This facilitates the training of children to fit into molds prepared for them by other institutions. That is, it becomes easier to specify and meet the educational needs of institutions because one institution controls education. For example, if the military sees a need to build satellites, as it did when Sputnik was launched, this can be quickly translated into a systematic effort to train future engineers by emphasizing science in schools.[18]

By requiring that education occur in schools we also create a special group of people whose responsibility is education, our teachers and educational administrators. In doing so we give up primary responsibility for educating our children. Not everyone can be or wants to be a teacher. However, there are many people who are not teachers, who could teach children, and who are kept away from children. This makes for an enormous burden on teachers. Even the best ones—those who try to help children obtain meaningful experiences—occasionally become authoritarian, because children are forced to relate to them in order to be educated.

In short, education in schools provides experiences that are isolated from the real world and that promote a psychic disposition to fit into the existing hierarchic order of society. This is the structure of children's experiences that we should change if we are to provide a new political education.

A New Structure for Political Education

The experiences that children should have as they are educated are those that would enable them to find psychic self-fulfillment in the context of the larger political world. They cannot find meaning for themselves on a personal level, and so control their own lives, unless they have a meaning for themselves in the political system. In order to do this, they must understand the system; that is, they must experience it.

This will be as true in a reconstructed political order (one based on nonhierarchic associations, that holds people to be prior to property and production) as it is in the present order. The structure of society will still influence psychic dispositions because it will continue to affect the way in which people interact.[19] Moreover, the children of a reconstructed society would be active participants. In contrast today, we isolate 52 million people in schools.

Our present educational structure is compatible with the hierarchic, competitive, product orientation of our society, and therefore supports it. Likewise, a society that is primarily oriented to the self-fulfillment and personal development of people would require an educational structure that supports and reinforces such an orientation. By creating an educational system that embodies a new orientation we might begin to undermine existing social structures, but the social structure cannot be changed merely by altering the educational system, because education is only one of the supports of the whole system. Changing the educational process alone cannot change society.

It was efforts in the 1960s to change society by altering the educational system—a process often called social engineering—that both characterized educational reform and made it impotent.[20] For example, liberals fought hard to integrate schools, in the expectation that black children would thereby gain equal educational opportunity and thus be equal in society. But the "failures" of blacks are far more the result of the racism and inequality of the society, than the lack of "quality" education for blacks.

The structure of experience in a new education cannot be designed, then, with the intent to change the existing political order. A new education should first enable children to survive under the existing order—which would probably mean that it would assist them in challenging the order. Second, its structure should be compatible with a new political order that we would hope to create. In discussing proposals for a new educational system, we will focus on its political aspects, as we focused on the political aspects of the present system. It is the politics of an educational system that make it important to us.

The structure of children's experiences for a new political education must be in the world, not in a school.[21] To talk about a structure of experience may raise some bristles among you because we tend to think that structure inhibits freedom and denies an opportunity for self-fulfillment, but to structure experience is not inimical to generating personal fulfillment. As Dewey forcefully contended, and as children who have been reared without any guidelines by parents who have misread Dr. Spock would agree, experience without structure is a denial of freedom.[22] Self-fulfillment and growth come by relating experiences. Repeating the same experience—which is often the practice in school—leads to boredom. Unconnected experiences provide no meaning, as the new experience stays isolated. If a person cannot relate a new experience to what is already familiar, then it does not mean anything to him. This may not be a significant problem if the necessary connecting experiences are within close proximity, so that a person is likely to stumble on them at random. This is the way children learn what they know in their earliest years. But it is a significant problem in regard to political education.

The structure of experience would need to be different for each person; it would be determined by what he has experienced in the past. For example, a black child in the ghetto is likely to have had different experiences with bureaucracy, perhaps through the welfare department, than a middle class white child in the suburbs. To begin to examine the nature of bureaucracy, then, the white child would need to relate new experiences to his past experiences—we cannot assume that the welfare bureaucracy has much meaning for him.

The task of structuring experience is not as insurmountable as it may appear because children from similar backgrounds share similar basic political experiences. But it does require that someone, akin to a teacher, select experiences in an ordered, meaningful way for a group, and within the group assist individuals in relating personal experiences.

Bear in mind that the purpose of a new education is to free

people politically. Therefore, experiences must connect in a way that helps a child to understand the political world. He should begin to feel how political decisions affect people, especially himself, and how their objective circumstances relate to his own. His intuition, or tacit knowledge, about power and inequality, and about its manifestations, should be developed. He must begin to know how organizations operate, how decisions are made, what the antecedents of decisions are.

Political education based on experience in the world is a process that requires a faith on the part of "teachers" that children are learning something meaningful to themselves because children cannot be expected to report how much they know about politics. As with the example of the face in the crowd that one could recognize but not describe, it may not be possible to articulate some feelings. A conceptual political sense that can be articulated comes after much experience with doing politics. But how can children do politics? Where will children learn if not in a school? What specifically does it mean to learn politics in the world?

First, it is clear that children cannot learn about the political world all at once. Political education is a developmental process— it is not a curriculum that can be taught in a year or two. It is a process that should be started early, perhaps at about age ten when a child begins to expand his interests beyond his family and neighbors, and begins to be curious about the larger world around him.[23] From there the education will proceed over a long period of time, with new experiences providing additional meaning. In this way, we begin to prepare people to use change for their own benefit rather than to be its pawn.

Based on experiences children have had, they should begin to work in their community with people who make decisions, in the institutions where the decisions are made. Some children might begin, for example, at a television station to learn how programs are made, artistically and technically. This might lead to work in offices from which a station is run, or it might lead to work in an institution about which a television program was made. Some children, on the other hand, may choose to learn more about the technical aspects of television and to seek out factories where electronic equipment is manufactured. Similar experiences can be seen to derive from most of the institutional bases in a community that make decisions to how people in the community live their lives. Health care can begin to be considered by working with doctors, examining sources of disease such as pollution, or working in a hospital. The organization of leisure can be explored by starting at museums, a baseball stadium, or a record studio. Children have daily experiences from which the structure of political education can begin. As children experience more institutions the base from which new experiences become meaningful naturally expands.

Obviously, institutions as they are presently organized could not accommodate children in the manner described here. Space must be provided in institutions for children to work along with those who work there now. The temptation would be to provide a separate place, physically within an institution but effectively isolated, for children. But this would only have the effect of re-creating schools.

Those who work in these institutions could become the skill transmitters. Mathematics, reading, computer techniques, and other so-called essential skills can be taught by the many people who have these skills. It should be the responsibility of everyone to teach children; institutions should be organized so as to facilitate the execution of this responsibility. Children would not be forced to learn skills. But if they wanted to learn them, as they found a need for them, skill transmitters could do the teaching. Nevertheless, there would still be a need for teachers. Not only would teachers need to assist in structuring the experiences of children. Teachers must protect children. Without the support of teachers, children could easily be co-opted by the institutions in which they were working.

In general, we look for support from the people with whom we work. We thus tend to bow to social pressures in order not to lose support—and this would be especially true of children. They would thus need a source of support that is separate from the institution in which they work, an alternative to which they can turn. Support from teachers can maximize the potential children have to respond creatively to the situations that they experience. Teachers would thereby be encouraging a constructive opposition children may have to existing structures.

Similarly, without teachers children may merely learn to be apprentices while they work in institutions—they would be practicing to fit into the existing structures. Teachers must be present in institutions to encourage children to question institutional operation, and to support children when they express feelings. Children should not be taught to deny their real feelings in order to take on the emotions defined by hierarchic roles, as children are taught to do in school today. It would be their reliance on accumulated feeling that would guide them in creating new and more people-oriented structures.

For a teacher whose job it is to defend children, the task of helping children to be self-fulfilled is a natural concomitant. This differs from the position of today's teacher, who is assigned the contradictory task of defending the established order. That is, a teacher today must teach the skills called necessary by the technocracy, and work to "promote" a child to the next "higher grade." In doing so, a teacher serves to reinforce the hierarchic order that denies people control over their own lives.

As teachers foster children's natural curiosity in an institutional setting, a profound transformation could begin to take place in the institution. Constant scrutiny could make them responsive instruments for the people they serve. Institutions could be impelled to share their resources directly with the community instead of indirectly as they do now merely by paying taxes that support schools. The new openness could encourage workers, also, to question and reconstruct their institutions, giving them greater meaning in their work. Workers would also find meaning from interaction with a larger segment of the community than they have at present. A general consciousness of interrelationships develops as people become less isolated from each other.

Bringing the educational process to the workplace would also engender a spirit of continuous education. We would cease to foster the notion that learning ends when we leave school. It would help erase the distinction between an educated person and a working person. This distinction tends to generate hostility in the former and snobbery in the latter, both of which perpetuate divisions among people. And it would help to break down sex roles, because both boys and girls would work on tasks that are often reserved for only men or women today.

To be sure, not all children would want to engage in activities at institutions all of the time. In the first instance, children need a "safe" place that they can feel is their own, to which they can go and discuss experiences they have had, in which they can play, and where they can control the environment. In 1970 when I worked on an after school model of the type of experiential political education program described here, I found that the children were guarded, and often constrained themselves, when they were in an institution. When we provided a mere seminar room for their use, they grabbed the opportunity to talk with each other in a "safe" atmosphere.

School buildings can be that safe place to which children can go, although they are often too large and unmalleable to allow children to organize them as they would choose. A house or storefront would be better. In a house children might also consider developing an alternative family, that could include teachers and the other children in the program. Sleeping and cooking facilities would physically free children from their nuclear families, and this would make them less dependent on their parents and natural brothers and sisters for all forms of sustenance. In having available the possibility of an alternative family, a child thereby gains an additional opportunity to realize his personal development, because he can choose from which structure to take support; he is not compelled to experience the behavior patterns of his nuclear family.

In any safe place children could be free to pursue noninstitutional activities, such as painting, play, dramatics and reading for leisure. (Some of these activities could also take place in institutions such as theaters or art museums and workshops.) If they desired it could be used to develop their skills, or to pursue traditional academic subjects in relation to what was being done in an institution.

In another instance, children might want to "drop out" from the formal education process altogether, and they should be allowed this freedom as well. Similarly, adults should be encouraged—perhaps through a national educational credit system that provided financial assistance for sixteen to twenty years of education at any point in a person's life—to continue their education alongside children, by "dropping out" from a job.

The after school model in Washington, D.C. was called the Mini School.[24] Two relevant generalizations can be distilled from the project. First, the children responded very positively to this type of program. They continued to participate in the program until the end, even though this meant that they gave up their afternoons, attendance was not compulsory, there were no fees, and it was explicitly an educational program. Second, even in those institutions where people had expressed great enthusiasm for the Mini School, efforts were made to separate the children from the operation of the institution, and to discipline them. Yet the willingness of institutions to participate at all suggests some room for development.

The children worked in an architect's office, a hospital, television studio, an art gallery, and school, and simply made visits and talked with professional workers at a community health center, the U.S. Congress, and a city planner's office. The experiences were not always meaningful, perhaps because they were unrelated to what the children had experienced before, and they lost interest quickly in these cases. But the Mini School was promising enough to warrant an attempt at a full-time program the following year. The failure of this attempt suggests some serious obstacles that face the restructuring of political education in America.

Obstacles to Change

There were three fatal stumbling blocks for the Mini School: lack of community support, the hostility of the District of Columbia school administration, and a lack of financial support. We had hoped to start the school with thirty children from two Southeast Washington public elementary schools. In order to secure accreditation for the children who would participate, and to make an impact on public education with the model, we sought to make it an adjunct program of one of the elementary schools, with the principal of the school as the nominal supervisor of the program. Funds were to come from private sources so that there would be no fee in order to enroll a child.

It is important that a local community support such a project, because the community's participation increases the vitality of the program, and parents can easily undermine a program by obstruction. In this case the community was apathetic. They had been poorly informed about the program, and did not attend the few informational meetings that were called. In effect, we did not develop the project in concert with them, but tried to impose it on them. Consequently they offered no support to us in conflicts that we subsequently waged and lost.

In fact, their lack of hostility was surprising. We were a white group coming into a black community, to run an educational innovation. Minority groups often feel, with good reason, that their children have been experimented with too often by white liberals, to the detriment of the children. They want "quality" education for their children, by which they generally mean the education white suburban children receive. As urban schools become increasingly non-white, this obstacle to innovation in urban public schools increases. Urban parents must come to learn about the deadness of suburban schools and the way in which even "quality education" is not in the interest of their children because it functions to support the existing political order. Similarly, white middle class parents must come to see what schools are doing to their children before they are likely to embrace an educational system that undermines schools. They presently misperceive schools as embodiment of their values.

Second, the public school administration would not allow the Mini School to become an adjunct program of one of its elementary schools. The Superintendant expressed his opposition this way: "Such projects lead to dissolution of the public school system and I do not intend to preside over this process." What he was expressing very plainly was the classic bureaucratic dictum to maintain control over as many people as possible. As almost all schools are organized through bureaucratic structures, it is not reasonable to expect that public school systems are likely to foster the political education we propose. On the contrary, they are likely to fight such an innovation. They are primarily concerned with the basis of their organization, namely, schools. Even when during his first year, the head of the New York City public school system attempted to institute reforms that only began to touch on the bureaucracy's control, he was quickly thwarted and his own job security seriously threatened by the opposition that was mounted.[25] The strength of public school bureaucracies is likely to wane only in the face of broad public opposition and changing societal organization that diminishes the reliance on schools.

Alongside of the bureaucracy in the public school system are the teachers, many of whom might be expected to oppose a new political education. I would like to believe that teachers go into their profession because they enjoy working with children, and if given the opportunity to be freed from the constraints of school and to be the defenders of children, they would grab it. However, circumstances seem otherwise.

Teaching is the most accessible profession for women. Certainly there are some women who would rather have been in other professions, but were forced into teaching by sex discrimination practiced in other fields. It is through detachment or aloofness from children and association with other teachers in school that such people find professional dignity. The same would seem to hold true for minority group members who are teachers because they have been denied access to other professions. In addition, most of us probably know a poet or frustrated philosopher who teaches in order to pay his rent.

Perhaps more significant is the fact that teaching has been a means of entering the mainstream of American society for immigrants. They achieved "success" through a merit system based on school certification. That this certification serves now to deny success to blacks and other minorities does not weaken the staunch defense by second generation teachers of the system that seemingly raised them up.

Moreover, the spread of unionization among teachers is facilitated by the existence of schools. If teachers are isolated from each other, working in separate institutions, their ability to organize, to make demands for higher wages and to secure their jobs would diminish. That they would begin to find an identity with workers other than teachers would also tend to threaten the unity of the union. Unions, like bureaucracies, have an organizational life beyond that of their constituent members. The union organization is likely to challenge any change that threatens its existence.

To the extent that teachers do care about children, though, they will see in a new political education opportunities for their own self-fulfillment as well as that of the children, and will then be a group generating demands for such educational change. In their 1971 contract talks, the progressive Washington, D.C. teachers' union included as one of its demands that some teachers be given the resources to create an experimental school as they chose to do it, which conceivably could be one modeled on the lines of a new political education. It is also instructive that a new child-centered education in the infant schools in England is succeeding in producing a more human education. It employs the same teachers who were formerly authoritarian, and who are now adapting very readily to an open classroom environment.[26]

That the Mini School was unable to raise sufficient funds from foundations may have been due to the state of the stock market, although a few did say it was "too radical." Our financial crisis does raise the question, nonetheless, of where money for teachers and materials is to come from for such an educational innovation. To charge tuition relegates such a program to only the wealthy, and foundations cannot be expected to fund innovative programs on a mass scale. This is a troublesome question faced by the alternative school movement, if it hopes to have a signficant impact on the nature of mass education. At present, alternative schools benefit only a few, and their models are not likely to be taken up voluntarily by public school systems if they are truly innovative and reconstructive models.

In theory the financial support for the proposed educational scheme would come from the community—especially from the institutions that would provide so many resources. Yet the proposals are likely to be viewed as threatening to institutions because they would do away with schools as they are now structured to reinforce the hierarchic order of institutions, and they would bring children into the midst of the institutions.

Still, institutions are constituted of people, and there are many people in institutions who are alienated from these structures—as we found in the Mini School's after school project. These people form an internal base of support that must be reinforced. The possibilities of enlisting their support, and the support of parents, will determine how optimistic we can be about achieving a new political education.

Possibilities for Change

The possibility of changing our present educational structure and of substituting a new political education will be determined by several changes occurring now in society. I will examine a few of these here. If they coalesce in one direction, it will facilitate diverse groups in demanding a new political education.

Years of formal schooling is becoming a meaningless criterion for job selection. Many companies have created in-service courses to train employees. Slowly people are realizing what statistics have described—that achievement in school is unrelated to competence in the workplace and should thus not be the basis determining rewards of employment at various levels. This has been underlined by a recent (1971) Supreme Court decision. Speaking for the unanimous court in *Griggs et al.* v. *Duke Power Company*, Chief Justice Burger declared that requirements of either a high school diploma or a certain level of achievement on a general education test, as a condition of employment, are prohibited under the 1964 Civil Rights Act.

Thus, although credentialism is still rampant, there is movement away from it. The federal and state governments, with their large employment rolls, could take a very important first step in this regard, by not basing their civil service classifications on years of formal schooling. The increasing number of college dropouts also suggests that people are beginning to challenge credentialism and formal schools on a personal level. These changes could lead people to forsake education for its supposed value of providing social mobility, and to demand an educational process that has more meaning for their lives than one based in schools can have.

One institution that is central in the current educational process is the university. It is the pinnacle of the education pyramid, and it is the training ground for school teachers. Not only is its certification used by the society's dominant institutions to structure the lives of people, but its resources are used to provide the necessary knowledge to maintain the existing order.

Students who demand control of their universities sense the university's centrality. The particular issue at hand may be the Indo-China war or military recruiting, but the fundamental issue students raise is how the university operates to perpetuate a social structure that students sense denies them self-fulfillment.

In this context, some professors' demands for academic freedom as the salvation of free universities are specious. It is the students who are trying to free the university. The allegedly pure knowledge generated by professors is often used to support the existing political structure, and professors' control over the students through powers of accreditation makes them supporters of the hierarchic society. As students attempt to gain more control over their own lives in universities, in effect as they come to control universities, these institutions can come to assist in the development of a new political education. They could then be one place where teachers for a new political education might be educated. Students at universities might undertake projects in the new education—working with children in institutions—and this might grow to be an accustomed part of university education.

Sometimes a reform that initially only modifies the basic structure of an activity, creates movement that can generate profound change. Such may be the case with the increasingly popular new progressive movement in education.

For nearly a decade educational theorists and practitioners such as John Holt, Jonathan Kozol, James Herndon, Herbert Kohl, Peter Marin, Ronald Gross, and George Leonard have advocated a change in education to place the needs of children, rather than those of a school or mystical curriculum, at the center of attention. They argue that if children do not "fit into" a school well, then the school should be changed, not the children. Their goal is clearly very human; they see a child's realization of personal meaning as the primary goal of education.

Their ideas have come to even more attention, now, as the highly respectable Carnegie Corporation's study of education, *Crisis in the Classroom* by Charles Silberman,[27] strongly endorsed them. In turn, the New York City teachers' union has endorsed Silberman's book.

These reformist moves can prove to be very significant for two reasons. First, they may commit many educators to a new way of thinking about education, about the needs of children rather than about the ways to manipulate children; about personal development rather than school flow charts. Second, I believe the stated goals are bound to be frustrated, because the intended reforms take place within the context of schools. Even the best schools in the new school movement necessarily isolate children by virtue of being schools, and so make children susceptible to being overwhelmed by the political world when they leave the supportive protection of the school.

If the goals are frustrated and many people are committed to them, there is the possibility that this group will channel their frustration into demands for an educational structure that can more realistically satisfy their goals. That is, they will have the impetus to forsake schools.

At the same time, a collateral movement for "schools-without-walls" is emerging. Programs to free high school students from school bonds and to allow them to learn in other institutions—usually cultural institutions such as museums—have been started in Philadelphia, Chicago, and Washington, D.C. While there is little effort to structure experience in these programs in order to develop political understanding, and their focus is administrative (increasing the resources available to students, without increased cost, by using cultural institutions; increasing the effective capacity of existing school buildings by removing some of the children), they legitimize two essential concepts: that meaningful education can occur outside of a school, and that other institutions beside schools have a responsibility for educating children.

These two movements in education, changes in the university, and the changing relationship between formal education and jobs can all serve to open people's eyes to the need for systematic change and this may promote the creation of demands for a reconstructed educational process.

To Commence

Unless the dominant institutions of society are willing to accept those people who effect values other than hierarchic ones, a new political education would create misfits in the society. They would be in tension with the existing order and soon could be crushed by it. A reconstructed educational process must be accompanied by manifold changes in society—that is, the society itself must also undergo reconstruction.

Other changes would necessarily involve the nature of work and the organization of the workplace; the nature of our leisure activities and our communications; the way in which we relate to people in other countries and how our government relates to other governments. The changes would affect the distribution of power in society, giving individuals greater control over their own lives, and probably the organization of the government. As we wrote earlier, a new educational process can contribute to the process of overall change, but it would ultimately be thwarted unless other societal changes do occur.

Marcus Raskin contrasts reconstruction to revolution and reform in maintaining that under the latter two processes changes occur through and in relation to the hierarchic order, and thus the order tends to remain intact. Reconstruction would invert basic social patterns as it focused from the start on nonhierarchic arrangements, with the intention of promoting freedom for the individual.[28] Reconstruction may require force as a first step, especially where violence is used to maintain a hierarchic order, as is the case with Third World people here and abroad. But force tends to serve antithetical ends to broad change, as it focuses attention on the subject of force rather than its underlying antecedents. Moreover, in victory the object of force—for example, the central government— may be preserved to justify to supporters the death and destruction that was involved in achieving victory, and to keep the victory secure.

A new political education is necessary for reconstruction, because an educational structure works to support and reinforce a societal structure with which it has a complementary logic and set of values. The goal of a new political education, then, is to support the development of a reconstructed political order based on personal self-fulfillment. What I have tried to explore here is the nature and theoretical underpinnings of the proposed change in education. I have not provided a detailed plan for generating a new political education. Its creation must come within the context of the reconstruction that we all undertake.

References

1. This idea is elaborately developed by Marcus Raskin, *Being and Doing* (New York: Random House, 1971), ch. 4.
2. Ivar Berg, *Education and Jobs: The Great Training Robbery* (New York: Praeger, 1970).

3. Viktor Frankl, *Man's Search for Meaning: An Introduction to Logotherapy* (New York: Washington Square Press, 1963), p. 167.
4. *Ibid.*, p. 169.
5. *Ibid.*, pp. 159, 172–173.
6. *Ibid.*, p. 191.
7. *The School and Society* (Chicago: University of Chicago Press, 1900), p. 22.
8. Frankl, *Man's Search for Meaning*, p. 174.
9. Michael Polanyi, *The Tacit Dimension* (Garden City, N.Y.: Doubleday, 1966), p. 91.
10. For a fuller treatment of this position see Eugene Gendlin, *Experiencing and the Creation of Meaning* (New York: Free Press of Glencoe, 1962), especially chapter 1.
11. Polyani, *op. cit.*, ch. 1 and 2.
12. *On Knowing, Essays for the Left Hand* (Cambridge, Mass.: Harvard University Press, 1962), p. 123.
13. *The School and Society*, ch. 3.
14. *Experience and Education* (London: Collier, 1963), ch. 7.
15. John Dewey, *Democracy and Education* (New York: Macmillan, 1916), pp. 90–91.
16. Neil Postman and Charles Weingartner, *Teaching as a Subversive Activity* (New York: Delacorte Press, 1969).
17. *How Children Fail* (New York: Delta Books, 1964).
18. James E. McClellan more fully details the interrelationship in *Toward an Effective Critique of American Education* (New York: Lippincott, 1968), ch. 1.
19. Erich Fromm and Michael Maccoby, *Social Character in a Mexican Village* (Englewood Cliffs, N.J.: Prentice-Hall, 1970), pp. 21–22.
20. Peter Schrag, "End of the Impossible Dream," *Saturday Review* (September 19, 1970).
21. Paul Goodman calls such education "incidental learning," which he strongly advocates instead of schooling: "The Present Moment in Education," *New York Review of Books* (April 10, 1969). However, Goodman feels structure impedes growth.
22. *Experience and Education*, p. 75.
23. Prior to that age a child still need not go to school to be educated in reading and other basic skills. For example, Ivan Illich has proposed a model of an educational process that would be based on open resources such as skill centers. See his "Education Without School: How It Can Be Done," *New York Review of Books* (January 7, 1971).

24. Kenneth Fox and I developed and operated the model from plans conceived by Marcus Raskin, who worked as a consultant on the project.

25. Joseph Lelyveld, "Chancellor Harvey Scribner, The Most Powerful Man in the Public School System—On Paper," *The New York Times Magazine* (March 21, 1971). David Rogers, in a full-length study, examines the "inbreeding, over-centralization, over-conformity to rules and insulation from parents" that characterize urban public school bureaucracies in *110 Livingston Street* (New York: Random House, 1968).

26. Joseph Featherstone, "The Primary School Revolution in Britain," *The New Republic* (1967).

27. New York: Random House, 1970.

28. *Being and Doing*, ch. 7 and 8.

Beyond Left and Right

ROD MANIS

The old Left and Right are dying and in their place a new polarization is emerging. On the one side is the political instincts of the new culture—libertarianism. Freedom of the individual is its goal and the diffusion of power is its means. On the other side is the politics of the old culture—authoritarianism. It holds that some elite—government, church, state, majority, etc.—knows what is best for us and all power should be concentrated in its hands.

But these political changes are only a part of a whole cultural

Rod Manis (Research Associate, Stanford University) previously taught economics at Alabama A&M College. He is the author of numerous articles. Among his varied political activities he has been Area Director of the Los Angeles County Republican Central Committee, and California State Chairman of Young Americans for Freedom.

revolution that will profoundly affect every aspect of our lives. Some of the forces that have brought about this revolution include our affluence, electronic communication, education, drugs, and inflexible and repressive institutions. The new culture fundamentally is the ability and willingness to think for oneself instead of blindly following social convention. We can only begin to see where this new awareness and independent thought will lead us. However, the political directions of the new culture can be sketched.

The new culture demands an immediate end to the war, a halt to all pollution of the environment, the repeal of all laws infringing personal liberty, fundamental restructuring of the institutions of education and welfare, and a drastic reduction of government power.

The new culture will bring about a radical decentralization of power away from the central government and down to the community and individual level. Such a political decentralization will not only allow greater individual and community freedom, but will make possible the wide degree of experimentation essential to solving present and future problems.

Most importantly, the new culture will go a long way in liberating man from the control of other men and ideas. More than ever before the individual will be free to do with his body and his mind as he wishes. In this way the new culture will unchain a creative force that we can now only begin to imagine.

Libertarians of the Left

What we think of today as the Left is a coalition formed by Roosevelt in the 1930s. It brought together liberal intellectuals, unions, minorities, and poor with the Democratic party of big city political machines in the North and traditional Democratic voting in the South. It obtained a political majority and working control of the nation for more than three decades before the coalition began to disintegrate in the late 1960s.

Liberal intellectuals felt that with the power of the federal government in their hands they could overwhelm the rulers of the corporate giants and override local bigots to push through important social and economic changes in the country. They did not fear expansions of the power of the central government, but rather felt that they were in control. They sought, therefore, to augment what they considered their own power. The coalition brought significant changes to the nation.

In the 1950s, however, some liberals began to question the results of this work. The sociologist C. Wright Mills began saying that a corporate, military, and bureaucratic elite was controlling power in America and suggesting that its purposes and programs were not good.

Revisionist historians such as Professor William Appleman Williams of the University of Wisconsin pointed out that this had been true throughout our history. His student Gabriel Kolko, in *The Triumph of Conservatism*, showed that even the reforms of the Progressive period, around the turn of the century, such as railroad regulation, actually benefited the corporate elite and not the customers, farmers, union members, poor or minorities as expected and believed. The Interstate Commerce Commission and other regulatory bodies were controlled, if not created, by corporate interests, and used their government powers to protect the big corporations from the competition of smaller businesses. Thus, they created monopolies and cartels that restricted the quantity and quality of services and raised prices to consumers.

Kolko and other students of Williams also believed that the interventionist American foreign policy was not for the benefit of the world's people and for democracy, a dogma of liberal faith, but like domestic policy, for the benefit of the corporate elite. Thus a split began in the Left, as the New Left emerged in the early 1960s.

The story of the rise of the New Left and its political organization, Students for a Democratic Society, is familiar. Fed by the Civil Rights Movement in the early 1960s, and the new culture in the late '60s, its philosophy came to dominate the political thinking of the new generation. But the new culture was to permanently transform the New Left.

The conflict between the politicos and the new culture people emerged as early as the beautiful summer of 1967 when the flower children converged on Haight-Ashbury and many hard-core Berkeley radicals began turning on and dropping out.

The politicos are mostly straight expounders of activism and violent confrontation. They talk in stale Marxian terms or the lyrics of Maoism. They are primarily concerned with power and organization and see the new culture as something to exploit.

The new culture people are turned off by fanaticism and violence and power seeking. They want a completely new life and consciousness. They want to enjoy their lives and their minds and nature and each other. They know intuitively that to put all their energy into liberating themselves is the best way to liberate the world.

When SDS lost its early anarchistic, decentralist character, it was deserted by the new culture and left to the squabblings of its power-minded factions. One such faction, the Weathermen, gained control and developed a program of bombings and other violence to attack the Amerikan Corporate Imperial System. Such a violent response is natural. It is deep in the old culture. It is animal instinct to fight back when attacked and kicked around by police and prison guards, as well as parents, schools, and the Army.

If the Establishment is going to bomb and machine-gun the people of Vietnam, drag away young people to be slaves in the Army, arrest and harrass them because of what they smoke, how long they grow their hair, and what life-styles they adopt, then we must expect some of these young people to react violently. But the responsibility lies entirely with the Establishment, not with the new culture that makes every effort to promote the much more effective nonviolent methods. And the new culture has been enormously successful. Even the Weathermen have begun shifting over to culture and away from violence as the latter has been found futile and dangerous.

The struggle between libertarian and authoritarian groups in radical movements has a long history. Libertarians have usually been anarchists, while authoritarians have usually been state socialists.

Anarchists believe that it is a moral imperative for all governments and other institutions of violence and coercion, to be abolished and replaced by systems of voluntary association. They oppose all violations of individual rights and see the governments as the greatest violators of all. In place of the present systems in which some men rule others, anarchists would substitute any and all forms in which people freely agree to live and work together.

Since the doctrine of the Divine Right of Kings fell into disrepute in the 1700s, the theory of the Social Contract has served as the rationale for governments. It argues that because individuals have a right to defend their rights, they can voluntarily associate and empower their representatives to protect them—thus police and armies.

Anarchists readily agree with the theory, but make the simple observation that governments of the world are closer to the Divine Rights of Kings than the Social Contract. You and I did not sign the Constitution, as Lysander Spooner observed, and therefore it (and the institution it created) has no moral or legitimate power over us. However, if we ever are allowed to freely form our own communities and agree to their governance, then they would be legitimate.

Some anarchists believe in syndicalism under which workers own and control their factories. Other anarchists emphasize decentralized power and community decision-making. Still others believe in laissez-faire economics and the ability of the free market to efficiently coordinate the productive activities of free men. All anarchists oppose authority and stand on the side of more personal freedom and autonomy on every issue.

Unfortunately, anarchists around the turn of the century resorted to bombings and assassinations which turned most citizens against them. The new culture prefers not to look back into history, even for its own roots, so most people in the new culture are unaware of the writings of such anarchists, as Kropotkin, Bakunin, Proudhon, Stirner, Tucker, Spooner, today's Murray Bookchin (who puts out *Anarchos*), and Paul Goodman, the famous sociologist and commentator on education. Yet together these anarchists have expressed most of the ideas of the new culture.

State socialists on the other hand, seek a centralized, powerful government that can control and plan much of the economy and life of the nation. Like anarchists, they see many of the evils of the present system and work for its overthrow. But, unlike anarchists, they desire a powerful elite, such as a party or a bureaucracy.

The conflict between the two runs deeper than peacetime debates. In times of violent revolution and upheaval the state socialists have usually turned on the anarchists and killed, imprisoned, and exiled them. Lenin first worked with the anarchists in the early stages of the Russian Revolution, even adopting the strategy of "all power to the Soviets" (the local assemblies). But then as he consolidated his power, he had anarchist workers and intellectuals rounded up.

The sailors and people of Kronstadt rebelled against the central power of the Supreme Soviet and were brutally crushed. Their slogan is the essence of anarchism: "Where authority begins, the revolution ends." In the May 1968 General Strike in Paris the anarchist students took the lead. But what may have been a revolution was betrayed by the Communist party which, in effect, supported De Gaulle's Government.

The new culture has been completely turned off to state socialism by the examples of its control in Eastern Europe. Its repression of personal freedom makes it no improvement over state capitalism. Anarchism, the turning against all states, has thus become the only radical position left. In Europe the exploits of Danny Cohn-Bendit, Fritz Teufel, and the Dutch Kabouters are renowned.

In the United Sates anarchist ideas and organization have become widespread in the radical movement—decentralization, affinity groups, rejection of central discipline and authority, and emphasis on personal efforts and autonomy. Black revolutionary groups are demanding decentralized, community control of the police and other institutions. Women's Lib has lateral communication and no leaders.

Even the state socialist economics of central planning and control have been discredited. Czechoslovakia tried to decentralize her economy to eliminate the tremendous waste of central economic decision making. She also tried to extend personal freedoms, but the Russians invaded and stopped her liberalization. Sweden has never gone in big for government management of production (socialism); only redistribution of wealth and social services (welfare state). Current British efforts to switch from universal benefits to selective benefits for the poor only, with the middle and upper classes paying their own way, indicate the new direction in welfare State thinking.

So the young Left is moving toward the anarchistic, libertarian new culture.

Libertarians of the Right

As with the Left, the coalition that formed what we now think of as the Right came together in the New Deal period. The authoritarians were mainly Southerners, religious fundamentalists (upset by the repeal of prohibition), and some wealthy interests who felt threatened by President Roosevelt.

The libertarians of the Right were largely Midwesterners, isolationists, anti-militarists, and defenders of the free market. They opposed the expansion of the federal government's powers because they felt it threatened personal liberty.

It is fascinating to return to the ideas of these early Right libertarians in light of current political thinking. For men like Senator Robert Taft ("Mr. Republican") a large military, an interventionist foreign policy, and engagements in foreign wars were perilous to our freedoms and wasteful of our resources. Garet Garrett in his book *Rise of Empire* (1952) saw America becoming an empire like ancient Rome. He pointed out that power was concentrating in the hands of the central government, especially the executive branch, and said that we would go the way of the Romans. Indeed, an empire abroad and a garrison state at home was the primary fear of these libertarian conservatives.

The Right libertarians' domestic policy of limited government and free enterprise took much of its support from the economics of the Austrian School. Beginning in the nineteenth century and carried forward by Ludwig von Mises and Friedrich von Hayek, this school argued for complete laissez-faire. It saw the greatest production of goods and services that people most desired coming from the unregulated, unrestricted free market where scarce resources would be put to their highest valued use.

The Right libertarians therefore opposed the increase of central government power primarily because they believed it reduced the freedom of the individual and also because they felt that it was economically inefficient and would not produce the desired results that liberals expected. These ideas were carried on through the 1940s and '50s by men such as Frank Chodorov (founder of *Human Events*), Robert LeFevre (President of Rampart College), and Leonard Read (founder of the Foundation for Economic Education). However, in the early 1950s Senator Joe McCarthy began his Communist witch-hunts. His activities stirred up patriots, anti-Communists, religious fanatics and others who became active on the Right. Being primarily concerned with protecting America from the "International Communist Criminal Conspiracy," they had little patience for civil liberties and thus greatly increased the authoritarian wing of the Right.

In the mid-1950s William F. Buckley, Jr. began his *National Review* with a host of authoritarian conservatives such as L. Brent Bozell (a Catholic theocrat), Russell Kirk (a stanch traditionalist), several ex-Communists (who saw their old cause as *the* threat) and others who revered either Catholic dogma or the old European aristocratic virtues and values.

Two important Right libertarian movements emerged in the early 1960s that would greatly widen the gulf on the Right. First, Ayn Rand (author of *The Fountainhead, Atlas Shrugged,* and several other books) was dogmatic enough about making a "virtue of selfishness" to appeal to much of the Right. But she also propounded atheism, Austrian laissez-faire economics and opposition to big government. Her Objectivist movement, fed by lectures, tapes, and books from the Nathanial Brandon Institute, became an important force among intellectual Rightists.

At the same time the brilliant and persuasive Milton Friedman (professor of economics at the University of Chicago) was having a profound effect on both the Right and the economics profession. (His monumental contribution to monetary theory is bringing about a revolution against Keynesian economics and his eminence has been recognized by his election to the Presidency of the American Economics Association.)

Friedman has brought about a dramatic shift in free market economic strategy. Rather than simply opposing each new statist innovation as the Right had been doing unsuccessfully since the New Deal, the "Chicago School" began examining the present economic-political mess and proposing radical changes (such as the negative income tax, tuition vouchers, a volunteer military to end the draft, etc.). Even liberals would have to recognize many of these as improvements though they led away from big government controls. Moreover, the Chicago School's analysis was much the same as that of the New Left,—that government programs and regulation worked to the benefit of the rich and powerful and to the detriment of the poor and minority groups that they were intended by New Deal liberals to help. The result was an agreement on a broad range of current issues between libertarians of the Left and Right and the grounds for the eventual split within the Right.

Finally, late in the 1960s the new culture began to affect the libertarian Right. Insulated from the new life-style by its own up-tight, straight living and from the libertarian Left by fear of "radicals" and antipathy to Marxist jargon, the thought of a realignment was slow in coming. But when grasped this revolutionary change was accomplished in a year—1969.

No one better exemplified this metamorphosis than Karl Hess, Senator Barry Goldwater's speechwriter. He penned that unforgettable phrase in Goldwater's 1964 Republican Presidential nomination acceptance speech: "Extremism in the defense of liberty is no vice; moderation in the pursuit of justice is no virtue."

By 1969 Hess had become an anarchist. In March of that year he wrote "The Death of Politics" for *Playboy* magazine attacking both the Right and the Left for their authoritarianism and put forth a libertarian analysis that was to electrify the young libertarian Right. Someone who had been where they had been was saying what they were beginning to think.

That summer Young Americans for Freedom (YAF), appropriately labeled the nation's largest young conservative fund-raising organization, held its convention in St. Louis.[1] About half of the delegates leaned libertarian. The other half were traditionalist (the name for the authoritarians), *National Review* fans, and newly recruited up-tight college kids who wanted to "hit a hippie for God and Country." The polarization began with the slogan "Sock it to the Left," the national YAF office's theme for the convention. It delighted the junior "hard-hats" but appalled nonviolent libertarians who saw much to be admired in the ideals of their contemporaries across the spectrum.

By the end of the year one-third of the delegates had left YAF to form a new libertarian movement. They took most of the talent and energy of YAF along with several major state organizations and thirteen of the twenty local chapters named outstanding by the YAF national office at the convention. Across the country these young libertarians first started their own publications, conferences, organizations, speaking tours, seminars, and other efforts. Then they began to merge into the new culture bringing new ability and insight. The realignment that Carl Oglesby (former SDS president) had called for in his 1967 book *Containment and Change,* had come to pass.

The young libertarians from the Right only had to change their attitudes about foreign policy and life-style; their economics and politics were perfectly consistent with the new culture. They remembered the warnings of their isolationist forebearers. They realized that the United States government could fight the spread of tyranny about as well as it could fight poverty or deliver the mail—badly. They decided that it was more likely to imitate totalitarian systems than effectively to stop them.

If we want freedom to prevail in the world, libertarians believe we should become a model of it. People in the United States should concern themselves with defense against direct attack, not in interfering with the political systems and aspirations of the rest of humanity.

Also, because of their association with the Right, these young libertarians had some qualms about where the new culture was leading us. They shared the fear that we would "go the way of the Romans" if we became "immoral," decadent, soft, and effeminate. This myth is deep in our Western culture and few are aware of its origins.

When barbarians sacked Rome in the fifth century, the Christian Church faced a serious threat. Many were observing that the Empire had declined over the past four centuries as Christianity spread. To defend the Church, Saint Augustine penned *The City of God* in which he shifted the blame for the decline and invasion to the "immorality" and easy living of the Roman people. This defense became Church dogma and was thus passed on to us.

Libertarians, however, contend that Rome declined because power was concentrated in the hands of the Emperor and the people were therefore less free in the Empire period than they had been in the Republic. Such powers allowed Emperor Diocletian to issue his "Edict on Prices" in 301 A.D. These maximum price and wage laws, along with heavy taxation and rapid inflation, seriously disrupted the economy and destroyed the prosperity upon which the civilization rested, making invasion inevitable. People will naturally enjoy the wealth they produce. To fault them for it makes the whole creative process rather pointless. Libertarians argue that if we are to avoid the path of the Romans, we must maintain and extend our freedom. Right libertarians found themselves perfectly at home with left civil libertarians. They had always opposed laws that infringed the individual's right to do as he pleased with his life and possessions.

It may be surprising to some to realize that the economics of these young libertarians from the Right were also perfectly consistent with the new culture. First, one must realize the enormous difference between a free market and capitalism. As Karl Marx made clear, capitalism is a system in which government uses its power for the benefit of the owners of capital and exploits workers and others—for example, maximum wage laws, suppression of unions, monopoly privileges, tariffs, subsidies, tax privileges, protection from competition, and on and on.

Force is absent in a free market, and everyone can trade voluntarily. This guarantees that precious resources will be directed to produce what the people want instead of what bureaucrats or aristocrats dictate. We may not like the tastes of the masses (and many intellectuals do not), and we may attempt to change their values, but we must not interfere in a system that best satisfies public tastes.

Both New Left libertarians and libertarians from the Right, starting from different economics, arrived at the same conclusion: that the Amerikan Corporate State, like all governments, taxes, spends and regulates for the benefit of the rich and the powerful at the expense of the poor, the minorities, and the powerless. They are joining in a movement that demands the end of such a system.

The New Culture

What is the new culture? What caused it? Will it survive and perhaps prevail? If so, what changes will it bring? Of all that can be written about the new culture, some answers to these four questions is all that will be attempted here.[2]

The new culture is thinking for yourself! If you could boil down all the vast divergence of the new culture—the changes in hair, clothes, music, values, life-styles, institutions, religions, and interpersonal relations—you could find one fundamental essence. The people of the new culture are questioning all of society's axioms and coming up with their own independent answers.

Members of the old culture are tightly bound by what their parents, teachers, ministers, media, and government tell them. They worry about what others will think. Conformity of thought and action, submission to the ideas of society, authority, and others is the essence of the old culture. The changes we call the new culture require a supreme confidence in one's own self and ideas and a total loss of faith in the establishment. Young men have let their hair grow in a pseudo-masculine culture. They have stood up to the Amerikan Imperial Army and said, "Put me in jail if you will, but you cannot use my body to kill people of Vietnam." Young people wear wild clothes, leave home, hitchhike across the country, arrive in a new city without skills, and "make it" on their own. People with training abandon secure career plans in order to take up new jobs that are more important and fulfilling. What has brought about this radical change in attitude?

Three causes can be suggested. First, increased affluence and education has made the new generation more aware and confident. Education, of course, does not mean schooling. It is television that has brought the world to the new generation and vastly increased their awareness of it.

Second, psychedelic drugs have played a vital role by their chemical effects on the consciousness and by contributing to a tremendous loss of confidence in an establishment that tries to prohibit their use. Marijuana simply produces a pleasant feeling and a relaxation of tensions. The stronger hallucinogens such as LSD, mescaline (from peyote), psilosybin (from mushrooms), and many others produce a profound effect. Ordinarily the perceptions coming into the brain from the senses go through what Aldous Huxley called a reducing valve.[3] Only the very strong sensations reach the conscious mind. This is, of course, essential for survival because it allows the brain to spend most of its time handling the problems of living. But what if, for a while, you could be aware of all that your senses were telling you about your surroundings? You won't be able to function very well, but it will only last a few hours and you can arrange your environment so that you do not have to function for that period.

The psychedelics usually create a very pleasant feeling and a playback of thoughts and images. In addition, you will see the world in an entirely new way. You will be much more sensitive to your own feelings than you ever were before. The drugs cause your mind to flow through all of your memory banks. If there are areas that you try to keep closed, such as self-doubts and feelings of inefficacy, then you will create anxiety in trying to force your mind away from those thoughts instead of dealing with them openly.

When it is over, you will realize that you have had an experience that few others have ever had and you will feel apart. You are on the road to thinking for yourself, for you know that you have a special insight. All of society's ideas are now open to question and subject to your own reason. You will seek out others who have shared your experience and will find them more sensitive and self-aware and, therefore, more loving and open than anyone you have known before. You will observe that they have consciously questioned and chosen new and different ways of thinking and living that are usually valid, though nonconforming. Soon you too will join the new culture.

You will first lose respect for the Establishment for trying to suppress the drugs. Then as you realize that what you are doing is a felony and that the system is trying to capture you and put your sheltered, middle class body in jail, you will grow to fear the Establishment. As you live in that fear and become aware of the injustice and insanity of the repression all around you, you will come to despise the Establishment.

The third major cause of the new culture, then, is the actions of the Establishment itself. The drug laws have caused a lot of the disillusionment. The Vietnam war contributed mightily. In getting us into it, LBJ really "ripped his breeches" with the new generation. Perhaps most importantly, the Establishment has failed to live up to its own proclaimed ideals of peace, justice, freedom, and democracy. The new culture takes such principles seriously and cannot put its faith in a system that has fallen so short.

The new culture will survive and prevail because all of these forces that created it are still with us. There is no sign that a new enlightenment will cause the Establishment to reverse and redeem itself.

Drug use, especially among educated young people, is skyrocketing. A Gallup Poll has shown that marijuana use among American college students increased from 5 percent in 1967, to 22 percent in 1969, to 42 percent in 1970. The proportion who took LSD or other hallucinogens increased from 1 percent to 4 percent to 14 percent in those same years! Seventeen percent said they used pot on the average of once a week.

Finally, the affluent middle class society from which the new generation is coming is the dream of the old culture. The irony is that as the whole world successfully drives itself to industrialization and suburban living, its children will join the new culture. The greatest period of danger for the new culture is the decade of the 1970s. By 1980 half of the voting population will be of the generation that was under thirty in 1970. Politicians then will have to respect, if not reflect, most of the new culture values and institutions. The big question is: how repressive will the old culture be in this decade? Will it seek to kill and imprison what it considers the leaders and many of the followers of the new culture, or will it seek to smooth and make peaceful the inevitable transition?

One has to understand the values of the new culture in order to imagine the kind of world it will bring us. We can think of the ideas of the new culture as a resolution of the conflicts in the assumptions of the old culture:

Conflict between men: The old culture saw men as basically antagonistic. They saw a Hobbesian world in which man's life would be mean, brutish, and short without powerful authorities to suppress his basic destructive urges. Upon this view rest our institutions of force and repression.

The new culture, however, recognizes man's interests as basically harmonious. It believes that if man has the proper attitudes, he will work together with his brothers to produce the life he desires. He needs the love and the material and spiritual contributions that his fellows can provide. It sees individual freedom not as dangerous, but as essential. The new culture sees no conflict between men that is not created by the values of the old culture. Such conflicts will disappear as the values that are essential to the new culture win over the old. A new sense of community will emerge in which love for and responsibility to one's brothers and sisters will dominate the thoughts and actions of people.

Conflict between self and society: The old culture saw a dangerous conflict between the individual and society. All man's basic drives were destructive to the social good. Therefore, the individual had to be tightly controlled from within and without. Laws and social customs were combined with internalized brainwashing and uptightness to produce a robot who must not enjoy or love, but must blindly sacrifice himself, his dreams, his desires, his ideas and his principles for the good of society.

The new culture realizes that such people are as bad for society as they are for themselves. Only by devoting one's total energy to maximizing one's happiness will the total happiness of society equal the greatest sum.

Conflict between work and leisure: The old culture had it that work is a painful, boring, alienating experience that one must endure so that he can survive. Then one can rush around on weekends or retire, when one is too old to enjoy many of life's pleasures, and cram in some socially approved recreation.

The new culture sees creative activity as a joy; the kind of thing one experiences when one solves a puzzle or builds something one is proud of. The people of the new culture will busy themselves with fulfilling, creative achievements that fully employ their abilities and totally involve their being and, thus, completely satisfy their creative drive. The new culture will not need to buy happiness outside their work hours—work and leisure will be indistinguishable. It appears to many that the young people of the new culture are lazy, will not make it, can't shape up, are doomed to poverty. And, indeed, in the short run, when most jobs are structured by and for the old culture, this view is understandable. But it must be remembered that most new culture people are young and that alternative institutions and life models are in their infancy. So the new culture for some time will consist of a lot of groping about. For now, each person will have to find out, individually, how to work and live.

Conflict between pleasures and duty: The old culture is convinced that pleasure is a sure sign that you are doing something wrong. H. L. Menken defined puritanism as "the haunting fear that someone, somewhere is happy." The old culture could think of sex as sinful and getting killed or maimed on the battlefield as virtuous. The new culture believes that pleasure is your duty. The individual's pleasure-pain mechanism, developed over a million years of natural selection, is still a very good guide in spite of recent feeble improvements in human reason. It is tightly bound to those things that promote our survival and is suppressed only with the most grave consequences. The sex drive, for example, is as legitimate as the creative (work) drive and both should be satisfied in the natural harmony of a healthy, balanced life.

These value changes and many others, along with the new technology, will profoundly affect our future lives. The new culture most certainly does not reject technology, only its misuses. The new culture will use technology to produce a life that is consistent with the nature and desires of human beings.

Take electronic communications as an example. We are rapidly approaching a time in which each of our homes (communes) will have a computer consol connected to central data banks where eventually all human knowledge will be stored. Projected either before you or around you in three-dimensional color will be any program you select for your entertainment or any fact you seek for your information.

Most of us will "work" by using the equipment to get the information we need for decision making and communication. (Even today people have achieved reading rates of over 100,000 words a minute. At such rates vast amounts of information could be scanned so that with this electronic extension of our brains we will see creatively that which we cannot now imagine.) Thus, we can see how absurd is the fear that this new generation "won't amount to much." Indeed, only the new culture that values independence, flexibility and imagination in thinking, and joy in creative work is consistent with our future technology and life style.

To understand the political changes the new culture will bring, one must realize that it will be totally unlike the power struggles of old. As Charles Reich writes:

> There is a revolution coming. It will originate with the individual and with culture, and it will change the political structure only as its final act. It will not require violence to succeed, and it cannot be successfully resisted by violence. This is the revolution of the new generation.

The new culture will change the world by the very simple, yet irresistable process of each individual changing his own values, and his own life. Almost incidentally the political structures will be transformed.

Immediate Political Demands

It is useful to divide the political goals of the new culture into immediate and long run. Today some important reforms can be carried out that will not only improve our lives significantly, but will alleviate the worst abuses of the present system and thus lessen the violence of the revolution.

End the war: Because murder is man's worst crime, ending American genocide of the Vietnamese must be the first item on any list of libertarian demands. It is not necessary for our own defense nor for the protection of the "freedom" of the Vietnamese to engage in this war.

Stop all pollution of the environment: The government is the biggest polluter in the nation. From federal agencies such as the TVA down to municipal sewer districts this pollution must be stopped, and the costs passed on to the users and beneficiaries of these programs. In addition, the common law protections of property rights against pollution must be restored. At one time anyone who was harmed by pollution could go to court and have the polluter forced to stop and/or to compensate those harmed. Most people are confused on this issue. They think property rights entitle one to do what he wishes with not only his land, but with the air above and the water on it. The common law, however, took the position that your property rights entitled you to protection from damage to your property. The court would prevent anyone from polluting your air or water or even your view just as they would prevent anyone from dumping garbage on or firing guns across your property. But in this century business and government agencies have usually been exempted from such court rulings often in the name of progress and just as often through bribery and corruption. Even the very stiff Refuse Act of

1899 has not been enforced. Government is not the answer. More commissions and agencies simply create a protective shield behind which the polluters will continue. Instead, the new culture demands that government stop its own polluting and stop protecting private polluters from court actions by those injured.

Repeal laws that infringe on individual rights: We must repeal the draft, and laws that restrict or prohibit drug use, sex acts, gambling, prostitution, pornography, alternate life-styles, and all other "crimes without victims." Every individual has the right to do as he wishes with his life, body, labor, what he creates or obtains in voluntary exchange with others, so long as he does not violate the same rights of others. Morally, force can only be used to protect individual rights. If someone uses force to impose his will, whether he be a thief, a religious fanatic, or an officer of the law, he is morally wrong and the victim has the right to resist with force, though it may not be practical to do so. If we wish to prevent anyone from doing something that harms only himself, we have a whole arsenal of weapons of persuasion. We should never resort to force. "If you protect every man from his folly, you will raise a nation of fools." Because every man has a right to experiment with his own life and possessions, and because it is to the benefit of us all to have such experimentation (we can learn from it), the new culture demands that all laws restricting that right must be repealed.

Replace the welfare mess with a negative income tax: Like education, the welfare system is also being attacked on all sides. It is as harmful to recipients as it is wasteful of the people's money. The problems of the poor can be divided into two categories: the lack of money, and the lack of skills and motivation and education and opportunity to get and hold jobs. The latter will require a multitude of efforts on many fronts. Communities can do a lot, but no one has all the answers. Much experimentation and personal effort will be needed. But the simple problem of getting immediate financial help to the poor, consistent with helping them to help themselves, has been badly bungled. A negative income tax program (NIT) should be instituted and the huge welfare bureaucracy should be scraped.

Under the NIT program those with incomes below some base

amount—say $6,000 a year for a family of four—will report their income like taxpayers do. The government will then send them a check (on a monthly basis) for some percentage—say 24 percent— of the difference between what they earn and the base amount. For example, a family of four that had no income in a year would get $1,500. With $2,000 in earnings, they would get an additional $1,000 for a total of $3,000.

Here are just a few of the advantages of such a system. We currently spend over $100 billion dollars a year in programs that were sold to the American people as helping the poor. Most such programs do not help those in poverty, but rather those well-to-do power groups that pushed the programs through. For a small fraction of that amount we could substantially increase the amount of money in the hands of the poor. We could also do away with the welfare bureaucracy that not only gobbles up a major part of the welfare dollar, but snoops into and regulates the lives of the poor in ways that no free people should have to tolerate.

Under the present system there is a strong incentive to stay on welfare. If you go out and earn money it will simply be deducted from your check. You find that you are working for nothing. Also, if you get off welfare to get a job and lose that job, it will be weeks before you can get back on welfare. Under the NIT you can keep 75 percent of everything you earn. Thus, there will be a much greater incentive to get a job, learn new skills and work yourself out of poverty and dependence.

The Nixon Family Assistance Program is a step in the right direction, but still retains the welfare bureaucracy, rent subsidies, and the food stamp program (a subsidy to agriculture), that distorts the graduated aspect of the NIP. At some income levels more than 100 percent of earnings are deducted from benefits. A much purer NIT will have to be adopted if its benefits are to accrue.

Power to the people: The radical decentralization of power away from the central government down to the community level that will characterize future political developments must begin now. Central government taxation, regulation, and expenditures, that primarily benefit the politically powerful, must be radically reduced. Demands by blacks, Chicanos, Indians, and others to control their own communities must be satisfied now. Because psychedelic drugs offer such fantastic promise, their use must be allowed. Since sexual hang-ups play such an important role in the psychological problems of most people, the sex laws must be repealed so that we can begin to overcome the serious harm that repression has brought.

Restructure education beginning with tuition vouchers: A few years ago attacks upon the methods and results of public education were nastily dismissed as the work of ignorance or bigotry. The public schools were holy and their every failure was used as an argument for more money. Today angry attacks are coming from all directions. Educators such as John Holt, A. S. Neill, George Denison, and many others have seen and reported that it is discipline and order, not education, to which teachers devote most of their energy. The destruction of curiosity and initiative is the result.

Minority groups are enraged that the public schools not only fail to help their children out of poverty through the miracle that education promises, but the schools actually handicap minority children. Paul Goodman points out that "in many under-privileged schools the IQ steadily falls, the longer they go to school,"[4] and Martin Luther King observed, "The sad truth is that American schools, by and large, do not know how to teach—nor frequently want to teach."

Research has seriously discredited the public schools. From the famous Coleman Report (with a $1.25 million HEW grant and a sample of 600,000 students) and dozens of other studies, no correlation has been found between either expenditure per pupil or teacher-pupil ratio and results on standardized tests. The fundamental dogma of the public schoolmen, that more money and smaller classes would solve all problems, simply isn't true. It further raises the question of whether the public schools are educating at all, or whether they are simply prisons to keep children out of the home and the labor market.

The new culture found the schools to be more than a waste of a beautiful time of life. They are jails in which every effort is made to crush out the children's individuality and impose old culture values. As Jerry Farber, professor at California State College, Los Angeles, wrote in this book *The Student As Nigger* (1969), "School is where you let the dying society put its trip on you." In response, thousands of free schools have sprung up across the country in which real education can take place in a new culture environment. But their growth has been seriously inhibited by the huge money sponge of the public schools.

Those who are aware of what new techniques and technology can do in the field of education are frustrated with the inertia of the schools. But when you realize that the public schools are a monopoly with virtually no competition, you can understand why there is no incentive to change.

Many of these insights about education and its future were presented to the 1971 White House Conference on Children by a committee headed by Dr. John I. Goodlad, dean of the Graduate School of Education at UCLA. The paper, entitled "A Radical Concept of 'School' in A.D. 2000," said:

> School is but a part of the learning environment. Until recently, we believed that it was the most powerful part of that environment: we now know that it is not.
>
> Compulsory attendance will be a thing of the past. School as we know it will have been replaced by a diffuse learning environment involving homes, parks, public buildings, museums, business offices and guidance centers.
>
> Modern technology will help us realize our goals. Each home could become a school, in effect, connected via an electronic console to a central educational computer system, a computer-regulated videotape and microfilm library and a national educational television network. Whether at home or elsewhere, each student will have, at the touch of a button access to a comprehensive "learning package," including printed lessons, experiments to be performed, recorded information, videotaped lectures and films.
>
> No longer will they [teachers] need to function as ineffective machines imparting "facts" by rote—real machines will have taken over that function. Some will spend many hours perparing a single lesson to be viewed by thousands or even millions of individuals of all ages; others will evaluate such instructional programs. Some will spend many hours preparing a single lesson to be viewed by thousands or even millions of individuals of all ages; others will evaluate such instructional programs. Some will staff counseling centers. Others will be engaging with groups of all ages in dialogue designed to enhance human communication and understanding.[5]

It is clear that in the long run schools will disappear and children will learn partly from TV-computer programs and partly from experience in the real world. In the short run, both for immediate improvements of education and for the transition to future forms, the monopoly of the public schools must be broken.

Voucher checks should be issued to the parents of any children wishing to attend nonpublic schools. The checks should be for the amount the government pays per pupil in the public schools ($400–$1,000 depending upon the State). Students will take the vouchers to the school of their choice—free school, religious, vocational, etc.—and turn them in. The school can cash the vouchers with the State. (Racially segregated schools should not qualify.) Thus, greater freedom of choice will be available to every student and his parents. All schools, including the public schools, will have to start improving in order to attract students and their money. Then and only then will new techniques and technology be introduced and real advancements made. Then students will be treated as respected customers rather than as prisoners. The new culture demands liberation from the public school monopoly and the voucher plan is an essential first step.

Where We Are Going

As the new culture comes to prevail in the remaining decades of this century, the present system of relatively centralized government, controlled by various elites—corporate, wealthy, aristocratic, military, bureaucratic—will be replaced by a radical decentralization of power down to the community level.

The greatest single threat to freedom is the concentration of power. It attracts the power freaks whose egomania drives them to impose their every mad whim upon the people they can control. Power rightfully belongs only to the individual. As he comes into conflict with others and disputes develop he finds it in his interest to form voluntary associations to settle such disputes. Man has the most disputes with those closest to him—his family, his community, his nation, and his world in that order. He will therefore allow his family and community a greater degree of control of his life than his nation or the world. He is most free when each level has the minimum power consistant with settling the conflicts at that level.

The Articles of Confederation, under which the Colonies fought the American Revolution and were governed until the Constitution took over, is an example of a decentralized political system. The Confederation Congress was a voluntary association of the several Colonies. It had the assigned task of winning independence from Britain, but no power to tax or regulate within the Colonies.

We are taught in high school history that the Confederation did not work. In fact, it not only enabled us to win the war, but was a real check on the concentration of power that men like Alexander Hamilton desired. He wanted a monarchy. The Constitution was a compromise between the two extremes. Now we can see that it was no compromise at all. It was only a matter of time until the central government, and especially the executive, usurped immense powers. Patrick Henry, as well as many other libertarians of the time, argued against the Constitution:

> Shall we imitate the example of those nations who have gone from a simple to a splendid government? . . . If we admit this consolidated government, it will be because we like a great, splendid one. . . . When the American spirit was in its youth, the language of America was different: liberty, sir, was then the primary object. . . . But now, sir, the American spirit, assisted by the ropes and chains of consolidation, is about to convert this country into a powerful and mighty empire.[6]

As long as the technology of defense is the same as it is today, it may have to be handled on a large regional basis. However, a noncorporate defense may be more effective. Sweden is considering teaching her people to resist conquest through civil disobedience. But defense is about the only thing that a "national" organization should handle. It could manage our defense so much more cheaply and efficiently if it concerned itself with this matter alone and depended upon voluntary contributions from the "States" (or associations of communities). NATO (the North Atlantic Treaty Organization) is an example of an association for defense without sovereignty. It worked satisfactorily as long as the threat was credible.

Today we are spending about $80 billion on defense. However, only $8 billion goes for strategic forces—the missiles, submarines, and aircraft that carry nuclear weapons. If we add research and development ($5 billion) and the National Guard and Reserve ($3 billion) in case someone lands troops on the continental United States we only have $17 billion (before subtracting tremendous waste that could be eliminated from these operations).

The rest of the defense budget goes to the Vietnam war ($20–$30 billion) and the incredible stupidity of maintaining a huge land Army ($30–$40 billion). Such an Army is not only useless in modern warfare (except to maintain an empire), but mostly stationed in Europe and Asia where the Germans and the Japanese have demonstrated their ability to defend themselves.

Therefore, our defense (even based on current assumptions that are highly questionable) should cost no more than $100 per person per year. That is not a big amount to obtain voluntarily from the "States." (Federal taxes today take over $1,100 per person per year.) In short, if we decide to simply maintain our defense and not our empire, we could do it relatively cheaply and voluntarily. Furthermore, the new culture may make any such destructive and dangerous defense unnecessary.

International associations may handle many problems as they do today (such as the International Postal Union, International committees on weights and standards). All other questions can be settled at the community level. There the "laws" that most affect one's life will be made. Community structures will vary greatly. Some may be quite similar to present day governments. Others may be collectively owned, while still others may be privately operated. Some may be theocracies where a particular religion dominates, while others may be secular. Some communities may ban not only pot, but long hair too; while other communities may allow the individual complete freedom in these areas.

There are at least four major advantages to this decentralization of power to the community level. First, a community will more perfectly represent the wishes of its constituents. Blacks will run black communities in their own way; other minorities can do the same. Second, there will be a greater freedom of choice so that anyone can find a few communities that are very close to his ideal. People can live in the community closest to their preference. Third, there will be less exploitation of minorities as is common in large political units. Few realize that modern American cities are empires in which wealthy, downtown interests control the surrounding communities and exploit them.[7] Fourth, because there will be a greater variety of community structures, each will be an experiment from which others can learn. As some communities prosper and some decline, as some are tranquil while some are disorderly, their systems will be studied. Good ideas can be copied and mistakes avoided. Those who are afraid of change should remember that many communities will be run just like those today. They can continue to live with today's institutions and not fear the new developments. Those who desire collective ownership in order to avoid what they consider exploitation can form their own communities. Because the change will probably be peaceful, these collective communities will usually buy up adjacent land and pool it. They can then set up their own structure for collective control and decision making.

Some will prefer the proprietory community.[8] An area of land which may be residential, or commercial or industrial, or recreational, or agricultural, or some combination, would be owned and managed by an individual or by selected managers hired by stock holders living either inside or outside the community. In such a proprietorial system there is a strong incentive for management to efficiently operate the services and land use practices of the community in order to either maximize profits, or in the case of stockholders living within the community (a kind of collective ownership) the values of the residents. They will have to pay strict attention to the effects of their actions on the ecology of the land because it is their land and if its value is reduced, they lose. For example, the managers would not allow any factory to pollute the air and drive down the value and rents from their residential or commercial property. On the other hand, they would desire factories to provide jobs for their residents. So they would impose upon any factory owner that they allowed to operate on their land strict pollution controls that would balance the residents' conflicting desires for both jobs and clean air. The associations of communities would establish some form of arbitration of disputes in which pollution from one community harmed those in another. The polluters would be required either to stop or to buy the permission of the harmed community.

This desire to maximize the total value of their land will also drive managers to seek the most efficient services for their communities, e.g., water, electricity or gas. They will also have a strong incentive to find the optimal land use patterns and designs to take into account every factor such as transportation, communication, beauty, safety, future value and use, protection, etc.

Let us look closely at the very serious problem of crime and the police and see what improvements could be made. Today the police have a monopoly of much of the protection business. They behave like any monopolist; they actively act to maintain their monopoly and restrict their output below and raise their prices above the market level—that is, the level that should be established if competition were allowed.

The tremendous inefficiency of the police is pretty well understood, even by people who never contemplate alternatives. First of all, 50 percent of all arrests are for drunkenness, disorderly conduct, vagrancy, drug and sex crimes. (All crime statistics are from FBI Uniform Crime Report, 1969.) Therefore communities that ended these laws would realize considerable savings in the $8.5 billion cost (as of 1969) of police, courts, and prisons. Even more savings will come because a major portion of big city crime is by drug addicts who need money to pay the high prices of dope. Without narcotic laws both drug prices and addict crime will fall to a tiny fraction of the current level. Then the problem can begin to be treated as the disease that it is.

Of the crimes reported, the police cleared by arrest only 46 percent of the violent crimes and 16 percent of the property crimes. Only 5 percent of all crimes were cleared by convictions as charged, 7 percent went to juvenile court and 1 percent were convicted of lesser offenses. But these are just reported crimes. A study of the National Opinion Research Center of the University of Chicago, cited in the report of the President's Commission on Law Enforcement and Administration of Justice (1967), showed that only about half of all crimes are reported. The study also found that the most frequent reason people did not report crimes was that they believed the police could not be effective or would not want to be bothered.

Those sent to prison find what President Nixon calls "universities of crime" where they learn from others how to commit more crime.

The commission found that roughly one-third of offenders released from prison would be reimprisoned within a five year period.

The answer to crime is clearly not more money for police, courts, and prisons for this system is as much a part of the cause as the solution. But communities could make significant improvements. Indeed, almost any experimentation by any community would be an improvement. Even while suffering under the illusion that the police are protecting them, Americans invest over $5.5 billion a year in private crime fighting services and equipment. Burglar alarms and private patrols abound. For example there are 2,000 private patrolmen versus 3,000 police in Washington, D.C. The rent-a-cops will drive down a protected street on the average of every ten minutes. They actually work to prevent crime, rather than showing up later to make a report. Where they operate, they have brought down crime rates to almost zero. Yet they only cost about $10 per month per protected home.

New technology already exists and much more could be developed and employed in communities that sought to keep up property values by keeping down crime. Private detective agencies hired by individuals and communities would develop all kinds of new and effective techniques and equipment to stop crime. Few realize that the Pinkerton Detective Agency in the nineteenth century developed most of the techniques that the FBI uses today. Two-thirds of all law enforcement officers in the United States are on private payrolls already.

The community associations of an area would establish some system of justice, perhaps like our courts. Or they may allow the prosecution and the defendant to agree upon some arbitration group that had built a reputation on fair and just decisions. The group might intensively investigate the matter and render its verdict as cheaply and quickly as possible. An unjust decision would hurt its reputation and result either in defendants or prosecutors refusing to accept it in the future. Also, appeal courts and/or arbitration agencies might also be established.

The system of prisons would probably be abolished and replaced by fines as punishment. The fines would be set to compensate the victim and pay for the average cost of apprehending the criminal. Eighty percent of Sweden's convicts are not imprisoned. They are allowed to keep their jobs, but must pay one-third of their salaries until their fines are covered. Those who are put in prison work in adjacent factories for wages, receive training and other benefits with the result that the repeater rate is only 15 percent.

With the freedom to experiment communities could attack the causes of crime, deter crime, apprehend more criminals, insure more justice, treat convicts more fairly and humanely, provide more training and rehabilitation, and therefore reduce recidivism. All of this can be done by myriad reforms that the present system is too inflexible to attempt.

The new communities could also make a substantial contribution to helping the poor. First the poor would run their own communities and end their exploitation by outside interests. The patrolmen would have an incentive to protect them from crime and treat them respectively as customers rather than colonial subjects. Technology is available today to create much better housing for the poor at much lower costs. The main obstacles that could be abolished are building codes that prevent new materials and techniques, and the construction union's power to keep out minority group workers and greatly increase labor costs. Important job opportunities would then be available to minorities if the white middle class grip on unions was broken.

With inexpensive TV-computer education the poor child and adult would have the kind of training that will give them a real chance, but which the public schools will never provide. With the help of a multitude of private efforts inside and outside of the community the poor would be much better off than they are today.

The new culture is constantly being asked, "But what will you put in place of the present system?" The answers usually given are abstract or theater. So an effort was made here to give some concrete glimpses of our new culture future. In summary, it will be decentralist and libertarian. We will live our own lives for our own sakes and by our own decisions. The new culture will make it possible for us not to dominate or control, but to inhabit and enjoy the whole universe.

References

1. See the anarchist faction's "Tranquil Statement" and other libertarian writings in Henry J. Silverman, *American Radical Thought: The Libertarian Tradition* (1970).
2. For excellent treatments see Charles A. Reich, *The Greening of America* (1970), Tom Wolf, *Kool Aid Acid Test* (1968), and Theodore Roszak, *The Making of a Counter Culture* (1968).
3. *Doors of Perception.*
4. *Compulsory Mis-Education* (1967).
5. *Where Do We Go From Here?* (1967).
6. Debates in the Virginia Ratifying Convention (June 5, 1788).
7. See Milton Kotler, *Neighborhood Government: The Local Foundations of Political Life* (1969).
8. Spencer H. MacCallum, *The Art of Community* (1970) is about the only treatment of this revolutionary idea.